Aging and Human Motivation

The Plenum Series in Adult Development and Aging

SERIES EDITOR:
Jack Demick, *Suffolk University, Boston, Massachusetts*

ADULT DEVELOPMENT, THERAPY, AND CULTURE
A Postmodern Synthesis
Gerald D. Young

AGING AND HUMAN MOTIVATION
Ernest Furchtgott

THE AMERICAN FATHER
Biocultural and Developmental Aspects
Wade C. Mackey

THE CHANGING NATURE OF PAIN OVER THE LIFESPAN
Richel R. Thomas and Ranjan Roy

THE DEVELOPMENT OF LOGIC IN ADULTHOOD
Postformal Thought and Its Applications
Jan D. Sinnott

HANDBOOK OF AGING AND MENTAL HEALTH
An Integrative Approach
Edited by Jacob Lomranz

HANDBOOK OF CLINICAL GEROPSYCHOLOGY
Edited by Michel Hersen and Vincent B. Van Hasselt

HANDBOOK OF PAIN AND AGING
Edited by David I. Mostofsky and Jacob Lomranz

HUMAN DEVELOPMENT IN ADULTHOOD
Lewis R. Aiken

PSYCHOLOGICAL TREATMENT OF OLDER ADULTS
An Introductory Text
Edited by Michel Hersen and Vincent B. Van Hasselt

PSYCHOLOGY OF THE CONSUMER AND ITS DEVELOPMENT
An Introduction
Robert C. Webb

Aging and Human Motivation

Ernest Furchtgott

Late of the University of South Carolina
Columbia, South Carolina

With the assistance of

Mary Wilkes Furchtgott

Kluwer Academic / Plenum Publishers
New York • Boston • Dordrecht • London • Moscow

ISBN: 0-306-46074-2

©1999 Kluwer Academic / Plenum Publishers
233 Spring Street, New York, N.Y. 10013

10 9 8 7 6 5 4 3 2 1

A C.I.P. record for this book is available from the Library of Congress

Printed in the United States of America

Foreword

I first met Ernest Furchtgott twenty-five years ago after joining the faculty of the College of Social Work at the University of South Carolina. At that time, Ernie chaired the Department of Psychology. In the following three years we collaborated with an Academic Committee on Gerontology in conceptualizing and shaping the University's Certificate of Graduate Study in Gerontology Program, guiding it to final approval by the South Carolina Commission on Higher Education. For twenty years we team-taught our graduate-level course, "Psychosocial Approaches to Gerontology," involving colleagues from related disciplines. Over the years, we examined and jointly graded hundreds of research posters prepared by our graduate students in gerontology as their final course requirement.

Several years ago, Ernie formally retired from the university. He instantly agreed to my request that he continue teaching the psychology of aging portion of our interdisciplinary course. On campus nearly every day since retirement, Ernie frequently telephoned to discuss a recent article in *The Gerontologist* or a paper presentation that had excited him at the Gerontological Society's annual scientific meeting. He maintained a clear presence in the academic community.

Over the years we discussed such diverse topics as the economics of aging, family caregiving issues, volunteerism by older adults, the ups and downs of our university's athletic program, South Carolina's higher education system, and even synagogue politics. A few days before his sudden death, we had a long discussion about the importance of reshaping the nation's long-term care system for older adults. Given the opportunity and a forum in which to advocate for long-term care reform, Ernie would have made a compelling argument pertaining to the needs of our nation's growing older population. At other times, he often shared with me his pride in the many achievements of his children and grandchildren. He was extremely devoted to his family, and with his wife, Mary, looked forward to visits at the beach and in their homes throughout the year.

In many ways, *Aging and Human Motivation* reflects Ernie's understanding of the multidisciplinary nature of the expanding fields of gerontology and psychology. The book not only defines and extends our understanding of motivational forces in human behavior; it also shows the author's respect and grasp of the knowledge being generated by researchers from numerous disciplines in the humanities and sciences. He intended for this book to be useful to the many disciplines that conduct research and provide direct and indirect services for older adults.

This book provides readers with an important understanding of the psychosocial aspects of the aging process. Chapters devoted to coping, the self, the meaning of life, social relationships, and achievement motivation indeed provide glimpses of the author's personal journey from middle adulthood toward retirement and into healthy older adulthood. The importance of social motivation, reduced isolation and loneliness, and meaningful social roles convey his underlying message that gerontologists and other helping professionals need to direct greater efforts toward health promotion, psychological wellness, and creative uses of leisure time for older adults. Ernie's continued thirst for learning, commitment to research and teaching, and his participation in community and religious organizations were indicative of his personal motivation and energetic approach to older adulthood.

Ernest Furchtgott earned his doctoral degree from the University of California, Los Angeles, in 1950. He served as a member of the Psychology Department at the University of Tennessee until 1969, when he came to the University of South Carolina, Columbia, as Professor and Chair of the Psychology Department. During a long career in higher education, he conducted research with grants from the National Science Foundation, the United States Naval Radiobiological Defense Laboratory, the Atomic Energy Commission, the National Institutes of Health, and numerous other government agencies. His research focused on the neural, genetic, and behavioral effects of atomic radiation, associative learning, and aging.

At the University of South Carolina, he taught courses in experimental psychology, the psychology of aging, and developmental psychology. He was the first graduate director of the Certificate of Graduate Study in Gerontology Program and first director of the South Carolina Center for Gerontology. He received many professional honors and awards and was a member of numerous professional, scientific, and community organizations.

GERALD L. EUSTER
Professor of Social Work and Director
  of the Certificate of Graduate Study
  in Gerontology Program
University of South Carolina
Columbia, South Carolina

Preface

Interest in motivation can be traced to the earliest stages of recorded history and, today, many of its aspects permeate numerous disciplines in the humanities and various sciences. The public shows much concern with problems in motivation; some examples include using motivational indices in the selection of students for admission to colleges, the popularity of speakers who sell "motivational" programs to businesses, the efforts of the leisure industry to attract retirees to relocate to certain areas of our country, and why and how people cope with various stresses. Though, in the past, courses in motivation were frequently taught in departments of psychology, currently, this practice is uncommon. Chapter 1 attempts to develop the rationale for the publication of this monograph, which deals primarily with the motives that are important in the lives of our older, relatively healthy people, who are becoming an increasingly large part of our total population.

This volume should be useful in undergraduate and graduate courses in motivation, as well as a source of supplementary readings in various areas of gerontology. Technical vocabulary is minimal, which should make it useful in disciplines other than psychology.

My interest in motivation began a half-century ago in graduate school, though all of my early publications were based on animal research. As I aged, my interests gradually shifted to the human level; this was abetted by personal experiences and insights, as well as a perceived need to combine information about motivation that is scattered in various disciplines. Many colleagues and students, too numerous to mention, have been very helpful in clarifying the issues in this amorphous domain. Special thanks, however, go to Professor Keith Davis, who made comments on the chapter on social interactions. The editorial and secretarial assistance of D. Coleman, J. Noble,

N. Park, and C. Traywick has been invaluable. Last, but not least, my wife, Mary, has provided me not only with much psychological support but has also contributed technical assistance; therefore, this book is dedicated to her.

Contents

1. Introduction **1**

Why This Monograph? 1
Motivation 2
Definitions of Aging 14
Our Focus 17
Reprise 18

2. Biological Foundations **21**

Introduction 21
Cerebral Metabolism 22
Neurotransmitters 24
The Endocrines 27
The Immune System 34
Cardiovascular Functions 37
Conclusions 39

3. Sleep and Fatigue **41**

Sleep 41
Summary 48
Fatigue 49
Summary 63

4. Pain and Discomfort Avoidance **65**

Introduction 65
Motivational–Emotional Aspects 66
Perception and Measurement of Pain 68
Interpretation of Symptoms 72

Culture 73
Personality 74
Conclusions 78

5. **Eating and Drinking** **81**

Introduction 81
Eating 82
Drinking–Fluid Intake 90
Conclusions 90

6. **Sexuality** **93**

Introduction 93
Biology 94
Culture 96
Surveys 97
Physical Health and Psychological Wellness 99
Conclusions 103

7. **Health Behaviors** **107**

Introduction 107
Definitions 108
The Role of Motivation 109
Theoretical Underpinnings 110
Perception of Health Status 123
Health Care Services Utilization 128
Health Promotion and Preventive Health Behaviors 132
Conclusions 137

8. **Stress** **139**

Introduction 139
Definitions 141
Theories 144
Aging and Stress 154
Classifications and Measurement 156
Biological Effects 161
Psychological Effects 170
Conclusions 184

9. Coping **187**

Introduction 187
Coping Styles and Strategies 190
The Age Factor 198
Wisdom and Religion 202
Conclusions 204

10. Ecological Studies of Stress and Coping **207**

Introduction 207
Measurement 208
Caregiving 209
Summary 221
Bereavement 222
Summary 230

11. The Self **231**

Introduction 231
The Self and Social Motivation 232
Some Definitional Problems 232
Aging 235
The Temporal Factor: Past, Present, and Future Selves 243
Conclusions 245

12. Purpose or Meaning of Life **247**

The Construct 247
Modern Expositors 249
Relationship to Other Constructs 252
Empirical Studies 253
Conclusions 256

13. Social Relationships **259**

Introduction 259
Theoretical Perspectives 263
Theories 264
Isolation and Loneliness 264
Factors Affecting Close Contacts 270
Conclusions 270

14. Achievement Motivation **279**

   The Construct 279
   Some Data on Older Populations 283
   Conclusions 286

15. Leisure **289**

   Introduction 289
   Theories 292
   The Role of Motivation and Its Assessment 298
   The Life Course 302
   Some Determinants of Leisure 306
   Adult Education 311
   Amenity Migration 312
   Volunteering 315
   Conclusions 319

16. Epilogue **321**

   References **327**

   Index **381**

CHAPTER 1

Introduction

WHY THIS MONOGRAPH?

Most young adults are employed or enrolled in educational institutions to prepare for employment, whereas only a small percentage of older persons is working for pay. Not only are there distinct settings of daily activities in which there are age differences in the frequency of participants, but also in most significant aspects of life, we find major age-associated behavioral differentiation. Among the most striking overt behavioral differences between young and old persons, readily evident by gross observation, are decreases in vigor, speed of movement, motor coordination, and physical strength. All of these constructs denote an energetic component and they all exhibit a progressive decline with age. Similar types of changes are also apparent during aging in members of most lower species. These organismic decrements will lead to quantitative as well as qualitative changes in various gross behaviors. Younger persons are more likely to be found on tennis courts, ski slopes, and in many other leisure areas requiring sustained physical exertion, while older persons are more likely to sit on park benches and enjoy the tranquillity, or they tend to congregate in shopping malls.

Aside from the differences in activities requiring energy expenditures, ascribable to biological decrements, preferences between age cohorts are also apparent in the choice of clothing, living arrangements, entertainment, and other aspects of everyday living. Thus, older and younger persons differ not only in terms of activities that entail energy expenditures or that depend on optimal sensorimotor functions, but an age factor is also present in the preferences for objects and goals in which energy expenditure may be minimal. Some of this diversity may be attributed to cognitive and/or cultural factors. Age differentiations; though not necessarily in the same domains of life, are apparent in all cultures. We may speculate that these changes are somehow related to

1

biological decrements; however, there are other possible factors, such as the perceived finitude of life, current Western society's belittling the role of older people, and other social phenomena that also may contribute to the observed changes in behavior.

Since the dawn of written history, most references to aging have contained descriptions of similar changes in behavior, many of which are considered to be decremental. For example, Ecclesiastes (XII: 1–7), in describing the latter part of life, speaks of "the evil days . . . in which there is no pleasure . . . strong men are bent . . . one fears to climb a height . . . and the caperberry can no longer stimulate a desire." von Mering and Weniger (1959, p. 282) note that in the modern literature on aging, the specific advice concerning a sound later maturity includes "the control of exhaustion, the development of high motivation [sic] and special recreational activities and hobbies." Such recommendations are not very different from what could have been gathered from reading ancient writings. For our purposes, however, it is interesting to note that von Mering and Weniger refer to the importance of motivational concepts as keys to healthy aging. They indicate, of course, that today we can go beyond description to the measurement of some of these factors.

MOTIVATION

People have always speculated about the "why?" of action. There is usually a desire to understand the basis of one's activities; some of this may be attributed to mere curiosity but, more likely, it is an attempt to control or influence one's behavior. From many perspectives, it is an effort to minimize discomforts. With the growth of science, a hallmark of modern societies is the effort to improve people's lives, including the debilities of advanced age. *Successful aging* or *aging well* have been popular phrases, appearing not only in the scientific literature but also in the general media. To achieve such a state requires that we first determine the meaning of the phrase and the factors that may contribute to success or wellness.

Aristotle characterized soul in terms of two faculties, one of which was movement or activity (*On the Soul,* Book III, Chapters 9–11). The seventeenth-century philosopher Spinoza postulated that "the primary fact about man is his *conatus,* striving" (Roth, 1929, p. 105). In most Western European languages, the term *motive,* derived from the Latin root for motion or movement, was used to denote excitement, cause, desire, want, drive, and other similar concepts, each of which is related to activity or a disposition to act. The historian of psychology, Boring (1950, p. 692), defines *dynamic* psychology as the psychology of motivation, a term that he attributed to Woodworth. The term is derived from the Greek root for power or strength. We see here a juxtaposition of movement and strength, charactertistics that decline during aging.

In the past 100 years, during which gerontology developed as a science, there has been a frequent call to understand the importance of motivation in tracing aging changes. For example, in the introduction to his chapter on muscle in the *Handbook of the Biology of Aging,* the biologist E. Gutmann (1977) began his review with the observation that "old age is a period when disorders of the locomotor system prevail" (p. 445). He then goes on to say that "from a physiological point of view, the marked decline in the efficiency of motor functions is a very complex phenomenon and includes changes in motivation [sic], receptors, nervous pathways, central synaptic mechanisms, and effectors" (p. 445) Guttman begins his analysis of the locomotor changes by specifying motivation as one of the factors that contributes to the age-associated declines, but there are no further specific references to any research on motivation in his review, though all of his other factors are discussed. Again, in the section on the dynamic output in senescent muscle, Gutmann indicates that a decrease in motivation may be an important factor in the loss, but here, too, this is not elucidated (p. 458).

In 1993, six major American science organizations concerned with behavioral gerontology released a report on research needs, entitled "Vitality in Later Life" (American Psychological Association, 1993). Though the term *motivation* does not appear in the document, several of the major issues implicitly include a search for a better understanding of the motivational factors influencing the later stages of life. Indeed, the term *vitality* implies energy, drive, and related motivational aspects. Among the many recommendations in the report, there is a section that suggests research efforts be directed toward an understanding of a person's perception of control, coping strategies, adherence to health regimens, seeking of medical treatments, maintenance of independent living environments, and productivity. All of these issues refer to motivation and many of them will be addressed in this monograph. George (1996b), in commenting on the status of the psychology of the life course, deplores the lack of attention that has been given to the analysis of individual motivation. She points out that people seek environments that make them healthier and happier. Yet this field has been relatively neglected.

The Role of Motivation and Some Modern Definitions

Koch (1941), in his analysis of the various uses of the concept of motivation, classified them into seven categories that included force, control of energy expenditure, and a process for initiating activity. Since organismic activity is usually not random, a directionality factor must also be included in a definition of motivation.

In 1974, Madsen reviewed and compared 30 modern theories of motivation, with a special emphasis on American psychology. A descriptive status of the theories was followed by a systematic metatheoretical analysis of the hypothetical and abstract levels of each approach. It included the epistemological and ontological bases of each theory, the units of analysis, and the nature of the hypothetical terms and variables that were employed. There was no overall synthesis of the theories— most likely an impossible chore. Madsen's treatise had little impact on subsequent work in motivation. There are no references to it in any of the volumes of the *Nebraska Symposium on Motivation* or in any volume of the *Annual Review of Psychology,* both publications that presumably cover significant developments in the field.

In a thoughtful essay, McReynolds (1990) noted that it has been difficult to articulate a rigorous definition of motivation, though there has always been a need to explain behavior using conative constructs. As already noted by Aristotle, the latter is one of the characteristics of a person or an organism. To clarify a complex construct, scientists have frequently resorted to the use of metaphors, analogies. Among examples in the physical sciences McReynolds mentions benzene rings in chemistry and Rutherford's model of the atom.

In his historical review of the role of metaphors applied to motivation by philosophers and psychologists, McReynolds (1990) classified them into five basic categories:

1. Persons as pawns; a metaphor not currently in vogue in psychology.
2. Persons as agents; readiness to act and choices. Currently, this metaphor is seen more frequently in the writings of philosophers than psychologists.
3. Inherent tendencies; these include the modern constructs of instinct and sundry genetic concepts.
4. Persons as organisms; the concept of organismic movement and various hydraulic metaphors, including drive and cathexes, fall into this category.
5. Persons as machines; this is the predominant modern metaphor.

These metaphors do not preclude the simultaneous application of those classified in categories 2, 3, and/or 5.

It is apparent that there is much overlap between the categories. McReynolds uses five categories, but not all of them are in common use today in the psychological literature. Though theorists usually do not acknowledge it, metaphors usually reflect the prevailing worldview (e.g., the current use of computer metaphors in cognitive psychology). McReynolds also postulates that the metaphors employed tend to be topical. There have been minimal attempts to apply the same metaphor to encompass the role of motivation in a variety of behavioral situations. In his summary, McReynolds points out that metaphors have served a useful purpose in clarifying some motivational issues. Specifically, there is the distinction between the concept of force or strength and direction of motivated behavior. It is apparent that this dichotomy is based on a physical energy metaphor.

An example of the fusion of various metaphors may be seen in the personality psychologist Stagner's (1977) approach. He viewed motivation; as general energy mobilization, specific motives are the results of deprivations or *discrepancies* between expectations and existing resources. For Stagner, the basic motivational mechanism is a discrepancy-detecting and -reducing system. Such an analysis is applicable not only to the motives involved in the maintenance of a biological state of equilibrium or homeostasis, but also to such psychological constructs as adaptation level, dissonance, social comparison, and so on. Cofer and Appley (1964, pp. 326–329) suggested that it is also appropriate to use the term *social homeostasis* when the action of two or more organisms acting in concert (e.g., a family, community, etc.) requires adaptation. In ecology, the construct homeostasis, without the modifier *social,* has been applied to population units (e.g., nest building in insect colonies, foraging in various species, etc.). Some critics have faulted the extension of homeostasis from an individual organism to groups, since a condition of *stability* or adjustment for a group may be contrary to that needed by an individual. Cofer and Appley could not resolve this discrepancy and it would take us far afield to analyze the relationships between the needs of individuals and those of a group.

The concept of homeostasis is discussed in Chapter 9 on stress. It is in the context of the latter concept that Lazarus (1991), in his treatise on emotion and adaptation, refers to a "somewhat portentous [*sic*] term the motivational principle" (p. 92). For Lazarus, motivation is both a personality trait describing an individual's striving to achieve certain goals and a reaction to certain environmental conditions. The two usages are related. An environmental reaction is a function of the individual's latent disposition or trait to achieve certain goals, be it positive or negative. The latter occurs when an individual seeks to escape or remove certain environmental contingencies. The second usage of the term is transactional or relational, in that the individual seeks out environments that are consonant with his or her motives and, conversely, attempts to remove him- or herself from harmful environments. This approach requires an evaluation of the characteristics of the environment to determine congruence with the person's motives. Thus, Lazarus is proposing a cognitive–motivational relationship theory. Thus, even psychologists who do not subscribe to a machine metaphor of motivation still apply an energetic component when they measure motivation.

Appley (1991) analyzed the more recent status of motivation and concluded that despite the current popularity of cognition in psychology, with its emphasis on the self and growth, the concept of equilibrium, balance, stability, or homeostasis is still a viable principle in the analysis of motivation. The popularity of constructs such as intrinsic motivation, stimulus seeking, growth induction, or self-actualization have led to the construct of "cognitive homeostasis." As in Cofer and Appley (1964), the second author again discusses the appropriateness of the term *homeostasis* to activities or behaviors that are not associated with the maintenance of physiological equilibria or the bodily machinery to which those concepts were originally applied.

Robinson (1985, Chapter 4), in his theoretical analysis of motivation, notes that any stimulus impinging on a resting organism is disequilibrating, and most human motives, even the so-called biological ones, sometimes referred to as drives, are not primarily in response to a serious physiological disequilibrium.

A very broad " common sense" psychological definition (Kelly, 1992) of motivation has been presented by B. Weiner (1992, pp. 1–2). The author "simply" asks why animals or people choose to behave in certain ways. In contrast to McReynolds's (1990) five metaphors, B. Weiner dichotomized modern theories of motivation into (1) those that use a machine, mechanistic, metaphor and (2) those that apply a God-like metaphor akin to the classical Cartesian mind–body dualism. In the latter, the emphasis is on the rational judgments that people make in choosing specific behaviors. According to Descartes, most human actions originate with the "will," which is difficult to reduce to simple mechanistic principles (Boring, 1950, pp. 163–165). At first glance, it would seem that Weiner's dichotomy implies that, broadly speaking, motives that can be associated with certain biological mechanisms fall into the machine category while those that are more difficult to associate with specific biological activities fall into the other category. However, Weiner is careful not to make such a simple distinction. Lewin and Heider, who researched primarily in the psychosocial domain, are classified by Weiner as adherents of the machine metaphor, since they both stressed the importance of balance, presumably the maintenance of an optimum internal milieu—homeostasis. We need to remember that on the human level, even the satisfaction of simple biological needs, such as eating, entails various rational choices.

A slightly different dichotomy was proposed by Subbotsky (1995) based on the work of the Russian psychologists Rubinstein and also Leont'ev (1978, Chapter 5), who postulated that *needs* only arouse a person and the actions that are then taken are directed by motives. In addition, *needs* lead to *activity*, and this in turn then produces other *needs*. Most human motives result from activities that in the past led to the satisfaction of some needs. This resembles Allport's (1947) *functional autonomy of motives*. For Subbotsky, (1995) there are pragmatic or mechanistic motives based on biological needs, largely independent of social and cultural factors, and nonpragmatic motives, such as those based on self-esteem, empathy, moral values, and so on. In essence, however, Subbotsky adheres to the traditional biological and social dichotomy, with a considerable overlap based on the development of non-pragmatic motives from the activities pursued in the satisfaction o biological needs. Subbotsky's dichotomy cannot be accepted literally. Ir assuming that there is an overlap between the pragmatic and nonprag matic motives, he admits that the boundaries between them are fuzzy

Current Status of Research in Motivation

The *Nebraska Symposium on Motivation*, which, starting in 195 was one of the premier annual publications in the field, gradually in th early 1970s switched from reviewing motivation to analyzing other to ics in psychology. It was not until 1990 (Dienstbier, 1991) that the pul lication returned to its initial goals of analyzing problems pertaining motivation; it also included a volume devoted to aging (Sondereggc 1992). In much of experimental psychology, the recent *Zeitgeist* led the information-processing metaphor, with the computer as its tool ar model. *Input, storage, retrieval, parallel processing,* and other comput terms entered cognitive psychology and, by extension, much of expe mental psychology. Since, presumably, computers have no motiv emotions, or choices, these areas were neglected by experimental p chologists. In some areas of "soft" psychology (e.g., personality, soci and clinical), problems pertaining to motivation continued to engage searchers. It should be noted, however, that under the hegemony neobehaviorism, with its concept of drive and the popularity of anir experiments, much of the research on motivation from the 1920s to 1950s dealt with studies on food and water deprivation or electric sh stimulation. The effects of these motivational variables may be easily served in subhuman animals and they can be extrapolated to a very limited extent to the human level. The similarities between the animal and human observations can be seen to a large extent on the physiological level. The use of animal paradigms in experimental psychology is well known. During the first half of this century, psychology and the other social sciences tried very hard to emulate the physical sciences, which in Western culture were looked upon as the archetype of science or even scholarship. In the Golden Age of Theory in American psychology, 1920–1950 (Leahey, 1991, Chapter 7), most studies of motivation by experimental psychologists were devoted mainly to animal behavior. It was assumed that animals could be the models for all, or most, human behavior. At first glance, it seems ironic that the absence of motivational constructs in much of present-day, traditional, experimental psychology, dominated by cognitive theories, makes it appear that in this respect it follows a path similar to Skinner's behaviorism, which also eschewed the concept of motivation in its analysis of behaviors. Leahey (Chapter 13) noted other similarities between information processing, one of the modern forerunners of cognitive psychology, and radical behaviorism. Avoidance of motivational terms by current cognitive psychologists is even more ironic if we consider that for most of the early advocates of cognitive approaches to psychology in the twentieth century, such as Tolman, G. W. Allport, and Lewin, motivation was a core concept in their systems. However, beginning in the 1980s, there has been a gradual revival in the application of motivational constructs even in cognitive psychology. Simon (1995), one of the most influential figures in the application of computer models in psychology, exhorted his colleagues to reconnect cognition with affect and motivation for progress in instructional psychology, since, in addition to cognition, it is necessary also to take motivation into account. Some have already taken this to heart. In the previously discussed theory, Lazarus combines motivation and cognition as a core construct in the analysis of adaptation and coping. This theory encompasses human–environment relationships (Bem, 1995). The reemergence of the concept of motivation should not be surprising. American psychology, almost since its founding, wanted to be recognized as a science that has practical applications in contrast to philosophy (Leahey, 1991, p. 224). Since in many applied fields, such as education or industrial management, the benefits from the use of motivational concepts never diminished, the renewed attention to motivation in scientific psychology was bound to occur.

It is interesting that *Psychological Science* published an essay review (Pervin, 1992) of a book on industrial psychology by Locke and Latham entitled *A Theory of Goal Setting and Task Performance* (1990).

Pervin was glad to see the reintroduction of motivation as a central component of social cognition. However, he faults the authors for not stating what is the determiner of a goal or goals. Also, what is the relationship of a goal to other goals? People have many goals. How are they related? Finally, what is the basis for behaviors that do not appear to be rational or volitional when persons claim that they did not intend to do what they actually did do? Dweck (1992), in a commentary on Pervin's review, also raises the issue of classes or hierarchies of goals. Also, how and by what are behaviors, cognitions, and affect (motivation) coordinated? In another commentary, Deci (1992) reiterates two questions raised by Pervin (1992), namely, what is the basis for energization toward a goal, and how do we differentiate intentional or motivated behavior from unintentional activities? Furthermore, Deci faults Locke and Latham (1990) for neglecting the qualitative aspects of performance. Deci goes so far as to equate his questions with the very broad philosophical issue, what is "human nature?" These review essays introduce and pose questions pertinent to many current cognitive concepts that seem to omit references to motivation. These commentators were not averse to reintroducing classical philosophical/psychological concepts, such as volition, intention, goal, and expectancy, that may be difficult to define.

In the 1991 *Annual Review of Psychology,* in a chapter entitled "Social Motivation," Geen (1991) observed that, until recently, motivation as a construct was seldom used by social psychologists, though the effects of motivational processes were frequently inferred from such specific behaviors as maintenance of self-esteem, persuasion, and so on. Interestingly, the topics covered in the three reviews in the *Annual Review of Psychology* during the 1980s, bearing the title "Social Motivation," had very little in common. This seems to prove the definitional problems plaguing the field.

How Will We Define Motivation?

Definitional problems in psychology are not restricted to motivation. The *1975 Nebraska Symposium on Motivation* was devoted to the conceptual foundations of psychology. Parenthetically, in this volume, the philosopher Mischel (1976) in his analysis of the status of psychological explanations, uses Freud's 1915 paper on instincts, a motivational construct, to illustrate the difficulties in using "clear and sharply defined basic concepts" in our field. Mischel then goes on to indicate that disagreements about foundational issues during the past 60 years have been increasing rather than decreasing. There is not much evidence that the current situation is any different from what it was in 1975. The plethora of definitions of motivation applies also to most other general concepts in psychology (e.g., cognition, perception, learning, personality) as well as to "psychology" or "behavior" in general. However, similar definitional problems also trouble other life sciences, such as physiology. What is a stimulus? In his textbook of general physiology Scheer (1953, p. 432), in his introduction to the role of stimuli, recommended that "it is unwise, in physiology, to attempt exact definitions" (p. 427). More recently Smedslund, (1991) also bemoaned the lack of any conceptual analysis of psychological definitions this, then, frequently leads to trivial empirical studies.

As indicated earlier, among the most noticeable features of aging are changes in behaviors related to what has been usually labeled motivation. Baltes (1987), in his analysis of the theoretical propositions employed in life-span developmental psychology, listed age-related increases in specialization of motivational and cognitive resources and skills. His examples and general discussion focus solely on the changes in cognitive resources and skills. He had little to say about motivational aspects. Yet Thompson (1992), in commenting on a symposium on the psychology of aging, notes that the way older individuals evaluate their own life experiences and how some individuals adapt to various changes in the environment is a topic that is underresearched, though it is very relevant to psychosocial well-being in later life and to what has been labeled "successful aging."

We do not attempt to use a rigorous definition of motivation. Rather, we have adopted, à la Kelly (1992), a "common sense" definition of motivation in which we examine where appropriate biological, behavioral, and/or phenomenological indices of a person's disposition for action and the resulting direction or choice. Many, if not most, human motives are most readily observed or inferred using common, linguistically meaningful terms, or attributions. Many energetic biological and behavioral indicators are frequently used interchangeably. Theoretically, the directional factor can be measured only by observing the stimuli to which an organism responds or the targets toward which behavior is directed. However, in many situations, we record verbal preferences for specific activities or goals. In a few instances, projective tests have also been used when the investigator interprets a person's responses to ambiguous stimuli. We assume that the objective or projective expressions are to some extent veridical indicators of motives. In a few instances, there have been comparisons between people's self-description of their motives and those of their spouse and peers (McCrea & Costa, 1986). We review some studies that have addressed this issue. Verbal report of preferences is the technique most commonly used in applied settings (e.g., consumer research, public opinion polling, etc.). Government agencies and businesses frequently rely on polling data.

There is a circularity in inferring motivation from the directionality of behavior (Robinson, 1985, p. 132), but this problem is analogous to that encountered in the use of concept reinforcement and other, similar widely used concepts in psychology. The two factors, strength and direction, interact. The intensity or energy that an organism exhibits in a behavioral situation is influenced by the nature of the target or goal variables as well as the characteristics of the organism, which include age and genetics, as well as lifelong experiences. Similar parameters may be discerned in describing the direction of behavior.

Classification of Motives

Motivations, or more appropriately, motivational systems—since each motive consists of numerous specific types of behaviors—may be classified hierarchically from simple biological motives to complex social motivational systems. Maslow (1973) proposed a theory of human motivation modeled as a pyramid whose base consists of the physiological needs of hunger, thirst, and so on, followed by higher psychological needs of affiliation, acceptance, and so on, and topped by the need for "self-actualization," a weakly defined construct, at the apex. "Growth," an enhancement of values or needs throughout life, is a human characteristic. Thus, in the analysis of motivations through the life span, attention must be given to "higher order" needs. This leads to progressively more difficult definitions and measurements as one proceeds from the base to the apex. Buck (1988) later also proposed a similar hierarchical theory of motivation and emotion, starting with reflexes at the bottom and progressing though primary drives to linguistically based motives and emotions at the apex. His is a progressive phylogenetically based system that reflects species requirements. Lower organisms' activities consist solely of reflexes and instincts, whereas higher organisms' motives are influenced by learning and, on the human level, the cultural experiences and language, with the latter playing major roles in directing much of behavior. Thus, many current treatments of human motivation distinguish biological from social motives.

Since the early 1970s, the *Annual Review of Psychology,* for example, has had separate review chapters for biological and social approaches to motivation. This division does not necessarily assume that the coverage treats distinct systems, but for heuristic purposes, it is sometimes beneficial to review them separately to avoid an unmanageable mishmash.

Recently, some social cognitive theorists have distinguished three broad classes of motivation (Bandura, 1991). One class consists of the biological motives that develop from (1) various tissue needs and (2) aversive conditions. The former must be satisfied and the latter must be removed. People must anticipate the occurrence of these needs (e.g., we construct shelters prior to the appearance of inclement weather contions). The second class consists of learned motives that operate through social incentives. For example, infants learn early in life the rewards associated with a mother's smile in contrast with the negative consequences following her scowl. People seek the approval of others and will refrain from activities that lead to disapproval. In this class are motives that depend primarily on the reaction of others. The third class, also a group of learned social motives, consists of cognitively based anticipations. People set goals for themselves and their behavior is guided by these self-determined expectancies and perceptions. For cognitive theorists who champion this viewpoint, analysis of the multifaceted self-concepts is a major task in explaining motivation.

In this monograph, we first discuss some of the motives that are to a considerable extent dependent on relatively easily measurable energetic and genetic factors but also have a large learned and environmental–cultural component. Today, we do not eat solely because of a need for food, and neither do many animals. Since at least the 1920s, experiments have demonstrated that fishes, chickens, rats, and other animals eat more when other members of their species are present (Allee, 1951, p. 98). Similar considerations also apply to other motives that are frequently labeled as biological. Allee (1951, p. 101) describes research with worker ants that demonstrated individuals start digging sooner and work more rapidly when placed together with other ants. On the human level, in most instances, it is difficult to determine the relative contribution of biological and psychosocial factors. We have, therefore, omitted the label biological motivation, though for many motives the biological factors are more readily discerned than the motives that depend primarily on the relationships of people living in a society and the approval or disapproval of others, and this includes also those motives in which self-regulation plays a major role. An energetic component is much more difficult to measure in many of these motives. Here, too, however, there are biological consequences, such as cardiovascular or immunological changes, when some of these motives are thwarted.

It cannot be overemphasized that many frequently used divisions of motivation into biological and various types of social motivation are arbitrary, and that on the human level, both innate and experiential factors influence most internal as well as publicly observable activities. Thus, constructs from social motivation are important factors even in what is frequently referred to as biological motivation. We may go to a restaurant to eat because we are hungry, because we want to socialize, or to please a partner. Though we eschew dividing motives into biological and social types, we discuss some individual motives in an order that might be construed as following traditional classifications of biological and social types. We cannot be exhaustive in analyzing motives, since this would encompass a review of all behaviors that have been studied.

The Temporal Framework

In general, biological or genetic factors in motivation have their major impact initially on short-term states, while psychosocial motives have a much longer temporal framework. Short- and long-term parameters are relative. As with genetic and environmental factors, the short- and long-term motives interact. The interplay between biological and psychosocial factors makes it very difficult in most instances to develop a multiperspective theory of specific motives, especially if we attempt to apply such a theory to an analysis of the motivational changes that occur with aging, since the organism's biological substrates are in a continuous state of flux. Health and sensorimotor abilities play a major role in motivation, and it is unnecessary here to describe the continuous decrements in health and physical abilities during aging. Similarly, the psychosocial components of motives are influenced by a host of interacting, long-term experiential factors that are difficult to subject to rigorous, traditional scientific methodologies. Furthermore, research findings are constrained by cohort and time of measurement factors that places limits on the generalizations that can be made (Schaie & Willis, 1991, pp. 258–259). Older individuals had experienced during their lifetime a variety of social changes, many of which can have a major influence on their motives. Growing up during a period of economic depression will affect a person's goals very differently from childhood experiences during an era of economic boom (Elder, 1974). Similarly, the stresses associated with military experiences in war may have long-term effects (Elder & Clipp, 1994). However, it is a daunting task to disentangle hazardous combat experiences from the social supports a person has at home and in the military, the public attitudes toward the military during and after the war, as well as a myriad of other psychosocial factors. In comparing posttraumatic stress disorders in combat veterans of World

War II and the Korean war, Spiro, Schnurr, and Aldwin (1994) noted that war experiences may be a hidden variable in the study of the psychology of aging of a large cohort that lived through these periods. It is time consuming and expensive to require participants in aging studies to recount all of their life experiences. Also, we do not know which experiences may be critical for an analysis of health, motivation, or other factors.

DEFINITIONS OF AGING

While there are numerous difficulties attendant to the concept of motivation, equally troublesome are the attempts to define aging. Birren and Cunningham (1985) pointed out that psychologists rarely use rigorous definitions of aging in their studies. Even with reference to such an easily controlled variable as chronological age, there have been no standard criteria for defining "old" age. Wherever available and important for our analysis, we at least specify the ages of the study participants. In different studies, the age ranges of "older" participants have varied from the 50s to the 90s. True, in diverse environments, a given chronological age may represent various psychological stages of development, but, ultimately, this then leads to a multiplicity of assumptions about the age factor in psychogerontology. While in some biological and psychosocial phenomena, such as menopause or retirement, age may be specified relatively discretely, most changes that occur during aging do not have a definite transition point. Frequently, however, in both biomedical and psychosocial sciences we use arbitrary conventions (e.g., in the definition of hypertension or poverty). Birren and Bengtson (1988) edited a volume devoted to an analysis of the disparate assumptions about age made by biologists, psychologists, and sociologists in gerontology. Passuth and Bengtson (1988), in their chapter, argued that, at the present, it is futile to attempt to develop a multidisciplinary general theory of aging encompassing biological, psychological, and sociological factors, since definitions of aging vary in each of these domains.

Biomarkers

Mooradian (1990) reviewed the issues arising from attempts to develop biological markers or indexes of aging. Although he points out that some gerontologists have maintained that this is akin to looking for the "Holy Grail" and that it probably will not lead to any useful application, others have identified several goals that may result from the development of such biological parameters. Among the benefits that could be achieved from the identification of a biomarker(s) of aging would be (1) an under-standing of the various mechanisms of aging; (2) standardization of geron-tological studies; (3) determining the impact of various interventions and or hazards on the rate of aging; (4) estimation of life expectancy; and (5) possibly determining maximum life span. Biomarkers should not be con-fused with normative age-related alterations of various biological para-meters. According to Mooradian, a biomarker should be directly linked to aging and be independent of disease states and metabolic derangements that commonly occur in aged organisms. Such biomarkers are not yet available. Mooradian's proposal, however, assumes that environmental factors that impact on the biomarkers are uniform in a population, and that is unlikely. A paper by Hochschild (1990) reports on a study on 2,462 persons in which 12 physiological measures were correlated with a num-ber of demographic variables (e.g., state of residence, education, parental longevity, etc.) and a number of lifestyle factors (e.g., alcohol consump-tion, amount of physical activity, etc.), where for each of the latter there are some normative data on morbidity and/or mortality. Hochschild em-phasizes that these are primarily correlational tests of physiological func-tioning related to environmental variables that may be useful in developing a risk index, which, with additional tests, may ultimately pro-duce a battery of tests serving as a biomarker(s) of aging. While compre-hensive studies even in a single domain such as biology are limited, there are data in some restricted substantive areas, such as life expectancy, in which the combined or interactive roles of biological, psychological, and sociological factors are examined to some extent, at least qualitatively. Such analyses are usually limited and do not encompass the multiple as-pects of human existence. Also, since for ethical and practical reasons ex-perimental approaches to human age-related changes are not possible, we must be content with descriptive and retrospective analytical studies. Yates and Benton (1995) speak of the problem of "reading genomic tea leaves" in the prediction of human life trajectories. Costa and McCrea (1995) criticized the search for biomarkers or functional measures of aging by stressing the statistical confounds that are associated with the large number of indices that have been used in this endeavor. They also emphasized that it is important to know not only which functions dete-riorate with aging, but also which remain stable.

Psychological and Sociological Markers

Biomarkers address primarily biological parameters. Psychological and social markers are even more difficult to specify. Dannefer (1988a; 1988b) presented a broad sketch of the heterogeneity of older populations. Not only are there intercultural differences, but even within a given culture there are large interindividual differences, and diversity increases with age. This diversity is not restricted to cohort effects that exert a powerful influence on a variety of biological, psychological and social factors, but within a single cohort, heterogeneity increases with age due to a variety of diverse biosocial life experiences. In addition, intraindividual differences also increase with age. For example, on many reaction-time tests for the same older individual, the responses from trial to trial are frequently more variable than they are for a younger person. Berkman (1988), an epidemiologist, reviewed some of the factors producing heterogeneity in life expectancy and functioning. The large heterogeneities pose difficult problems for different aspects of social policy.

Though increases in individual variabilities with aging have been known for a long time (Baltes & Willis, 1977), little consideration was given to this important phenomenon even by gerontologists. Nelson and Dannefer (1992) analyzed 127 gerontological studies published in well-established journals of gerontology or development between 1982 and 1987. Only 43% of the articles with empirical data reported any measures of dispersion (standard deviation, variance, range, or standard errors). In the articles that did report dispersions, variability showed aging-associated increases in 83% of the longitudinal and 65% of the cross-sectional studies. In only 17% of the studies, both longitudinal and cross-sectional, did variability decrease with age. Finally, only 21% of the authors discussed the variability found in the data, and only 10% discussed them in their concluding remarks. The lack of attention given to variability makes it more difficult to arrive at reliable generalizations and it is more likely that discrepancies will be found between apparently similar studies. This is especially the case in an area such as motivation.

Maxson, Berg, and McClearn (1996) used a cluster-analytic approach to study some health and psychosocial factors as predictors of dementia and mortality. In a nonrandom sample of 335 men and women in Sweden, aged 70 years, they collected data on several measures of self-reported health, cognitive performance, functional capacity, social contacts, and subjective well-being (SWB). Survivors were retested at ages 75 and 79. Multiple analyses of variance were used to obtain five clusters of participants. Cluster A consisted of participants who scored above the sample mean in all domains. In Cluster C, the participants had the highest scores on SWB, the second highest on cognitive performance, but their health scores were low. Nevertheless, this group had the lowest incidence of dementia, and their mortality was not different from that of participants in Cluster A. Though the sample size in this study was relatively small and the validity of some of the measures may be questioned (e.g., self-reported health), it poses difficulties for defining successful aging.

OUR FOCUS

We have briefly presented some of the obstacles to the analysis of aging changes in motivation. In contrast to the research covering childhood or adolescence, there are logistical problems in following and observing an individual from early through late adulthood. In addition to the relatively long duration of the human life span, the recent rapid technological, sociopolitical, and cultural changes result in increasingly greater variabilities in individual life histories. This creates a much greater challenge for the development of generalizations about late adulthood than it does for the construction of a theory for the early part of the life span, which encompasses only a short time frame. A brief time period reduces the difficulties inherent in empirically testing changes in motivation that are influenced by the continuous shifts of environmental factors. Also, since in our society reinforcements or support for research are to some extent contingent on obtaining closure in an empirical investigation, it is much easier to study longitudinal motivational development in childhood than in adulthood. A number of scholars have taken a pessimistic view about the feasibility of developing an integrated theory of psychological science in general or even of subfields, such as personality or motivation (Koch, 1993; Magnusson & Törestad, 1993). In 1977, Baltes and Willis referred to theories of aging as being prototheoretical, incomplete, and of insufficient precision and scope. Thirteen years later, Birren and Birren (1990) came essentially to the same conclusion. In 1996, Birren and Schroots concluded that the psychology of aging is data rich but theory poor. Most of the efforts on theory construction have been on limited aspects of aging, primarily cognitive capacities. Among other shortcomings, they mention the lack of attention paid to the *needs* of the elderly.

In summary, except for a few personality theories that usually attempt to describe broad, all-encompassing approaches to developmental stages and are typically poorly anchored to testable empirical theorems, psychologists have failed to analyze some of the disparate generalizations about *gerodynamics,* the continuous aging changes in behavior (Birren & Schroots, 1996). If we can view motivation as an integrating psychological concept (Appley, 1991, p. 22) that attempts to explain broad aspects of behavior, it would seem worthwhile to examine at least some of the major changes during aging or among the aged in various domains in which motivation plays an important role. A considerable emphasis will be given to homeostasis in terms of the appearance of stress and coping, since, traditionally, it is assumed that aging manifests itself in a loss of balance.

While aging is associated with numerous somatic and psychological pathologies that have profound consequences on motivation, we attempt to examine primarily studies conducted on relatively healthy older people who represent the great majority the elderly. We define "old" in terms of commonly adopted social criteria in Western societies (e.g., age of retirement from work, eligibility for various social benefits, and diminished expectations). Societal needs have directed much of gerontological research and writing to investigations of older persons who have major disabilities and need special services. By focusing our review on motivational factors in healthy persons, we may provide some guidance toward an understanding of "successful aging" in the fastest growing segment of our population. Many of the findings are, of course, applicable also to individuals who have health and other problems commonly occurring in an older population.

REPRISE

During the past 30 years, experimental psychology has shown relatively little interest in motivation, though the construct has been widely used in applied fields, and a somewhat similar situation has occurred also in gerontology in general. While there has been much research in nonapplied gerontological psychology, research on motivation has lagged. Until recently, most of the research emphasis both in the United States and in other countries has been on the problems faced by disabled older persons, rather than an analysis of aging in normal, "healthy" individuals. At the same time, it is necessary to remember that there is a continuum between normal healthy aging and pathological changes (Birren & Schroots, 1996). Similarly, there is a continuum between elderly who are living independently and those who are institutionalized. Do scientists reflect the public's stereotypes about aging (i.e., that most older people are incompetent or disabled; Barrow, 1992, Chapter 2), or are they partially responsible for the stereotypes? Kelly (1992) discussed the impact of common beliefs on scientific propositions. Also, there is considerably more financial support for the solution of visible social problems than for nonapplied science. The biologist

Adelman (1995), in a paper on "the Alzheimerization of aging," bemoaned the overemphasis of research support in the United States on applied problems. It seems to me, however, that it is not always easy to separate applied from basic research. Thus, a review of the information on various motives, some within an applied setting, may contribute to some understanding of the behavioral activities of the continuously growing older cohorts of our population.

We cited McReynolds's (1990) observation that references to metaphors in motivation have been topical. This is not surprising, since it may be assumed that most human activities, aside from some basic physiological functions, have a motivational component. Attempts to develop overarching theories of behavior appear to be difficult, if not impossible. Perforce a review of motivation, or of any other topic in psychology, cannot be exhaustive and must be limited by the author's predilections.

CHAPTER 2

Biological Foundations

INTRODUCTION

This chapter reviews several biological functions that in the past have been most directly linked to changes in motivation during aging. For heuristic purposes, it discusses the changes on the organismic or physiological rather than the cellular level, though it is assumed that, ultimately, the cellular mechanisms lead to the organismic changes. The biologist Cristofalo (1996), in his review of recent theories of aging, observed that aging refers to several phenomena. There is no singular biological change that can be used as a criterion of aging. He also recommended that we dissect (his term) the various aspects of aging.

Most organismic systems exhibit some changes during aging. Since this is not a treatise on the biology of aging, selection was necessary. McCarter (1995) noted that, historically, aging has been associated with a loss of the intensity of energy metabolism. Since the Introduction indicated that, traditionally, many psychologists have defined motivation as the energetic aspect of behavior, an understanding of age-associated changes in energy metabolism is critical for the analysis of aging and motivation. There are numerous ways that the intensity of energy utilization can be studied, either in an organ system or in the whole body. In humans, the most common technique is to measure whole body basal metabolic rate (BMR) to determine total energy expenditure (McCarter, 1995). There is much literature on this topic, though aging per se does not seem to affect the intensity of metabolism. Changes in body composition in various organismic systems, however, do play a major role (McCarter, 1995). There have been no recent studies relating BMR to motivation or other specific behavioral variables. We, therefore, omit this topic. In Chapter 3 we examine fatigue, which in many cases may be related to metabolic changes.

A number of neuroendocrine and hormonal factors modulate metabolic rate by affecting sensory and motor activities and thereby motivation. We review, therefore, age-associated changes in cerebral metabolism, several neurotransmitters, some of the endocrines, the immune system, and cardiovascular (CV) functions.

CEREBRAL METABOLISM

The brain is a heterogeneous organ and aging produces a variety of structural and functional changes in its different parts. In 1890, Roy and Sherrington first proposed that functional activity of the brain is related to the cerebral blood flow (CBF) of the region associated with a specific organismic activity in order to meet its metabolic demands. We can, therefore, measure metabolic activity in the brain by measuring CBF, or regional CBF ($_r$CBF), and oxygen, or regional oxygen metabolism ($_r$CMRO$_2$). The required energy for neural activity is obtained by the oxidation of glucose. Hence, the regional glucose metabolic rate ($_r$CMR$_{glc}$) can be determined either under resting or active states.

Several techniques are available for each of these measures. For example, for $_r$CMR$_{glc}$, a minute quantity of a radioactive isotope, a positron-emitting tracer analog of glucose, is injected intravenously; the person then performs the task for which the glucose metabolism is to be measured. During the task performance, the skull is scanned with radiation detectors connected to a computer. This technique, positron emission tomography (PET), makes it feasible to localize and quantify the rate of glucose utilization. More recently, magnetic resonance spectroscopy, a noninvasive technique, has also been introduced in measuring brain functional activities. There are several sources available for brief descriptions of the various methods (Coffey, 1994; Pietrini & Rapoport, 1994).

Under resting conditions, $_r$CBF, $_r$CMR$_{O_2}$, and $_r$CMR$_{glc}$ measures of brain metabolism show relatively high positive correlations with each other, but during activity, these relationships can change. There are numerous factors influencing the measurements. Foremost is the selection of the participants. Are studies to be conducted on "average" persons of a given chronological age, or is there a selection based on health status? Small brain insults, not detected by behavioral or by "usual" medical examinations, may affect the results. The role of several behavioral factors during the measurement procedures complicates the interpretation of the results. For example, Pietrini, Horwitz, Grady, Maisog, *et al.* (1992) found that the metabolic indices during a cognitive task, watching a film, are more pronounced in young than in healthy older persons. What could have contributed to this change? Were the older persons paying less attention to the task? Though this was not reported, it is possible that this, indeed, was the case. Presumably, no behavioral measures were recorded. But it should be also noted that in psychology, attention is at the present still a difficult-to-measure, ill-defined construct (Kinchla, 1992). Numerous sensory factors are also important. Most likely, there were "stronger" sensory inputs in the younger persons. CBF and CMR_{O_2} are correlated not only with specific behavioral activities, but also with the effort or "arousal" associated with the activity (Ingvar, 1982). The concept of arousal has been applied to increases in the activities of the central nervous system (CNS) or autonomic nervous system (ANS). CBF is much higher during anxiety or a high level of excitation than during less arousing activities. The latter, in turn, are associated with higher CBF than resting states or sleep. Attention to a speaker or apprehension about responding to a speaker enhances $_rCBF$.

Grady and Rapoport (1992) published a brief review of some studies on cerebral metabolism and aging, with a special emphasis on changes associated with various dementias. Many, but not all, of the studies they reviewed had reported some decreases in $_rCBF$ as well as in $_rCMR_{O_2}$ and $_rCMR_{glc}$. More recently, Pietrini and Rapoport (1994) again summarized additional studies of $_rCMR_{glc}$ in older people. The reviewers noted, however, that in most studies, sensory inputs were not controlled, though animal studies have indicated that sensory stimulation affects CBF as well as CMR_{O_2}. Since many older individuals have pronounced sensory deficits, it is inappropriate to compare young persons who have relatively intact sensory inputs with older persons who have sensory deficits. They concluded that in healthy older persons, $_rCBF$, $_rCMR_{O_2}$, and $_rCMR_{glc}$ are minimally affected in the resting state, with changes probably not greater than about 12%. During behavioral activities, however, there are larger age differences. We mentioned previously the potential role of sensory effects and motivational or emotional factors that may contribute to the observed decrements. In most studies, these had not been controlled. The authors also reviewed data showing decreased correlations in older persons of $_rCMRO_{glc}$ between different cortical areas. This may reflect localized small structural insults.

Though even persons with some diminished CBF, when presented with a cognitive task, can temporarily respond with increased flow, perhaps by exerting extra effort. But persons with "substantial decrements" in flow, associated with more pronounced structural changes, cannot compensate with increased CBF activity when they are faced with cognitive tasks, and they usually perform more poorly than healthy individuals of the same age (Wang & Busse, 1975). Also, $_rCMR_{glc}$ correlations in the resting state between areas in the frontal and parietal lobes and the temporal and occipital lobes are higher in younger than in older persons (Pietrini & Rapoport, 1994).

The relationship between reduced resting cerebral metabolism and functional impairment is most noticeable in Alzheimer-type dementia (SDAT) patients (Haxby & Rapoport, 1986). The results of $_rCMR_{glc}$ are very similar to the data on CBF, even though the correlation between these variables is not extremely high. As with CBF or $_rCBF$, $_rCMR_{glc}$ in dementias and other cerebrovascular disease will differentially affect regional functional activity. Thus, large changes in brain metabolism are strong indicators of pathology.

In short, at the present, cerebral metabolic activity is not a useful index for the assessment of motivational–affective factors. Also, most of the data that we have on brain metabolism have been obtained cross-sectionally with the concomitant shortcomings of this experimental design. Logistical difficulties make it unlikely that much longitudinal data will be forthcoming in the near future.

NEUROTRANSMITTERS

Introduction

The energetics or activity of the nervous system depend on the availability of various neurotransmitters, and the list of putative transmitters appears to be constantly growing. Several pathological conditions associated with aging have for a number of years been linked with a loss of certain neurotransmitters, while the levels of neurotransmitters associated with aging have been vigorously investigated, both on the animal as well as the human level. Rogers and Bloom (1985), in their review of this topic, noted the discrepancies in the reported experimental findings: "There is virtually no metabolic step for any of the neurotransmitter systems where at least two conflicting reports on the effect of age cannot be cited" (p. 665). They then go on to consider some of the difficulties that have led to this confusion. Among the factors, they claim, that need to be considered are (1) differences in the definition of "old"; (2) differences in the regions that were assayed; (3) interaction of various pathological changes; (4) postmortem changes, especially in most human studies where measurements of transmitters occur after death; (5) the person's prior environment, including disease history; (6) influences of manifold drug treatments; and (7) a lack of standards for comparison. Later, Morgan and May (1990) came to essentially the same conclusions, as did Rogers and Bloom (1985) five years earlier. Morgan and May (1990) referred to their chapter only as a "progress report" awaiting substantially more research. More recently Cotman, Kahle, and Korotzer (1995) also concluded that shifts in individual neurotransmitters are only minor in healthy older adults. These authors also emphasize the important role of neurotrophic factors, endogenous signaling proteins, such as nerve growth factor and cytokines. These proteins promote the growth and survival, as well as the plasticity, of neurons, and they are especially important in the reorganization after injury. Such adjustments are, therefore, especially important during aging, yet few studies have been devoted to their status during aging. Though decremental activity in an isolated subsystem may be small, considered *in toto,* the impact may be large. There may be a cascade in which an imbalance in one system spreads and influences other changes. The commonly observed decrements in the ability of the older organism to respond to challenges (Massoro, 1995) also apply to the brain. Several compensatory mechanisms that help the young to absorb small changes in a neurotransmitter system tend to be deficient in the older organism (Cotman *et al.,*1995).We briefly examine some of the aging effects where there seems to be substantial agreement among various investigators. Whether these changes represent incipient pathological conditions, similar to those producing decreases in CBF, described previously, cannot be ascertained. Most of the data are cross-sectional; thus, they are age differences rather than age changes.

Acetylcholine

The oldest identified neurotransmitter is acetylcholine (ACh). It is widely distributed in both the central and peripheral nervous systems, as well as at the neuromuscular junction. The enzyme choline acetyltransferase (CAT) is needed for its synthesis, and many studies of age changes measured CAT activity. While results on CAT activity have been inconsistent in healthy, aging individuals, decreases seen in SDAT patients seem to be one of the most significant neurobiological symptoms of the disease.

Catecholamines and Serotonin

The neurotransmitter in the sympathetic nervous system (SNS), as well as in many CNS structures, is norepinephrine (NE), one of the catecholamines. In the cerebral cortex and the hippocampus, most studies report no changes in NE with age. However, in the hypothalamus, there seems to be some decline in NE (Morgan & May, 1990). At the same time, most studies report increased levels of plasma NE. The mechanism(s) for this excess in the plasma are still uncertain; it is not the result of increased secretion (Lakatta, 1990), but possibly a consequence of changes in body composition and low levels of physical activity (McCarter, 1995).

Dopamine (DA) shares with NE several enzymes in its synthesis and catabolism. According to most investigators, DA levels show large age-associated decreases in human neostriatal structures (Morgan, May, & Finch, 1987, 1988). However, there have been several studies that have reported no changes even with large samples, and the inconsistencies between findings are difficult to interpret. The sole explanation for the discrepancies offered by Morgan and May (1990), and Morgan *et al.* (1987) are the large within-samples variabilities in each study. The presynaptic losses occur mainly in the nigrostriatal pathway. Postsynaptic responsiveness indicates even greater declines as measured by a loss of D-2 receptor density (Wong, Broussolle, Wand, Villemagne, *et al.*, 1988). DA losses are implicated in Parkinson's as well as in SDAT disease. In nonpathological states, the role of DA has not been established thus far.

While aging does not seem to affect presynaptic serotonin levels, postsynaptically, changes have been reported, especially in SDAT patients (Morgan & May, 1990). First, it is not possible to provide a brief summary of all neurotransmitter changes with age. It is analogous to the question, how are brain functions affected as a person ages? Aside from the technical difficulties in the assay of dozens of putative transmitters, the fundamental problem of separating "normal" aging changes from "pathological" disturbances remains. Second, at what point in the life span do we start tracking changes? Finally, we must remember that the brain is a structure of immense complexity, in which anatomical and functional transformations are constantly in progress. Several psychologists have emphasized that it is futile to look for close relationships between a single neurotransmitter, enzyme, or hormone and motivation or personality traits (Depue, Luciana, Arbisi, Collins, & Leon, 1994; Zuckerman, 1995). Most psychological factors depend on a number of physiological variables, and most of them interact. We have already mentioned the same caveat with reference to aging and neurotransmitters (Cotman, *et al.,* 1995). In major geriatric diseases such as SDAT or Parkinson's, there are gross transmitter losses, and most of the research efforts on the human level have been concentrated on the analysis of these effects.

THE ENDOCRINES

The endocrine system, or more properly, systems, also play a vital role in the maintenance of bodily homeostasis. Loss in the effectiveness of some of the endocrine or combined neural and endocrine systems has played a prominent role in theories of aging since the beginning of interest in the later stages of life (Timiras, 1988, p. 53). Several of them are especially closely tied-in with ANS functions and, thus, with activation and motivation. Aside from their role in modulating ANS functions, several endocrine systems are closely linked with many basic biological *needs,* such as eating, drinking, and temperature control. In the second edition of the *Handbook of the Biology of Aging,* in a chapter entitled "Neuroendocrine and Autonomic Functions in Aging Mammals," Finch and Landfield (1985) ascribe a major role to this system in the control of cellular aging. The pituitary, with its connections with the hypothalamus and the adjacent brain regions, which are frequently referred to as the limbic system, is usually considered to be the central structure regulating biological motivation. However, it needs to be emphasized that many endocrine-associated disease states of the elderly, such as diabetes mellitus, will have major consequences at any age. These effects are, therefore, more properly associated with pathology rather than eugeric aging or "normal" aging. For purposes of this review, we consider primarily those glands that play a significant role in the energizing, thus in the motivational, aspects of behavior.

The Pituitary and the Adrenal Cortex

The anterior lobe of the pituitary shows relatively few structural changes with age, and the secretion of adrenocorticotrophic hormone (ACTH) remains stable throughout life. The hypothalamic–pituitary–adrenocortical (HPA) system is activated during stress. Sapolsky (1992), in his review of the adrenocortical axis changes in aging humans, also indicates that "the most striking feature of adrenocortical function in aged humans is its normalcy" (p. 315). Not only are basal functions maintained, but responsivity to stress via the secretion of ACTH also seems to remain intact through adulthood in healthy individuals. However, it is difficult to test this relationship because it is unethical to induce stress in people, and the limited available data are based mostly postsurgical cases and some experimental hypoglycemia studies (Sapolsky, 1992).

The adrenal cortex secretes three classes of steroids: the glucocorticoids, mineralocorticoids, and androgens. Cortisol, the principal human glucosteroid, which has excitatory effects on the nervous system, shows only minimal changes in older people (Nelson, 1995). During the past two decades, a considerable amount of research in psychiatry has been devoted to studies in which the synthetic steroid dexamethasone (dex), which suppresses ACTH production in the pituitary, is administered to psychiatric patients, mainly to depressed persons. In healthy individuals, ACTH stimulates cortisol production, and cortisol in turn reduces ACTH release—a negative biological feedback mechanism. Since dex inhibits ACTH release, cortisol plasma levels will also be suppressed after dex administration. When disturbances affect the HPA system, the negative feedback system may not be functioning properly, and dex may not suppress plasma cortisol levels. For example, in some forms of depression, such as melancholic, characterized by anhedonia, loss of weight, and sleep disturbances, there is hyperactivity in the HPA, resulting in overproduction of ACTH, and standard doses of dex will not result in the suppression of cortisol (Ritchie, Belkin, Krishnan, Nemeroff, et al., 1990). Thus, administration of standard doses of dex and subsequent measurement of plasma cortisol have led to the development of the dexamethasone suppression test (DST) as a tool used in psychiatric diagnosis. As such, the roles of several variables, including age, have been investigated. In many of these studies, it has been reported that with increasing age, some older individuals do not show the same level of cortisol suppression after DST as do younger persons (Sharma, Pandey, Janicak, Peterson, et al., 1988). The contributions of age to the post-DST hypercortisolemia seem to vary from study to study. Some have reported that only 8% of the variance may be attributed to age (Weiner, 1989), while others have reported a greater effect (Maes, Jacobs, Suy, Minner, et al., 1990). While methodological variables may account for some of these variations, concurrent medical illnesses (Cooke, Warsh, Stancer, Hasey, et al., 1990) as well as depression, which is usually more common in older individuals, may contribute to the higher levels of dex nonsuppression in more older than younger persons. Also, there seems to be some evidence that in approximately 50% of SDAT or multi-infarct patients, there is some dex resistance (Sapolsky & McEwen, 1988). It is plausible that in many studies in which older persons exhibited dex-resistant depression, early stages of SDAT were present, but the latter are usually difficult to ascertain. It has also been reported that hypercortisolemia and dex nonsuppression do occur more frequently in the old-old, those over 80 years of age. The two factors tend to combine so that older SDAT patients show greater hypercortisolism and dex resistance than do younger patients.

Sapolsky (1992), in his review of HPA changes, speculates that older depressed persons may be more hypercortisolemic because, cumulatively, they have experienced more episodes of depression than have younger depressives. Alternatively, the incidence of mild forms of depression, often associated with diverse somatic ailments is indeed higher in older than in younger populations; in many older persons who live in the community, depression may not have been diagnosed, and some of their deviant behavior, such as sleep disturbance, may be attributed to aging rather than to depression.

Another hypothesis was also advanced by Sapolsky (1990), based primarily on an extrapolation of animal data. Glucocorticoids have an effect on certain brain structures, most prominently on the hippocampus, which is rich in glucocorticoid receptors. In turn, the hippocampus modulates the release of ACTH, a negative-feedback relationship. The research on the interaction of the hippocampus and the pituitary–adrenal system has been conducted primarily on the rat (McEwen, DeKloet, & Rostene, 1986). With age, there is a loss of the glucocorticoid receptors, and there are also decrements in the pyramidal cells in the hippocampus. In the rat, long-term exposure to corticosteroids produces hippocampal aging, that is, loss of cells (Kerr, Campbell, Hao, & Landfield, 1989; Finch & Landfield, 1985); numerous behavioral changes in aging have been ascribed to the atrophy in the hippocampus (Landfield, 1988). Finch and Landfield (1985, pp. 578–580) concluded their review by emphasizing that much more work is needed on the relationship of adrenal steroids and aging, and that the former cannot account for the various hippocampal aging changes. Sapolsky (1990) speculates that in aged humans, the normal feedback sensitivity of the glucocoticoids to ACTH stimulation may be close to a threshold of dysfunction; thus, any disorder, such as depression, SDAT, or psychotic disorders, may reveal pituitary–adrenal dysfunctions. As in other organismic systems the HPA becomes dysfunctional when major stressors or stimuli that deviate very much from a "normal" level impinge on the organism. It is difficult, however, to quantify major deviations.

The Adrenal Medulla

The adrenal medulla is part of the SNS, and it has rich vascular connections with the adrenal cortex. The adrenal medulla secretes epinephrine (E) and NE. In addition to the adrenal medulla, NE secretion also originates in the brain, and in the adult, its predominant origin is in the sympathetic nerve endings (Goldstein, Mc Carty, Polinsky, & Kopin, 1983). Our previous analysis of the glucocorticoids needs to be kept in mind when we review the adrenal medulla. Most studies have found that plasma NE actually increases with age in humans (McCarter, 1995; Raskind, Peskind, Veith, Beard, et al., 1988). These increases are primarily the result of an increased appearance of NE, rather than to lowered clearance, though the latter also contributes to the elevation of NE in plasma. During isometric exercises that elicit a diminished cardiovascular response, there is a greater serum catecholamine rise in older people. At the same time, the return to a basal level is slower in older than in younger persons (Finch & Landfield, 1985). The mechanisms for these changes have not been determined. Florini (1989) analyzed in general the problems in explaining age-related changes in hormone levels. In the case of insulin, for example, there are at least four different possibilities in accounting for the commonly seen decrements in the hormone level in older persons. Also, the sensitivity of different target tissues changes differently with age, and sensitivity to catecholamines may also be influenced by other hormones, such as glucocorticoids that themselves show aging changes. Thus, several mechanisms may be involved in the observed increases of NE during aging. Secretion of NE is associated with increased SNS activity, perhaps the result of increasing stresses. Since sympathetic outflow to different vascular beds is not uniform, and hypothalamic stimulation and baroreceptor stimulation also result in quantitatively dissimilar outputs, different stressors will result in quantitatively different NE responses (Goldstein et al., 1983; Kopin, 1995). Therefore, an analysis of age-associated changes in catecholamines involves separate analyses of changes in the specific organs innervated by the SNS.

The Thyroid

Slowing of activity and reduced metabolic rate, typical signs of aging, have been traditionally associated with decreased thyroid activity. It would be expected, therefore, that thyroid activity should show decrements during aging. The size of the thyroid gland decreases after maturity and there are various microscopic changes in the cells. In most healthy older individuals, the level of thyroxine (T4), the major hormone secreted by the thyroid gland, remains unchanged, even though the secretion rate for the hormone may have been reduced. Here, too, as with the glucocorticoids, the lowered secretion is compensated for by decreases in clearance rate (Timiras, 1988, pp. 241–257). By the ninth decade, T4 metabolism may be reduced by 50% from the adult level. Impairments in the hypothalamo–pituitary–

thyroid axis with age are also evident (Reymond, Donda, & Lemarc-hand-Béraud, 1989) in that decrements in both the thyroid-releasing hormone and thyrotropin have been found, and the prevalence of hypothyroidism is higher in older individuals. This may represent an accumulation of thyroid disturbances occurring over several decades (Runnels, Garry, Hunt, & Standefer, 1991). The results with the thyroid resemble those seen with the glucocorticoids. It would seem that the reduced organismic reaction to the thyroid hormone is primarily a change in target-tissue functions (Florini, 1989). The extent to which various changes in thyroid functions are related to the existence of age-associated nonthyroidal illnesses is not easy to determine. At the same time, strict selection of experimental participants, presumably healthy elderly, has demonstrated that age-related changes in the thyroid do occur. The latter can contribute to the development of various diseases (Mariotti, Franceschi, Cossarizza, & Pinchera, 1995). Thyroid alterations may be associated with a number of energetic changes, such as weakness, fatigue, anorexia, and depression. In the analysis of aging and motivation, little attention has been paid to the thyroid, but its role needs to be considered.

The Pancreas and Carbohydrate Metabolism

No account of energetics or activation is complete without a brief consideration of carbohydrate metabolism. While several hormones are involved in the regulation of carbohydrate metabolism, insulin and glucagon secreted by the pancreas play major roles. Age-associated impairment in the ability to maintain blood-glucose homeostasis after ingestion of glucose has been known since about 1920 (Timiras, 1988, p. 258). Even in healthy individuals, there is a slight rise in fasting blood glucose levels with increasing age. This increase is, however, small compared to the rise seen after the ingestion of glucose, referred to as glucose "tolerance," the ability to dispose of ingested glucose. Plasma levels of glucose are measured before and after the ingestion of a standard oral load of dextrose. About a half of older persons have mean blood-glucose concentrations 1–2 hours after the dextrose administration that are 2 *SD*s above the mean for young people (Andres & Tobin, 1977). In one national survey, it was reported that the prevalence of diabetes mellitus, the disorder denoting a metabolism deficit, increases from 2.1% in the 20–44 year age group to 17.9% in the 65–74 year age group (Goldberg & Hagberg, 1990).

Several mechanisms have been proposed as contributors to the loss of glucose tolerance in older persons. These include impaired insulin secretion and its metabolism; an increased glucagon level, which has effects antagonistic to those of insulin; failure of secreted insulin to inhibit glucose output; resistance of target tissues to respond to insulin; and interaction with other hormones, such as growth, NE, or corticosteroids (Florini, 1989; Halter, 1995; Timiras, 1988, p. 260). As in many other functional changes seen in aging, it is not clear to what extent the decreases in glucose tolerance with age are normal and to what extent they are exacerbated by various lifestyle factors such as adiposity, lack of exercise, presence of various illnesses (hypertension), the use of prescription and other drugs, or dietary conditions (Halter, 1995). Several studies have shown increased glucose tolerance in older persons who had participated in regular physical activities, exercise regimens, and/or reduction in percent body fat (Goldberg & Hagberg, 1990).

Pituitary–Gonadal Hormones

Aging of the reproductive system has been known since the dawn of history. Indeed, until modern times, aging has frequently been defined as the cessation of reproductive activities. The earliest scientific attempts at rejuvenation by Brown-Séquard in 1889 involved the injection of older men with testicular extracts (cited by Andres & Tobin, 1977).

In the human male, aging is associated with a fall in the serum level of free or bioavalable testosterone (bT) (Schiavi, Schreiner-Engle, White, & Mandeli, 1991; Vermeulen, 1991). While some investigators report no changes in total serum-testosterone levels (Schiavi et al., 1991), several others have reported changes even in this index (Vermeulen, 1991). There are large interindividual variabilities in both of these indices, and almost all of the data are based on cross-sectional studies. A pilot longitudinal study on a small sample (Vermeulen, 1991) found changes similar to those reported in the cross-sectional studies. The decreases are more pronounced in men who suffer from various health problems such as diabetes mellitus, hypertension, and other cardiovascular diseases. Even though androgens decrease with age, most men do not lose fertility. The decrements are primarily of testicular origin, though there are also some alterations in the hypothalamo–pituitary functions. The clinical signs associated with the androgenic decrements include asthenia, decreased bone and muscle mass, loss of sexual motivation, and in extreme cases, impotence. Schiavi et al. (1991), in a cross-sectional study of 77 healthy married males between the ages of 45 and 74 years, measured total serum testosterone, bT, luteinizing hormone (LH), estradiol, and prolactin, and at the same time they asked their participants to recall the recent frequency of several of their sexual behaviors, such as arousal, coitus, masturbation, and orgasms. In general, age produced a statistically significant negative correlation between age and bT, but a positive one with LH. Total testosterone and estradiol also tended to decrease with age, while prolactin showed increases, but the aging effects were less pronounced than those between bT and age. The various behavioral measures were significantly correlated with bT and the ratio of bT/LH, but not with the other gonadal hormones. However, the age- related bT (bT within an age group) was a more important determiner of the behavioral indices than the effect of bT independent of age. The correlations between the hormonal levels and the behavioral frequencies were in the range of $-.34$ to $-.51$, with $ps < .002$ and lower. The authors acknowledge, of course, that a number of psychosocial factors other than hormone levels play a significant role, most likely a more important one, than do the hormones in sexual behavior. For a more detailed discussion of the psychosocial factors and sexual behavior in general, see Chapter 6.

Aside from reproduction, testosterone is also related to certain emotional states. Gray, Jackson, and McKinlay (1991), as part of a larger study in Massachusetts, obtained data on anger and dominance using a self-report measure and 17 endocrine variables from a random sample of 1,521 males aged 39–70 years. They found that about 3% of the variance on measures of dominance and anger could be attributed to bT. However, it should be noted that of the 105 computed correlations, only 8 reached the usually accepted levels of significance. It would seem, therefore, that testosterone plays only a minor role in the previously named emotional states.

In women, urinary excretion of estrogens begins to show gradual declines throughout adulthood (Talbert, 1977). With the approach of the menopause, there is a dramatic decrease in these hormones as well as progesterone and androgens. While low levels of all gonadal hormones are still present even after the menopause, they are produced from nonovarian sources (Harman & Talbert, 1985). The plasma concentrations of the pituitary-produced gonadotrophin, follicle-stimulating hormone, and LH actually show large increases after the menopause, reflecting the low levels of circulating estrogens that act as a negative feedback mechanism for the secretion of gonadotrophic hormones (Talbert, 1977). Aside from the reproductive system, the decline in the gonadal hormones has major impacts on several physiological functions in women, especially on the cardiovascular and skeletal systems. Based on animal data, it might be assumed that the decrements in the secretions of gonadal hormones would affect sexual behavior in women, but the limited available data do not support such a relationship. In a small sample of premenopausal women, reproductive hormones were not seen to be related to sexual desire or activity (Schreiner-Engel, Schiavi, White, & Ghizzani, 1989). Both Cohen (1990) and Corby and Solnick (1980) note that men are more commonly affected by the use of drugs and health factors than are women. Just as sexual activities do not seem to depend on the decrements of gonadal hormone secretions, there is not much evidence that the hormonal changes induce depression. A number of studies found no evidence that the menopause, with its dramatic drop in estrogens and progesterone, leads to any increases in clinical depression (Matthews, 1992; McKinlay, McKinlay, & Brambilla, 1987). We can conclude, therefore, that the gonadal hormone changes associated with aging in women have their major influence on the cardiovascular and musculoskeletal system. The commonly observed behavioral changes during the menopause are mainly the results of changes in other organismic systems affected by the gonadal hormones. More frequently, the behavioral changes are the consequences of psychosocial factors that are present during this stage of life, since in many cultures, the menopause, the end of the reproductive period, serves as a convenient landmark for denoting the beginning of "old age." Again, a more detailed analysis of sexual behavior of older women, with emphasis on psychosocial factors, is discussed in Chapter 6.

THE IMMUNE SYSTEM

During the last two decades, psychologists have begun to investigate the relationships between behavior and the immune system, especially in conjuction with chronic stress. Among the many reviews, O'Leary (1990) wrote a good, brief introduction to psychoneuroimmunology that included some of the basic concepts. Cohen and Williamson (1991) analyzed potential relationships between psychological stressors and the development of infectious diseases. In their review, they noted that stress may influence both illness behavior and pathological changes. None of the studies they reviewed involved older individuals. Schneiderman, McCabe, and Baum (1992) edited a volume on stress and disease processes, with the majority of contributions devoted to an analysis of immune functions, but this volume has few references to studies of older persons.

Declines in the circulating levels of natural antibodies in older humans have been known since the 1920s (Makinodan, 1977). Many diseases that occur more frequently in the aged have been ascribed to declines in the immune system, and this has led to biological theories of aging implicating the immune system (Makinodan, 1977). Support for such theories comes from the well-known observation that there are increasing incidents of certain infections and cancers with age that have been linked to lowered functions of the immune system. In addition, the development of autoantibodies that are reactive against self-antigens may lead to several autoimmune diseases, some—but not all—occurring more commonly in older people. These include some forms of arthritis, anemias, and nephropathy. Not all declines of immune functions begin at the same stage of life or show the same rates of decrements with age, and the interindividual variabilities of most immunological parameters increase dramatically in the aged (Hausman & Weksler, 1985). The latter fact poses major difficulties in the analysis of empirical data. The variabilities in immune functions are associated not only with genetic factors, but also with such environmental conditions as nutrition, exercise, and various diseases. Since interindividual variabilities in environmental factors increase with age, generalizations concerning aging effects become progressively more difficult in older populations. Furthermore, immunity affects the expression of many diseases that commonly appear in older persons and, in turn, these diseases affect immunity (Hausman & Weksler, 1985).

It has been proposed that there are bidirectional communications between the CNS and the immune system (Ballieux, 1992; Cotman *et al.,* 1995; Moynihan & Cohen, 1992), especially during stress. The individual's immune reactivity is partially determined by the perception of the stressor. Conversely, the perception of the stressor may be influenced by the state of the immune system. This relationship is probably an expression of the interdependence of the immune system with neuroendocrines, mainly the hormones in the HPA system and the neuropeptides (Goya, 1991). Along with the relatively well-established evidence for certain neuroendocrine changes during aging, the immune system is also likely to be affected. The interactions of these systems exacerbate gerontological investigations and the control of possible confounding variables; nevertheless, there is ample evidence that the immune system changes with age, though the mechanisms may not have been clearly established thus far.

Many of the age-related deficits in the immune system result from the involution of the thymus after sexual maturity, with a consequent decline in the production of lymphocytes and the subsequent capacity of the T cells to function effectively (Hausman & Weksler, 1985; Miller, 1990, 1995). There is no consensus, however, about the effects of age on the strengths of B cell responses (Miller, 1990). Similarly, there are discrepancies in the results on the function of human lymphocyte natural killer (NK) cells, which are important in the resistance to viral infections before other immunological responses are activated (Miller, 1995). Miller believes that NK function in human blood is very sensitive to numerous variables, such as the emotional state of the person or prior exercise, and most of these factors are not controlled in most laboratory studies. In addition, assay procedures do not tend to be uniform.

A given stressor may either enhance or decrease immune responses, and different stressors may produce qualitatively or quantitatively different changes. Some of the factors that are important in response to stressors, aside from those that affect the "normal" nonstressed level of the immune system to which references were made previously, are such parameters as the duration of the stressor, chronicity, the immune status of the individual, the effects of various stress hormones, and coping ability of the organism (Moynihan & Cohen, 1992). Though numerous studies have shown that changes in the immune system covary with stress, it has not yet been shown unequivocally that the immune system mediates the stress–disease link (Miller, 1995; Stone, 1992). As noted previously, the immune system influences health status, but health status itself affects the immune system. Finally, while the immune system may not mediate health status, it may be a moderator. However, health status is difficult to specify. More research using finer multivariate statistical analysis techniques may provide clues to elucidate some of the complex relationships (Stone, 1992). Data on age-associated changes in psychoneuroimmunology are sparse.

There have been several investigations of the relationship between depression, a frequently occurring condition in older people, and immunity. Some of the earlier studies were reviewed by Weisse (1992). The relationship between depression and immunocompetence, protection against pathogenic processes, is complex. While most studies have reported reduced immune processes in clinically depressed persons, others have found no changes, and a few have even reported increases in lymphocyte reactivity (Weisse, 1992). Usually, more severely depressed and older persons show greater deficits of immunocompetence (Weisse, 1992). However, Darko, Wilson, Gillin, and Golshan (1991) found, paradoxically, that less depressed, less retarded patients actually had a greater reduction of lymphocyte-proliferative responses, the most consistent immune changes observed among the clinically depressed, than did the clinically more depressed patients. Depression was measured with the Hamilton Rating Scale. As we have previously indicated, numerous environmental factors, hospitalization, or drug usage, which frequently occur in a depressed population, will influence immune reactivity. Depression may be conceptualized as the consequence of exposure to a major social stressor, such as loss of a loved one or help-lessness. Thus, the decrements in immune functions in individuals who have been exposed to stressors are not unexpected. Even the anticipation of stress may reduce T cells (Kemeny, Cohen, Zegans, & Conant, 1989). The extent to which the reduction of immune functions is the direct consequence of depression, or is secondary to the various functional changes associated with depression, such as changes in sleep or diet, has not been ascertained. Finally, it is important to note that older individuals experience a variety of health problems, and they may also receive drugs and other therapies, many of which affect the immune system. Simultaneously, the illness and/or its treatment may produce a depression, making it difficult to determine causality in the changes of immune functions in many older individuals.

In one of the few studies comparing young and old participants' responses during a laboratory-induced stress, Naliboff et al. (1991) found no age effects asociated with the performance of arithmetic problems in several immunological indices, except for a decrement in NK cell reactivity in the older individuals. At the same time, older subjects showed lower heart rate (HR) reactivity and less skin conductance than did the younger participants. Were the older participants less stressed by the task demands?

In conclusion, it seems well-established that the immune system, especially the T cells, function less effectively with increasing age. We also know that the immune system is closely linked with the stress-responsive neuroendocrine system, particularly with the neuropeptides and the glucocorticoids. Because numerous environmental conditions influence immune functions it is difficult to obtain clear-cut data that are not contaminated by various concomitant factors. Much more longitudinal research is needed in this developing field before human psychoneuroimmunology can provide us guidance in gerontology.

CARDIOVASCULAR FUNCTIONS

In his review of the cardiovascular system, Kohn (1977) begins with the statement: "Changes involving the cardiovascular system are central to major questions about aging. Aging of the cardiovascular system may underlie, in part, the generalized physiological decline and progressive debilitation that characterize the aging syndrome" (p. 281). He also cites a study indicating that Leonardo da Vinci wrote about the thickening of the veins as the cause of aging and death (Kohn, 1977). In her analysis of activation, a construct denoting motivation and emotion,

Duffy (1962, p. 29) pointed out that cardiovascular measures often show predictable relationships to overt behavior. Studies on the role of the cardiovascular system in activation or affect were conducted in Wundt's laboratory over a century ago (1887).

Cardiovascular diseases increase exponentially with age (Lakatta, 1985), and this confounds changes that can be attributed to aging per se. For a researcher, the task of selecting participants for a study by screening out persons with cardiovascular abnormalities is difficult, since in many people, the disease is occult, not easily detected. Occult coronary diseases can be frequently diagnosed by exposing the individual to an activity such as treadmill exercise, which exerts cardiovascular stress (Lakatta, 1990). In a large autopsy survey, it was found that approximately 60% of men who died in the sixth decade of life had a 75–100% stenosis of at least one major coronary artery (Lakatta, 1990). In healthy community-dwelling individuals, resting cardiac output, a product of stroke volume and heart rate (HR), does not change very much with age (Lakatta, 1985). However, systolic blood pressure (SBP) does increase with age, and this necessitates an age-related change in myocardial energy metabolism, with an increase in myocardial oxygen consumption. While changes at rest are small, the responses to stimulation may be considerable. In the supine position, HR in healthy individuals is not influenced by aging, but in the standing position, HR is higher in young than in older individuals (Schwartz, Gibb, & Tran, 1991). The same investigators also reported that beat-to-beat variation (SDs) of HRs are smaller in the older person. Cardiac output of older persons reaches its peak at a substantially lower work rate than it does in young adults. However, when maximum effort is not exerted, older healthy individuals may reach the same cardiac output as do younger persons (Shephard, 1987, pp. 71–72). Maximum HR, O_2 consumption, and cardiac output responses to strenuous physical activity decline in older persons and the ejection fraction of blood during exercise decreases from resting levels in older persons. Many of the age-related changes are attributed to altered responsiveness following adrenergic stimulation and/or changes in the peripheral vasculature (Lakatta, 1985). Also, there is a blunting of beta2-adrenergic mediated vasodilation and a preservation of alpha2-vasoconstriction. Older persons require a longer time for HR, BP, and ventilation to attain equilibrium at a given work rate, and conversely, the recovery following effort takes a much longer time (Shephard, 1987, p. 77). The slower recovery of HR after effort can be seen even after older persons perform a 12-item free-recall task. Slower recovery after the performance on an arithmetic and a memory task was seen already in a 40- to 59-year-old group compared to a 23- to 39-year-old group (Furchtgott & Busemeyer, 1979). Increasing HR activation in older persons occurs not only in response to physically demanding tasks, but also in mental tasks, such as when a requirement for episodic memory (recalling a list of random digits) is coupled with a reaction time (RT) task. Under such conditions, older persons show greater HR acceleration than do young ones (Jennings, Nebes, & Yovetich, 1990).

Several studies have examined the role of exercise training on various biological and psychological variables. Blumenthal, Emery, Madden, George, *et al.* (1989) studied 101 men and women aged 60–83 years who were free of clinical manifestations of coronary disease. The participants were randomly assigned to an aerobic exercise group, a yoga and flexibility group, or a waiting list control group. The exercise group participated thrice weekly in a 45-minute exercise program, which included bicycle ergometry and walking/jogging. This regimen produced a significant improvement in peak O_2 consumption (V_{O_2}) and a significant increase in cardiorespiratory fitness, consisting of HR at rest and at submaximum workload, duration of time on the bicycle, and peak V_{O_2}. The other two groups did not show an improvement in their cardiorespiratory fitness. There were other physiological benefits derived from the exercise regimen, but psychological measures of mood, psychiatric symptoms, and neuropsychological functioning were not affected by the training. This study illustrates the importance of environmental factors in assessing the cardiovascular status of an older person.

To summarize, it appears safe that decrements in cardiovascular functions during aging are most evident when the individual is engaged in some physically or psychologically strenuous activity. Reserve capacity is reduced. There seems to be an increasing impairment in the maintenance of normal functions with increasing task demands.

In contrast to the small functional decrements seen during rest or low-level activities, age-associated changes are most pronounced during activities in which environmental demands are high. Thus, activities induced by high levels of motivation are more likely to show differences between young and old. For many functions, the older organism requires more time to reach the optimum level of activity for a particular function, and it cannot reach the same maximum potential performance level that can be achieved by a young organism.

CONCLUSIONS

The preceding brief summary can be also applied to most other biological systems important for motivation. Aging effects are most pronounced when the person is active rather than at rest. Some theories of homeostasis assume that all organismic activities, by definition, result in some disturbances in equilibrium. This has been labeled as "stress." Not only cannot the older organism reach a high peak performance, it probably cannot maintain maximum functioning for as long a period as a younger one, and at the conclusion of the activity, the older organism requires more time to return to the preactivity baseline level. Age-related changes in physiological responses apply not just to large environmental challenges; even for moderate demands, some of the physiological responses change with age. For any given workload, the physiological responses are greater in old than in young individuals, and the rate of recovery of O_2 uptake and CO_2 elimination is slowed down (Shock, 1977). Similarly, lowered HR responses and slower return to a baseline are also seen after performance on mental tasks. The various bodily systems do not operate in isolation. Thus, the decreased efficiency of various physiological control mechanisms cannot be attributed to a single system. Changes in the functions of the nervous, endocrine, immune, and cardiovascular systems are not parallel, and alterations in any one of these or other systems that we have not discussed can profoundly influence all bodily functions. Even "simple" behavioral functions involve numerous biological mechanism. There are dynamic feedback functions whereby the biological substrates influence behavior and vice versa. Also, as Cristofalo (1996) has noted, there is no one biological change that can be used as a criterion of aging.

An obvious factor that interferes with normal activity is health. Unfortunately, it is not easy to specify "normal" health independent of chronological age. A hallmark of increasing chronological age is an increasing incidence of health problems. Though there have been numerous criticisms of a machine-like "wear and tear" theory of aging, Yates and Benton (1995) do find it useful to some extent, at least on a population level. Many health problems in older individuals may be attributed to the prevalence of certain lifestyles. However, some biological changes may have only minimal behavioral consequences, and some may even be adaptive. For example, Katzman (1995) has pointed out that the presence of neural plaques is commonly identified as a biological symptom of Alzheimer's pathology, but the correlation of this observation with cognitive measures is small. Thus, this index is of little help in the assessment of normal aging. Similar difficulties apply also to other biological measures. We have also noted that there have been very few long-term longitudinal studies of biological functions.

CHAPTER 3

Sleep and Fatigue

SLEEP

Introduction

In the previous chapter, we discussed some of the biological mechanisms that are related to motivation. Most definitions of motivation include an energetic factor. Sleep and/or fatigue imply low levels of overt activity. The desire for sleep may be considered to be a powerful motive, and a reduction of this activity leads to efforts to satisfy this need. Numerous disciplines from biochemistry to psychology have contributed to our understanding of this phenomenon. In 1995, *The National Institute of Mental Health* convened a task force on basic behavioral research needs. One section of the group's report covered emotion and motivation, and the latter included a statement that "the need for sleep is powerfully motivating."

The importance of this state to the general well-being of an organism has led to numerous reviews of the overall changes or some aspect of this activity in older adults (Bliwise, 1993; Dement *et al.,* 1985; Prinz, Dustman, & Emmerson, 1990; Richardson, 1990; Woodruff-Pak, 1985). Among the most common complaints of older individuals are difficulties in falling asleep, daytime sleepiness, restless sleep, an insufficient total amount of sleep, and early awakening. Since sleep disturbances are symptoms occurring frequently in depression and other mental problems associated with aging, as well as various somatic illnesses, there have been a number of reviews of sleep within these contexts (Bliwise, 1993; Hoch, Buysse, Monk, & Reynolds, 1992).

Epidemiology

Several studies have reported that as many as 35–50% of people over the age of 65 years have some sleep-related problems (Hoch, Buysse, et al., 1992; Mellinger, Balter, & Uhlenhut, 1985). In a recent survey of 9,000 community elderly, 50% reported some sleep problems that were associated with respiratory symptoms, physical disabilities, depression, use of nonprescription medication, and poorer self-perceived health (Foley, Monjan, Brown, Simonick, et al.,1995). Thus, almost any health problem encountered by an older person may interfere with sleep. Several studies have reported that sleep complaints are related to gender, socioeconomic status (SES), and race (Blazer, Hays, & Foley, 1995; Mellinger et al., 1985). But as Dement et al. (1985) caution, it is not clear to what extent the age-related changes are the consequences of the increases of various pathological changes or whether they are intrinsic to "normal aging." Difficulties associated with the definition of normal aging have been noted previously. This is especially the case with sleep, since Bliwise (1993) has noted that several common sleep changes occur at a chronologically much earlier age than do many other physiological functions. Also, as is true of other aging phenomena, expectations of changes may affect many self-reports of sleep.

Methodology and Laboratory Findings

Since a person cannot tell an observer that he or she is asleep and gross observations by others are not very reliable, we need to record some physiological indices. The three most commonly used ones are electroencephalograms (EEGs), electrooculograms (EOGs), and electromyograms, measured with a polysomnograph (PSG). The standards for the parameters are based on data from young persons (Dement et al., 1985). Combining EEG and EOG patterns, five stages of sleep can be identified.

In the first four stages, EOGs are relatively quiescent; they are referred to as nonrapid eye movement (NREM) states, while during the fifth stage, eye movements are rapid and thus labeled the rapid eye movement (REM) period. During the first two NREM stages, EEG voltages are low and frequencies are high. There are some differences in the parameters between the two stages, but for our purposes, it is not necessary to elaborate on this. In NREM Stages 3 and 4, frequency decreases and amplitude increases. These characteristics are especially noticeable in Stage 4. The last two stages are sometimes called slow-wave sleep (SWS). Stage 4 is the deepest state of sleep, as measured by the amplitude of the stimulus that is necessary to awaken the sleeper. In this stage, delta waves of 0.5–2.0 Hz predominate. In mature adults, each five-stage cycle lasts about 90–100 minutes. Figure 3.1 is a schematic diagram of EEG patterns in the four NREM stages.

There are a number of well-established changes of the sleep architecture in older individuals (Dement *et al.*, 1985; Hoch, Buysse, *et al.*, 1992). The most important changes are numerous short-duration (3–15 seconds) midsleep awakenings (between nocturnal sleep onset and the final awakening), the increased amount of time spent awake in bed, and perhaps most significantly, a decrease in SWS. There is an absolute as well as relative decrease of nocturnal NREM Stage 4 in older persons. Since Stage 4 is the period of deepest sleep, many older individuals report that they do not feel rested even though they spent a considerable amount of time sleeping. It has been speculated that SWS serves a biological restorative function in the CNS (Dement *et al.*, 1985). The SWS decrements begin early in life, so that from middle age on, the changes are small. For example, in one cross-sectional study in healthy older persons from the seventh through the ninth decade of life, the decreases were small, especially in women (Reynolds, Monk, Hoch, Jennings, *et al.*, 1991). In this study, aside from the small decrement in SWS from

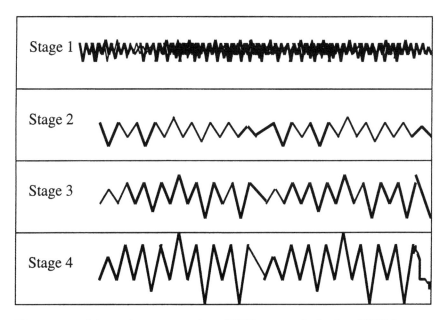

Figure 3.1.   Schematic representation of EEG patterns in the four NREM stages.

the ages of 60 to 91 years, other indices of sleep efficiency (latency to sleep onset, time spent asleep, and awake after sleep onset) did not vary, and with these measures, men tended to maintain greater stability. The authors were unable to explain the paradoxical findings since in many studies, women report fewer age-associated changes (Reynolds, Kupfer, Taska, Hoch, *et al.,* 1985). An examination of their data indicates that more 70- and 80-year-old women were on medications than similarly aged men. This part of the study also needs to be contrasted with another comparison from the same laboratory of healthy 20-year-olds and octogenarians. On almost all self-rated and laboratory measures, the older people slept more poorly than the younger (Monk, Reynolds, Buysse, Hoch, Jarrett, *et al.,* 1991) and their SWS was only about 20% as much as that of the 20-year old group.

There is much disagreement concerning the proportion of REM sleep in older persons (Bliwise, 1993). Many studies have reported no changes, while others have shown decreased rates, though the changes have been small. Bliwise attributes the discrepancies to methodological differences in laboratory studies that can never mimic the *ad libitum* normal sleeping environment. Animal studies have been equally ambiguous and cannot be used to resolve the discrepancies in human data.

There have been major controversies concerning the daily need for sleep as people age. Some have argued for a decreased need, others have claimed that there are no changes. There have been even reports that older people need more sleep (Bliwise, 1993). What is not controversial, however, is that the diurnal pattern frequently changes with age.

Circadian Rhythms

A common phenomenon is that older people retire earlier in the evening and rise earlier in the morning than do younger adults (Hoch, Buysse, *et al.,* 1992). Many older individuals also exhibit a redistribution of their diurnal sleep cycle from a monophasic wake–sleep pattern during a 24-hour period to a polyphasic pattern in which naps occur between the daily major nocturnal sleep periods. At least three factors have been postulated to account for daytime naps. First, if we assume that the total need for sleep does not change, there is a need to compensate for nocturnal sleep interruptions, such as periodic leg movements (myoclonus—spasm of leg muscles) and sleep-related respiration disturbances (SRRD), primarily apneas (transient suspension of respiration), occurrences present even in many otherwise healthy older persons who do not seek help for sleep problems. However, there are a few reports that downplay sleep apneas and causality may sometimes be in the opposite direction: that the sleep interruption from other causes induces the SRRD (Bliwise, 1993). Similarly, the significance of myoclonus for sleep quality is not well-established (Hoch, Buysse, *et al.*, 1992). In addition, cardiovascular, gastrointestinal, prostate, menopausal, respiratory, and other somatic problems may also result in nocturnal sleep fragmentation (Bliwise, 1993; Dement *et al.*, 1985). Polyphasic sleep patterns are most pronounced in nursing home residents and/or dementia patients. Second, older persons report more incidents of fatigue, which will be reviewed below. Third, it is necessary to consider the possibility of a disturbance of a circadian rhythm. There have been a number of reports of changes in various neuroendocrine circadian rhythms, such as plasma testosterone, estrone, estradiol, and plasma somatostatin during human aging (Richardson, 1990), and the sleep–wake cycle is another manifestation of this change. However, most studies of circadian rhythms have not separated the environmental time cues, the "entrained" rhythms from the "endogenous" rhythms. The observed circadian rhythm is a composite of the endogenous biological pacemaker and an entrained rhythm, and it is not always easy to separate the two (Monk, 1991). Animal data show a marked decline in the amplitude of the sleep–wake rhythm in older laboratory rodents in which, presumably, the entrained factors are minimal. Richardson believes that both a change in the circadian rhythm and various occult sleep-related pathologies in older people may contribute to the polyphasic sleep patterns seen even in healthy adults. This does not exclude, however, the contributions of various environmental factors, such as long periods of bed rest, boredom, loneliness, or decreased physical activity, to the observed sleep changes. However, Richardson (1990) cites data that indicate some of the changes in the sleep–wake rhythm are independent of the absolute amount of activity. Young volunteers living for several weeks in an isolated environment in which most temporal cues were removed typically selected an approximately 25-hour circadian sleep–wake cycle and volunteers in their 70s and 80s tended to select a shorter cycle approximating 24 hours. Monk (1991) believes that this may partially explain older persons' tendencies to become sleepy earlier in the evening and to awaken earlier in the morning. The variations in the endogenous free-running sleep–wake rhythm necessitate the development of environmental entrainment mechanisms to keep the rhythm on a 24-hour cycle (Monk, 1991). In a comparison of 9 healthy old men ages 80–86 years and 9 healthy young men ages 20–28 years, Monk, Buysse, *et al.* (1992) found that during 36 hours of continuous wakeful bed rest, the endogenous rectal temperature rhythm was not altered in the older group. However, during the same period, measures of global affect, self-rated vigor, manual dexterity, visual search speed, verbal reasoning speed, and visual vigilance showed a linear decline in the older group, with only a few of these participants exhibiting the normal superimposed 24-hour rhythmicity on some measures. In most of the younger individuals, the rhythmicity was apparent and for most of the measures, the differences were statistically significant, though the sample sizes were small. The authors speculate that some of the sleep problems commonly seen in older people are the result of a misalignment between the endogenous rhythm, as measured by rectal temperature, and the entrained rhythms, which are homeostatic and affect psychological processes.

Monk, Reynolds, *et al.* (1992) attempted to determine the role of environmental factors influencing the circadian rhythm in the sleep disturbances of older community-residing men and women (ages 71–91 years). Data were also obtained from young controls. The participants recorded their activities in a diary each day, including the presence of other persons. Some of the included items were time of breakfast and the presence of other persons and activities following this meal, and so on, continuously, for the whole day. In this study, the older individuals participated in as many activities and had as much other-person involvement as did the young group. What was especially important in testing the role of external circadian time cues was the finding that the older persons showed greater temporal regularity in their daily social activities than did the younger group. Yet the older group exhibited the normal age-associated sleep impairment. The data thus did not indicate that the social time cues of daily activities affected the sleep–wake rhythm. It should be noted that the sample size was small.

Neuropsychiatric Factors

Just as in younger persons, the changes in the sleep–wake cycle in older adults may be symptoms not only of physical health problems but also of depression or various psychosocial stresses. Benca, Obermeyer, Thisted, and Gillin (1992), in a meta-analysis of 177 studies with data from 7,151 patients and controls, showed that most psychiatric groups have significantly reduced sleep efficiency. No single sleep variable characterized a specific disorder; thus, sleep changes cannot be used for diagnosis, but there were patterns associated with some categories of psychiatric illnesses. Reductions in SWS time and percentage of SWS occur in affective disorders; this phenomenon is similar to what is also found in healthy older adults. There is some evidence for a significant age × diagnosis interaction for the sleep-efficiency variable in affective disorders. In their analysis, Benca *et al.* (1992) used an age of 19 years to dichotomize the age variable. Published at about the same time, another meta-analysis of 30 PSG studies, but restricted to insomnia, depression and narcolepsy (Hudson, Pope, Sullivan, Waternaux, *et al.*, 1992), found that the three disorders are arrayed on a single continuum of progressively more disturbed sleep and that the disturbance worsens with age. All EEG measures except for the amount of REM activity per minute of sleep became poorer with age. Several studies, some based on large community samples, have reported that the incidence of persistent (lasting over 1 month) insomnia or hypersomnia is high in late-life spousal bereavement (Hoch, Buysse, *et al.*, 1992). Insomnia may be a symptom of a depressive disorder, although it may occur even when a person does not exhibit a major depression syndrome (Lamberty, Bieliskaus, & Holt, 1994; Pasternak, Reynolds, Hoch, & Buysse, 1992; Reynolds, Hoch, Buysse, Houck, *et al.*, 1992; Rodin, McAvay, & Timko, 1988; Vitiello, Prinz, Avery, Williams, *et al.*, 1990). This is not surprising, since insomnia can range from a brief, one-night reactivity to a temporary stressor to more persistent changes associated with more enduring disturbances resulting from major interferences with one's life goals. Vitiello *et al.* (1990) stress the importance of rigorous health screening of participants and obtaining samples that have not been self- or physician-referred. Friedman, Brooks, Bliwise, Yesvage, and Wicks (1995) compared the self-reported level of stress in 42 "good" and 42 "poor" older sleepers as measured by the Elders Life Stress Inventory (ELSI) and the State–Trait Anxiety Inventory (STAI); depression was also measured on the Geriatric Depression Scale (GDS). There was no difference in the level of self-reported life stresses between the two groups on the ELSI or on the GDS, but the poor sleepers scored higher on the STAI. The poor sleepers reported problems with both falling asleep at night and morning awakenings. The latter finding is somewhat counterintuitive: The authors admit that the recruitment of participants for this study may have been biased, since only persons who were not taking hypnotics were tested. Because the level of current life stresses as measured on the ELSI was the same in the two groups, the authors speculate the poor sleepers had greater difficulties adapting to previous stressors, which did not register on the ELSI, but did manifest itself on the STAI. The authors also hypothesize that life stresses, with their attendant sleep problems, may lead to poor sleeping habits that tend to be maintained.

Not just overt health problems interfere with normal sleep; there is also evidence that physical fitness contributes to more effective sleep and daytime alertness. Edinger, Morey, Sullivan, Higginbotham, *et al.*

(1993) obtained PSG data on 12 aerobically fit and 12 sedentary healthy older men following both a day with and a day without aerobic activities. The aerobically fit men had shorter sleep-onset latencies, less wake time after onset, and more SWS than did the sedentary individuals. The authors caution the reader that perhaps better sleepers feel more alert in the daytime and are more likely to exercise; this was a study with a small sample of men only.

Cognitive Effects

While there have been extensive studies of electrophysiological and other biological measures of older populations, and most have found that sleep efficiency shows a decline, the relationship of these decrements to cognitive functions has been investigated sparingly. This is not surprising, since in the past, the major interests of sleep researchers in aging have been oriented more toward issues of health, including the performance of individuals afflicted with depression and SDAT disease, than toward cognitive abilities of healthy persons. It is also assumed that older people are retired and work-related performance is of only minor concern.

Several studies, mostly cross-sectional ones, were unable to find any significant relationships between daytime self-reported sleepiness or various physiological measures of sleep and laboratory assessments of performance on standardized tests of intelligence or vigilance (Berry & Webb, 1985; Bliwise, Carskadon, Seidel, Nekich, et al., 1991; Hayward, Mant, Eyland, Hewitt, et al., 1992; Hoch, Reynolds, Jennings, Monk, et al., 1992; Prinz, 1977). The absence of measurable laboratory performance decrements in sleep-deprived individuals is not unusual, since enhanced effort may compensate for any potential energetic losses associated with sleepiness (Dinges & Kribbs, 1991). In addition, there are some reports that in healthy young adults, even a chronic shortening of the" normal" sleep duration may have few behavioral consequences (Harrison & Horne, 1996).

SUMMARY

The importance of sleep for the well-being of organisms and its disturbances in older persons and in various pathological conditions has led not only to numerous studies of this phenomenon but also to a large number of reviews in the gerontological literature, including several recent statistical meta-analyses. Some of these publications emphasize basic science findings, while others are oriented toward specialized health professionals such as internists, nurses, psychologists, and psychiatrists. There is also an abundance of publications for laypeople.

In general, sleep quality deteriorates during aging. Several of the changes are associated with various physical or mental health disturbances. However, alterations in sleep have been observed even in some presumably healthy older people. In several surveys one-fourth to one-half of community-dwelling older persons have reported some sleep problems. First, the most common changes in the sleep architecture of older persons is a decrease in the amount of Stage 4, the SWS, the deepest stage of sleep. Second, nocturnal sleep of older persons is frequently interrupted by a variety of physiological disturbances. This sleep fragmentation may induce daytime sleepiness and a concomitant increased incidence of naps, but there is little evidence that laboratory test performance of cognitive activities is adversely affected by the periodic sleepiness occurring in some older persons. We lack long-term studies of "sleeplessness" in mature people. To what extent sleep losses are compensated by additional motivation in the performance of various tasks is difficult to evaluate. Since most older people do not have jobs or other responsibilities that require continual high levels of alertness, efforts to obtain such data need not have a high priority.

FATIGUE

Introduction

The previous section has discussed the normal age-associated decrements in sleep. A related concept is fatigue. Actually, Chapter 2, on physiological changes, could have included a section on the loss of energy or activation that colloquially is referred to as fatigue, a decrement in various physiological and behavioral functions, or in practical terms, decreased work output or interest in an activity or activities. Even when performance does not decline, older persons frequently experience increased fatigue. Skinner (1987, pp. 150–152), one of the most eminent modern behaviorists, who typically eschewed "mentalistic" terms, wrote about his experiences of fatigue when he was in his early 80s. Even more remarkable is his statement that "the kind of fatigue that causes trouble has been called mental [sic] perhaps because it has little to do with the physical fatigue of labor." In a pilot study of a small sample of noninstitutionalized persons ages 62–98 years, Brody and Kleban

(1983) found that 65% of "normal" and 70% of participants with diagnosed functional mental health problems reported experiencing fatigue, weakness, or dizziness during four 24-hour periods.

During the last few decades, Western societies have experienced the rise of a new illness, chronic fatigue (CF; Lewis & Wessely, 1992). It is not clear whether it is a symptom or a syndrome. While many physical illnesses such as arthritis, anemia, or hypotension, as well as many mental disorders, are associated with fatigue, thorough physical and mental examinations cannot always attribute CF to a specific disorder. For Fuhrer and Wessely (1995), and others, CF is the modern version of the classical neurasthenia or the conversion disorders. These investigators analyzed medical records of 3,723 patients ages 18–64 years, who saw a general practitioner in France. CF was the major presenting complaint of 7.6% of the patients. The complaints were inversely related to age. CF is frequently associated with depression and, to lesser extent, with other psychological disorders. Since the prevalence rate for major depressions and less severe mood disorders decreases after young adulthood until about the age of 75 years (Gatz, Kasl-Godley, & Karel, 1996), CF complaints tend to be parallel. It is necessary, of course, to exclude individuals with reliable diagnoses of physical illnesses. The validity of epidemiological data of CF based on older patients who visit professionals is questionable. Many older people who may perceive fatigue assume that this is the norm for the elderly, and they will not turn to a professional for assistance. In our treatment of fatigue, we minimize references to studies of persons who seek professional help for CF.

Despite the high prevalence of complaints about fatigue among older people, in most textbooks of gerontology and geriatrics, or even in handbooks, the term appears very rarely, if at all. This is in contrast to sleep, for which there is a plethora of reviews. Since in our culture fatigue is frequently associated with work, and older people are not expected to work and are supposedly disengaged from activities, little attention is given to fatigue. When it is mentioned, it is usually in the context of depression (Stenback, 1980). But even this relationship is not always emphasized. For example, the second edition of the *Handbook of Mental Health and Aging* (Birren, Sloane, Cohen, Hoyman, *et al.,* 1992) omits any references to fatigue, lassitude, or similar terms in the index. Some mental health professionals have suggested that the word should be discarded from the professional lexicon (Widlocher, 1982). Nevertheless, it would seem appropriate to examine the term in the context of motivation. Again, it needs to be emphasized that fatigue is a symptom in many physical ailments common in older people as well as in many psychiatric disorders, most prominently in depression.

Definitions

In 1947, Bartley and Chute, following an exhaustive review of the literature, were able to categorize the uses of the term *fatigue* into three classes. According to them, the term may denote the following:

1. A physiological state of temporary impaired capacity of muscles or sense organs resulting from previous activity in which a rest period leads to the restoration of previous capacity; most physiological treatments of fatigue adhere to this definition.
2. Deterioration of performance or work decrement; this is the definition most commonly used in ergonomics and more recently in human information processing. Several papers in a volume edited by Hockey, Gaillard, and Coles (1986) use this definition in the analysis of mental effort and the "intensive" aspect of behavior. Though a variety of topics are discussed in this treatise, aging is only mentioned in one chapter (Rabbitt, 1986) and the data pertain to speed differences in various information processing tasks with aging characterized by speed decrements.
3. A subjective feeling of lassitude or tiredness; psychopathologists and personologists most frequently apply the term *fatigue* in this context.

Bartley and Chute (1947) emphasized the interrelatedness of the three uses of the construct. The frequent difficulty of inferring the presence of only one antecedent condition led them to assume that the term *fatigue* is a multifactorial construct and as such may lack clarity. They preferred to restrict the usage of the term *fatigue* to the subjective feelings of tiredness and to use the terms *physical impairment* and *work decrement* for their two other categories. They also pointed out the importance of differentiating short-term or acute fatigue, applicable primarily to the physiological and sensory decrements, from the long-term or chronic effects that tend to be more descriptive of the psychopathological effects.

Holding (1983) was also unable to arrive at a simple definition of fatigue, and he believed that it is premature to try to apply the construct to different behavioral phenomena. Although Bartley and Chute (1947) describe and devote part of a chapter to aging, their treatment of the topic is very limited. Fatigue of the aged is described in one paragraph as the consequence of thwarted aspirations and "the collision of the individual with his surroundings" (p. 301). Holding called for the discovery of the conditions that induce fatigue in older persons, a task that has not attracted many investigators. In a later elaboration of the concept of fatigue, Bartley (1981) again reiterated his position that fatigue should be treated as a self-assessed state colloquially labeled as tiredness or weariness. He cautioned psychologists not to use fatigue as a synonym for work decrement, which may be the result of lack of motivation or other factors that also affect performance, and impairment should be reserved to physiological structures or systems that are not functioning. Cofer and Appley (1964) essentially followed the Bartley and Chute exposition (1947), but, again, they did not review fatigue in older persons.

There have been a number of theoretical analyses of fatigue (Broadbent, 1979; Cameron 1973; Hockey *et al.*, 1986; Kahneman, 1973), mainly in the context of work. These approaches are of limited interest to gerontologists. Kahneman (1973), in his theory of effort and attention postulated that if the demands of the task are high, fatigue may be compensated for by increased effort. Thus, operationally, fatigue cannot be differentiated from low motivation. Fatigue may interfere with performance, just as low motivation does, and either state leads to low output. While a person may indicate the presence of fatigue, the antecedents of this state are ambiguous. Thayer (1989, p. 61) uses the construct energetic arousal and its converse, tiredness or fatigue, in his biopsychological theory of mood. He relates energetic arousal to readiness for action, which, as we have previously discussed, is usually denoted as motivation. Thayer, however, limits his construct of energetic arousal and fatigue mainly to perceptions or feelings, Bartley and Chute's (1947) third definition of fatigue. He, too, does not clarify the relationship between fatigue resulting from physical activity or illness and perceptions of tiredness that are the results of lack of interest in performing certain activities. Thayer (1989) does not deal with aging in his monograph. For Lazarus (1991), illness or fatigue only potentiate emotional states; they do not cause them. Lazarus (p. 316) adopts a dualistic position in his usage of fatigue: "The role of physical fatigue is to alter for the worse the power balance that is sensed between demands and coping resources; fatigue per se, though influential, is not as I see it the direct cause of the distress; the appraisal of a weakened capacity to cope is." He does not define fatigue, nor does he describe the antecedent conditions. In this monograph, Lazarus makes no references to aging, a stage of life in which fatigue is more prevalent than at an earlier age.

Stress and the Perception of Fatigue in the Elderly

The complex problem of stress will be treated in more detail in Chapter 8. For the present purpose, we adopt a broad definition of stress, to wit, a disequilibrium or major change from a previous level of adaptation. Aging is associated with various losses: spouses, other relatives, close friends; health, including sensory and motor capacities; cognitive powers; economic wherewithal, jobs, and earning potentials; and roles and status symbols in Western societies. A common response to a loss or losses is a feeling of discomfort or illness, and weakness or fatigue is one of the symptoms in a variety of illnesses. Depression and fatigue are thus a frequent concomitant of losses. Seligman's theory of "helplessness" or "hopelessness" (Schaie & Willis, 1991, pp. 484–486) focuses on losses. Older individuals perceive the various losses to be of a magnitude that is beyond their ability to handle due to diminished capacity. Illness, fatigue, or exhaustion may be present, or these may be acceptable rationalizations for failure to develop other means to cope with some of the losses. In our society, we view such responses to stressors as normal. In a similar vein, Selye (1946), whose theory of the General Adaptation Syndrome (GAS) during stress has had a profound impact on theories and research, viewed aging as the result of exhaustion of adaptation energy. For Selye, this exhaustion is the result of long-term exposures to various stressors. Exhaustion is, after all, the extreme form of fatigue. This commonsense view is the adaptation of the well-known physical phenomenon of wear and tear. In metallurgy, the term *fatigue* is applied to a progressive cracking of a metal following repeated application of stress (Considine, 1977). Unfortunately, the term *exhaustion* is vacuous.

Physiological Impairment

In Chapter 2, we analyzed some of the physiological changes associated with aging. We reviewed a number of decrements in several physiological systems that occur during aging. Since these are long-term, permanent changes, they were not referred to as fatigue, though in some folklores, fatigue is the major hallmark of the aged. On the other hand, a temporary loss or decrement of any system, motor or sensory, resulting from prolonged activity, is usually referred to as fatigue. In this section, we analyze fatigue in older people that follows prolonged activity of a system or part of a system. Physiologists frequently differentiate peripheral from central fatigue. Most of Bartley and Chute's first category, physiological impairment following extended muscular and sensory stimulation, is referred to by physiologists as peripheral fatigue. Human research is of limited value, since we cannot separate fatigue from effort, as we have previously indicated, and ethical reasons limit the type of research that can be performed, especially with older individuals, since we are not certain under what circumstances the losses from prolonged activity will not be temporary, but will produce permanent impairment.

In neuromuscular physiology, fatigue has very specific connotations. It has been defined as a failure to maintain a required or expected force (Edwards, 1981). Either peripheral or central factors may be the major contributors. While peripheral variables have been investigated, the potential CNS processes are still unknown (Edgerton & Hutton, 1990). Aging leads to decreases in muscle fibers and in some energy supply—enzyme activity (E. Gutmann, 1977). Data on rats probably underestimate losses with age of human muscle fibers, especially motor nerves of fast motor fibers (Faulkner, Brooks, & Zerba, 1991).

A major factor in maintaining peripheral muscular activity is cardiac output, the ability to deliver O_2 to working muscles. During maximum physical effort, about 75% of the cardiac output is directed to the active muscles (Shephard, 1987, p. 73). Shephard also discussed (pp. 68–69) the reduced mechanical efficiency of older persons during motor performance resulting, among other things, from poorer motor coordination and joint stiffness, which will increase the O_2 cost of effort. Poor peripheral circulation and a sluggish response of the heart to effort will increase the accumulation of lactic acid even in submaximal work situations. While many textbooks of exercise physiology specify primarily the plateaus reached in maximum O_2 consumption rate (V_{O_2MAX}) and lactic acid accumulation as the major factors in fatigue, Noakes (1988) emphasizes the need to pay attention to the limitations of muscle contractility. The varying contributions of these and other factors mean that for older persons, the increased physiological costs will be greater in some than in other activities. For example, the relative costs are greater for bicycle ergometer work than for treadmill running. Since maximum work capacity, V_{O_2MAX}, and muscular contractility decline with age, for any given level of effort, the older individual is closer to his or her maximum capacity; therefore, the available reserve capacity is lower. Thus, some decreased capacity for work in older people can be accounted for even in the absence of reduced motivation. Kennedy (1988) in a review of fatigue and fatigability, pointed out that in work situations, fatigue occurs long before a nerve–muscle unit is incapable of contracting. Fatigue is a protective function for the organism. In normal individuals, subjective ratings of fatigue and physical exertion are related to HR and to V_{O_2} (Borg, 1977).

Performance Decrements

Peripheral Factors.   From a motivational standpoint, most of our interest is on performance decrements. In the previous section, we briefly discussed the neuromuscular changes that follow activity. Shephard (1987, pp. 81–86) discussed the impracticality of obtaining data on maximum oxygen intake or aerobic power in older persons during exercise testing. The best measurement of a person's physical work capacity is V_{O_2}, but many old persons will cease exercising before reaching an oxygen plateau. Effort may be limited by the person experiencing some shortness of breath, muscular weakness, and, most significant from a motivational standpoint, a fear of overexertion, compounded by the lack of recent experience that many older persons have in engaging in strenuous activities. In one study, apparently well-trained young-old individuals (56–68 years) were able to reach "definite" oxygen plateaus (Shephard, 1987, p. 81). There is actually a controversy about the advisability of pushing older individuals to a plateau in an overall physical fitness program, since it is hard to determine what should be the limiting factor. V_{O_2} intake does decline with age, so that by the age of 65 years, it is typically 30–40% less than that of a young adult (Shephard, 1987, p. 91). Muscle strength, measured in various ways, such as by hand grip, trunk extension, or wrist flexion, shows decreases with age (Shephard, 1987, pp. 105–108). Here, too, some of the changes may be attributed to losses of muscle fibers, reduction of adinosinetriphosphatase (ATPase), enzyme activity, motivation, and fear of injury. Though we have much evidence for changes in the muscular, cardiopulmonary, and endocrine systems with age, we have little evidence of the relationships of these biological changes to performance decrements. There have been few studies in which performance decrements were studied simultaneously with physiological costs. DeVries, Brodowicz, Robertson, Svoboda, *et al.* (1989) tested the physical capacity for work at the fatigue threshold in older individuals who were subjected to increasing workloads on a bicycle ergometer. Measurements included electromyograms (EMG) from the quadriceps muscles, HR, $V_{O_{2MAX}}$, and ratings of exertion made by the participants. The investigators reported that the onset of fatigue as stated by the participants was better predicted by the EMG indexes, than the $V_{O_{2MAX}}$. The study also found that physical conditioning improved the resistance to fatigue. These results were similar in terms of the indexes of fatigue to those that this group of investigators had previously found with younger persons, though the workload at which fatigue was first observed was lower in the older participants (Devries, Tichy, Housh, Smyth, *et al.*, 1987). Norris and Shock (cited by Shock, 1977, p. 655) have shown that even at low or moderate workloads, the physiological costs of work are greater, and the rate of recovery is slower in older persons. Kennedy (1988) in his review of fatigue and fatigability, called attention to the side effects of many centrally acting drugs that reduce motor activity and ANS functions, for example, monoamine oxidase inhibitor (MAOI) antidepressants, antihypertensives, antihistamines, neuroleptics, and hypokalemics. Since many of these drugs are used much more frequently by older than younger persons (Hershey & Whitney, 1988), fatigue should be more frequent in an older than in a younger population.

Central Factors.   In the preceding section, we dealt with performance decrements that result from certain changes in biological states. We now consider decrements that are less dependent on peripheral or specific biological states and more on what physiologists refer to as *central fatigue* and what has sometimes been labeled *mental fatigue* (Mulder, 1986). Many cognitive psychologists, stimulated by Kahneman's (1973) concept of effort, use the terms *mental effort* and *mental fatigue.* In the monograph by Hockey *et al.* (1986) on energetics and human information processing, references to fatigue occur in several chapters. Mulder (1986) defines fatigue as the inability to continue to exert control over the CNS to carry out attention-demanding tasks. The tasks are not necessarily physically demanding, but the necessity to perform too many operations simultaneously and/or perform them under time pressures will lead to an overload of the system, or mental fatigue. Mulder (1986) illustrates his concept of mental fatigue by using data from a study of city bus drivers, who constantly face somewhat conflicting tasks demanding time-constrained attention. Efficiency of information processing as measured by HR decreased, and this was attributed to the presence of mental fatigue. Other investigators have found changes in pupillary diameter in persons engaged in "fatiguing" tasks. Hockey (1986) introduced another factor, "phasic fatigue," that occurs when the individual must maintain a complex cognitive task set, which then may lead to a loss of central control, a là Mulder (1986), and this leads to a temporary blockage of performance. Such temporary involuntary lapses in performance due to mental fatigue will occur when the task is monotonous. A person who works all day and then drives at night in light traffic on an interstate may experience temporary lapses of attention. Experimental data in support of this concept have been known since the 1930s (Warburton, 1986). Homogeneous task conditions probably lower the person's mental effort and the attendant activation of physiological functions that are essential for maintaining attention. Mental fatigue may arise either because of the presence of very difficult time-constrained task demands or because of the opposite condition, a monotonous homogeneous task. This inverted U-shaped relationship seems to support the commonsense notion that is the basis of the classical Yerkes–Dodson "law" (Heemstra, 1986). This "law" postulates that performance is optimal when the motivational level is neither too high nor too low, as illustrated by Figure 3.2.

Lacey and others (Appley, 1991) have been emphasizing that there are several dimensions to activation and arousal involving the CNS, ANS, the endocrines, or the viscera, and there are further divisions within each system that may be differentially activated. Futhermore, various pathologies increase the differences between the reactivities of the various components that contribute to arousal. Thus, in older persons, the correlations between various indices of arousal are greater than they are in younger cohorts.

As Bartley and Chute (1947) already indicated, mental fatigue does not necessarily imply that it is analogous to peripheral muscle fatigue. Brain energy metabolism is not always impaired in mental fatigue (Van den Berg, 1986). A person who in the late afternoon complains and exhibits symptoms of fatigue in the office may go home and perform strenuous yard work or play tennis.

The literature on performance decrements due to fatigue in older persons is sparse. Welford (1958), in his monograph on aging and

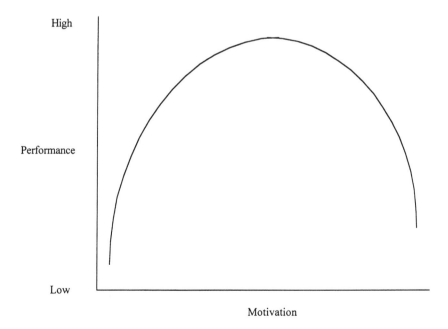

Figure 3.2. Yerkes–Dodson law relating performance to motivation.

human skill, discusses fatigue only briefly. First, he notes that performance decrements may be the results of attentional or motivational changes, as well as the presence of more rapid endogenous impairments in older persons. Second, Welford reminds us that it is difficult to perform laboratory experiments of prolonged duration that would compare to activities in real-life situations. Third, it is possible for an older individual to compensate for potential performance decrements by exerting more effort, which increases the physiological costs, but information on such trade-offs is lacking and operationally difficult to achieve. Stagner (1985), in his *Handbook of the Psychology of Aging* chapter on industrial psychology, makes no references to fatigue. Botwinick and Shock (1952) tested 50 individuals ages 20–29 years and 50 individuals ages 60–69 years on six tasks: writing digits, uniting words, addition of 3, 6, and 9 digits, and a digit-substitution test. There were decrements in performance with continuous work on all the tasks except the speed of writing. However, the decrements were greater in the young than the old group. Since the average educational level of the young group was 13.6 years of schooling completed, while for the old group it was only 6.9 years, it is possible that the motivation for the tasks may have been higher in the older individuals, and this may have compensated for any possible fatigue effects. Perhaps the older persons were trying to demonstrate that they were still competent. No physiological measures or verbal questions pertaining to interest in the tasks were gathered. Bleecker, Bolla-Wilson, Agnew, and Meyers (1987) tested "healthy" participants, ages 40–90 years, on a simple visual reaction time (RT) task. Each participant received 44 trials. While there were age differences, as expected, fatigue was not a significant factor. Perhaps 44 trials was not sufficient to induce fatigue.

Psychologists performing intellectual assessments of older persons have been concerned about the possible adverse effects of fatigue. Several studies on the Thurstone's Primary Abilities Test or the Wechsler Adult Intelligence Scale showed no or minimal effects of fatigue induced by the prior administration of some unrelated tasks such as letter cancellations (Cunningham, Sepkosky, & Opel, 1978; Furry & Baltes, 1973; Furry, & Schaie, 1979; Rust, Barnard, & Oster, 1979). We may conclude that brief pretests do not induce sufficient fatigue to affect appreciably performance on standardized cognitive tests, which usually last less than 2 hours. This finding is of practical importance, since older individuals are frequently assessed for various purposes, and studies would seem to indicate that we probably do not have to be concerned about the individual's cognitive activities prior to taking standardized tests.

Perception of Fatigue

Bartley and Chute (1947) preferred to restrict the use of the term *fatigue* to the subjective experiences of tiredness or lassitude, or what others may refer to as the perception of fatigue. They emphasized psychological conflicts as the source of fatigue, and as such, the concept differs from one that implies physiological impairment and/or performance decrements. Woodworth (1938, p. 234), in his *Experimental Psychology,* described certain intraorganic states such as hunger, thirst, and fatigue as emotional states. Buck (1988, p. 23) rephrased it by defining emotion as the "readout" of motivational states. Motivation and emotion, according to Buck, are two sides of the same coin, and according to this viewpoint, fatigue is an emotional state.

Some community surveys have reported that some symptoms of depression are present in almost all elderly persons (Thompson, Gong, Haskins, & Gallagher, 1987). One of the major symptoms of depression is severe fatigue. Fatigue is included in the operational criteria for depression in the *Diagnostic and Statistical Manual of Mental Disorders* of the American Psychiatric Association (DSM-III), the Beck Depression Inventory, the Hamilton Rating Scale for Depression, the General Health Questionnaire, the Zung Self-Rating Scale for Depression, and most other instruments used in the diagnosis of depression. For many elderly patients, the physical symptoms of severe fatigue and sleep problems may be the first manifestations or precursors of a diagnosis of depression (Manu, Matthews, Lane, Tennen, *et al.,* 1989; Pfeiffer, 1977). Symptoms of fatigue and sleep problems in depression are not unique to our culture. In a study in India (Chadda & Kulhara, 1987), in a group of 59 patients with depressive disorders, 90% complained of sleep problems and 88% reported fatigue. Of course, the symptoms may have been the basis for the diagnosis of depression. Kennedy (1988) raises the question of whether the fatigue seen in depression is independent of the other features of the disorder. It seems that it is frequently difficult to test, and at times it may be impossible. For example, fatigue and sleep disturbances are frequently associated with depression; however, loss of sleep and fatigue may also occur when the individual is highly motivated to work on a task and there are no other symptoms that are usually associated with depression. Nevertheless, feelings of fatigue can occur following prolonged muscular or sensory activity, as an aftermath of overarousal when the individual can no longer cope with environmental stressors (or at least believes that he or she cannot cope), or as the side effect of various illnesses or drugs.

As we indicated before, physiologists differentiate central from peripheral fatigue (Edwards, 1981). Peripheral fatigue is due to impaired neuromuscular transmission, or the impairment in the excitation–contraction coupling. Fatigue is not necessarily a perception of weakness. This can be demonstrated by paralyzing a muscle with curare. A person trying to move a partially curarized limb feels weakness, not fatigue. The latter is experienced after prolonged contraction. In attempts to move a partially curarized limb, the individual feels that he or she is exerting a great deal of effort to make a movement. On the other hand, while attempting to move a limb that has been fatigued by prolonged contraction, the individual does not feel that he or she is exerting the maximum effort (Grimsby, Hannerz, Borg, & Hedman, 1981). When an individual says that he or she has run out of energy, it does not mean a lack of energy in the biochemical sense of the concept. Muscular fatigue is associated with a perception of weakness in a muscle, which is present even when the muscle is not used (Edwards, 1981). Our previous example of the tired office worker attests to this proposition.

It should now be apparent that measuring the perception of fatigue is not easy. In 1962, Borg (1977) developed a psychophysical scale, RPE (rating of perceived exertion), with which a person rates the amount of exertion required to perform a task. On the scale, a rating of 6 or 7 represents very little exertion, while a rating of 19 or 20 represents the maximum exertion a person can produce. The scale was developed on young individuals, with the values meant to represent roughly normal HRs (×10) with values of 6–7 corresponding to a resting HR of 60–70 beats per minute (bpm), 13–14 corresponding activity requiring exertion at which HR is around 130–140 bpm, and so on. It should be noted that this is not an interval scale (Borg, 1982) and HR changes in older persons, including the maximum attainable rate, differ from that applicable to a younger group. Since the introduction of the RPE scale, a large number of studies, mainly with young individuals, have been performed using it. Sidney and Shephard (1977) tested 26 men and 30 women, ages 60–70 years, some on a bicycle ergometer and others on a treadmill, and obtained HR or O_2 consumption measures as well as RPE ratings. As in the studies with younger persons, there was a significant linear relationship between the physiological measures and the rating of exertion, though, as expected, compared to that of younger persons, the slope was displaced. All of the volunteer participants in the study reported that their habitual activities were "above average."

While the RPE scale is applicable to older exercisers, a number of studies have found that several psychological factors influence the ratings. Pandolf (1978, 1982) and Dishman (1994), in their reviews, found that not only local muscular and cardiopulmonary variables affected RPEs, but so did motivational variables such as interest in the task, expectancies, anxiety, and other similar states. The importance of previous experience with the task, which may include motivational or practice effects in RPE ratings, was actually initially postulated by Borg (1977) when he developed his scale. More recently, Dishman (1994) also cautioned that RPE estimates tend to reflect various physiological responses better at high intensities of exercise. They tend to measure a subjective Gestalt of sensory information associated with many physiological responses to exercise. The estimates are more accurate at higher intensities of exercise.

Rejeski (1985) presented a model of perceived exertion based on a parallel processing model similar to several models in current cognitive psychology, but more specifically, it is based on a model of pain perception developed by Leventhal and Everhart (1979). Rejeski proposes that physical work is associated with certain sensory cues in the muscle receptors, which give rise to certain emotional responses as well as to certain memory cues previously associated with the responses from the muscle receptors. The model can be used to explain the role of previous experiences in the assessment of exertion, the expectation of the duration of the task on RPE, and a number of other motivational variables that play a role in the rating of exertion (Figure 3.3).

The role of expectancy in RPE ratings may explain the results reported by Sidney and Shephard (1977). For a given workload, HR and RPE were lower for treadmill performance than for the bicycle ergometer. The authors explain this difference in terms of the greater strain on a single muscle, the quadriceps, during the bicycling. However, an equally plausible alternative is that the participants were more familiar with walking than bicycling, and they believed that the latter requires

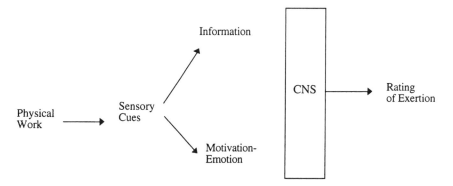

Figure 3.3.   Rejeski's model of rating of exertion associated with physical activity.

more exertion than does treadmill walking. An even stronger case for the role of expectancy or an experiential factor in the same study can account for the results of a 34-week physical conditioning regimen with the same participants. Conditioning lowered HR at a given treadmill speed and slope, but RPEs remained constant. The authors were puzzled by this outcome, and they proposed several physiological hypotheses to account for the anomalous ratings. However, none of their hypotheses seemed to be satisfactory. A simpler psychological explanation might be that the individuals remembered the previous ratings after exposure to a given workload, and they discounted the lowered physiological costs that resulted from the training regimen. An early study by Borg and Linderholm (1967) also produced data that seem to underscore the role of experiential factors in the ratings of exertion. In a group of 61 lumberjacks, ages 27–63 years, *Mdn* 45 years), and in a "mixed" group of subjectively healthy professionals, clerical workers, students, and retirees ages 18–79 years, HRs and RPEs were obtained while the participants were subjected to different workloads on a bicycle ergometer. While in general, with increasing age, the workload resulting in a rise in HR was rated as more effortful, the differences were much more dramatic in the group that was relatively sedentary compared to the lumberjacks.

The role of motivational factors, mainly expectancy, in the perception of fatigue in older persons, which we have illustrated in the context of several laboratory studies, can be seen even more vividly in various systemic illnesses as well as in psychosomatic and psychopathological conditions. Weakness and lassitude or fatigue have traditionally been the symptoms of most forms of human illness. We began this chapter with some epidemiological data on the prevalence of fatigue in older patients who seek help for medical problems. Since aging is associated with the prevalence of various ailments, it should come as no surprise that society expects to see fatigue and lassitude as a common characteristic of the elderly. Zung (1980, p. 354), in a review of affective disorders in later life, states, "The primary symptom of aging is fatigue." If a well-known geriatrician makes such a generalization, the perceptions of the general public cannot be faulted. Zung attributes fatigue both to the presence of physical illness and to denial. He refers to the latter in the context of frequent complaints by elderly patients that there is "nothing wrong with me; it's that I have (some physical disorder) and I feel tired, that's all." The over-the-counter preparation Geritol was marketed for a long time as an elixir for "tired blood." Today, various vitamin supplements are advertised to reduce fatigue in older persons. Stenback (1980), in his chapter on clinical depression in the elderly, also states that "a pervading somesthetic (or cenesthetic) feeling of fatigue or fatiguability is frequently an integrated part of the depressed affect" (p. 618). Since the prevalence of mild depression in this population may be very high, Zung's statement, and other similar characterizations of older persons, should not be regarded as improper. Not only do older people have more illnesses and depressions, but they may also be more likely to exhibit hypochondriasis, which is frequently associated with depression, though the two syndromes may not be identical. Busse and Blazer (1980, p. 404) reported that in one study of community-residing elderly, between 10% and 20% considered their health to be poorer than that of other older persons in their community.

SUMMARY

Since symptoms of fatigue that tend to occur in older populations are infrequently discussed in the standard textbooks in gerontology, it seems fitting to analyze the concept in the context of motivation of older individuals. The concept of fatigue, like many other motivational and psychological concepts in general, is used by both physiologists and psychologists. The definition of fatigue is similar, though not identical, in the two disciplines. Physiologists focus on impairment in biological systems, while psychologists emphasize either performance decrements or a perception of low energy level. There are physiological changes in energy metabolism during aging that result in an earlier onset of muscular and sensory fatigue. Even in younger persons, the physiological changes cannot be separated from certain psychological factors that produce feelings of fatigue. Among the physiological contributing factors are various illnesses that beset older persons, the frequent use of various drugs by the elderly, many of which induce fatigue or drowsiness, and a normal decrement in motor and sensory abilities. From a psychosocial standpoint, older persons lose many familial, social, and economic resources that may directly or indirectly exacerbate performance impairment, which may then be labeled *fatigue.* Even one's perception of aging and the expectation that older people are supposed to be tired may contribute to fatigue. As Kennedy (1988) indicated in his review, we cannot separate the feelings of fatigue that result from certain definite physiological changes (e.g., prolonged muscular activity) from those that have a psychological, expectations, or psychiatric etiology (e.g., depression). However, in the case of fatigue resulting from physiological impairments, there are measurable physiological indices such as lactic acid, HR, V_{O_2MAX}, and EMG, which do seem to correlate fairly well with self-reported ratings of fatigue (Borg, 1982). This does not negate the significance for motivation, the initiation or maintenance of action, in perceived fatigue in the absence of biological signs. Increased effort by the introduction of incentives or information that the person has the competence to perform may mitigate the effects of fatigue.

CHAPTER 4

Pain and Discomfort Avoidance

INTRODUCTION

Hedonism, the doctrine that human action can be attributed primarily to the desire to gain pleasure and avoid pain and discomfort, dates back to ancient times. The writings of Socrates's pupil Aristippos (ca. 400 B.C.) were among the earliest to refer to this theory (Boring, 1950, p. 704). More recently, in both Darwin's and Freud's theories, hedonism was one of the basic postulates. Such a view was prevalent in many twentieth-century behavioristic theories of acquired drives, especially in animal models (Hilgard, 1987).

Pain and suffering have fascinated and been studied by theologians, philosophers, physicians and various biomedical scientists, psychologists, pharmacists, sociologists, anthropologists, and a variety of other professionals concerned with human existence. Interests by such a diversity of scholars inevitably leads to multifaceted approaches to the conceptualizations and definitions of pain and discomfort.

Cofer and Appley (1964), in their introduction to the topic on pain and motivation, note that "pain which arises from tissue injury or disease, however, is not the lot of a substantial portion of the population." The last statement seems to be less applicable to older populations, since one of the hallmarks of aging is the increase in the incidence and prevalence of a variety and multiplicity of chronic diseases and injuries. In most instances, diseases are associated with pain and/or discomfort. The modern technological and information explosions have led to a greater awareness of health problems (Opler, 1967). These developments have produced an increase in life expectancy in most societies, with a rapid growth in the number of older people who are experiencing more pain, illnesses, and discomforts.

MOTIVATIONAL–EMOTIONAL ASPECTS

Young (1961, pp. 563–564), in his discussion of emotional distur-bances and health, notes that there are two groups of words in the En-glish language that contain the same Greek root *pathos,* namely, one referring to sickness, such as pathology and psychopathy, and the other to emotions, in words such as empathy, sympathy, and apathy. Thus, it seems that there has traditionally been a close relationship between the emotions and sickness. Parenthetically, currently, in American English, pain is used as a metaphor for many negative emotional states, and this only leads to confusion. For example, it would seem more appropriate to say, "I am sad, or unhappy, or disappointed," rather than to say "I feel pain" when one's favorite sports team lost, unless the person feels that the loss produced a headache, stomachache, or some other somatic symptom. Such a view does not preclude the appearance of pains or ill-ness that are the sequelae of psychological stresses.

Psychosomatic medicine, which emerged as a separate area in med-icine and forged its identity in the 1930s, attributed major roles to behav-ioral factors in illness. Indeed, any homeostatic concept of organismic functions assumes that individuals will be motivated to avoid behaviors that induce pain or discomfort, and to seek relief from pain. The modern field of health psychology (Chapter 7) includes the application of the principles of basic pain physiology and psychology to problems of health.

Gate Control Theory

The most influential modern neurophysiological theory of pain, the gate control theory by Melzack and Wall (1965), was developed after much evidence was accumulated that motivational factors, such as anx-iety or excitement, affect CNS activity to aversive stimuli. The descrip-tor *gate control* refers to a physiological mechanism in the spinal cord that controls the access of the signals to the somesthetic brain area. The gate is influenced by the activity of descending fibers from the brain, which are responding to ongoing cerebral activities such as arousal. For example, it has been well known that soldiers wounded in battle may not feel pains from a wound but complain about a vein puncture in the hospital. Figure 4.1 is a block diagram of the gate control theory. While the specific neurophysiological mechanisms of the theory have been criticized (Weisenberg, 1977), the importance of nonsensory factors in the perception of pain seems to have been widely accepted. According to Casey (1978, p. 213), a neurophysiologist and a member of the Wall

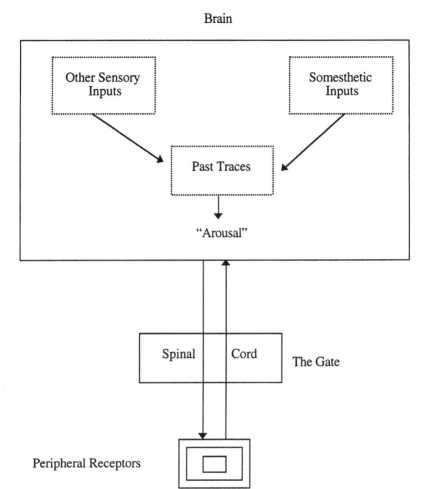

Figure 4.1.   Block diagram of gate control theory.

and Melzack team, "Pain is a highly motivating experience accompanied by autonomic and emotional responses."

Melzack and Wall (1965) proposed a multidimensional theory of pain. The first dimension is sensory–discriminative, and it concerns the (1) detection of the quality, (2) intensity, (3) location, and (4) the duration of the signal. The second dimension is motivational–affective and involves the perception of the aversive characteristics generated by the perception of pain, and the third is a cognitive–evaluative dimension and asks how does the pain influences current or future activities. This model has helped to bridge the gap between basic research and clinical applications (Chapman, 1978). As is true of most psychological constructs, the three dimensions are not completely independent; there are interactions between several of them. Usually, an increase in the intensity of the pain, the sensory dimension, also leads to an increase in the aversiveness of the stimulus. A similar differentiation of factors probably applies as well to illness and discomfort in general. Lazarus (1991, 1993), in his theory of emotions, uses a similar model. However, for Lazarus, pain is not an emotion unless it is appraised; thus, his concern is not with pain as a sensory–perceptual event, but primarily with its consequences in terms of the motivational–affective and the cognitive–evaluative dimensions. Unfortunately, as Weisenberg (1977) has noted in his review of pain, most research has focused on the sensory rather than the motivational–affective aspects of pain. In his book, Lazarus (1991) treats in some detail the problems of illness and discomfort. We discuss his approach more fully in Chapter 7 on health behaviors and again in Chapter 8 on stress, a major source of discomfort. Indeed, it could have been feasible to incorporate the analysis of pain in either of these two chapters. However, in most formulations, stress is not limited to the consequences of what are traditionally classified as pain experiences, as we have noted in the Introduction.

Another concept pertaining to the affective–motivational aspect of pain is suffering. Since ancient times, it has led to numerous conceptualizations. Price and Harkins (1992) note that there are several possible meanings associated with this sensation. The first is that the suffering is interrupting one's thoughts, plans, and well-being. The second is a feeling that the person is a burden to the caretakers and society. The third possible meaning is the fear associated with the potential harm or even death that might befall the sufferer. Finally, the sufferer may feel a sense of isolation or separation from his or her surroundings (Bakan, 1968). These conceptions overlap, and they may be interrelated in many instances. They may also give rise to a variety of emotional responses such as depression, anger, or anxiety. We attempt to highlight primarily some motivational factors applicable to pain and discomfort avoidance, and to illness in older individuals.

PERCEPTION AND MEASUREMENT OF PAIN

Introduction

We have already discussed some of the difficulties in differentiating "normal" from "pathological" aging. Some believe that the distinction is arbitrary, since we are dealing with a continuum in the measurement of most biological structures and/or functions. While, from a scientific viewpoint, such categorizations may be unimportant, pragmatically, for social and economic reasons, they are essential. Many controversies in the health fields, such as the training of the treatment provider or compensation for the professional, center around the issues of classifications. It is also appropriate to differentiate between "disease" and "illness": Disease is usually defined as a specific diagnosis (e.g., arthritis or atherosclerosis). "Illness" refers not only to the presence of a specific disease, but also to a person's perceptions and responses to the disease (Ouslander & Beck, 1982). A person may have a disease and not feel ill. Conversely, a person may feel weak and ill, yet no specific pathophysiological condition can be observed. Physicians sometimes use the term *sign* when physically measurable "objective" indices are present, and the term *symptom* is applied to the patient's perception or complaints, such as a headache. The example, however, illustrates the arbitrariness of the distinction. Pains are the most common accompaniments of pathology, yet there are at the present no "objective" measures to identify them. Turk and Melzack (1992), after reviewing the literature, found that there is no isomorphic relationship between physically determined pathology and pain. They also cite studies that found low correlations between persons' reports of pain and their behavior. The lack of objective measures is not restricted to pain. It also applies to other sensory functions, such as the simple and most commonly used measurement of visual acuity. First, since, in most instances, biological changes are not discrete but represent a continuum from what is considered normal to some state conventionally labeled pathological, the distinction between health and illness is frequently difficult to discern. For example, how elevated does BP have to be to be labeled as hypertension? Second, in many early stages of pathology, it is difficult to obtain objective signs. Third, many physiological changes are transient, and the organism returns quickly to a normal state without the benefit of any interventions. Finally, the examiner, being human, may miss a pathological sign. Some of these problems in diagnosis are especially applicable to what have been referred to as psychosomatic or psychological disturbances. Fatigue, a perception of discomfort, has been previously reviewed in Chapter 3. With reference to pain, Katz (1996) postulates that it is not possible to separate mental and physical health, such as depression in later life, frequently associated with pain. This state may result either from psychological or physiological stressors. Because of the high prevalence of pains and diseases in older individuals, much has been written about this topic.

It is a truism that to seek help for a health problem, the person must first perceive the presence of a deleterious condition. The importance of motivational–affective and cognitive factors precludes a simple objective measurement of pain, and it requires sophisticated self-report procedures. Bakan (1968, p. 59) cites the pharmacologist Beecher, who concluded his review of pain measurement with the statement that "pain cannot be satisfactorily defined, except as every man (person) defines it introspectively for (her) himself." Nevertheless, recently, there has been some progress in the development of techniques that permit us to measure certain aspects of the pain experience.

The measurement of pain ideally requires separating the discriminative from the motivational–affective and the cognitive–evaluative factors (Melzack & Katz, 1992). In the 1970s, Melzack and colleagues developed the McGill Pain Questionnaire (MPQ) based on the model he developed with Wall, which includes the three separate aspects: sensory–discriminative, motivational–affective, and cognitive–evaluative psychological dimensions. Though a number of investigators have questioned the independence of the three dimensions (Price & Harkins, 1992), especially in clinical studies, the MPQ has been probably the most widely used scale. Melzack and Katz (1992) defend the utility of the MPQ's framework, and they cite studies showing its potential in the differential diagnosis of various pain syndromes, though they acknowledge that high anxiety may limit its discriminative capacity. Price and Harkins (1992) use only a sensory and an affective dimension in measuring pain. However, they differentiate between an immediate cognitive meaning given to a sensation, called Stage 1 affect, and a Stage 2, in which the implications of the pain are evaluated, including how the pain will influence one's life and/or future. Several other pain assessment instruments, including a shortened version of the MPQ, are described in the volume edited by Turk and Melzack (1992). There are also self-report measures of suffering and disability (Jensen & Karoly, 1992). In their edited volume, Turk and Melzack (1992) note that at present, the relationships of pain to pathology, functional impairments, and the degree of disability are poorly understood. This should not be surprising, since Melzack espouses a tridimensional theory of pain in which motivational–affective and cognitive factors contribute to pain perception. Thus, every person will have a somewhat different developmental history, including pain experiences, that influences his or her perceptions and actions. In Chapter 8, we again refer to a similar approach in the analysis of stress, a concept that is closely related to pain and discomfort. Lazarus (1991, pp. 361–362), in his treatise on emotion and adaptation, refers to several of the studies on pain to which we have made references. As do many reviewers in other fields, Turk and Melzack (1992) ask for more normative information on specific populations, a plea well understood by gerontologists.

Aging

As might be expected, most surveys and epidemiological studies have found that rates of persistent pain in community-dwelling individuals increase with age (Harkins & Price, 1992). Though many of the surveys were beset by numerous methodological biases (Von Korff, 1992), it should be obvious that the increases in health problems with age should also lead to increases in the experiences of pain, especially since many older adults experience a multiplicity of chronic ailments, and some of the interactions exacerbate the perception of pain. Since most sensory functions exhibit decrements during aging, it has been traditionally assumed that this also applies to pain (Harkins & Price, 1992). Studies of cerebral evoked potentials to noxious stimuli do show decreased magnitudes and increased latencies in older subjects. However, numerous laboratory studies using standard psychophysical techniques with various noxious stimuli (electric shock, radiant heat, pressure) have produced contradictory results. Some have found that thresholds increase with age, others reported decreases, and still others found no changes. On the other hand, in three studies, pain tolerance actually decreased in the elderly. Tolerance is the maximum pain level that the individual is willing to accept in the laboratory (Sternbach, 1978). Though this measure may be more significant for an understanding of clinical pain, ethical concerns limit these types of studies, and they are rarely performed nowadays. Harkins and Price (1992) have noted that all of the studies thus far have been cross-sectional. Since cultural factors influence the reporting of pain and other aspects of pain experience, longitudinal studies would be preferable. Also, many investigators in the past have neglected to control previous and current health problems common in older persons, and these may affect the perception of pain. A person who has experienced various illnesses in the past may evaluate pain differently than a person who has not had many health problems. Harkins and Price attribute the discrepancies in the reports of the laboratory studies to (1) difference in the stimuli used (radiant heat, contact heat, electric shock); (2) the part of the body that was stimulated; (3) the differences in the psychophysical method employed; and (4) criteria used in the selection of subjects. The latter need to consider not only current health status but also past experiences with pain. The logistical problems in getting appropriate samples seem to be great.

Many older persons have health problems and experience chronic or intermittent pain. However, several studies of chronic pain patients using self-report scales of the intensity, unpleasantness, and other affective responses have been unsuccessful in revealing age-associated differences (Harkins & Price, 1992). Even the presence of greater physical pathology in older than in younger patients does not produce a greater impact of the pain experience (Sorkin, Rudy, Hanlon, Turk, & Stieg, 1990). Keefe and Williams (1990), in a study of chronic pain patients aged 21 to 65+ years, found no aging effects in coping strategies except for a greater tendency in the older sufferers to use prayer and hope. However, the role of cohort was not mentioned. Since, in the past, religion may have been a more significant factor in people's lives, there may have been a greater emphasis on religious activities in previous cohorts. Similarly, the perceived effectiveness of the coping strategies employed did not correlate with age. The authors note, however, that their sample size was small.

INTERPRETATION OF SYMPTOMS

When pain and other forms of discomfort are perceived, the person interprets the meaning and significance of the symptoms and the action that ought to be taken. Perception of illness is a function of the previous experience embedded in the cultural context of the individual. In a diary study of a random sample in upstate New York, Stoller (1993), obtained data from 669 community-dwelling participants ages 65 years and older (mean 74). While the age of the oldest participant was not given, 8.6% of subjects were above 84 years, with women constituting 60% of the sample. The participants were asked to keep a health diary for 3 weeks. They were to record symptoms they experienced and how they interpreted them from a checklist of 26 items. Except for heart palpitations and vision problems, none of the other bodily symptoms were considered to be "definitely serious" by the respondents. A large number of participants tended to assume that many of the symptoms are normal in older persons; only 16% attributed their symptoms to nonmedical factors. Prior and current health experiences were the major influences in the interpretations. The correlations between perceptions of pain or discomfort and interference with normal activities ranged between .60 and .85 for different symptoms. Those who rated their overall health status as poor reported more negative interpretations of their symptoms than those who perceived their health status to be good. The perceptions of stress, measured by the Geriatric Life Events Scale, and social support played minor roles in the interpretation of many, but not all, symptoms or in the interference with usual activities. Stoller admits that the latter finding is difficult to interpret and that her study did not permit her to analyze the basis for what appears to be contrary to findings in most previous studies on social support. Also, individuals with multiple roles tended to report more symptoms and interferences with normal activities, which is contrary to the assumption that multiple roles are a source of support in buffering stress. However, as Stoller indicates, an individual with many roles is more likely to perceive interferences by a variety of symptoms than a person with a narrower range of activities. Another aspect of this study (Stoller & Forster, 1994) examined the relationship between pain and physician contacts. Uncertainty regarding the seriousness of the problem as well as the level of pain or interference with normal activities triggered a professional consultation. With a smaller sample of participants ages 66–91 years, Cook and Thomas (1994) obtained similar results. Pain did not increase medical services utilization unless it was severe. Many elderly accept mild levels of pain as a normal part of aging and resort to nonprescription analgesics to manage the discomfort.

CULTURE

Large cultural (ethnic) variations in response to painful stimuli, which have been observed in well-controlled laboratory studies and in a host of descriptive ethnographic accounts, would seem to contribute to the motivational–affective factor. Sternbach (1978) reviewed studies in which Yankee, Irish, Italian, and Jewish women showed differences in the laboratory to pain tolerance to electric shock stimuli and ANS changes to the noxious stimuli. In interviews, members of these ethnic groups expressed different attitudes toward pain and its expression. Sternbach also cites interviews with surgical patients in a Veterans Administration Hospital and their families, conducted by the anthropologist Zborowski, which indicated that there are ethnic differences in the United States in attitudes toward pain and pain expression. The sociologist Mechanic (1992) also noted that in the United States, visits to physicians and taking of medications vary in different religious groups.

The contributions of ethnicity overlap with a related factor, personality encompassing both genetic predispositions and environmental experiences in the perception and tolerance of pain, especially in chronic clinical conditions. Merskey (1978) begins his chapter on pain and personality with quotations from the Book of Lamentations in the Bible, most likely predating Aristotle (384–322 B.C.), relating that a person who saw the sacking of Jerusalem has an experience like fire in his bones, a burning pain. Thus, the perception of pain and suffering cannot be separated from the predominant ethos of the times.

PERSONALITY

A major impetus for the Melzack–Wall gate theory (1965) were the reports from both field and laboratory studies that anxiety, usually classified as a personality factor, plays a major role in pain perception. In a later exposition, Melzack (1993) relates pain to his new conceptual nervous system, the *body–self neuromatrix*. In this schema, pain cannot be attributed solely to the activities in the cortical pain center or to the limbic system, but it encompasses both. The limbic system is a diffuse, variously defined group of neurons in the cerebral cortex, the basal ganglia, the thalamus, the hypothalamus, and other structures associated with motivations and emotions. Pain is, therefore, a multidimensional concept consisting of sensory, affective, evaluative, postural, and perhaps other dimensions, all of them components of personality, according to different theorists. In many personality inventories, for example, the Minnesota Multiple Personality Inventory (MMPI), pain sensitivity is one of the measures used in the classification of personality. Merskey (1978) and Weisenberg (1977) reviewed some of the earlier literature that dealt primarily with younger adults. There has been little research on older adult pain–personality relationships, and practically none was based on longitudinal observations. One of the factors that has been studied is personal control, the perception that individuals have to some extent the ability to determine their actions. Since many facets of control apply also to health practices and health services utilization, we are deferring a discussion of this factor to Chapter 7 on health. Instead of discussing the numerous personality variables that may affect pain perception and reactivity, we focus on just two, often considered to play major roles in the aged.

Hypochondriasis

A personality variable that traditionally has been assumed to occur frequently in the aged, especially among older women, is hypochondri-

asis (Busse & Blazer, 1980). Hypochondriasis is defined as the exaggerated concern with bodily symptoms, including the perception of pain,
in the absence of physiologically detectable pathologies. It is usually associated with mental disturbances, most commonly with anxiety or depression (Blazer, 1996), and the incidence does not seem to be higher in
older than in younger persons (Costa & McCrea,1985b). The more frequent utilization of medical services by the elderly is related to a higher
frequency of pathological physical diseases, but there may be important
motivational factors that might differentiate some cases in the young
and the old: In younger persons, hypochondriasis is frequently the result of certain psychosocioeconomic factors, such as job dissatisfaction,
that may lead to workers' compensation or problems with the spouse or
children. These factors associated with hypochondriasis may be less
common in older populations. On the other hand, older adults experience various chronic health problems and social losses that threaten
their self-esteem and independence (Hayslip, Galt, Lopez, & Nation,
1994). They may seek secondary gains in the form of attention from
family members and caring professionals (Busse & Blazer, 1980). The
flip side is the overevaluation of one's health that occurs in the elderly
about as frequently as hypochondriasis (Blazer, 1996).

Depression

Depression is probably the major personality factor influencing
pain and illness perception. While epidemiological studies have reported that major depressive disorders (MDD) are less common in community-dwelling older than in younger people (Gatz *et al.,* 1996),
depressive symptoms associated with various losses and adjustment
needs do occur frequently in the elderly. This apparent paradoxical
finding may be attributed to the atypical symptoms seen in older "depressed" individuals that are not equivalent to those seen in young
MDD patients. In hospitalized medically ill older patients, the prevalence of depression is high and is related to the severity of the illness. In
general, depression is related to the degree of functional disability or
impairment with normal functioning. In a large scale study of 598 elderly nursing home and congregate-apartment residents ranging in age
from 61 to 99 years, Parmelee, Katz, and Lawton (1991) administered
the MPQ, several scales measuring depression, a scale of self- and/or
staff-assessed functional disability, and obtained self-ratings of impairment of 14 body systems (e.g., cardiac, endocrine). Small, statistically
significant correlations in the .18 to .41 range were obtained between

pain intensity or localized pain complaints and depression; individuals diagnosed as depressed exhibited higher correlations than those not diagnosed as depressed. However, even for the latter, some of the correlations were statistically significant, though the highest r was only .22. Except for headaches and joint pains, the differences between the depressed and nondepressed elderly were statistically significant: Depressed persons who reported less anger and greater vigor experienced greater pain. Those who were diagnosed as suffering from a major depression were more likely to have a specific complaint than those with only minor symptoms of depression, and the latter had more complaints than nondepressed persons. The differences between the groups were significant only when possible physical pathologies were present. This implies that depressives are more sensitive to somatically explainable pains and aches. While functional disability was a significant covariate of pain intensity, the relationship between pain and depression remained significant even when this factor was controlled. Thus, functional impairment cannot explain the pain–depression relationship and neither did age contribute to the relationship between pain experience and depression. While the investigators established a small relationship between pain and depression, accounting for about 5–15% of the shared variance, the causal mechanisms could not be determined in this cross-sectional study.

In a cross-sectional study of 228 mainly low SES community-residing adults 55 years of age and older who were outpatients at a university clinic, Williamson and Schulz (1992a) measured depression, pain, and self-reported activity restrictions, and obtained a physician's evaluation of health status. Data on the age variable were not reported. For the whole sample, symptoms of depression were positively correlated with pain ($r = .3$), activity restriction ($r = .4$) and physical illness ($r = .2$). All three correlations were much higher for those having high scores on the depression scale. To clarify the relationships between the variables, a path analysis was used to test the model in which the effects of both activity restriction and physical illness were assumed to affect symptoms of depression. Other potential models were not tested. However, with only six paths, the outcome was not very different from that obtained in the initial correlation matrix, and the results corroborated the Parmelee *et al.* (1991) findings. Though Williamson and Schulz emphasized the role of activity restriction as a major factor in the relationships between experiences of pain and depression, other potential path models were not tested. As was indicated previously, a cross-sectional correlational study provides few clues about the potential causal mechanism. In another report on basically the same sample ($N = 230$),

Williamson and Schulz (1992b) reported on the relationships between depression, pain perception, physician-evaluated health, self-evaluated health activity restriction, use of pain medication, and several psychosocial and demographic factors. Though this study would have better lent itself to a path analysis than the previously reported one, the technique was not utilized. In addition to these reported relationships between depression, activity restriction, and physician-evaluated health, the authors also reported that symptoms of depression were associated with poorer self-reported health and the use of pain medications. The latter is to be expected, since many analgesics produce drowsiness. After controlling for physician-diagnosed physical illness symptoms, self-report variables accounted for an additional 13% of the variance in depressive symptomatology, but this included the use of pain medication, which contributed 6% of the variance. Financial worries, problems with transportation to the clinic, low social support, and other worries, such as feeling useless, and lonely on holidays and similar occasions, also contributed to the symptoms of depression beyond the effects of physical illness. While 25% of the variance of depressive symptomatology could be attributed to health factors, 22% could be accounted for by the psychosocial factors, although the authors are aware of many of the limitations of this cross-sectional study. Finally, though the participants were obtained from an outpatient clinic, it is not clear whether the problems that necessitated the clinic visit(s) were chronic or acute. In a third study, Williamson and Schulz (1995) compared young and old (an age range of 30–90 years) home-residing cancer patients. The sample was dichotomized into those under the age of 65 years and those who were older. There were two measurements 8 months apart on patients receiving radiation therapy. Symptoms of depression, activity restrictions, and other chronic health conditions were recorded. Initially there were 268 participants, but at the second measurement, the sample was reduced to 161. The attrition rate was not related to age, but to the level of pain, depression, and functional impairment at the initial point. The 8-month testing period revealed an increase in pain perception, activity restrictions, and depression, with routine activity restrictions more distressing to the younger individuals; presumably, activity restrictions are more debilitating to a younger individual. Age per se did not affect pain ratings, and in both young and old patients, there was a slight decline in pain ratings. No biological criteria were correlated with the psychological measurements.

Causality is difficult to determine in clinical studies. Does depression intensify the perception of pain, or does pain enhance depression? Also, are depressed individuals more sensitive to pain, or are they more willing to acknowledge and express it to others? It would appear that activity restrictions may be a key factor in the relation between pain and depression. Whether personality characteristics contribute or moderate the experience of pain or illness, or whether the reverse is the causal sequence, is a much debated issue. Even if personality factors are involved, the extent of the relationship is uncertain (Friedman, 1990).

CONCLUSIONS

Pain and discomfort avoidance are frequently considered to be the most fundamental motives. Since aging is associated with the development of diseases, it seems appropriate to examine the changes in pain perception in older persons. Pain avoidance or relief is one of the major concerns in health maintenance and in well-being. Pain is a multidimensional construct, and the Melzack–Wall theory, currently the major guide to research in the field, postulates three dimensions: (1) sensory–discriminative; (2) affective–motivational; (3) cognitive–evaluative. As is true of most psychological constructs, the dimensions are not orthogonal. Information is available primarily on the sensory–discriminative changes during aging, though the affective–motivational dimension is important for an analysis of the activities of a person who experiences pain.

There are large individual differences in pain sensitivity and reactivity, many related to personality and cultural factors. Since there are numerous theories of personality, each encompassing a large number of complex dimensions, it is difficult to determine the quality and magnitude of the relationship. Only cross-sectional data are available on the effects of aging on laboratory pain perception, and the results have been contradictory because of differences in the aversive stimuli that have been employed, the methods of measurement, and the heterogeneity of those tested.

In chronic pain, a common problem in the elderly, coping strategies do not seem to be affected by age. However, prior experience with pain seems to be important. Depressive symptoms brought on by health problems and various psychosocial and economic losses seem to exacerbate chronic pain, especially when activity is restricted. The restrictions, however, tend to be more deleterious in younger persons. Older individuals expect to have pain and activity restrictions, and these may lead to less depression. Unfortunately, the causal sequence of this relationship is not known.

Knowledge concerning the perception of pain and the motives engendered by it are of great importance in the field of health. Reactions to symptoms and health services utilization seem to depend on the intensity of the discomfort and the activity restrictions engendered by the pain, as well as on some personality variables. Hypochondriasis, an exaggerated preoccupation with the interpretation and bodily symptoms of pain and discomfort, does not seem to be more prevalent in the elderly, and there is usually comorbidity with various diseases. The possible motivational factors in hypochondriasis are frequently different in the young and the old.

CHAPTER 5

Eating and Drinking

INTRODUCTION

In animal studies of motivation, hunger and thirst have traditionally been the most thoroughly investigated motives. In the *Handbook of the Psychology of Aging* (1977), Elias and Elias begin their review of motivation with animal studies of hunger-induced drives. This biologically based motivation is not reviewed in their section on human motivation and the subsequent editions of the *Handbook* do not discuss this topic. The 1977 review is of limited value for understanding these motives on the human level.

Eating and drinking are determined not only by biological factors but also on the human level, largely by hedonic (sensory) factors and by developmental influences—habits, social settings, and culture. In an introduction to a conference on nutrition and the chemical senses during aging, Hegsted (1989) observed that most nutritionist have concerned themselves with what we should eat rather than with why we eat, what we eat, and what we like to eat, which are the basic motivational questions. In adition to age, numerous cohort and time of testing or observation factors play important roles. Most of these interact to complicate any analysis. It should be noted that there are several methodological problems in dietary intake data that typically are based either on recall data or on records kept for 3–7 days (Ausman & Russell, 1990). Hegsted (1989) cites several studies in which the intraindividual variabilities during the periods of study were greater than the interindividual variations. For many persons in our society, especially for the relatively well-educated, who are the most common participants in diary studies, there is a great variety of available foods. Thus, generalizations from short-term studies may be somewhat limited.

In a recent review not dealing with an age factor, Herman (1996) observed that despite the huge amount of research, there is no comprehensive theory of human eating. We do not know how different factors that are causally related to eating combine to determine what and when we eat. Much human research on eating is saddled with assumptions based on laboratory animal studies, and there are even controversies about several physiological details of hunger and satiety on the human level. Adding the various psychosocial factors complicates the analysis of eating behaviors. Herman also notes that most research efforts have been focused on disordered rather than "normal" eating. It seems, therefore, that we are far from understanding in people the aging changes in motives that have been of major importance in the development of many twentieth-century behavior theories. Our treatment of the topic is mainly descriptive.

EATING

Biological Factors

In aging, consideration must be given both to normal aging changes and health disturbances that commonly occur in older people. In healthy individuals, there are relatively few major physiological aging effects that have an impact on nutrition. For example, the gastrointestinal (GI) tract maintains, on the whole, normal physiological activity well into advanced age (Nelson & Castell, 1990; Norton, 1995). There are, however, some alterations in GI functions, especially during stress, such as a decline in mastication, gastric acid output, and some decline in small intestine absorption for certain substances, as well as some alterations in the colon, rectum, liver, and pancreas. GI symptoms, such as indigestion, heartburn, and epigastric discomfort, are common complaints of older people. These discomforts may have some effects on eating habits, or they may induce anxieties. More importantly, numerous health problems, many of them occult, not apparent upon a simple clinical examination, affect eating, and some occult health problems also involve the GI system (Norton, 1995). Oral health and dental dysfunctions also affect food intake. In addition, various prescription drugs used by older people influence appetite.

In animal studies, aging is associated with a decrease in endogenous brain opioid peptides (Morgan & May, 1990; Morley, 1990) that enhance hunger and eating, and there is an increase of cholecystokinin, probably an opioid antagonist, which is a satiety factor (Morley, 1990). Several recent human studies also point toward decreased internal control of eating in the aged. Roberts, Fuss, Heyman, Evans, *et al.* (1994), with a small sample ($N = 9$) of healthy older men (mean age 70 years) and a young control group ($N = 7$, mean age 24 years), tested the effects of overfeeding. A 10-day baseline phase was followed by a 21-day over-feeding phase, during which the participants consumed approximately 1,000 kcal/day above their baseline, an 8.9% increase. In a 46-day follow-up phase, the young participants rapidly decreased their body weight to the preexperimental level, while the older group could not dissipate the excess energy intake that occurred during the overfeeding phase and kept the extra weight. In a symmetrical experiment, again with a small sample of other young and old participants, the regimen was underfeeding. The results were parallel to the overfeeding experiment, with the young exhibiting decreased resting energy expenditures (REE) during underfeeding, while the old participants did not reduce their REE. The experimenters accounted for their findings in terms of changes in age-associated REE that become less sensitive to food intakes. No measures of hunger or satiety were taken. The latter factors were investigated in another small population study by Rolls, Dimeo, and Shide (1995); 16 younger and 16 older (ages 60–84 years) participants were fed several different fixed preloads of yogurts that varied in energy densities (i.e., compositions of fat and carbohydrates) 30 minutes before they had access to an *ad libitum* self-selected lunch buffet. Ratings of hunger and satiety, and the amount of various nutrients consumed during the meal were measured. The young were better able to compensate for the preloads and therefore ate less for lunch. Though the older men rated themselves as less hungry and fuller than the young, this was not reflected in their food consumption. A minor problem of this study was the large percentage of the older men who were taking prescription drugs. de Castro (1993), in a 7-day diary study of food intakes and activities in 307 healthy adults ages 20–80 years, found that the reported hunger was less affected by meals in the older than the younger participants. The small number of participants in the laboratory studies, the relatively short observation periods, and the difficulties in controlling for health status seem to call for additional work on this important topic.

In summary, the various, normal age-associated physiological alterations may be invoked to account for the inability to regulate body weight, leading to both the presence of anorexia and obesity in some older people. However, the internal factors are not sufficient to explain much of the variance in eating changes with aging in healthy individuals. It is most likely that psychosocial factors, either directly or in an interaction with the biological factors, are prepotent in determining food intake in healthy older persons.

General Health

While eating and food choices are associated with psychological, sociological, cultural, and economic factors, in many instances, the psychosocial factors may be secondary to age-related health problems such as diabetes mellitus, hypertension, viral infections, or SDAT, which affect appetite (Murphy, Cain, & Hegsted, 1989). Also, there are many undiagnosed subclinical physiological changes that may affect appetite. Arthritis, tremors, and other neuromuscular handicaps may also affect the choices for obtaining, preparing, and consuming specific food items. Poor dentition will also influence eating.

A fairly common health problem affecting nutrition of older individuals is depression, which may be the result of illnesses or psychosocial losses. The diagnosis often may be overlooked by assuming that the observed symptoms are normative for the aged. Morley and Morley (1996) report that depression is the major cause of undernutrition in both community-dwelling and institutionalized elderly. Other stress-related health conditions also affect eating in older individuals, just as they do in younger cohorts.

Hedonic Factors

Smell, taste, visual stimulation, and possibly other senses, as well as the social–perceptual context, all play a role in eating. There have been many studies showing that some or all olfactory thresholds increase with age; suprathreshold odors are weaker, and what is even more significant for everyday living, the discrimination, identification, and memory for various odors gradually deteriorates (Bartoshuk & Duffy, 1995). Somewhat smaller losses are seen in taste. The changes are not uniform for all smell or taste qualities, and they are affected by the response measures that are used (Bartoshuk, 1990; Cain & Stevens, 1989; Cowart, 1989; Wysocki & Gilbert, 1989). Deterioration of vision and other senses may decrease the esthetic quality of food substances. Many older people, especially widows, lack companionship at mealtimes, which also reduces the hedonic quality of the food (de Castro, 1994)

Food Preferences

A number of studies have found that total caloric intake per kilogram of body weight decreases with age (Elahi, Elahi, Andres, Tobin,

et al., 1983; McGandy, Barrows, Spanias, Meredith, *et al.,* 1966). Wurtman, Lieberman, Tsay, Nader, *et al.* (1988) measured calorie and nutrient intakes during a 4-day period in healthy noninstitutionalized
elderly (ages 65–94 years) and in young individuals (ages 21–35 years)
while they were residing at the MIT Clinical Research Center, where
they had access to unlimited quantities of specific foods during breakfast, lunch, and dinner. They could select from a variety of high protein
and high carbohydrate foods. The types of foods offered were chosen to
represent meal items normally eaten in the Boston area. In addition,
participants had continuous access to eight different snacks. All food
intakes were carefully monitored. The elderly participants consumed
significantly fewer calories, carbohydrates, and fats than did the
younger group, both on an absolute basis and when adjusted for differences in body weight. Older participants consumed almost 85% of their
calories from meals, while the younger adults consumed only about
72% from meals, with the rest coming from snacks. This was a descriptive study that did not attempt to determine the basis for the age differences. Is snacking, for example, associated with certain changes in our
culture affecting young people more than the elderly? Since snacks are
heavily advertised on television programs aimed at younger audiences,
it is not unreasonable to assume that this will influence their food consumption. It would appear that in addition to certain physiological
changes with age, a number of psychological and social factors play
major roles in food choices, amount consumed, and other variables involved in eating.

Habits

Perhaps the most potent factor affecting human eating is previous
experience. It is difficult to modify lifelong habits in dietary patterns,
many or most having been acquired in childhood. There is a strong resistance to change food habits except for health reasons (Betts, 1988; Peters & Rappoport, 1988). Jägerstadt, Norden, and Åkesson (1979) noted
that the main difference between the nutrient intake of a group of older
retired persons and a comparable group of middle-aged people could be
ascribed to differences in food habits. In their study, the elderly consumed more fish and milk but fewer vegetables. The latter were less
available when the older group was growing up and establishing food
habits. Well-established food habits will persist even when public
health recommendations advise a change. Persistence of habits applies
especially to less educated older people or to those who are more influ-

enced by traditional cultural mores. Angulo (1988) cites a study in which Cubans in Florida continue to fry food, a cardinal feature of their cuisine, even when this is against medical advice. Because of changes in height and body composition, obesity in the elderly is not easy to specify (Ausman & Russell, 1990). When it does occur, it must be attributed, to some extent at least, to eating habits, just as is the case with younger cohorts. With decreases in energy needs due to decreases in basal metabolism and activity, the need to reduce caloric intake is counteracted by strongly established food habits. In a survey by the National Center for Health Statistics of 3,479 persons ages 65–74 years in 65 locales in the United States, obesity in elderly women ranged from 19% to 36% (Ausman & Russell, 1990); more recent data show an even greater prevalence of obesity (Elahi, Dyke, & Andres, 1995). Surveys also found deficiencies in the daily intake of several nutrients based on the Recommended Dietary Allowances of the National Research Council (Ausman & Russell, 1990), and this is most likely associated with long-established dietary habits.

It should not be assumed, however, that the elderly cannot or do not change their eating habits. Currently, there is much emphasis in our media on a healthy lifestyle, with nutrition as a major component, and many older persons seem to pay more attention to this aspect of eating than do younger people (Rappoport & Peters, 1988). In a longitudinal study of volunteers over the age of 60 years (median age 72 years; range 60–85 years), Garry, Rhyne, Halioua, and Nicholson (1989) asked their participants to keep a consecutive 3-day food record each year. Data were collected over a 6-year period, but data were available for only 5 years. From the original group of 304 elderly, complete records were analyzed for only 157 participants. Weights of the participants and daily energy intake remained relatively constant over the 6-year span. There was, however, a gradual decline in fat and cholesterol intake during the study. The results on these volunteers reflect the impact of the public's awareness of the role of fat and cholesterol in cardiovascular and other diseases. It is noteworthy that data over the 6-year period could only be obtained on about half of the original volunteers. The media seem to be more important in influencing healthy food habits than are family or friends (McIntosh, Fletcher, Kubena, & Landmann, 1995); in their study of 424 adults ages 58 years and older, these investigators found that over 60% reported that they had reduced their red meat intake and that the changes were not the result of health problems. In a longitudinal study in the Netherlands, Kromhout, Coulander, Obermann, Van Kampen-Donker, *et al.* (1990) collected dietary histories from men ages 40–59 years in 1960, 1965, 1970, and again in 1985. Of the initial sample of 872 men in the 25-year period of the study, a number had died, could not be located, or were too ill to participate, leaving 315 participants for whom complete data were obtained. Data on a small new sample of 40- to 57-year-old men were again collected in 1985. During the 25-year span, the initial group decreased significantly its consumption of bread, potatoes, eggs, milk, legumes, and vegetables, while it increased its consumption of fruits, nuts, pastries, and alcohol. In other food groups, no significant changes were observed. The data for the independent sample in 1985 were similar to those of the longitudinal participants collected the same year. This study lends support to the hypothesis that changes in nutrition are less dependent on age than on prevailing cultural changes in food preferences. The diet in 1985 was nutritionally better than in 1960 but still far removed from the recommendations of the Nutrition Council of Netherlands. Thus, well-established cultural patterns of food intake are difficult to change even in a quarter of a century. When new developments in the health sciences suggest that there are benefits to be derived from lifestyle changes, including nutrition, they are most likely to occur in educated, financially well-off, married older persons (Duffy & McDonald, 1990). Elahi et al. (1983), in their combined longitudinal and cross-sectional study of nutrient intakes in highly educated upper-middle-class males from 1961 to 1975, found that the year in which the dietary diaries were taken influenced the relative intake of carbohydrates, polyunsaturated fatty acids (both increased in later periods), and cholesterol (decreased over time). These data tend to support the role of culturally induced changes in diet in well-educated persons, who are probably more familiar with the information on nutrition and health.

Social and Economic Factors

A number of social factors, some mentioned previously, influence eating. Elahi et al. (1983) showed that living alone may affect the hedonic quality associated with eating and/or a reluctance to prepare normal meals. Usually, eating with a spouse or family extends the time spent on meals due to increased social interactions. McIntosh, Shifflet, and Picou (1989) used a 24-hour nutritional recall with 170 low SES elderly (mean age 69 years) at a federally funded nutrition site. They found that poor diets were related to stressful events and strain, and to low social support. Those with more friends and companions fared better than did isolates. The study emphasized the importance of mealtime company.

In another similar study of 2,195 older Australian men (Horwath, 1989), poor dietary intake was most common among those who lived alone. This condition, however, was associated with low SES and physical inactivity. de Castro (1994) found that even young people have a greater food intake when they eat with family than when alone or with strangers. Shifflet and McIntosh (1986), in a study of 805 older persons at 13 nutrition sites over a 2-year period, found a small positive correlation between positive future-time perspectives and age-appropriate food habits. Those living with a spouse had a stronger future-time orientation than those living alone, and a higher income was also significantly associated with a more positive future orientation. Rosenbloom and Whittington (1993) studied 50 recently widowed persons (mostly women) and 50 age, gender, and race-matched married persons; ages ranged from 60 to 85 years. An analysis of 3-day food intake diaries and interview data showed that widowhood had negative effects on eating behaviors and consumption of nutritious foods. The effects were not related to a loss of financial resources but could be interpreted to changes in the social context of eating. It seems apparent, therefore, that companionship is important for maintaining adequate motivation for good food habits. However, there are numerous psychosocial variables associated with companionship, and it is difficult to specify the variance attributable to each of the factors that influences food intake.

Lack of transportation also imposes problems on the ability to obtain a variety of foods or affordable items. Corner grocery stores are disappearing from the American scene, and supermarkets may not be easily accessible to older persons. Older people may be living with relatives or in situations with limited food storage and preparation facilities, which also hinders nutritional choices. Financial problems have been considered to place special constraints on the quality and quantity of available essential nutrients. The development of various national and state nutrition programs for older citizens was based on the assumption that many elderly in our society lack adequate nutrition. However, Hendricks, Calasanti, and Turner (1988), in a brief review of studies on the relationship between income and dietary intake, noted that the results have been mixed. While some investigators have reported that there is a positive relationship between monetary resources and nutrition, other studies have not found any relationships. The authors note that SES is not only a function of how much money a person has, but also how it is spent, and that includes expenditures for food. Cohort, historical, and cultural factors will affect how a group or an individual will distribute available resources among a host of goods and services, including food, which can be obtained with the resources on hand and with those expected in the future. People do not eat merely to satisfy basic nutritional needs. Thus, we are dealing with complex motivations. Hendricks *et al.* (1988) cite studies that analyzed the symbolic value of food for different groups or individuals. Most cultures use meals and special foods for celebratory and other specific occasions. In some ethnic groups, older people retain their habits to a greater extent than do those in other cultural groups, though data on this topic are scant. While Calasanti and Hendricks (1986) recommended that research be conducted on the relationship between physiological, psychological, socioeconomic, and cultural factors that may shed light on the motivation for maintaining adequate nutrition, available dietary intake data do not show any major qualitative or quantitative changes with age in the absence of health or economic problems. However, it is difficult to obtain detailed, valid longitudinal data using recall measures: Kohrs and Czajka-Narins (1986) indicate that even 24-hour recall data have a limited reliability. Written records are better, but as the number of days required to keep them increases, the degree of cooperation of the participants decreases. Thus, valid long-term records are not available, and it would probably be difficult to develop a program that would produce them. However, dietary histories based on questions of general food patterns and habits can be obtained by trained interviewers, and they do seem to have some validity, though they rely on the memories of the participants, with all of the problems associated with recall in the elderly. At the same time, it is essential to keep in mind that cultural changes in diet are continuously taking place, with emphasis on the health components of nutrition becoming increasingly important in our culture. An analysis of changes in eating as a function of aging must, of necessity, also control the societal changes in food consumption. Despite these caveats about general cultural changes in food consumption, there is some evidence, not surprising, that in some cultures, eating habits established in childhood and adolescence tend to be stable. This is apparent in the few studies that examined eating patterns in ethnic groups that show low assimilation, and in older, less educated individuals who are less influenced by media promotions of health-enhancing diets. The impact of habits may also be deduced from the reports on a large percentage of elderly who are obese, or who exhibit deficiencies in the intake of certain essential nutrients when the requirements may change with age.

Finally, nutrition information is now fairly frequently presented in our schools and in the mass media, but this seems to reach primarily young people and the more educated segments of our older populations.

DRINKING–FLUID INTAKE

There is not much information on age-associated changes in drinking or fluid intake. Just as eating is affected by a large number of both biological and environmental factors, drinking is influenced by a whole host of acquired nonhomeostatic environmental variables. In a classic study, Phillips, Rolls, Ledingham, Forsling, *et al.* (1984) demonstrated that in healthy older active males (ages 67–75 years), 24 hours of water deprivation produced less thirst, as measured by rating of thirst and subsequent drinking, than in young men. In this study, all 7 men remarked that they felt surprisingly little thirst, and one reported that he was not thirsty at all. There appears to be a reduced osmoreceptor sensitivity to water deprivation in older persons, a physiological deficit that increases the risk for developing dehydration and hypernatremia, a high level of plasma sodium resulting from the inability to compensate for renal and extrarenal fluid losses (Solomon & Lye, 1990). Just as in eating, it was found that the influence of the opioid system lessens in older animals; Silver and Morley (1992) also found that in humans, its role in fluid ingestion seems to be absent.

These findings were based on studies in which body fluid homeostasis was challenged. DeCastro (1991) obtained 7-day diaries of *ad libitum* food and water intake of 262 adults ages 20–82 years, finding no age differences in overall fluid intake or the perception of thirst. There is practically no information about the role of psychosocial factors in fluid intake in the elderly.

CONCLUSIONS

Animal studies on hunger and thirst have played a major role in the development of theories of motivation. On the human level, this approach is of little utility, for in most Western societies, people do not eat and drink solely to satisfy biological needs.

While there are some minor changes in the GI system that may induce some discomfort, they do not seem to be of major significance in eating and fluid intakes. Of greater import is some recent evidence that the perceptions of hunger and satiety, as well as thirst, tend to become poorer with age. The internal feedback mechanisms following overeating or undereating, and the reduction of age-associated decreases in resting energy expenditure are weakened in older persons, which may lead to anorexia or obesity.

The normative changes in the internal feeding mechanisms probably play a smaller role than do the numerous health problems that afflict older people is eating. Various chronic physical conditions and the drugs prescribed for their amelioration require dietary changes; persons with diabetes, hypertension, and osteoporosis, for example, need to adhere to special diets. Certain health problems, such as reduced mobility or sensory inadequacies, may interfere with meal preparation. Major depressions and other psychological illnesses manifest themselves in changes in food intake. Some more educated older people are aware of the role of diet in the maintenance of health. In Chapter 7 on health, we refer to studies on some motivational variables in the development and adherence to nutritional regimens.

There are several major psychosocial factors that determine eating. Culture and long-established food preferences are major determiners of what a person eats; companionship influences how much and, to some extent, what we eat. Since many older persons are widowed, this will affect food intake. Economics and access to food stores may also influence diet.

The small amount of information on fluid intake seems to indicate that changes with aging occur mainly when normal homeostasis is interrupted (e.g., when the person is deprived of liquids for some length of time or is under thermal stress). However, even when such a homeostatic balance is altered, the responses of older persons are less pronounced than they are in younger populations. Nutritionist often remind older persons to maintain an adequate intake of fluids.

In short, the traditional animal models of motivation based on hunger and thirst have had little utility for our analysis of motivational changes in human aging. The interaction of several psychosocial factors with the normative changes in metabolism and feeding mechanisms clearly point out the problems in the analysis of human motivation in older individuals. We covered this topic primarily because, historically, in psychology, eating and drinking were the "bread and butter" in the studies of motivation.

CHAPTER 6

Sexuality

INTRODUCTION

Sex is frequently classified with hunger and thirst as a basic or biological motive. For example, Wigdor (1980), in her review of drives and motivation in the aged, discusses sex in the section on basic drives, though she notes that "this drive is most subject to learning and the influence of social conditions" (p. 247). Beach (1956), one of the major figures in psychological research on sexual behavior, believed that it was inappropriate to equate sexual behavior with hunger and thirst as a primary motive. First, abstinence from sex does not cause death as does the absence of food and water. Second, food and water deprivation and the associated hunger and thirst sensations produce depletion of body tissues, but this does not occur in sexual deprivation; on the contrary, it is sexual behavior that may cause exhaustion. Finally, at least for primates, though there is some evidence for it even at lower phyletic levels, sexual behavior is determined to a much larger extent by environmental or social factors than are most of the other so-called biological motives. The gerontologist Comfort (1980, p. 887) points out that the importance of social factors in primates precludes any generalizations from animal to human sexual activity. We saw already in the previous chapter that even the animal studies on hunger and thirst provide little guidance for the analysis of human eating and fluid intake. This caveat is even more applicable to sexual behavior.

Hill and Preston (1996) noted that there is no widely accepted theory of human sexual motivation. Various cognitive, affective, and motor activities occur in achieving the goals that are labeled sexual behavior. In their study of college students, using questionnaires, they were able to identify eight relatively stable motives that lead to sexual behavior, including (1) the experience of pleasure; (2) expressions of closeness toward another person; (3) power or conquest; (4) reproduction; (5) feeling valued; and (6) relief of tension. These motives are situationally determined and many of them interact. They found gender differences, with the young men more oriented toward pleasure and relief of tension and the young women focusing on emotional closeness. The authors admit that the responses may have been influenced by social desirability, a problem common to many questionnaire studies. There are no comparable data with older participants to determine aging changes in sexual motivation. In most instances, except, usually, for reproduction, many of these motives also affect older persons. In addition, often there are expectations of receiving assistance and care, though these may be subsumed under category 2 of Hill and Preston's study (1996).

The increased interest in sexuality in our culture during the past 50 years has had an impact on various behavioral patterns in all age groups in our population, including older adults. It should not be surprising, therefore, that there have been increasing numbers of studies and an even larger number of publications for both professional and lay audiences on the topic of sexuality of older individuals. It is safe to say that the consequences of the heightened interest in sexuality may have been greater in the older segment of our population than in the other age groups, since, traditionally, the latter were supposed to have been asexual because sexual activity was linked to reproduction.

The modern interest in human psychosexuality may be traced to the beginning of this century, with much of the scientific and professional impetus arising from Freud's writings. However, the intellectual father of sexual awareness maintained the prevalent attitudes of his times toward old age. He was afraid of old age, and in rare references to it, he demeaned it (Kahana, 1978). With few exceptions, most of his early followers adopted similar stances in the realm of sexuality. Thus, initially, older people were not included in the growth of sexual awareness in our culture; it was not until after World War II, with the sharp increase in the number and the improved well-being of older people, that an interest in gerontological sexuality became widespread. For example, the best known empirical studies of sexual behavior in the United States, conducted in the 1940s (Kinsey, Pomeroy, & Martin, 1948; Kinsey, Pomeroy, Martin, & Gebhard, 1953), included only 182 adults over the age of 60 years in a sample of 18,000 respondents. Since the aforementioned study, there has been a virtual flood of publications on sexual behavior of older persons.

BIOLOGY

Though much information has been collected on normal sexual physiology and the changes associated with aging (Masters & Johnson, 1966), major gaps remain. Some of the findings were presented in Chapter 3. Considering the multiplicity of motives for sexual behavior and the important roles of various biological and psychosocial variables, it is not surprising that we lack data even for young persons on the mechanisms that occur during various early stages of sexual behavior, namely, the thoughts and desires that may lead to arousal. Schiavi and Seagraves (1995), in their review of the biology of sexual functions, concluded that in men, the mechanisms of action for androgens are not completely understood. In animals, the median preoptic hypothalamus controls the gonadal steroids and polypeptide hormones, but there is no comparable good human information. Since, in people, the role of the CNS in sexual behavior is of greater significance than in animals, knowledge of the triggering mechanisms would seem to be desirable. If we, then, further inquire about aging changes, the problem becomes still more complex. As with other age-associated physiological and behavioral changes, there are large individual differences.

Males

For the male, one major age-asociated change may be characterized as a slowing of the response cycle. Penile erection takes longer to induce; once achieved, it may be maintained for extended periods of time without ejaculation, and the refractory period before another erection can occur after an ejaculation is much longer. When ejaculation occurs, it is less forceful than in younger men. Nocturnal and morning penile erections are much less common (Schiavi, Schreiner-Engel, Mandeli, Schanzer, et al., 1990), and erection is more dependent on physiological stimulation and less on psychological factors in older men. The onset and magnitude of the physiological changes are relative, and many of them begin in men's twenties, but in some individuals, major decrements in some of the factors are not observed until men's sixties. There are also decreases in the secretion of testosterone, but the changes usually do not begin until the sixth decade of life.

Females

The age-associated physiological changes, except for menopause, are even less pronounced in the female. Following menopause, the reduction in estrogen production produces a thinning of the vaginal mucosa and reduced level of secretants that permeate the vagina during sexual arousal; these changes may produce pain and irritation during intercourse. The undesirable effects may be remedied with the use of personal lubricants or, in severe cases, with estrogen cremes or suppositories. For women, external stimuli may play a more significant role than the neurophysioplogical mechanisms (Schiavi & Seagraves, 1995).

CULTURE

Prior to discussing current U.S. survey data, a brief digression may be of some interest, since it may shed some light on sexual behavior in general. The important role of cultural factors in the sexual behavior of older individuals is apparent from the information available on preindustrial and traditional societies. Winn and Newton's (1982) Human Relations Area Files contains data on sexuality in 293 cultures, representing a variety of geographical regions of the world. In only 106 of them were there references to sexuality in the aged, and in only a few of these were they discussed systematically. Furthermore, in many instances, age is often defined imprecisely, and in many field studies, age was estimated by an observer from appearances. Finally, it should be noted that the reviewers did not mention that the life span in many of these societies differs greatly. In 20 of 28 cultures (70%) for which ages were available, sexual activity in males continued into "very old age," a poorly defined construct. Specific ages mentioned ranged from over 50 to beyond 100 years, though the validity of some of this information may be questionable. The nature of the activities ranged from intercourse to cunnilingus and "carnal passion." In the other 8 societies, observers reported inactivity or disinterest in older men. Similarly, in 22 of 26 societies for which information was available, older women were reported to have sexual contacts. Ages ranged up to 80 years, although the majority of the reports made references only to "older" women. Interestingly, in 18 of the 22 reports of sexual activity in older women, the characteristic coupling was between an older woman and a younger man. Winn and Newton associate this with the greater probability of widowhood of older women and the unavailability of older men; thus, even in these societies, social factors play an important role in sexual behavior. In a more recent study from Israel, Antonovsky, Sadowsky, and Maoz (1990) reported that sexual activity of 121 older women, ages 65–85 years, was higher in those of European or American origin than those who immigrated from Asian or African countries.

The major problem that older women face in Western cultures is lack of a partner; women live longer, tend to marry younger men, and in our society, men tend to prefer younger sexual partners (Botwinick, 1984; Turner, 1988). While, in our culture, physical attractiveness of the woman seems to play a greater role than does the attractiveness of the man, at least for younger individuals (Margolin & White, 1987), this may not be always the case with older persons (Martin, 1981).

SURVEYS

Methodological Difficulties

Valid data on sexual behavior, in general, are difficult to obtain, since in Western societies, it is almost impossible to get unbiased samples of respondents to sexual questions (Starr, 1985). Laumann, Gagnon, Michael, and Michaels (1994, pp. 35–47), in the introduction to their large-scale study of sexual practices of U.S. adults ages 18–59 years, which began in 1988, noted that there had been no extensive surveys of sexual behavior that met even the most elementary requirements for the study of a representative sample of the population. For example, Laumann *et al.* (1994, p. 46) cite the popular *Janus Report* (Janus & Janus, 1993), based on some 8,000 cases from sex therapists' offices and their friends, which estimated that in the 51–64 year age range, 81% of men and 65% of women are having sex at least once per week. On the other hand, Laumann *et al.* (1994) refer to a more valid General Social Survey (GSS) report, according to which the percentages were 43% and 25%, respectively, for these two groups. The discrepancies between the *Janus Report* and GSS are even greater for the 65+ age group. While in the *Janus Report* the percentages for men and women in the active group were 69 and 74, respectively, the GSS found them to be only 17% and 6%, respectively.

In our culture, many people, especially older individuals, were brought up to believe that sexual activities are a private matter that need not be discussed with others. Using a probability sample of 2,058 US adults, Leigh, Temple, and Trocki (1993) found in self-administered questionnaires that the refusal rate and the number of incomplete responses were higher in older (60+ years) than in younger respondents. Similar findings were reported by Mulligan and Moss (1991) in a mail survey of 427 veterans. For questionnaires of older adults, response rates in the 20–30% range are not uncommon (Bretschneider & McCoy, 1988; Steinkee, 1994).

Also, what aspect of sexual experience is to be measured? Is it only frequency of intercourse? In the Introduction, we referred to the multiplicity of motives that are implicit in human sexual behavior. As part of a large study on health in a Charleston, South Carolina county, in a stratified sample of the population (Keil, Sutherland, Knapp, Waid, *et al.*, 1992), the investigator merely asked whether the participant was "sexually aroused" by a partner, lest the question be misinterpreted. Bretschneider and McCoy (1988), in their study of sexual activities, collected data also on masturbation and on nonintercourse-associated touching and caressing. Many sex therapists and researchers prefer to emphasize "pleasuring" rather than any specific sex act in their definition of sexual behavior. Pleasuring refers to any sexual experience, not just intercourse and orgasm, which the person perceives as being pleasant. However, Mulligan and Palgutta (1991), in interviews of male U.S. Veterans Administration nursing home residents, found that coitus was the preferred form of sexual activity. Could this have been related to the relatively low SES of the residents? The same group of investigators (Mulligan & Moss, 1991) found similar results with a mail survey of noninstitutionalized veterans.

Some Findings

Despite these methodological problems, most research, to no one's surprise, indicates that there is a decrement in sexual activities with increasing age. We review primarily some more recent surveys to take into account the time of observation factor.

A 1987–1988 U.S. National Survey of Families and Households based on a probability sample of over 13,000 adults reported that age was the single factor most associated with marital sexual frequency. The steepest decline occurred between the fifth and sixth decades of life (Call, Sprecher, & Schwartz, 1995). Surveys by Diokno, Brown, and Herzog (1990) and by Matthias, Lubben, Atchinson, and Schweitzer (1997) also found that age and marital status were related to sexual activities, especially in women.

There is a frequently cited study on an unusually old sample of 80- to 102-year-olds (mean 86) residing in a residential retirement facility in California (Bretschneider & McCoy, 1988): out of a potential pool of 598 healthy residents who were not receiving any daily medications, 102 white men and 100 white women volunteered to participate. It was a highly educated upper-middle-class sample, with 40% having had postbaccalaureate education. The questionnaire consisted of 117 items pertaining to both past and present specific sexual behaviors. Not all participants answered all of the questions. The published report contains several inconsistencies that may reflect omissions of responses by some participants. For example, in their Table IV, in response to the question on frequency of intercourse during the past year, of 80 men, 30 answered "Never" and 50 checked categories ranging from "Sometimes" to "Very often." However, in response to the degree of enjoyment of this act (N = 79), 19 indicated "None" and 60 marked responses from "Mild" to "Great." Were there some respondents who answered the enjoyment question without responding to the frequency? Similarly for women, on frequency (N = 80), 56 responded "Never" and 24 "Sometimes" to "Often," but on the enjoyment question (N = 82), 50 indicated "None" and 32 "Mild" to "Great." Many of their other data also reveal discrepancies. The smallest total N is reported for the data on masturbation. The highest frequency of sexual activities were reported for nonintercourse touching and caressing. The authors also state, though they do not present specific data, that activity decreased between the ages of 80 and 90 years. The reported findings have been sometimes misinterpreted. For example, Barrow (1996, p. 144) states that at times, 62% of the men in this study had intercourse. Since only 80 men out of a total sample of 100 responded to this question, the actual percentage was 50% of those who participated in the study. The percentage for women is similarly overstated. We also must remember that only about one-third of the eligible participants volunteered for the study. While the quantitative aspects of this study are weak, they do indicate that at least some octo- and nonagenarians, and perhaps even some centenarians, possibly still engage in and enjoy several types of sexual behaviors.

PHYSICAL HEALTH AND PSYCHOLOGICAL WELLNESS

Physical Health

There are a number of medical conditions that frequently occur in older persons, as well as some drugs prescribed for several ailments, that will reduce sexual functions, especially in males. Organic conditions may be exacerbated by psychological factors. Approximately 50% of males with diabetes mellitus have some impairment of their erection, apparently associated with peripheral vasomotor neuropathy; while many patients with cardiovascular (CV) diseases are apprehensive about sexual activities, the deleterious effects in most instances are minimal (Corby & Solnick, 1980). Leiblum, Baume, and Croog (1994) reported that in a study of 60- to 80-year-old hypertensive women who were on medication, and who had a steady partner, a large percentage were sexually active. The major impediment to sexual activity was the partner's desire and/or health. The difficulties experienced by the hypertensive women were similar to those seen in "healthy" community-residing adults. On the other hand, in a large-scale community survey ($N = 1,290$) of males in the Massachusetts Male Aging Study (MMAS) in 1987–1989, Feldman, Goldstein, Hatzichristou, Krane, and McKinlay (1994) found that male impotence between the ages of 50 and 70 years was positively correlated with CV diseases, hypertension, diabetes, and the associated use of medications. Impotence in males may also be a self-fulfilling prophecy; the fear of losing the capacity to obtain an erection reduces the erectile response (Starr, 1985). While several psychosocial factor such as anger expression, dominance, alcohol consumption, and education each contributed between 11% and 15% of the variance, it is probable that several of them also affected health. Though it was impossible to determine causality, McKinlay and Feldman (1994) speculate that a comparison of MMAS data with other cross-sectional surveys of earlier cohorts tends to imply that there are "real" age changes rather than only cohort effects. The Leiblum et al. (1994) and the MMAS studies tapped similar cohorts, but whereas the former surveyed only women, the latter was a study of men. Thus, gender may also be related to age changes. Diokno et al. (1990), in a probability sample of 1,956 men and women ages 60+ years, found that incontinence, mobility difficulties, and mental problems were correlated with low sexual activities.

There are numerous medical and popular publications (including Gershenfeld & Newman, 1991; Walz & Blum, 1987) that discuss specific medical problems that may affect sexual behavior. In short, health problems, a difficult-to-define concept, tend to increase with age, and many of them can interfere with several sexual behaviors. However, we do not have clear-cut data to attribute all of the decrements to biological or health factors. Longitudinal studies that could untangle age and cohort effects are lacking, and such efforts probably have a low priority. Also, longitudinal studies might possibly tease out the contributions of life events and some time-of-measurement factors such as wars or economic upheavals (Levy, 1994).

Psychological Wellness

In his 1985 review of sexuality and aging in the *Annual Review of Gerontology, and Geriatrics,* Starr places much emphasis on the centrality of sexuality for physiological and psychological well-being. He believes that if it is unfulfilled, it may cause a variety of difficulties, though he does admit that more research to explore this problem is necessary. He also points out the importance of expectations, which result from the dissemination of information from scientific opinion-makers as well as from the modern popularization of sexuality in the mass media, advertising, and other facets of everyday life. Such an emphasis on sex may actually create anxieties in individuals who for various reasons cannot or do not engage in sexual activities.

Edwards and Booth (1994) reviewed the literature on sexuality, marriage, and well-being in the middle years. Even within the context of marriage, the results have been difficult to interpret. While recent studies have found a relationship between the quality and quantity of sexual activities and marital happiness, the causal directions are not clear. Does unhappiness unrelated to sexual activities reduce the latter? Or does reduction in sexual behavior cause marital unhappiness? The reviewers conclude that the relationship between sexuality and well-being is reciprocal; however, some couples report that the marriage is "bad" but "sex is great," and others report the reverse. In studies of married or cohabiting couples, it is usually difficult to disentangle the role of sexual activities from other close social relationships, and the meaning of sexual relationships may be different for older than younger persons (Thomas, 1982).

Edwards and Booth's review focused on middle-aged (less than 60 years old) married couples. With older individuals, Leiblum *et al.* (1994), in their study of 60- to 80-year-old hypertensive women, found that scores of quality-of-life measures did not differ between sexually active and abstinent individuals. Martin (1981) questioned his male participants about their belief that sexual activity may benefit health: In the "least active" group, 62% responded in the affirmative, while for the "most active" group, the percentage was 74, a small, not statistically significant difference. The large number of respondents who agreed with this hypothesis probably reflected a culturally accepted norm. Simultaneously, Martin found that in spite of their good health, over one-third of his 60- to 79-year-old, well-educated, economically comfortable, and maritally adjusted males reported no more than a half-dozen orgasmic responses per year, and 13% reported zero such experiences. These data are inconsistent with the frequently given advice in many textbooks of geriatrics that "it is desirable for the emotional, social and physical well-being of the older person that an active sex life be maintained for as long as possible" (Pfeiffer, 1969). Martin (1981) also quotes from an article in which the author claims that "the encouragement of sexual relationships in the elderly is of profound value in maintaining mental, emotional and physical health." Similar quotations from several other gerontologists are also cited by Thomas (1982) and, later, by Walz and Blum (1987), who "present our own case for the benefits of continued sexual activity in old age." However, they did not provide any data to support their claim. Hodson and Skeen (1994) even state that "recent studies indicate that a steady sexual life can reduce the negative effects of aging" (p. 226). Data by Persson and Svanborg (1992) contradict this assertion, at least for males. Similar data for females are not available. Martin (1981) also reported that sexual activity in the elderly males did not cease because their partners lose sexual attractiveness and/or because their partners did not enjoy sex anymore. Only 11% of the "least active" and 3% of the "most active" interviewees said that they no longer felt that their wives were sexually attractive, and fully half of these individuals hastened to add that this was due to their own lack of erotic reaction and not because of any loss of physical attractiveness on the part of their spouses. Thus, the overwhelming majority of even the inactive males did not associate their inactivity with the loss of sexual attractiveness of their partners. As to the decrease in activity because their partners may have lost interest in sex, 75% of the "least active" and 97% of the "most active" men believed that their wives usually or frequently enjoyed coitus. Turner (1988), in a study of 109 women and men between the ages of 60 and 85 years, also found that there are changes in the preferred sexual activity associated with age, and these were similar in the two sexes. The changes were not related to the psychological well-being of the individuals, to a low rating of satisfaction with sex life, interest in sex, or subjective pleasure, but the changes were primarily the result of aging in various physiological systems. Perhaps the most significant findings that run counter to a physical-need notion of sexual activity in the elderly arise from the responses to the question, "If there were some new medical discovery whereby a man's sexual interest could be restored to that of a 20-year-old without much trouble or expense, under your present circumstances would you seek such a treatment?" In the "least active" group, 66.7% responded "No" or "Doubtful" to that question, with an additional 4.8% who were undecided. The responses in the other two level-of-activity groups were similar. Thus, at least two-thirds of older healthy, well-educated, economically comfortable, and maritally adjusted men were satisfied with low or no sexual activity, and they did not feel the necessity for an enhancement of this behavior. Yet the same respondents who did not wish to enhance their own sexual vigor, even if it could be done easily and inexpensively, still expressed the belief that sexual activity may benefit health.

This is analogous to the frequently found discrepancies between health beliefs and positive health practices (Rodin & Salovey, 1989). It should also be noted that with increasing education in our culture, the old myths and stereotypes about sex and the elderly tend to be reduced (Steinkee, 1994). In a community-dwelling sample in Los Angeles of 1,216 persons aged 70+ years, Matthias et al. (1997) obtained data from 1,123 participants who responded to a question about the satisfaction with their level of sexual activity during the past month. The authors did not specify the behavior(s) measured by their question. They also obtained data on their mental health status and on depression. Though only about one-third of their sample reported sexual activity, over two-thirds stated that they were satisfied with this state of affairs. Those with a positive mental health status were satisfied with their sex life, regardless of the level of such activity. Men were more likely to be sexually active, but less likely to be satisfied than the women in this study. The various data on satisfaction in the domain of sexual behavior tend to support Hill and Preston's (1996) hypothesis that numerous motives are involved in sexual behaviors. Satisfaction in the sex domain is not solely a function of the frequency of intercourse.

Most forms of sexual behavior, excluding only masturbation, prostitution, and other related activities, involve close or intimate social relationships. Close relationships, in turn, involve a variety of cooperative and helpful interactions, though there are mixed motives in most sexual activities. In a review of interpersonal realtionships, Berscheid (1994) noted that it is conceptually difficult to integrate relationship research; even studies of love relationships seems to have different meanings to different people. Thus, disentangling the motives for sexual from other types of relationships seems like a very onerous chore, especially when we also introduce age, cohort, and other cultural factors. In addition, the gender factor must also be considered. We review the general topic of social relationships in Chapter 13.

CONCLUSIONS

The lengthy treatment of sexual motivation of older individuals serves as a good demonstration of the interactions of biological and psychosocial factors in age-associated changes in motivation in general. It is trivial to state that various forms of sexual behavior decrease during aging: in terms of the biological factors, the decrements seen in sexually motivated behavior depend on both normal aging changes in the peripheral neuroendocrine system involved in sexual activity and—

perhaps even more importantly—side effects from age-associated illnesses, drugs, and other treatments used to alleviate many ailments that
interfere with sexual activities. One of the most significant psychosocial
factors for females is the lack of a partner. In many studies, the specific
behaviors that comprise sexual activities are not specified.

Analysis of aging changes in human sexual behavior is challenging.
There are several methodological difficulties in obtaining representative samples, since, in our culture, many older individuals grew up during an era in which information about sexual behavior was a private
matter, and these people are not willing to talk to investigators. Also,
there are numerous motives that lead to sexual behavior. In addition to
arousal, there may be a need for emotional closeness, pleasing a partner,
or feeling valued. These motives may then lead to a variety of behaviors,
including touching, caressing, and masturbation, as well as intercourse.
While in most surveys the assumption is that only the latter is a measure of sexual behavior, in a few studies, a broader conception has been
used.

In terms of psychosocial factors, the role of sexuality in the context of the totality of all human activities will influence the effort individuals devote to this behavior. Secular factors are very influential,
as evidenced by an examination of the relatively rapid and frequent
changes of the role of sexual behavior in Western cultures, as well as
the anthropological data from various non-Western societies. The
growing emphasis on sexual behavior, engendered to some extent by
the mass media in recent times in Western societies, has also influenced gerontology. While in the past, sexual behavior was usually associated with procreation, at the present, the motivation is more
directed toward pleasure and social interaction. Therefore, older people who cannot procreate are expected to engage in and enjoy sexual
behavior. Some older individuals, who, for various reasons, do not engage in such behavior feel that they are missing something. Yet most
studies indicate that a lack of sexual activities in older individuals is
not necessarily associated with lack of life satisfaction. Since most
forms of sexual behavior involve social interactions, low levels, or the
absence of sex, may reflect the broader problem of low social relationships. An analysis of sexual behavior illustrates some of the difficulties in arriving at broad generalizations about human motivation
even in a given culture.

While most studies have found decreasing sexual behaviors with
age, it is difficult to determine the antecedent factors. Unfortunately,
there are no longitudinal data to unravel the roles of cohort, time of
measurement, and various lifestyle factors. Expectations of decrements

may also contribute to decreased activities, and they may exaggerate problems, increasing anxiety and leading to a vicious-cycle phenomenon. Though many believe that sexual activity is essential for general well-being and physical health, the evidence for this relationship is weak and causality cannot be specified. There are older individuals in good physical and mental health whose level of sexual activity is very low or nil.

CHAPTER 7

Health Behaviors

INTRODUCTION

Alcmaeon, one of the founders of Greek medicine in the early part of the fifth century B.C., referred to health as a state of organismic balance and disease as a rupture of that balance (Watson, 1978, pp. 11–13). Throughout history, the notion of distress or disease due to an imbalance of some external or internal forces acting on the organism was commonly accepted. Hippocrates's theory of humors also emphasized the importance of balance in the maintenance of health (Hothersall, 1990, p. 12).

Few will dispute the importance of health maintenance, and attempts to prevent and to ameliorate sickness constitute a major motive of most adults. With increasing age, this motivation grows (Bearon, 1989; Cross & Markus, 1991; Holahan, 1988; Nurmi, 1992). In two interviews with national probability samples of Americans 18 years of age and older, in 1974 and in 1981, 4,254 and 3,427 respondents, respectively, were asked how serious each of a list of life problems was for themselves and for "most people over 65" (Ferraro, 1992). In each of the two surveys, both in the self-referents and in the older-people referents, health issues of the elderly were near the top of the list as the most serious problem. It seems appropriate, therefore, to examine some of the motivational factors that are involved in the behaviors that prevent and/or remedy illnesses.

Though almost all human activities, whether eating, drinking, sleeping, exercising, working, or even leisure, may immediately or in the future affect health, in many instances, the potential health consequences play a small role in the decisions to engage in various activities, especially prior to middle or late adulthood. This was the gist of a thoughtful essay by the sociologist Mechanic (1992). However, many behaviors that usually lead to serious health disturbances are acquired early in life, and they become well-established automatic processes not requiring special effort to sustain them; for example, when we cut our-selves, we attempt to stop the bleeding, and we do not cross a street when we see a fast-moving vehicle approaching. In many behaviors that may be classified as "health directed," the motivation may be social rather than health maintenance. For example, people often go swim-ming or play tennis not because the physical activities promote health, but rather for an opportunity for socialization. As with most complex behaviors, mixed motives are the basis for many of our health-directed activities. In his essay, Mechanic (1992) concluded that the correlations between various positive health practices are modest and age is an an important factor.

DEFINITIONS

There are a variety of definitions of health and, thus, of health be-haviors, and they are difficult to circumscribe. In 1948, the World Health Organization defined health as "a state of complete physical, mental, and social well-being" (cited by Lawton & Lawrence, 1994). Such a broad definition implies achievement of a utopian state. For Lawton and Lawrence, health is a "fuzzy set" category that has many in-terrelated facets, but none is predictable. A person may have a specific sensory handicap but otherwise be healthy; thus, even in terms of overt somatic measurements, health is not a unidimensional construct. The difficulties in the definition of health have also been set forth by epi-demiologists (Bergner & Rothman, 1987; Patrick & Bergner, 1990). Health status, functional status, and quality of life are frequently used interchangeably: The importance attached to dysfunctions in various systems, limitations of general activity or specific functions (vision, lo-comotion, hearing), affective consequences, and other correlates will in-fluence the judgment of health status. Functional disabilities may be the result of psychological disturbances that at times are difficult to evalu-ate. Although there is a substantial comorbidity of psychological and physical disorders (Cohen & Rodriguez, 1995), no longitudinal data es-tablished that the onset of psychosocial difficulties invariably leads to depression or other mental health problems, or conversely, that the causal chain is reversed. Also, the relationship may be transactional, so that causality may proceed in either direction. The role of psychosocial stressors in the development of psychopathology is much less clear than are the roles of viruses, bacteria, tumors, or other agents in the onset of physical diseases (Adler & Matthews, 1994; Clark, Watson, & Reynolds, 1995). There is no metric for psychosocial stressors and for the coping mechanisms that alleviate or prevent their appearance. Most stressors are intimately related to the prevailing culture. Chapters 8, 9, and 10 are devoted to the analysis of stresses and coping. Finally, timing the specific onset of a health disturbance is problematic.

Health-related behaviors may be either (1) antecedents of illness or discomfort or (2) the consequences of responding to the presence of illness or discomfort. An example of the first is smoking; an example of the latter is visiting a dentist when a tooth hurts. Frequently, the two types of behavior interact, as when a person who overeats and gains weight develops health problems that lead him to seek professional help, during which he is advised to change his eating habits. The multiplicity of factors that may induce a given organismic dysfunction complicates a simple analysis. Aside from genetic factors, coronary diseases may result from an "unhealthy diet," lack of exercise, and repeated psychosocial stresses that activate the ANS and the endocrines. Several motives may affect diet, exercising, exposure to stressors, and so on.

The disequilibria denoted by stress are intertwined with health behaviors, since in most theories, stress is inferred from discomfort and illness. Also, prolonged exposures to environments that induce stress or the absence of coping mechanisms may induce physiological changes that may be temporary or relatively permanent. Thus, health disturbances are frequently used as a major sign of stress. Conversely, coping is usually defined as the amelioration of the signs or symptoms associated with stress.

THE ROLE OF MOTIVATION

There are elderly individuals who seem to lack the motivation to maintain healthy lifestyles and/or to seek assistance to ameliorate their health problems. This is not different from what occurs at younger ages, for many attitudes and behaviors that affect health are formed early in life and tend to persist. Since we have noted that most human activities may have a health component, though, in most instances, it may be negligible, it is difficult to determine the dominant motivations when people neglect their health. In addition, the health consequences of most behaviors may become apparent only after a prolonged period of time, frequently, not for decades.

In a broader context, several of the issues of the quality of life in old age and the "will to live" rather than to commit suicide are classical philosophical problems of much contemporary interest. Some of them are discussed by Moody (1992, Chapter 4) in a treatise on ethics in gerontology. The current promotion of "successful aging" assumes that people are motivated to adopt lifestyles or habits that enhance health. Similarly, efforts to extend life expectancy are directly related to maximizing purported effective health behaviors. There are some individuals who in their youth may be aware that in the long-term, their lifestyles may be harmful, but they prefer immediate gratification to longevity. Changing long-established habits that may impair health may be a particular problem for older people since they may have overlearned certain routines. Also, many behaviors that in the long term are injurious do not induce immediate health symptoms and the long-term experiences with such an activity may have extinguished the fear of the undesirable consequences. This factor might have more impact on an older than younger individual. The focus of this chapter is on health as a value or motive. This necessitates that we examine first the self-perception of health. In Chapter 4, we discussed the issues related to the perception of pain and discomfort. Next, after the person perceives that health problems may be present, a decision concerning a course of action will be made. Finally, we briefly look at health promotion that entails adopting or maintaining a "healthy" lifestyle. These behavioral categories are not mutually exclusive.

The importance of culture, cohort, and a person's prior experiences as factors determining the strength of health motivation cannot be overemphasized. This is especially important in the analysis of age-associated changes, since there is a constant, rapid flux of values and desires in most modern cultures. Landrine and Klonoff (1992) reviewed some anthropological and sociological studies that show the influences of culture and ethnicity on health-related beliefs and schemas. Kaufman (1996), in focus groups with small samples of urban African Americans and whites of similar SES, found that the former tended to define illness in terms of attitudes, while the latter stressed changes in activity. Though our interest is the motivation for various activities, in most studies, this variable was not examined, and it is usually implicitly assumed that people, at least in later adulthood, are motivated to maximize their health or level of comfort.

THEORETICAL UNDERPINNINGS

Health behaviors have been of concern not only to the medical sciences and epidemiology, but also to most social sciences. In a review, Moorman and Matulich (1993) referred to 22 health behavior models that have been proposed during the past quarter-century. While a multiplicity of health behaviors exist and each of them may involve several motives, most of the theories are applicable to only certain types of activities affecting health. Health behaviors in response to an illness or disability are coping reactions. Chapter 9 treats this topic.

Psychosomatic Medicine

At least beginning with the Greeks, since Hippocrates and his theory of humors, it had been assumed that individuals with certain personality characteristics are more prone to engage in behaviors that may be health-risk factors. Such beliefs, though never codified, continued through the history of medicine. The field of psychosomatic medicine, which arose in the 1920s–30s has looked at psychological factors, primarily personality dispositions, as they influence somatic illnesses (Dunbar, 1943). It was assumed that certain personality types adopt lifestyles that tend to lead to the initiation, exacerbation, or maintenance of physiological changes that ultimately result in somatic diseases (Busse & Blazer, 1980). Psychosomatic medicine was heavily influenced by Freudian theory, and most of the constructs in this approach were rooted in psychoanalysis. The classical psychosomatic approaches were not considered in a life-cycle perspective (Busse & Blazer, 1980). In the current psychiatric taxonomy (American Psychiatric Association, 1994), Axis II personality disorders include *somatoform disorders,* "the presence of physical symptoms not fully explained by a general medical condition." In this system, however, etiology is of less concern than it was in psychosomatic theory. The neglect of etiology in psychopathological classifications has created several problems (Clark *et al.,* 1995), such as defining the core of a disorder.

Behavioral Medicine and Health Psychology

With the waning influence of psychoanalysis, *behavioral medicine* and/or *health psychology* entered the scene. The two terms are used interchangeably. The usage mostly reflects the professional training and predilections of the user, analogous to speaking of behavior or psychology. In this field, personality factors, as in psychosomatic medicine, again play an important role, but the theoretical basis is usually not psychoanalysis. One of the seminal series of studies that gave impetus to this approach was by Friedman and Rosenman (1959), who attempted to correlate specific overt behavior patterns with cardiovascular (CV) diseases. Their Type A personality, prone to CV diseases, was characterized by an intense sustained drive to achieve, eagerness to compete, desire for recognition and advancement, performance under time pressures, and extraordinary mental and physical alertness. The cultural climate in the United States in the 1960s, with the growth of a counterculture movement, was a fertile ground for a wide acceptance of this model both by the scientific community and the lay public. Over the years, the validity of the original Type A measures as an index of CV diseases has been found wanting (Adler & Matthews, 1994). More recently, Type A personality has been associated with hostility and anger, but the correlations of these personality traits with CV diseases also are plagued by measurement problems (Adler & Matthews, 1994), as have been efforts to relate personality to various immune diseases (Cohen & Herbert, 1996). Since individuals with certain personality traits such as neuroticism are more sensitive in appraising and/or responding to pain and other bodily discomforts, they are more likely to seek professional help and thus be identified with having a health problem (Costa & McCrea, 1990). Other personality characteristics such as risk-taking are also related to health behaviors. However, personality theories per se are not theories of health behaviors, but they relate the motivations of the individual to engage in certain behaviors. We have omitted presenting models of personality that have been proposed to account for specific diseases, a major focus of psychosomatic medicine, since it would require an analysis of a large number of medical problems. Smith and Williams (1992), in a critique of health and personality, note several weaknesses in this research area. While there is an overabundance of personality constructs and theoretical models, their translation into measurement procedures has been lacking, incomplete, or haphazard. This has resulted in rather tentative links between the personality measures and health outcomes. Some of the models and their critiques are included in Chapter 8 on stress. Smith and Williams believe that reliance solely on static trait taxonomies is unlikely to advance our understanding of health behaviors, and they advocate studies in which the interaction of traits with relevant situational characteristics is examined.

Some Recent Models of Health Behaviors

The rise of social-cognitive psychology in the 1950s and some doubts concerning the utility of the personality trait approach has led to the development of several models that have been applied to health behaviors. Schwarzer (1992) has reviewed four such related theories of health behaviors and then presented his own synthesis of several of these approaches. These theories and several of their modifications are not specific to late adulthood, and most of the supporting evidence has come from studies primarily of young adults. Other models, not reviewed by Schwarzer, have also been influenced by the current growth of research in cognitive psychology.

The theories have much in common, and in studies, they are rarely pitted against each other; thus, all of them have a certain degree of validity (Weinstein, 1993). We briefly mention only those that may be most relevant to the health factors of older people and comment on their applicability.

Health Belief.   This theory, originally introduced by Hochbaum (1958) and later modified and extended by others, is based on the value–expectancy and decision-making models of Lewin, Tolman, Edwards, and others. Perceived susceptibility to illness results in an experience of threat; people will not seek preventive care or health screening unless they have relevant health motivation and feel vulnerable. A cost–benefit analysis triggered by cues to action, such as information obtained from the media or friends, will lead to health behaviors if the costs do not exceed the expected benefits. The motivation for health-related behaviors must be sufficient to override other motives. Since well-established habits are difficult to change, older people are less likely to adopt health behaviors that recent research has found to be applicable to the elderly. On the other hand, they are also aware that they are more vulnerable and will, therefore, pay more heed to various symptoms that are indicators of potential health problems.

Locus of Control–Self-Efficacy Expectancies.   A factor that has received much attention in gerontology, especially in the fields of health and stress, is locus of control (LC), sometimes referred to also as personal control. Rotter (1966) applied social learning theory to differentiate two levels of control: an external LC, when one's activities are directed by factors in the environment, mainly others, and an internal LC, when one is less influenced by others and is "a master of his or her own destiny." It is usually assumed that older adults experience decreased health, retirement, loss of spouse, and other normative stresses that are usually associated with the inability to control one's activities and increased dependence on others. There have been several definitions and measures of control in different research contexts (Rodin, Timko, & Harris, 1985; Rotter, 1966; Thoits, 1991). A belief that the consequences of certain events are contingent on the person's behavior or his or her personal characteristic is the most common definition currently in use. Kuhl (1986) differentiated between perceived and actual control. Low perceived control reduces motivation to initiate attempts to exert control, resulting in behavioral deficits that are greater than the available capacity. Actual control, on the other hand, is determined from the available behavioral repertoire of the person. A feedback mechanism also seems to affect the perception of control; an older person experiencing various physical disabilities will perceive having less control than objective indices might indicate, which further diminishes the perception of control and any efforts to exert control.

Rotter's (1966) 24-item scale to measure LC generated much research and was applied to a variety of situations and populations. This widespread use of the scale led Rotter (1975) to caution researchers about some misconceptions related to the use of the scale: Expectancies in each situation are a function of the previous experiences in the same and in similar situations and populations; thus, there is a need for LC measures in specific domains. The generalized scale is probably important in novel situations. LC is only one of many variables predicting behavior, with knowledge of the value of reinforcement being of greater significance. Expressions of external LC may also serve as a rationalization or defense. Finally, Rotter noted that his scale was standardized on American college students and that it may have less or no validity when applied to other populations.

Other scales measuring similar constructs appeared later (Lazarus, 1991, p. 140). Levenson's (1974) 24-item scale consists of three factors: (1) belief in internal control; (2) belief in the control by powerful others; and (3) belief in chance occurrence. The LC construct has been frequently referred to in studies of health of the elderly. Rodin (1986; Rodin *et al.,* 1985 and Schulz, Heckhausen, and Locher (1991) reviewed the LC literature in gerontology, but few studies had compared the influence of control on health in younger and older persons. According to these reviewers, some data support the notion that there is a relationship between internal control beliefs and health or health-related behaviors, but others show no relationships.

Two studies with young and old participants in samples of 285 and 563, respectively, (Shewchuck, Foelker, Camp, & Blanchard-Field, 1992; Shewchuck, Foelker, & Niederehe, 1990) cast doubts on the original three-factor conceptualization of LC. In these studies, nearly half of the Rotter's 24 items did not load reliably on any dimension purported to measure LC, and age affected the factor loadings. But Rotter (1975) had previously cautioned researchers about the usage of his scale with noncollege populations. If the same constructs have different mean scores in different age groups, does this imply that there is a shift in the relative importance of the same construct for people in different age groups, or do the properties of the construct themselves change with age? This indeterminacy applies to many studies in which the same measuring instrument is frequently used with young and old participants in comparing performance on cognitive or personality tests (Hertzog, 1987). It is also necessary to distinguish objective control from perceived control, which may or may not be veridical (Kuhl, 1986). For Sappington (1990), intellectually or factually based LC beliefs can be differentiated experimentally from emotionally based beliefs. Sappington cites a study showing that belief in one's own effort to control pain correlated significantly with LC beliefs that were intellectually rather than emotionally based. The importance attached to internal control in Western societies can be related to the influence of the Protestant Reformation, with its emphasis on the autonomous individual. In the West, people have been socialized to mistrust any situation in which they lack personal control.

We have previously noted that, in general, the same scale may be a measure of different constructs in young and in older people, though this potential confound is infrequently considered in aging studies. With this caveat in mind, however, we mention a few recent investigations. In a study in Berlin, Baltes, Wahl, and Schmidt-Furstoss (1990) found that the correlation between functional health and belief in personal control was high ($r = .67$; $p < .01$). Three studies by Lachman (1986) compared college students with elderly adults (age ranges 60–94 years) using Levenson's general scales of LC (1974) and domain-specific scales measuring control of (1) intellectual behavior and (2) illness and health. She also obtained intelligence test data, a self-evaluation of health, and the number of doctor's visits. On the Levenson scales of LC, there were no differences between the college students and the older adults. However, on the intellectual behavior and the health scales, the older adults were more external, believing that they personally had little control of their lives. Lachman concluded that domain-specific scales measuring belief of control relevant to specific activities, rather than a general concept of LC, are more useful. Krause (1988) found that persons with internal LC on the Rotter scale made fewer physician visits during periods of high stress such as bereavement than did persons with external control. On the other hand, routine physical checkups were not related to LC. The author notes that the data were cross-sectional, a global rather than a domain-specific index of control was used, self-report data measured physician visits, and the potential buffering effect of social support was not assessed. Data that do not support the role of an internal health LC factor in health service utilization were reported by Strain (1991). She interviewed 743 older Canadians (median age 70 years) concerning their physician's visits, hospital utilizations, and overall health services use. While some health beliefs, such as attitudes about the health care system, accounted for a small amount of the variance, health LC appeared to be unrelated to health care utilization. In contrast to Krause (1988), Strain (1991) did not separate different types of physician visits (i.e., routine checkups, visits for symptoms associated with life-stress events, or symptoms not directly related to major life events). Wolinsky and Arnold (1988) analyzed some of the issues in using health services utilization as a measure of health; they differentiated "objective" pathophysiological indicators of health status from "subjective" demand characteristics. Hospital utilization is a better reflection of an objective measure of health status, while initial visits to a physician include both objective needs and subjective perceptions of ill health. The latter are more likely to be affected by psychosocial variables, including perception of control. A few additional studies that reported positive relationships between internal LC and healthy lifestyles are reviewed later. In a large-scale study of 476 middle-aged adults, low-back-pain patients with high internal LC orientation benefited more from a combined physical and psychological treatment program than did patients with an external LC (Harkapaa, Jarvikoski, Mellin, Hurri, & Luoma, 1991). Stoller and Forster (1994) also found that an internal LC was inversely related to physician utilization. The latter, however, cannot be used as an index of pain or suffering. It is possible to perceive pain and not visit a physician and vice versa. The exaggerated perception of one's health status is probably also related to LC.

It is difficult to summarize the role of LC in health behaviors of older people. First, there have been few comparisons between young and old people. Though this is theoretically possible, practically, this is not realistic, since younger people have relatively few health problems and those they do have vary appreciably from those seen in an older population. Most young persons have acute diseases, whereas older people suffer to a large extent from chronic conditions. Second, there are several types of LC scales; some are global scales, while others are specific to health. Even for the latter, questions may be raised concerning their appropriateness for older persons with various impaired functions (Aldwin & Levenson, 1994). Third, there are numerous measures of health, including self-assessments, various kinds of health services utilizations, and health-related lifestyle habits. Fourth, in one of the few sequential studies in which both longitudinal and cross-sectional data were obtained, it was found that internal LC on the Rotter scale increased between 1971 and 1985 (Gatz & Karel, 1993). In Western societies, there probably has been an increasing emphasis on personal control, so it should not be surprising that the findings on LC and health relationships have been far from uniform.

A related approach was initiated by White (1959), who reviewed the status of motivation, drawing upon psychoanalysis as well as on traditional animal and human research. Many scholars in those fields have noted the organism's need for competence in order to interact with the environment. This includes a need for mastery or control, cognizance (having knowledge), and achievement; White dubbed this phenomenon *effectance motivation,* basing the construct on the common observation that people receive satisfaction from feelings of accomplishment or efficacy. An ill person, one experiencing pain or discomfort, is unlikely to believe that he or she is very efficacious and in control of the situation. This has led to an examination of the relationships between pain or discomfort and indices of control. White's theory provided the impetus for Bandura (1977, 1991) to develop further a construct of self-efficacy, or a belief that one is competent to perform certain acts or to have control of one's behavior in certain situations. Self-efficacy is influenced by retrospective judgments of one's performance, in which one attributes the outcomes to one's abilities and/or effort; the construct has led to numerous studies, primarily with college students. The related construct of control also is based on the commonsense notion in present-day Western culture that expecting to have control over the outcome of an activity is a moderately strong motive. While effectance motivation attempts to make attributions about the *causes* of events, LC specifies the *locus* of reinforcement. The two constructs overlap, but effectance motivation is a broader construct, since LC is only one factor in control (Peterson, Maier, & Seligman, 1993, pp. 144–146). People may believe that a certain outcome is determined by their own actions—internal LC, but if they do not posses the requisite skills, they will have low self-efficacy in this particular situation. According to Bandura (1991), people anticipate likely outcomes of their actions and select goals for which they have an expectancy that they are competent to achieve them. This theory has been applied to health behaviors; for example, a person must believe that quitting smoking will improve health and must believe that he or she has the competence to accomplish this before an attempt is made to extinguish this habit. Except for the greater emphasis on competence, this theory is very similar to that of Hochbaum (1958). The decreased competence of older persons in many domains should also impact their health behaviors, especially in extinguishing harmful habits. Also, self-efficacy is related to internal LC, a topic that was reviewed previously.

Protection Motivation Theory.   Rogers (1975) postulated that the perceived severity of a disease, perceived vulnerability, effectiveness of some actions, and self-efficacy expectancy determine health behaviors. This theory differs from the previously mentioned ones primarily in its specific attention to vulnerability. As such, it should be of special interest to gerontologists since a well-established phenomenon of aging is an increase in vulnerability. Gatz *et al.* (1996), in their analysis of the prevalence of depressive symptoms, theorize about the role of greater biological vulnerability with increasing age.

Schwarzer's Synthesis.   Schwarzer (1992) combined several aspects of the aforementioned theories. In the process, he differentiated between a motivation phase, in which the individual forms an intention to adopt a precautionary measure or change the risk behavior, and a subsequent action phase. The two phases are reminiscent of the "having" and "doing" perspective in personality (Cantor & Zirkel, 1990). The motivation phase is analogous to what others have called a decision-making stage, in which intentions are affected by outcome expectancies, including self-efficacy expectancies. The outcome expectancies are influenced also by the perceived severity of an illness and the availability of coping resources. But Schwarzer points out that intentions are not enough. People may want to lose weight but do little to accomplish it. Thus, it is necessary to postulate an action phase consisting of cognitive, behavioral, and situational levels. Actions are also influenced by the person's self-efficacy, which determines the amount of effort and persistence, and by social support. The action phase frequently requires the development of subgoals, and algorithms of action sequences. At other times various situational barriers may be inhibitory.

Schwarzer's effort and persistence factors appear to be personality traits, probably encompassed by Costa and McCrea's (1985a) conscientiousness (will) trait. However, if one subscribes to McClelland, Koestner, and Weinberger's (1989) distinction between "implicit" motives and traits measured by questionnaires, the determination of effort and persistence poses difficult assessment problems. Also, several other variables have been defined differently by various investigators.

All of these theories assume that people have accurate information concerning the risks resulting from specified activities. Many "risky" behaviors contribute only marginally to some illnesses. Furthermore, many of the consequences of health behaviors are often delayed, sometimes for decades, so that it is difficult for a person to perceive any causal relationships, and there may be differences in the motivations related to the initiation and the maintenance of a behavior. Individuals are also frequently willing to accept some health costs if the behavior leads to other benefits. Finally, these theories assume that people usually act rationally and consider all of the consequences of their actions, but human actions may be distorted by various motives (Ajzen, 1996).

Andersen's Sociological–Behavioral Model. A popular "behavioral" model of health services utilization was introduced by the sociologist Andersen (1968). The three major components leading to health services use are (1) predisposing conditions, (2) enabling conditions, and (3) need. The predisposing variables include demographic factors, such as age, sex, SES, and health beliefs; enabling factors include personal or family resources and availability of services; and the need component includes perception of the illness and the way the family or person responds to the illness. Others have added a social support component to Andersen's model.

Andersen (1995) revised his model by adding to the predisposing variables the psychological characteristics of the individual. He also added social relationships as an enabling factor. This reflects a broadening of the sources of support in our society as the size of families is beginning to decrease and kin become geographically dispersed. The present version has shifted from a largely behavioral–sociological model to a broad psychosocial one with a very large number of variables.

From an analysis of the literature, including studies with older adults, in which Andersen's model was tested, Krause (1990b) concluded that the earlier version has rarely explained more than 20% of the variance in medical care use, and most of it could be accounted for by various physical health-status measures such as the need component. In Andersen's model, motivation is only implied by the need to remove the aversive stimuli. The lack of specification of the psychosocial variables has been a subject of frequent criticisms of this model (Hansell, Sherman, & Mechanic, 1991).

Synthesis of Social-Cognitive and Behavioral Models. Krause (1990b) and others have noted that there is considerable overlap between the social-cognitive model and Andersen's original model. In both, the perception of physical symptoms and beliefs about the efficacy of medical treatments are important. While in Andersen's model, demographic variables are considered predisposing factors, in the cognitive social models, it is assumed that they influence symptom recognition and symptom attribution (Krause, 1990b). In a preliminary causal model, Krause proposed that various types of illness behaviors are dependent on several demographic factors, stressors, stress-focused support, symptoms of physical illness, belief in the efficacy of medical care, and availability of medical resources. He also pointed out that "information must be gathered on the intent or motivation behind specific self-care or informal care activities" (p. 235). Included in Krause's model is the presence of psychosocial stressors that may be the result of factors other than those associated with the current physical problems that have given rise to the current illness. For example, the present illness may be associated with a recent bereavement; however, this illness may be superimposed on a previous stress associated with conflicts with one's children. Consequently, Krause recommends that information concerning current illness symptoms be examined in the context of past illness behaviors. The very large number of parameters in the Andersen (1995) and Krause (1990b) models makes it difficult to test their power in the absence of large sample sizes (Hoyle, 1995).

Leventhal's "Commonsense" Model of Illness.   Leventhal and associates (Leventhal, Diffenbach, & Leventhal, 1993; Leventhal, Leventhal, Schaefer, & Easterling, 1993) dispensed with the prevalent social-psychological models of behavior and adopted instead what they have labeled a "commonsense model" of illness. It borrows heavily from Lazarus's (1993) theory of emotions, according to which individuals are active problem solvers; thus, their behavior is a product of their perceptions and emotional reactions to health threats, followed by the associated coping procedures. The responses are a function of the natural history of the disease, the social context, and several stable dispositions of the person (biological and psychological characteristics). The stimuli (inner/outer) or symptoms are the key factors in the cognitive representation of the illness (Cameron, Leventhal, & Leventhal, 1993). Perception of the somatic changes initiates a self-regulatory process. Figure 7.1 presents the proposed model.

The perception of the situation leads to activities in two parallel processing systems that interact. One system represents the illness threat and its attendant coping procedures, and the other, the emotional reactions with its attendant coping responses. Both perceptual and conceptual representations are constructed. A physician may tell a patient that she has peptic ulcers. In addition to the perceived symptoms, one of the processing systems, previously acquired information, including the label and/or experiences with this type problem, will affect the patient's responses. There have been several criticisms of Lazarus's approach, which will be discussed in Chapter 8 on stress. The same comments also apply to Leventhal's model. Among those taking a different approach have been Costa and McCrea (1990), who believe that

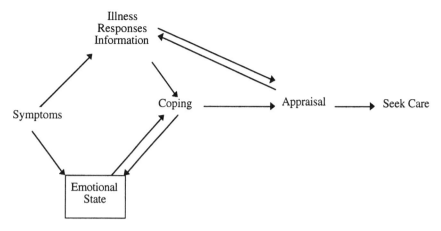

Figure 7.1. Model of Cameron, Leventhal, and Leventhal's (1993) care initiation steps.

a person's perception and appraisal of a situation is a function of his or her personality; they favor more objective measures of both the context and the symptoms.

Leventhal *et al.* (1993a) also hypothesize that older people are more risk averse in general and therefore more motivated to engage in health-promoting behaviors. We have previously reviewed the lower energy levels and greater fatiguability of the elderly. These age-associated changes should also lead to greater avoidance of activities that engender illness and the accompanying emotional arousal. The emotional component of Leventhal's complex theory for self-regulation of health provides a more specific role for motivational factors than do some of the other theories of health behavior. The authors also acknowledge that much work remains in fleshing out the details in the construction of specific representations of illness and the procedures for coping and appraisal. This model is fairly similar to Krause's (1990b) except that Leventhal *et al.* (1993a) place greater emphasis on the emotional variables and self-regulation of behavior. Theirs is also the only model that specifically takes into account age-associated changes involving a motivational–emotional factor. On the other hand, Krause, with his background in sociology, includes the role of perceived availability of medical resources and specifies the contribution of preexisting stresses.

Antonovsky's Salutogenic Model. According to the sociologist Antonovsky (1979, 1987, 1990), people strive to achieve a sense of coherence (SOC) whereby different aspects of their lives make sense. In general, SOC enhances health by a reduction of stress and illness. Social relations linked to a sense of coherence have been shown to reduce mortality (House, Umberson, & Landis, 1988). The person with a strong SOC is less likely to choose risky behaviors and more likely to adhere to social norms that are health promoting. It should be noted also that Antonovsky (1987, pp. 133–134) believes that his approach has much in common with Bandura's self-efficacy theory. Antonovsky's model could also fit in general into a social cognitive theory. What distinguishes his thesis from other cognitive models is the explicit reference to sociocultural resistance factors that are separate from the individual's resistance resources. Lazarus (1991, pp. 388–390) criticizes Antonovsky's holistic definitions of health, which include physical, psychological, and social factors. Lazarus believes that such an approach precludes separating antecedents from consequences; however, neither does Lazarus's transactional model differentiate stimuli (antecedents) from responses (consequences).

The Moorman and Matulich Health Consumer Model. On the basis of some of their research in marketing and consumer behavior, Moorman and Matulich (1993) developed a model in which the focus is on health-information acquisition and health-maintenance behaviors. In this model, motivation plays a key role, since health maintenance and the development of preventive behaviors are a function of the consumer's interest in performing health behaviors. Another important variable is ability, analogous to Bandura's concept of efficacy. The authors postulate that health is an important goal or value, and this stimulates people to engage in behaviors that enhance or maintain health. In their model, they propose eight specific hypotheses relating to health behaviors, primarily in terms of health knowledge, perceived health status, health LC, education, income, and age. They hypothesize that younger consumers will perform more health behaviors than will older consumers whose health motivation is low as opposed to high; this is based on the assumption that aged individuals have less ability to acquire health information and thus, when motivation is low, it will inhibit their acquisition of effective health behaviors. This is contrary to many other theories, which assume that, in general, older people are more motivated to engage in health-maintenance behaviors. In their research, Moorman and Matulich measured motivation by means of a questionnaire scale standardized on college students. However, McClelland *et al.* (1989) differentiated between self-attributed motives obtained from questionnaires and those inferred from projective tests.

Thus, depending on the measurement technique used, the strength of motivation will vary. Another problem with their model is the assumption that a unitary motive determines health behavior; we have referred previously to the multiplicity of motives that may influence any behavior that has consequences for health. To test their model, Moorman and Matulich (1993) asked their participants to rate their behavior and attitudes toward alcohol consumption, smoking, several nutrition variables, and visits to health professional, but there may be several motives for alcohol consumption or smoking. Finally, it should be noted that in their study, they found little support for their hypothesis that older consumers engage in fewer health behaviors when health motivation is low. Overall, they found that motivation and ability influences health behaviors, but the interaction of these factors varies for different behaviors. Their study supports the need to obtain information for specific health behaviors rather than for a global concept of health activities.

Summary.   We have described a number of health behavior models or theories. These approaches are in addition to the personality theories that ascribe a major role to the appraisal and response to stressors as an expression of a trait such as neuroticism. The summary presented after the description of the role of LC in health also applies to a large extent to all models. The major differences between the various approaches is in the variables, both the antecedent and the consequent, to which there are explicit references. Thus, it is difficult to pit the theories against each other in testing their validity. The large number of behavioral settings and motives that affect health may preclude the formulation of a generalized theory. Some models focus on prevention and health promotion; others focus on decisions after an illness has occurred. There are few explicit references to motivation. Most of the data are based on studies with college students, and few models explicitly refer to the diverse illnesses that an older person may have experienced during his or her lifetime. Given the limited available data, it may suffice to describe and model specific health-related behaviors applicable only to delimited aspects of human existence.

PERCEPTION OF HEALTH STATUS

The motivation for pursuing various types of health behaviors depends to a large extent on the initial ability to assess one's health status. In Chapter 4 on pain, we reviewed the perception of pain and noted the difference between the motivational–affective and the cognitive–evaluative factors (Melzack & Katz, 1992). Experience, including cultural and developmental variables, and personality play an important role in the perception of discomfort. Perception of health problems may be either the result of self-assessment or a professional's judgment. Under most circumstances, professional judgments occur only when an individual seeks help after he or she perceives some symptoms; self-assessed health status depends to a large extent on the perception and interpretation of symptoms. In Chapter 4, we reviewed some of the changes in pain perception that occur with age. The evaluation of specific dysfunctions in self-reports is also present in the judgments of global health status of professionals. Markides, Lee, Ray, and Black (1993) reported substantial discrepancies in two physicians' global ratings of health (i.e., "excellent," "good," "fair," or "poor") of middle-and old-aged Mexican Americans. Here, too, the authors could not determine the source of the discrepancy; agreement between physicians occurred only when several chronic conditions were present. Do some professionals use expected mortality as the criterion of health, while others take into account functional disabilities? In the latter case, there are most likely some individualized unknown metrics.

In some early studies, Friedsam and Martin (1963) and Maddox and Douglass (1973), using relatively small samples (Ns < 90), reported small but positive relationships between older persons' self-ratings of general health and physicians's ratings. While Friedsam and Martin found that patients tended to underestimate their health status, Maddox and Douglass found a trend in the opposite direction. A number of subsequent studies have confirmed the weak positive correlations between self- and physician's ratings (Rakowski, Hickey, & Dengiz, 1987). These studies, however, did not compare self-ratings and objective measures in older and younger persons. Such a comparison was attempted in a semirural area of Wisconsin by Levkoff, Cleary, and Wettle (1987), who interviewed 269 middle-aged (45–64 years) and 191 older persons (65+ years) who agreed to have their medical records reviewed. The older persons appraised their health as significantly worse than did the middle-aged who had comparable diagnoses in the musculoskeletal, digestive, nervous, and sensory systems. But as the authors note, the medical diagnoses did not include any measures of the severity of the disease. Thus, it is possible that the older persons' health status was actually worse.

In 1992, Idler reviewed six large-scale studies (Ns = 1078–6944), which found that global self-assessed health was a better predictor of survival during a follow-up period than were very extensive data from medical records. The studies were conducted in the United States, Canada, and Israel. What was noteworthy in the analysis was the elimination of a considerable amount of covariance with other measures of physical health. In these prospective studies, self-perception of health contributed independently to the prediction of mortality, which was not contained in the information provided by the "objective" measures. Idler admitted that the basis for this additional information in self-perception was not known; the magnitude and the meaning of the association between self-assessed health and mortality could not be ascertained. Were they based on information known only to the respondents? Were they the result of some idiosyncratic integration of a multitude of "subjective" and "objective" data by the respondents? Also, current perceptions of health and perceptions of pain are affected by knowledge of past health and expectations of the future. In her own study in an outpatient rehabilitation clinic, Idler (1993) examined the relationship between pain perception and a global assessment of health in a random sample of 200 clients who varied in age from 18 to 92 years. She found that pain perception influenced self-perception of health status, and conversely, global perception of health status influenced pain perception. Idler used cross-sectional data, based on patients who were mostly unmarried and who suffered from arthritis. However, the correlations were moderate.

Idler did not explore the possibility of a relationship between her findings and the existentialist (Frankl, 1962) construct of will to live. The latter would include the motivation to engage in a variety of health-promoting activities or avoidance of behaviors inimical to health. The availability of some scales that operationalize some of the existential constructs makes it feasible to relate these seemingly diverse approaches in exploring the motivation or purpose for living in older individuals.

Since Idler's (1992) review, several additional studies have shown that global self-assessed health is inversely related to mortality, especially in the young-old. Rakowski, Fleishman, Mor, and Bryant (1993) analyzed data from 7,000+ participants who were asked to compare their activity with that of their age peers. Those who were less active showed greater mortality than those were more active, not a surprising finding. These authors also noted that we do not have data relating self-rated health to such motivational consequences as nonadherence to prescribed health regimens, delay in taking action in response to symptoms, and other undesirable behaviors that may increase mortality. Thus, as mentioned earlier, there are several possible explanations for the observed relationship between self-perceived health and mortality.

In a study of community-residing elderly, starting with an initial sample of 2,583 participants, Idler (1993) obtained data on global self-assessed health status of 10 self-rated chronic conditions, a single-item screening instrument was used for the diagnosis of angina and scales of functional ability as indicated by various measures of activities of daily living (ADL), such as bathing, dressing, or eating as well as endurance and physical ability. All of these measurements were self-reports. Telephone follow-ups were conducted annually for 6 years, during which period mortality was ascertained from death certificates, hospital records, and proxies; complete follow-up data were available on the 1,319 survivors. Functional disability had the largest association with self-assessment, followed by education, arthritis (most likely associated with functional disability), age, and having had a heart attack. Multivariate regressions of self-assessed health indicated that respondents ages 77 years and older gave disproportionately positive health assessments relative to objective health status. This was most apparent in those ages 83+ years, who probably compared themselves with other members of their own cohort. In addition, there was a cohort effect: Earliest cohorts showed increasingly positive health self-assessment over time, while later cohorts showed self-assessments that were more nearly identical with predicted values of survivorships. Idler is cautious in drawing conclusions about cohort effects, since the length of her follow-up periods was short. Her youngest cohort was only 71–76 years old at the time of the study. Idler speculates that the earliest cohorts experienced more hardships in early life, having lived in an era when medical services were less available, daily living chores were more onerous, and the work week was longer. Having lived to a relatively advanced aged may have given them a feeling of satisfaction in having overcome substantial barriers. Finally, the data also support a hypothesis that "pessimists" have a higher mortality rate. However, it is not possible to determine the degree to which such an attitude affects survivorship. In short, age, cohort, and attitudes all may influence self-assessment of health. Chipperfield (1993) obtained self-ratings of health in interviews of 4,303 Canadians ages 65–111 years using an area probability sampling technique. On the basis of the subjective global ratings, the sample was divided into three groups: a "well," a "typical," and an "ill" group. Using the number of self-reported "objective" health problems, the sample was again trichotomized, but it should be remembered that the seriousness of each problem was not taken into account. Only 6% of the participants gave global ratings of health that were much higher than their self-reported "objective" indicators. Twelve years later, 1,518 of the surviving participants or their proxies were reinterviewed (2% could not be tracked down or refused to be interviewed). Death certificates were subsequently obtained for 97% of the deceased individuals. Mortality during the 12-year period was highest in the ill and lowest in the "well" elderly. But this group was the youngest, had the highest level of income, and exhibited the highest level of life satisfaction and the greatest level of functional independence. In the "well" elderly group, those who underestimated their health were more likely to have died during the follow-up period than those whose ratings were congruent. None in this group overestimated his or her health. In the "typical" group, those who overestimated their health were significantly less likely to die than those who provided congruent ratings, while there was no relationship between underestimation and mortality. Finally, in the "ill" group, those who reported significant overestimation of their health were significantly less likely to die than those who reported congruent health ratings. In summary, overestimation (optimism?) of one's health tends to be related to lower mortality.

Stoller (1993) concluded that medical interpretations of symptoms are frequently mixed with nonmedical ones. Those who experience few symptoms are more likely to assume that their health is "normal" and minimize the potential import of new and unfamiliar symptoms. This may reflect Costa and McCrea's view (1990) that illness is to some extent a manifestation of a personality factor, neuroticism, which sensitizes some individuals to appraise and respond to minimal pains while others have more stoic attitudes.

Mangione, Marcantonio, Goldman, Cook, *et al.* (1993) compared 247 women ages 50–69 years with 276 women ages 70–89 years prior to undergoing major elective noncardiac surgery. The patients had a low prevalence of comorbid conditions. Each participant responded to a standard questionnaire measuring health status. The results revealed somewhat contradictory relationships between age and measures of health status: Compared to younger patients, the older ones had worse role function and physical function scores, lower energy, higher fatigue scores, and poorer scores on the ADL scale. However, their global perception of health did not differ from that of the younger group, and neither did their mental health scores or pain perception. The correlations between the various measures differed in the younger and the older group, which implies that overall health perception is determined by different factors in the elderly than in the young patients. In the elderly, global health perception was not as strongly correlated with role functions and pain scores as in the younger group; older people tend to adjust to chronic pains and disabilities. Hays, Schoenfeld, and Blazer (1996) analyzed self-rated health in 3,756 older adults; data were also obtained on BP, functional status, presence of chronic diseases, mental status, and depressive symptomatology. Using least square regressions, poor health rating correlated most highly ($p < .001$) with depression scores, followed by poor functional status, presence of chronic diseases, age, income, and education.

The heterogeneity of chronic diseases and functional disabilities do not lend themselves to a simple metric of health. There may be varied interpretations of the common question, "How do you rate your health?" Though several studies have found a relationship between self-assessed health and survival, the mechanism of the observed relationship is unknown. As Idler (1992) and Wolinsky and Johnson (1992) have concluded, we are groping here in the dark.

HEALTH CARE SERVICES UTILIZATION

After a health problem has been perceived, a person has several options. First, he or she may decide not to do anything if the discomfort is not too severe. Leventhal *et al.* (1993b) reviewed studies indicating that, as a rule, symptoms that are intense and/or have sudden onset result in rapid seeking of medical assistance. Most frequently, however, the discomfort is of short duration and the symptoms disappear. Many chronic diseases of aging have a gradual onset that precludes determining the appropriate time for seeking professional help. Second, many individuals resort to self-care or assistance from family and friends before they seek professional services. A person with an occasional not-too-intense headache will ingest a store-bought analgesic. Self-care also encompasses routine habits that prevent illness, such as consumption of vitamins, immunizations, and exercise. There are few reliable data on age differences on many self-care or health maintenance behaviors (Dean, 1992).

Research efforts on self-care have begun to emerge only since the mid-1970s, and studies in industrialized countries indicate that the vast majority of symptoms of discomfort are not brought to the attention of health professionals. In a 2-week diary study of 142 community-residing older adults (60+ years), Rakowski, Julius, Hickey, Verbrugge, and Halter (1988) analyzed the type of action taken by the participants in response to symptoms (no action, medication, medical help sought, self-care, or nonprofessional advice). On the average, older persons, women, the married, and those with more illnesses recorded slightly more symptoms. Professional assistance was by far the least frequent action taken in this group. Only satisfaction with one's income was associated with a tendency to seek professional help, but the relationship was weak (partial $r = .18$).

It appears that in most instances, lay practices are deemed to be appropriate (Dean, 1992). Probably, the explosion of health information in public media, the introduction of health education concepts from kindergarten to college, and the present greater availability of health-care educational and community health services have made the public knowledgeable about many common health practices. There are a large number of motivational variables that influence the decision to use professional health services. In addition to motivation, decisions to seek professional health care are affected by an individual's information about health, functional abilities, the organization and financing of health services, kinship relationships, housing, and other sociocultural factors. Current studies in the United States cannot be compared with those in other countries that have other systems of health care. Much of the recent research has utilized Andersen's model (1968), which posits enabling factors such as beliefs. Thus, explicitly or implicitly, motivational variables play a role in health services utilization. Most of our data are from epidemiological studies in which important behavioral factors are usually not considered. While need or health status is usually the prepotent variable in health services use, much of the variability remains unexplained (Wolinsky, 1990, p. 45). After partialing out the numerous demographic, social structure, and economic factors, there is probably little variance remaining that can be attributed to beliefs and other motivational variables.

Reports of physician visits were obtained in a 1979 interview study of 2,051 noninstitutionalized older Virginians (60+ years) (Arling, 1985). Self-reports of health and functioning status, social support, psychosomatic distress, and economic status as well as several demographic variables were also ascertained. Medical conditions and ADL impairments explained approximately 13% of the variance in physician visits, while psychosomatic and emotional distress accounted for only 2.1% of the variance. Social support in conjuction with ADL contributed about 1% of the variance. Sex, race, marital status, or living arrangement were not significant factors. In contrast to studies reporting that psychological distress is linked to physician's visits for medical care among the elderly, Berkanovic and Hurwicz (1992), in a year-long longitudinal study of 940 Medicare recipients (aged 65+) who were members of a health maintenance organization (HMO), found that depressive symptoms did not influence the initial visit to a physician. Actually, depressive symptoms and illness were more likely to occur subsequent to physician visits. Apparently, depressive symptoms are likely to occur in response to health problems that lead the person to visit a physician rather than vice versa. These findings support Costa and McCrea's (1990) contention that hypochondriasis or psychological distress leading to overutilization of health care services does not increase in the older population, considering their "objective" health.

Leventhal *et al.* (1993) investigated timing decisions for obtaining medical care from outpatient clinic and emergency room patients. Excluded were persons who were under treatment for cancer, myocardial infarction, or stroke, and those with cognitive impairement. Interviews were conducted with 88 relatively well-educated middle-aged (40–55 years) and 80 community-residing older (66–94 years) adults who belonged to an HMO. The time from the onset of symptoms to the decision that these represent an illness was significantly shorter in the older adults. The geometric mean of the delay in days for the older group was .74 in contrast to 7.0 days in the middle-aged group. The difference between the cohorts was most pronounced when the symptoms were neither very severe nor mild. The delay from the time that illness was appraised until professional care was sought was also shorter in the older group. The authors hypothesize that older individuals are less tolerant of uncertainty when it pertains to health, probably because of their greater concerns about this, and the elderly are more willing to turn over responsibility to another person when their health may be at risk. When people are faced with difficult decisions and their knowledge is limited, they do not want to be accountable for their choices (Lazarus, 1991, p. 148). The difference in delay between the cohorts was unrelated to the number of symptoms associated with the presenting problem or the amount of pain experienced. Neither working outside the home nor having a spouse accounted for the age effect. The data analysis also ruled out the presence of significantly more preexisting chronic illnesses in the older group, the experience of pain reported, or fearfulness about the nature of the symptoms as significant age factors in seeking medical care. The authors note, however, that their sample was a highly educated group. In a second study, with older (65+ years) and middle-aged (45–65 years) adults, Leventhal, Easterling, Leventhal, and Cameron (1995), again found that the delay for appraisal and total delay prior to seeing a professional were shorter in the old group. These differences occurred even after controlling for perceived seriousness, disruption of normal activities, ruminations about the illness, and perceived vulnerability to illness. In their discussion, the authors refer to a subsequent longitudinal trial in which the delay behavior of younger and older persons with new symptoms produced similar results. The outcome of these studies is not too surprising. Older people, especially the educated, are aware of their greater vulnerability to the onset of most diseases and the potential for complications, as well as the slower recovery once a disease occurs. It is therefore reasonable for them to be motivated to seek professional care sooner than do younger persons. Also, older people usually have fewer job and family responsibilities that constrain the time available for exploring professional diagnoses and simple health care practices. The authors hypothesize that there is more risk aversion with aging, a general phenomenon associated with aging that seems not to be restricted to health (Botwinick, 1984, 177–180).

We already referred to Strain's (1991) study on health beliefs and LC. Health beliefs accounted for only 3% of the variance in the number of physician visits per year and 1% of hospitalizations. Overall, health beliefs contributed only 4% of the variance in health care utilization, and health LC did not affect utilization. As in most other studies, need for services emerged as the most important determinant of health services utilization. However, the need factor also included self-perception of health, which is probably confounded with belief and other psychosocial variables. Grembowski, Patrick, Diehr, Durham, et al. (1993) tested self-efficacy, ability to control one's behavior, and outcome expectations—a belief that certain behaviors may pose health risks—in exercising, dietary fat intake, weight control, alcohol intake, and smoking in a group of 2,524 Medicare recipients (ages 65–74 years). The relatively healthy white participants responded to a mail questionnaire pertaining to self-efficacy, health-risk status, perceived health status, and type of awareness. While there were some weak relationships between body awareness and health-care utilization, the authors acknowledge some of the limitations of their study. The sample could not be considered representative of the HMO population from which it was drawn because of the low initial response rate. Body awareness may have influenced the willingness to participate. A weaker than typical correlation between self-assessed global health and medical utilization may have been due to an unusually healthy sample. Nevertheless, body awareness may be a psychological factor that makes a small contribution to the perception of illness and/or care utilization.

In contrast to most of the previously cited studies and others reporting that psychosocial variables make only a small contribution to the decision to seek professional medical help, in a cross-sectional study in two samples of relatively well-educated community-residing women ($N = 112$ and 115, respectively) ages 65–85 years, Cheng (1992) found that a global self-report measure of health status accounted for 30% of the variance in self-reports of physician utilization over a 12-month period. Psychosocial factors, including somatization and undesirable life events, but primarily loneliness–distress, accounted for an additional 13–14% of the variance, while sociodemographic variables were not useful in predicting physician utilizations. Since the range of demographic variables was limited, it would seem that cultural factors

may have played a major role in the relatively high relationship between service utilization and psychosocial factors.

HEALTH PROMOTION AND PREVENTIVE
HEALTH BEHAVIORS

Since earliest civilization, it has been known that certain practices
promote health. At the present, we have scientific evidence, though
some of it is not universally accepted, that supports the relationship between illness and certain behaviors. The field of public health depends
on fostering education that promotes beneficial health behaviors and
much psychological research has been devoted to studying the relationship between attitudes, beliefs, and behavior (Fishbein & Ajzen,
1975), including practices that affect health.

Several reviews of health promotion were prepared by Hickey and
Stillwell (1991), Rakowski (1992), and Schwarzer (1992). We now
briefly mention some large-scale surveys published more recently. We
have previously referred to the social-cognitive theories relevant to
health (Schwarzer, 1992). Hickey and Stillwell (1991) discuss this topic
from a public health vantage point. In their article, there is not a single
reference to motivation or other psychological concepts. Rakowski
(1992), a sociologist, focuses on his discipline and on epidemiology. Not
only is there little overlap among the three reviews, but also Hickey and
Stillwell (1991) and Rakowski (1992) cite different sources. Studies of
health and health promotion are in the province of numerous disciplines, and investigators of the same topic frequently ignore references
to similar issues published in other disciplines. In his summary,
Schwarzer (1992) admits that we do not know much about the significance of the numerous factors, including the situational ones that determine health promotion. This limitation applies even to young
populations, which are typically more homogeneous than the older
ones, and where data collection with captive participants (students) is
easier to accomplish than with older adults. Since Schwarzer's essay appears in a publication that is not specifically oriented toward gerontology, his references to empirical studies come primarily from studies of
young adults. Hickey and Stillwell (1991) also conclude that there is little consensus regarding the efficacy of various health-promotion practices applicable to diverse older populations. Similar sentiments are
expressed by Rakowski (1992), who asks, "How will we know when the
health of the aging population has been optimized?" (p. 268). But this
question is equally applicable to younger age groups. In the introduction

to this chapter, we referred to Mechanic's (1992) contention that the correlations between various health-related activities are modest. Kane and Kane (1990, p. 424) also note that many claims for prevention in an elderly population are not supported by reliable data. The task is complicated by the large number of older individuals who suffer from various functional disabilities and chronic diseases. Health-promotion activities appropriate for younger people may not feasibly be implemented in many older groups. While in younger populations the emphasis is on enhancing health, in the elderly, it is on maintaining the current status or reducing the rate of undesirable decrements. Furthermore, preventive health behaviors depend on attitudes and beliefs that are strongly influenced by culture and change with advances in medical knowledge.

Ferraro (1993), in an analysis of interview data from the 1984 National Health Interview Survey of older Americans, compared 855 black respondents with a random sample of 3,000 whites. Blacks were less likely to report health-promoting behaviors, and this was more so for black women than men. Information was also obtained on self-assessment of health and functional morbidity. Health optimism–pessimism was then operationally defined as the residual of health assessment regressed on functional morbidity and health promotion. In terms of this measure, blacks showed more health pessimism than did whites. Ferraro noted that his analysis of these cross-sectional data did not rule out the influence of socioeconomic variables, including education. Ralston (1993), in her review of other data on health-promotion activities of rural black elderly, arrived at similar conclusions. Professional health care in some rural communities is viewed with suspicion, as exemplified by the expressions, "The doctor can't do me any good" or "Hospitals are considered a place where the ill go to die."

Prohaska, Leventhal, Leventhal, and Keller (1985) collected data at public health fairs from 173 younger (ages 20–39 years), 111 middle (ages 40–59 years), and 112 older (ages 60+ years) adults. The respondents were asked how often they performed each behavior that influences the development of several diseases, their perceived vulnerability to six diseases, and which of 16 symptoms they would consider as warning signs of a disease. Of 16 health practices, 15 showed significant age differences, with the older group showing an increased number of health-promoting behaviors; persons only performing aerobic or strenuous exercises showed decrements with age, and these activities are most likely not health promoting in the elderly. However, the magnitudes of the various effects was small ($rs = .04–.14$). Also, the intercorrelations between the various health practices were low. There were no age differences in the perceived efficacy of the 21 health practices in preventing illness. As expected, weakness and aches were seen less likely as signs of illness by the older than the younger respondents. There was a significant interaction between age and gender in the frequency of medical checkups. It should be noted that the data were obtained from individuals who visited health fairs, persons who probably had a greater motivation to maintain their health than a random sample of the population. More frequent health-promoting lifestyles in older adults in some health domains have been reported also by others (Walker, Volkan, Sechrist, & Pender, 1988). In that study, the older respondents felt more responsible for their own health. It also agrees with the data in the Leventhal *et al.* (1993) study in which older persons felt that they were more vulnerable to the onset of diseases.

Housee*t et al.* (1988) in reviewing the role of social relationships and health, differentiated between social support, which usually is beneficial to health, and social control in a relationship, which may be beneficial or damaging. It seems that there are complex interactions between gender, marriage, or living alone and preventive health behaviors and morbidity. In a cross-sectional study Potts, Hurwicz, Goldstein, and Berkanovic (1992) examined the relationship between social interactions and health-promotive beliefs and preventive health behaviors in 1,009 older (mean age 73 years) members of a health management organization (HMO). Interview data were obtained on several preventive health behaviors (exercising, nutritional practices, refraining from smoking, excessive alcohol consumption, and drinking caffeinated beverages). Health-promotive beliefs pertaining to five categories of the named behaviors and data on social support were also obtained. Weak positive relationships (rs = .09–.18) were seen between social support and each of the five categories of health-promotive beliefs; most of the correlations between demographic variables and beliefs were not statistically significant, except for alcohol consumption. In six of eight analyses, stronger social support networks were related to preventive health behavior, though, again, the correlations were marginal (rs = .07–.11). The two exceptions were consumption of fiber and excessive drinking of caffeinated beverages. In six of eight analyses, health-promotive beliefs significantly predicted their associated behaviors (rs = .11–.35). The exceptions were consumption of red meat and intake of vitamins/minerals. The rationale for these relationships was not presented. Supplementary analyses revealed that preventive health behaviors tended to be associated more strongly with beliefs in the elderly living alone (widowed, divorced, separated) than in those who were married. Apparently, a spouse may inhibit behaviors that a person believes to be health-promoting. Potts *et al.* (1992) noted that no data were obtained on the health beliefs or behaviors of a person's support-network member(s), which may have elucidated the apparently anomalous relationships between social support and living alone. Since during the same interview session, data were obtained on beliefs and practices, it is possible that some respondents may have given similar answers to two measures to give the appearance of consistency. Also, data on behaviors were given only for frequency of performance. A person who ate 4 ounces of meat three times per week would have received a worse score on preventive health behaviors than a person who ate a 16-ounce steak once per week. The authors acknowledge the difficulties in defining "good" health habits, but to this we may add the difficulties in quantifying them. Weak positive relationships between a supportive family environment and good health practices were also reported in a sample of 172 community-residing elderly by Rakowski, Julius, Hickey, and Halter (1987). Umberson (1992), in an analysis of interview data from a national two-wave panel survey in 1986 (N-3,617) and in 1989 (N = 2,687), found that gender and marital status interacted in regulating or controlling several health protective behaviors (physical activity, hours of sleep, alcohol intake, smoking). Marriage is associated with more efforts to control health for men than women. Females are more likely to control the health of others than are men. Most importantly, Antonucci (1990) in her review of social supports and relationships, emphasized the significance of the instruments in assessment, including questions in interviews in such a conceptually diverse field as social support and social relationships.

Speake, Cowart, and Pellet (1989) measured health LC, self-rated health status, and healthy lifestyle (health behaviors in terms of exercise, nutrition, stress management, interpersonal support, "health responsibility," and self-actualization) in 297 healthy volunteers ranging in age from 55 to 93 years. Seventy percent of the participants rated their health as excellent or good, and only 10% rated their health as poor. Internal LC and self-ratings of health status were significant predictors of healthy lifestyles. These two factors accounted for 24% of the variance in the composite score of lifestyle. The authors acknowledge that the sample consisted of persons who had more education and a higher income than their cohorts in the U.S. population. Also, it should be noted that except for the exercise and nutrition subscales of lifestyle, the other subscales were confounded to some extent with perceived health and LC. Grembowski et al. (1993), in a study of 2,524 well-educated, mostly female community-residing participants ages 65+ years, found two factors of healthy lifestyle efficacy expectations (belief that the person can control certain behaviors). One consisted of exercise, dietary fat intake, and body weight, and the other consisted of alcohol consumption and smoking. The usual correlation between socioeconomic scale (SES) and health-related lifestyles was modulated by self-efficacy measures. This would indicate that the relationship between health and SES is greatly influenced by self-efficacy. Tran, Wright, and Chatters (1991) used data from 581 respondents ages 55+ years in the 1979–1980 National Survey of Black Americans; poor subjective health, affected by chronic physical health, was predictive of lower levels of personal efficacy and subjective well-being (SWB). Stressful life events reduced personal efficacy and SWB. The authors caution the reader that the reliability for some of these indicators was not well established. Waller and Bates (1992) reported that older individuals with high internal LC beliefs who believe that they are competent or, in Bandura's terminology, that they have high general self-efficacy, are more likely to benefit from a health education program than those with an external LC and low self-efficacy. This study was based on a group of self-selected volunteers. But in this, as in most studies, the effects of the program were assessed soon after the program ended. Thus, the long-term benefits of health promotion programs are not always apparent (Lalonde, Hooyman, & Blumhagen, 1988).

Health promotion and the development of health-preventive behaviors are learning and performance tasks in which motivation is a critical variable. In the social-cognitive theories of health behaviors, expectancies and incentives play a key role, but there have been no studies in which motivation was explicitly investigated. Admittedly, the motivation for many health-promoting tasks, as is the case in many human activities (McClelland, 1992), may be difficult to discern. For example, is exercising performed to maintain or enhance health, or is the motivation companionship or physical appearance? Is it a visit to a physician for care of an illness, or is it a checkup that may be classified as preventive (Rakowski, 1992)? It is possible, of course, as part of large health surveys to have questions that probe the motivation for certain health-promotion or prevention activities, but this has not been attempted. However, as McClelland *et al.* (1989) have shown, the validity of some self-attributed overt motives may be questionable. Most of the studies have been cross-sectional. The increase in the educational level of our population and the media attention to health should boost health-promotion practices. On the other hand, certain cultural changes, such as the growing use of automobiles even for traversing short distances, may be contrary to good health practices. Some longitudinal studies may shed some light on this subject. Finally, as Mechanic (1992) has pointed out, the correlations between various health behaviors are low. Thus, health-promoting activities found in one domain, such as nutrition, may not generalize to other behaviors, such as exercise.

CONCLUSIONS

Health is one of the major values at all ages and increases in importance with aging. Chapter 4, on pain, contains material that overlaps with material covered here. Most behaviors encompass some health aspects, but people usually do not pay attention to them until later in life. Health behaviors include activities that relate to health maintenance, restoration, or improvement. Many of our health-related behaviors are automatic, and—as in much of behavior in general—they may be based on mixed motives. Stress may manifest itself in illness, and illness is a stress. Separate chapters are devoted to stress and coping in the elderly.

There are numerous models of health behaviors, since some address illness perception, and others, health promotion or restoration or decisions to seek professional health services. Individuals with certain personality traits, young and old, are more likely to appraise and respond even to minor pains and discomfort than others who have less responsive characteristics. Classical Freudian psychosomatic theories have been replaced by modern personality theories, based on social learning, such as the role of LC and several cognitive theories of health behaviors based on expectancy–value and knowledge efficacy constructs; they vary in terms of the number of explicit constructs they include. While there are studies that support each of the theories, it is difficult to pit them against each other. The available data are mainly cross-sectional, and there are few comparisons of younger and older persons. Since health problems change with age, it may not be practical to compare aging changes.

Global self-assessment of health frequently has been shown to be related to mortality even after controlling for physician-rated health. Those who overestimate their health, optimists, tend to live longer than the underestimators, the pessimists. This relationship occurs primarily in the young-old but the basis for this finding is unknown. In studies in which the Andersen behavioral model was used, self-perception of health is considered a need factor, and the latter is positively correlated with a tendency to seek medical assistance. Self-assessment may also be related to a high level of motivation to engage in health behaviors, such as adherence to prescribed regimens, which are not measured in most studies. Finally, there may also be a relationship with the existentialist construct of "will to live," but here, too, no data are available.

Older people, especially the more educated, have a shorter delay period in seeking professional help after the appearance of symptoms than do younger persons. But health beliefs, emotional factors, and social support contribute only a very small portion to the total variance, according to most studies, in seeking medical assistance. The physical condition of the individual and ADL impairments seem to be the major factors in seeking medical help.

There have been some studies on health preventive and promotive behaviors, but these involved mostly younger persons. The correlations between various health-preventive behaviors are low.

The few available data on older persons do not show any long-term effects of health promotion and the development of preventive habits. Though motivation is a key variable in these activities, and psychologists, in general, have made tremendous strides in studies investigating learning and motivation, little of this effort has been directed toward health. At present, our knowledge of health promotion and preventive behaviors is poor. The interaction of motivation for health behaviors with other motives is strongly influenced by cohort, including experiences and cultural influences. This creates difficulties in any attempts to disentangle the fuzzy relationships between health behaviors and other categories.

CHAPTER 8

Stress

INTRODUCTION

Origins

In Chapter 1, in the definitions of motivation, we introduced the concept of balance or homeostasis. Again, in Chapter 2, on the biological foundations, and in Chapter 7, it was necessary to integrate motivation with homeostasis or equilibrium. There have been different views on the usage of the terms *homeostasis* and *equilibrium*. Cofer and Appley (1964, pp. 302–366) and Appley (1991) review the history of the controversy, primarily in reference to psychology. In general, physiologists, following Cannon (1915), tend to use the term *homeostasis,* while most psychologists, including Appley (1991), express a preference for the more "dynamic" term *equilibrium,* which may be applicable to both closed and open systems. Equilibrium does not imply that the organism seeks to return to a prior steady state, and it can therefore be applied to such psychological concepts as expectancy or achievement. Similarly, the biologist Yates (Yates & Benton, 1995) introduced the term *homeodynamics,* since organisms are open systems and equilibrium denotes stillness. For our purposes, the distinction between terms is not too important. Motivation may be defined as the organism's attempt to achieve equilibrium or homeodynamics.

Current Conceptions

Currently, stress is one of the most ubiquitous concepts in psychology. For the period 1990–1996, *Psychological Abstracts* had an average of nearly 2,000 articles yearly in its index under the ascriptors stress, physiological stress, social stress, stress management, stress reactions, and various subcategories (e.g., occupational stress, environmental stress, and coping). Arousal and other concepts related to stress were indexed separately. Note the differentiation between physiological, psychological, and social stress. Coyne and Downey (1991) refer to Garfield's analysis of the *Social Science Citation Index* for 1983, which revealed that articles on stress, anxiety, and depression, the latter two being frequently used as indices of stress, were the most active research areas in the social sciences. Coyne and Downey believe that this momentum is likely to continue in the near future. Lieberman (1992) referred to stress studies as a growth industry in the behavioral and social sciences. The concept of stress has been invoked to account for numerous animal and human disequilibria to the point that almost all changes in the environment, the latter including both physical and biological conditions, and the social situation, are labeled as the consequences of stress. This was bound to lead to some criticisms of the concept, specifically, its vagueness. The basic philosophical assumption in the use of the concept of stress is that all or most changes affecting an individual are deleterious (Pollock, 1988).

In biology and the social sciences, the term was not used until the World War II period. Hinkle (1987) traced the evolution of the concept in medicine from terms in use since antiquity, such as *hardship, adversity,* and *affliction,* to later concepts such as frustration, strain, and pressure, to the current usage of the concept stress. The first usage of the term *stress* in *Psychological Abstracts* appeared in 1944. It should be noted that the *Abstracts* also referred the reader searching under the ascriptor "stress" to the term *emotion.* Among the four articles indexed under stress is one by Haggard (1943) that reported the effects on the galvanic skin response (GSR) during classical conditioning with electric shock (the stressor) while the participants were aware of the presence of a verbal cue, an investigation very similar to several others on aversive conditioning and the role of various cues. Previous investigators, however, did not use the term *stress* when they reported the outcomes of similar studies in aversive conditioning. Another article indexed under stress was by Freeman (1944) on the use of the Stress Interview. The author defined stress as the result of being highly motivated to succeed, but with limited time available to perform, or with the individual being told that he or she was failing. In *Biological Abstracts,* the term *stress* also did not appear until 1949. It is thus apparent that though studies that currently may be labeled as investigations of stress have been around for a long time, in the life sciences, the term is of relatively recent origin.

DEFINITIONS

The proliferation of the term *stress* in the scientific literature, covering the spectrum from basic biology to anthropology, has resulted in a variety of definitions. There are also many other current terms that do not refer to stress but cover similar phenomena, such as *life problems, life difficulties, strains,* or *frustration* (Wheaton, 1996). Some investigators have even argued that the concept is useless (Cohen, Kessler, & Gordon, 1995). Moreover, there are bothersome instances in which the user does not define the term; the definition is amorphous, or the usages by an author within the same context are inconsistent. Most commonly, the concept is used as (1) a stimulus, as in " It is a high stress job"; (2) a response, as in "Retirement produces stress for a person"; or (3) a mediating state or intervening variable, as when a person is told that her spouse is very ill and the resulting stress induces insomnia.

In general, the term *acute stress* has been invoked whenever an organism or, most frequently, a person, is faced by a challenge, harm, threat (Lazarus, 1993), or structural constraints (Wheaton, 1996). The last term, used primarily by sociologists, has been applied to restrictions in choice or social exchanges. All of these terms are also poorly defined and tend to overlap.

Selye's Influence

The most common usage in psychology of the concept of stress is based on the physiologist Selye's (1956) model. He used the term (1) *stressor* for the adverse stimulus; (2) the *general adaptation syndrome* (GAS) for the intervening physiological changes or *stress;* and (3) the *reactions* (responses) to the situation, be they adaptive or maladaptive. The GAS consists of increases in the activity of the hypothalamic–pituitary–adrenocortical system (HPA) that then trigger a variety of biological and behavioral responses. Related to the HPA is the activity of the sympathetic–adrenal system, first emphasized in homeostasis by Cannon (1932). Selye's definition of what induces stress was, of course, circular (i.e., a condition or stimulus was a stressor when a GAS occurred). This is reminiscent of the problem encountered in defining a stimulus discussed in Chapter 1).

As far as possible, we use the term *stressor* for the input or the stimulus, and *stress* as the mediating state in a *process* wherein the organism is faced with a challenge that disturbs the normal or expected equilibrium, which then produces some biological or psychological changes. If the consequences result in a relatively long-term psychological disturbance, we refer to it as distress. However, it is impossible to distinguish a momentary psychological disturbance, such as an inability to give a response to a challenging question, from a more serious disequilibrium or distress.

Selye's model commonly has been used when an investigator observes or measures the consequences of certain specific (1) "life events," such as loss of a loved one or surgery; (2) some other specific "threat," such as visiting a physician or an interview with an IRS agent; or (3) daily hassles and small annoyances, such as misplacing keys or being caught in a traffic jam (Kanner, Coyne, Schaefer, & Lazarus, 1981). In all of these situations, it is possible to specify, or at least describe, the nature of the stressor, and its duration is usually fairly limited. On the other hand, in many instances, especially in social relationships, there is a relatively prolonged stressor and/or the boundaries are difficult to circumscribe. Here, the term *strain* has been used, since it may lead to responses different from those to life events. For example, a person who lives in a deteriorating old house close to a noisy interstate highway or in a high-crime neighborhood is probably experiencing chronic stress. It is difficult to specify the stressor(s). The latter consist of a host of physiological (noise, poor temperature controls) and psychosocial factors. Older persons who have lived in such houses for several decades cannot specify at what point they began to experience stress. Almost every facet of a person's experience in that house may be attributed to stress.

Pearlin (Pearlin, Aneshensel, Mullan, Whitlatch, 1996) emphasizes the role of the *primary stressor* that engenders *secondary stressors.* Caretaking of an elderly disabled person, the primary stressor, may then affect the caretaker's interactions with other members of the family, a secondary stressor, creating chain effects resulting from the stress induced by a specific stressor. Though not separating primary and secondary stressors, the role of chronic or previous stressors on the response to new stressful events has been discussed by several investigators (Kessler, 1997; Taylor & Aspinwall, 1996). The proliferation of stressors is of particular significance when we analyze the lives of older people who are losing sundry specific resources, or who have previously experienced stress.

Biological versus Psychosocial Stressors

In the realm of biology, we have much information concerning stimuli or stressors that are potential inducers of stress. The same cannot be said about psychological stressors. Thus, some psychologists (R. S. Lazarus, 1990a, 1990b) state explicitly that they are addressing only psychological stressors in their theory; Lazarus (1993) believes that there are profound differences between physiological and psychological stress, though he does not elaborate on the distinction.

There are many environmental conditions that produce concurrently physiological, psychological, and social stresses or some combination of them. Death of a spouse may induce not only a social but also psychological and physiological stresses. Widowhood affects a person's role status and may also influence relationships with children and friends or financial well-being; it frequently engenders loneliness, depression, and other psychological problems, and many of these problems usually manifest themselves by physiological consequences. Widowhood is a good illustration of a frequently occurring stressor encountered by older persons that leads to a variety of interconnected physiological, psychological, and social stresses.

Kasl (1992), in reviewing the usage of the concept stress in the psychosocial sciences, concluded that at the present, it refers to a variety of social and psychological experiences that have an impact on health and it is premature to expect agreement among researchers. The sociologist George (1996a) also notes the strong links between stress and health. This view assumes a very broad definition of health, another concept that is difficult to define. Selye (1956) also used a very broad definition of stress as a nonspecific result of any demand upon whether the the effect is mental or somatic. Such a definition might imply that life itself, which continuously places demands on the organism, produces a constant state of stress. This potential paradox was already addressed by Selye (1974) when he asserted that many minor physiological disequilibria or stresses do not induce distress or awareness of discomfort. People also learn to adapt or cope with many stresses. From another perspective, Gove (1994) believes that the most meaningful activities in life are stressful. If a person is motivated to achieve a goal, he or she will face a challenge, which, according to our previous definitions, induces stress.

We may view the life course as a series of changes or transitions, and each of these places new demands on the organism, thus producing a series of different stresses during each stage of life or age. Sociologists emphasize the life-stage or role-change approach; for example, marriage or widowhood is a role change that may induce stress. To understand aging, therefore, special attention ought to be given to the analysis of stress. For Antonovsky (1990, p. 157) all living is potentially pathogenic. Except for potent stressors, however, the consequences of most common stressors are minimal. Other investigators, though phrasing their concepts differently, also arrive at very broad, all-encompassing definitions of stress.

THEORIES

Definitions of constructs are based on theories. Since stress permeates most important aspects of life, some attention needs to be given to some of the models or theories.

Biological Models

The General Adaptation Syndrome and Other Biological Models. We have previously referred to Selye's GAS. For Selye (1956, p. 54), "Stress is the state manifested by a specific syndrome" nonspecifically induced by a variety of stressors, whether drugs, bacteria, or neural stimuli. It manifests itself in a variety of symptoms such as fatigue, fever, loss of appetite, and/or sleeplessness, in addition to specific symptoms associated with the organ systems that are affected. For example, a stressor that affects the gastrointestinal (GI) system will induce GI as well as various other symptoms associated with the GAS. The general manifestations are commonly referred to as "being sick." Continuous stress will produce a state of exhaustion when the organism is no longer capable of responding to the stressor.

Sapolsky and others have proposed (1992, pp. 5–9) that with chronic stress, the neuroendocrine responses, specifically, the glucocorticoids secreted in large quantities over time, begin to have adverse effects, especially on the hippocampus. The evidence for this hypothesis is mixed (Nelson, 1995). Though the exhaustion phase is controversial, the other parts of Selye's model seem to have been supported, and his model has served as a major impetus for much recent biological research on stress.

More recent work has shown that in addition to changes in the adrenocortical and the autonomic nervous systems, stress responses involve a host of other physiological mechanisms such as the immune system, neuropeptides, enzymes, and other regulatory mechanisms. In Chapter 2, on the biological foundations, we briefly touched upon some of these systems. H. Weiner (1992) refers to Darwin's observations that the whole organism responds to various environmental challenges and that physiological and behavioral responses are *indivisible*.

There have been several biological theories of aging based on the "wear-and-tear" phenomenon seen in inanimate objects such as an automobile. Repeated heavy usage or misuse—stresses—will eventually result in the failure of the object. In the summary on current theories of aging, Massoro (1995) favors a concept of homeostatic failures involving many independent and interacting biological processes.

Potential Benefits of Mild Levels of Stress. Though this does not represent a model, it seems appropriate to introduce here an interesting biological phenomenon. In plants and lower organisms, we have evidence that some agents, which typically are considered stressors, in small quantities may have beneficial effects and enhance fitness. According to Sagan (1987) the term *hormesis* was coined in 1942, when it was reported that a naturally occuring antibiotic that at "normal" (high) doses suppresses the growth of fungi has at low doses the opposite stimulatory effect. Numerous studies have demonstrated similar nonmonotonic dose effects after exposures to various carcinogens, ionizing radiations, and various other toxins. Figure 8.1 is a schematic diagram of hormesis when low doses are beneficial to the organism and the opposite occurs after high doses.

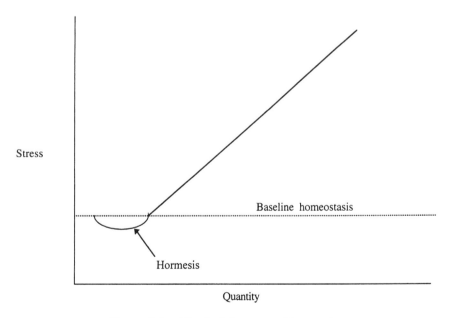

Figure 8.1. Physical stressor and hormesis.

Extrapolations of hormesis studies to people are difficult at the present. Macklis (1997) referred to some studies reporting that, in some cases, survivors of atomic bomb detonations in Japan at the end of World War II are outliving their nonexposed peers. Several factors in these epidemiological studies cannot be controlled. For example, did the exposure lead to better subsequent health practices?

Lazarus, Deese, and Osler (1952) reviewed some studies of the effect of World War II battle stress on performance. Though a few respondents claimed that their performance was enhanced, objective data were not available. In a subsequent analysis of the literature, Monat and Lazarus (1977, pp. 349–364) concluded that mild stress may sometimes facilitate performance. He proposes several possible mechanisms. One is the classical drive or motivation hypothesis that stressor-induced high anxiety may enhance performance on simple tasks but interfere with complex tasks. This is the modern version of the classical Yerkes–Dodson hypothesis (Appley, 1991). Lazarus favors a coping explanation, according to which threat of failure mobilizes the organism to search for adaptive, more effective forms of behavior. Antonovsky, in his theory of *stress resistance,* uses a similar model. Also, social psychologists (Janis, 1983) have introduced the concept of stress inoculation, in which individuals are provided information about expected threats and trained to develop coping skills to increase their tolerance to subsequent stresses. There is, however, a difference between biological immunization, in which a very low level of the infectious agent is introduced to develop immunity, and social stress inoculation, in which there is an effort to present the person with situations that mimic as much as possible the expected stressors and then teach the individual how to cope.

A somewhat related concept, developed from a few studies with small samples and several methodological shortcomings, seems to suggest that coping with various major life crises, such as a death in the family, rape, or permanent paralysis, may ameliorate subsequent responses to stressors (Holahan, Moos, & Schaefer 1996; Kessler, Price, & Wortman, 1985; Schaefer & Moos, 1992). These investigators assume that a substantial number of people who experience life crises develop new skills that make them more resilient when faced with other stressors. In addition to developing new problem-solving skills to cope with the stressors, the person may find new *meaning,* interpretation of the situation, and may, during a crisis, acquire new forms of social support, changes that the authors labeled *crisis growth.* These investigators also acknowledge that our information is scant concerning the generality of personal growth resulting from a specific stressor. Also, most of the data have been cross-sectional self-reports.

Though personal growth may be related to hormesis, the analogy is somewhat strained, since on the human level, subsequent stressors usually are different from those that initially affected the organism, and the contexts in which the initial and subsequent stressor occur may also vary. Since people usually learn from their experiences, it should not be surprising that a type of "growth" occurs.

Some Recent Psychosocial Theories

While Selye's devised construct of stress has had a broad impact on both biological and psychosocial investigations, there is probably no comparable model with a similar wide influence in psychology and sociology. Though many theories have been proposed, their impact has been limited; psychology and the related social sciences are amorphous fields that pose major difficulties for the construction of a broad theory. We examine briefly some more recent general theories that may have relevance to an analysis of motivation.

Lazarus.   The reemergence of cognition in modern psychology after World War II, with its emphasis on perception, thinking, and evaluation, has also had a major impact on studies of stress. Foremost in championing this approach has been Lazarus, who was trained as a clinical psychologist. His broad influence in the field was recognized by an Award for Distinguished Scientific Contribution by the American Psychological Association in 1989, and by the honor of his writing a prefatory chapter in the 1993 *Annual Review of Psychology.*

In one of the earliest reviews of the effects of stress on performance, Lazarus *et al.* (1952) defined psychological stress as an *intervening variable*—a concept much in vogue at that time—that is neither a stimulus nor a response. Stress was an interaction of motivation and emotion, a relationship resulting from difficulties in attaining a goal. It occurred either when a person was failing in the performance of a task or when the task was made difficult and required a great deal of effort; it was then necessary for the person to appraise or perceive the situation as currently or potentially interfering with her or his equilibrium. They also differentiated physiological stress in which a motivational component is presumably absent from psychological stress. Since motivation was not defined, it is not clear, however, how the two types differed. Is being hungry a physiological or a psychological stress?

After devoting 40 years to studies of psychological stress, Lazarus (1990, 1991, 1993) has not veered much from his original positions. He still differentiates physiological from psychological stress, and the latter is defined as a relationship between the person and the environment in which the environmental or internal demands tax or exceed adaptive resources (Monat & Lazarus, 1985). For Lazarus, stress is a transaction influenced by a host of mediators; thus, stress is neither an environmental input nor a disposition of the person, but indicates a conjunction of a person with certain motives and beliefs. The environment may be seen as posing harms, threats or challenges. The complex, multivariate process is not static; therefore, no single measurement is satisfactory. There are both short-term and long-term effects. Ideally, stress requires longitudinal observations. He admits that there is a certain degree of confounding between measures of distress, psychosocial manifestations of stress, and personality factors, including preexisting health.

Lazarus (1991, p. 185–188) addresses the relationship between physiological states resulting from illness, fatigue, or drugs and emotions or stress. He believes that the physiological states potentiate the emotional states, stressors, but they do not cause them. The physiological states are dispositions, and Lazarus admits that he espouses a mind–body dualism. Such a position is not indefensible. Rakover (1990, p. 393) believes that the mind–body problem cannot be solved within the context of current Western thought, and for many contemporary philosophers of science (Popper, 1991), the dualistic approach poses few difficulties. Though Popper does not favor talking about two interacting substances, he does recommend distinguishing between two kinds of interacting states (or events), a physicochemical and a mental one. We build houses that may represent to viewers a variety of mental states. Rychlak (1993) applied to psychology Bohr's construct of complementarity. In physics, for some purposes, light has the characteristics of a wave, while in other conditions, it is a particle. In psychology, some phenomena may be grounded in a physical, a biological, a psychological, or a social theory and method, and it is feasible to mix these approaches, since none are fundamentally more basic. In Lazarus's epistemology, concepts at different levels (i.e., the brain and psychological processes) are not parallel (1990a, p. 186). He believes that there are profound differences between physiological and psychological stresses, that what generates tissue damage—physiological stress—is different from what generates psychological stress (1991, p. 4) and that today, and for the foreseeable future, we will not be able to match physiological processes in the brain with psychological processes of coping or appraisal. Developments in the philosophy of science during the past 40 years, along with the rise of cognitive science, with its disregard for the unity-of-science reductionism and its rejection of strict operationism, in terms of observables (Greenwood, 1991, Chapter 4; Leahey, 1991, Chapter 15), have led to spirited debates concerning the foundations of psychological science(s).

Several criticisms of Lazarus's and other models of stress that rely on self-reports are based on the assumption that these methods lack objectivity. There have been many refutations of such a radical behavioristic position (Rakover, 1990, pp. 211–217; Slife & Williams, 1995, pp. 152–153). For example, if X reports that his foot hurts, and his behavior is similar to that reported by others who also state that their foot hurts, we have an "analogical inference to other minds" (Hyslop & Jackson, 1972, cited by Rakover, 1990, p. 212). The diverse approaches to stress research are testimony to the theoretical and methodological turmoils that currently occurr in many areas of the social sciences.

Lazarus (1991, pp. 392–396) points out that stress leads to impaired health, but impaired health also is a stressor. To use only objective measures of emotion may be theoretically possible, but not practicable. Furthermore, it would require assessment of the individual prior to the experience of the environmental event, the stressor, to measure changes, which is, again, not an empirically feasible condition. Also, many measures of health include subjective components, such as headaches, that at present cannot be assessed except by self-reports.

Finally, Lazarus claims that attempts to develop objective behavioral descriptions of environments have produced muddles that are inadequate for any systematic analysis. Lazarus (1990b) also notes that even in reports of natural disasters, where there are objective indices, different observers address different catastrophic events.

Costa and McCrea.   Costa and McCrea (1990) have championed a psychometric approach to stress. They are uncomfortable with the subjective judgments used in the measurement of stress by Lazarus, which arise from the necessity of using appraisal of the situation. They believe that responses to statements such as "I have trouble relaxing," "I have unexpected company," or "I am lonely" reflect individual predilections that are not comparable from person to person; instead, Costa and McCrea advocate using objective measures such as being a widow or having a myocardial infarct. Their studies also indicate that the effects of individual coping efforts add only small amounts of variance when removal of emotional distress is measured. Costa and McCrea (1990) also raise the issue that a person's perception and appraisal of a situation is a function of his or her personality: An event may be perceived as a stressor by an individual because of a high level of neuroticism, but another individual who is low on the trait of neuroticism may not experience the same event as a stressor. Costa and McCrea believe that Lazarus confounds the responses to stressors, such as feeling tense, with the antecedents (i.e., a person experiences stress because he or she is tense).

Antonovsky and Other Sociological Theories. A somewhat different approach to stress has been proposed by Antonovsky (1979, 1987, 1990) as part of his "salutogenesis" theory that places an emphasis on the factors promoting desirable health. For Antonovsky (1990), life is always potentially pathogenic, and at every point in time, people are experiencing some chronic stressors determined by biology, culture, social structures, and idiosyncrasy. Yet they adapt because of the presence of "generalized resistance resources" (GRRs), which include biological factors (the pituitary–adrenal system, immune system, ANS), artifactual materials (shelter, money), cognitive and emotional factors (knowledge–intelligence, ego identity), and sociocultural factors. The absence of some GRRs can become a stressor; for example, an older person who lacks knowledge concerning various health prevention techniques may become stressed when exposed to unfavorable environmental conditions that may not be stressors for a person familiar with appropriate health practices. In addition to the GRRs, there are also many specific resistance resources useful for a specific individual. Stressors have the potential for positive, neutral, or negative consequences. For example, retirement may improve a persons health, life satisfaction, or even finances. In other cases, it may have no effects, while for some persons, the consequences are harmful. It is, therefore, not always possible to predict the stressfulness of a specific life event or environmental change. In addition to the psychosocial GRRs, Antonovsky posits a mediating or buffer resource that provides feedback to the individual: the sense of coherence (SOC), a construct with cognitive, motivational, and instrumental components. SOC is defined as an orientation in which the person is confident that stimuli in the course of living are comprehensible, manageable, and meaningful (i.e., an optimistic view of life). Over time, possessing many GRRs lead to a strong SOC, "a crystallized, integrated view of the world" (Antonovsky, 1990, p. 159). Lack of GRRs, such as a low self-esteem, low social class, or cultural instability, lead to a weak SOC, which makes the person less resistant to many stressors. Thus, SOC is directly related to and predictive of health status. Chapter 12 addresses the issue of life's purpose or meaning.

　　Antonovsky (1990) presents data from a study of retirement in Israel that supports his construct of an SOC as a predictor of health and life satisfaction, and this approach is related to several personality theories that use constructs such as hardiness, self-efficacy, locus of control, or mastery. Antonovsky admits that his model needs to be refined and tested in a variety of cultures with people who experience different life events and possess various SOCs. His background in medical sociology is apparent in the theory he proposed, since it has been known for a long time in medicine that pathogens can not only depress immune responses, but they can also enhance resistance; this is the basis of the effectiveness of inoculation and/or increased resistance to subsequent stressors. Antonovsky (1979, pp. 95–96) cites a study in which some concentration camp survivors adjusted better to the rigors of Israeli life in the early 1950s than those in a control group. In interviews with 805 retirees, Sagy and Antonovsky (1994) found that both after retirement and 2 years preretirement, physical and psychological health were a function of a family's SOC. Previously, Ruff and Korchin (1967) described the benefits of training involving stress on the subsequent tolerance to stressors in astronauts. Similarly, in the volume edited by Appley and Trumbull (1967) in which the Korchin and Ruff paper appeared, there are several references to behavioral practices in different cultures where exposures to some minor stressors lead to enhanced stress tolerance. In Chapter 9, we refer to stress management that to some extent may be taught.

Other sociologists (Burke, 1991; Cohler, 1991; Pearlin & Schooler, 1978) who have influenced psychological analyses use definitions of social stress that emphasize changes in role status or identity, life changes that are not necessarily unexpected but occur primarily during various expectable role transitions, such as marriage or retirement. The response or coping to psychological stresses will also, by definition, consists of a variety of learned patterns of behavior.

Hobfoll. Another partially cognitive theory of psychological stress has been developed by Hobfoll (1988; 1989) and Hobfoll and Freedy (1990). This theory is to some extent a contraposition to Lazarus's model and borrows heavily from Antonovsky's theory (1987), with an emphasis on ecological congruence and resistance factors (Hobfoll, however, does not acknowledge his debt to Antonovsky). The major premises in Hobfoll's model that differentiate his approach from that developed by Lazarus are (1) the assessment of the personality and constitution of the individual and (2) the use of objective measures of the stress-inducing situation rather then a sole reliance on appraisals by the individual experiencing stress. Hobfoll espouses a *conservation of resources* theory that places more emphasis on objective events than does Lazarus. People have innate or acquired needs to conserve the quality and quantity of their resources, and they actively seek to protect, maintain, and build up their resources at a minimum cost. In this approach, psychological stress is a person's reaction to (1) a perceived threat to available resources; (2) an actual loss of resources; or (3) a lack of attainment of new resources following the expenditure of available resources. Logically, the third category is an extension of the second category. Hobfoll defines resources as (1) objects, various possessions; (2) conditions, such as marriage, seniority, socioeconomic status; (3) personal characteristics that enhance stress resistance, such as self-esteem, skills, traits; and (4) energy, which includes time, money, and knowledge. These categories are not mutually exclusive. It is not clear, for example, why money is considered energy when it could equally be placed into Hobfoll's category 1, objects. Social support may overlap several categories, and though it is effective in reducing psychological stress, in many instances, it is at a significant cost of resources; in psychological stress, people attempt to minimize the loss of valued resources. While this theory deemphasizes the appraisal function, its major construct, resources, also leads to circular definitions. If a personal characteristic such as optimism reduces psychological stress, then it is viewed as a resource, but if it impairs adjustment, then it is labeled as a negative coping style. It is tautological to say that the stress experienced during exposure to an aversive stimulus such as extreme cold is a loss of resources, unless Hobfoll also restricts his theory to psychological stressors and excludes in his theory all physical stressors. This does not, however solve the problem of how to categorize states such as hunger and thirst. A. A. Lazarus (1990) also finds the construct of loss of resources nebulous: What resources are lost when somebody feels stress in a traffic jam in the absence of a time constraint? Hobfoll's (1989) model also includes an appraisal of resources and the perception of a threat, constructs that are as circular as those proposed by Lazarus. Objects compose Hobfoll's first category of resources (e.g., gold); while the physical properties of gold can be objectively measured, its psychological characteristics, such as its reinforcement value, still depend on the appraisal of an individual.

Unresolved Dilemmas.   Lazarus (1991) and other psychologists concerned with stress have replaced Selye's original, all-embracing construct of stress and now make separate references to physiological, psychological, and social stresses. As noted previously, the problem with this trichotomy is that there are many stimuli in the environment that induce disequilibria on several levels, or an initial disequilibrium on one level generalizes to another level; for example, loss of a loved one, which first induces loneliness, may later affect health or finances. In many in-

stances, individuals actually seek to engage in activities that are pleasurable, and experience emotional or psychological satisfaction, yet
these activities may have deleterious physiological consequences, such
as use of some recreational drugs. Thus, many environmental inputs
may have different consequences for psychological and physiological
equilibria. Limiting measurements to the psychological domain, for example, may be inadequate, since the initial psychological effect may trigger physiological changes that will alter the initial psychological effects.

It is noteworthy that, initially, Selye (1956, pp. 37–39) also strug-
gled with the semantics of his concept. Trumbull and Appley (1986)
tried to introduce some "objectivity" in assessing the antecedents of
stress without jettisoning the perceptual factor. They proposed that
stress may be the result of taking into account "real" as well as perceived demands and capacities, though how this can be accomplished
was not spelled out. For Lazarus, personality may be at times an antecedent variable, and at other times a consequence (Lazarus, 1991, p.
204). Such a viewpoint has also been recently championed by Magnusson and Törestad (1993). They bemoan the dominance of a Newtonian,
mechanistic, unidirectional causality stumulus–response model of personality, and they favor instead a dynamic holistic model. Lazarus's approach is in this mold, in contrast to that of his critics, primarily Costa
and McCrea (1990), who are at forefront of reenergizing a trait approach
to personality that was somewhat neglected by the "situationists" during the past few decades (Wiggins & Pincus, 1992). Situationists downplayed the role of traits and focused on the situation as the primary
determiner of behavior. Most typically, however, there are few, if any,
measurements of the conditions preceding a stress. Since most stressors
are the result of real-life situations and for ethical reasons we cannot realistically simulate stress in the laboratory, the meaning of many personality indices is difficult to interpret.

In a thoughtful analysis of the definitional quagmire, Pearlin (1982)
recommended that the concept of stress be retained even though it may
involve different phenomena on the biological, psychological, and social
levels. One possible solution may be to examine what, if any, relationships exist between sundry physiological, psychological, and social measures associated with various environmental conditions that by various
definitions have been labeled stressors. Included under this label are also
various life events, such as marriage, retirement, and what others have
called life crises. In most situations, however, it is difficult to disentangle
biological from psychosocial and economic variables in stress.

The extent to which different kinds of stressors are autonomous or
interdependent is not clear. The issue of autonomy of psychological, so-

cial, and cultural variables relates to a fundamental definitional problem of various psychological and sociological concepts, such as emotions, motivation, stress, and their extensions to the modern constructs
of psychosomatic and somatopsychic illnesses. Most critiques of psychological models of stress have raised metapsychological issues about
the constructs. Whether such concerns are justified seems to be an empirical question. Rakover (1992) believes that there is no adequate solution of this problem, and previous psychological research programs in
which it was of central concern, such as structuralism or neobehaviorism, failed.

AGING AND STRESS

If psychological stress occurs whenever the organism is faced with
any demand, or at least, according to many in the field (Hobfoll, 1989;
Holroyd & Lazarus, 1982), with demands that tax or exceed the individual's resources, and aging is associated with a loss of biological, psychological, social, and economic resources, then all of these changes
imply that the whole area of gerontology—from the biochemical substrates of an aging individual to the economic spheres in which he or
she exists—may be analyzed as the organism's responses to stress. From
a biological viewpoint, it has been postulated that the various subsys-
tems of the organism show a certain degree of autonomy of function, but
with aging, some degree of this autonomy declines (Yates & Benton,
1995). Aging, therefore, results in some dynamic instability that increases the susceptibility of the organism to even moderate external or
internal stressors (Schroots & Birren, 1990). Some indirect evidence for
this hypothesis is seen in the disruption of various structures controlling diurnal rhythms (Richardson, 1990). Older persons are afflicted by
various bodily disabilities that ipso facto may be biological stressors.

But, some psychologists and sociologists dispute the stressfulness
of old age (Ruth & Coleman, 1996). According to Tornstam (1992), the
assumed negative consequences of aging can be ascribed to Western society's values after the Reformation; following this historical period,
work and productivity became the measures of life satisfaction and,
thus, of equilibrium. Currently, in Western societies there has been a
shift away from the work ethic, with evidence based primarily on some
studies in Sweden and other developed countries in which older people
do not report lowered global life satisfaction after retirement. Focusing
on only one potential stressor, such as employment, produces an incomplete picture.

Zautra, Affleck, and Tennen (1994) discuss some of the difficulties in the definitions of life events that induce stress in an older population. A person with a demanding job and a good pension plan may perceive little stress following retirement, whereas for that same individual, the loss of a spouse may be highly stressful. The stress resulting from widowhood may be influenced by the previous caregiving situation: A person who had a long period of caregiving may experience much less stress than a widow who never had any caregiving responsibilities and whose husband died suddenly; indeed, the long-term caregiver may experience relief at the death of her spouse.

Stresses are domain-specific, and it is difficult to assert that old age is a nonstressful period of life, since there is no denying that aging is usually associated with decreases in health, including various disabilities, financial constraints, and increases in the mortality of spouses and other attachments. Discussions concerning the relative stressfulness of aging again highlight the problem of separating physiological and psychological stresses.

We have previously noted that interindividual differences in general tend to increase with age; this is also apparent in stress responses in young people because of large individual differences in personality, constitution, available physical and psychological resources (including social supports), past experiences, and perception of the situation, all of which determine responses or coping strategies. The heterogeneity in responsivity becomes more pronounced with increasing age. Thus, research on stress and aging is even more problematic than that on other aging phenomena (Lazarus & DeLongis, 1983). Eisdorfer and Wilkie (1977) discussed some of the methodological issues in stress-related research with older individuals, stating that "age is generally assumed to play an important role in determining how a person reacts to stressors, but the parameters and mechanisms are not clear" (p. 254). Chronic illnesses and diseases are more common in older people and may be the stressors affecting various behavioral responses, the consequence of stress, or they may interact with some other stressors. An analysis of stress may, therefore, be more important in gerontology than in studies of the earlier stages of the life span. We review some of the extant data, beginning with biological effects that usually are associated with stress, and then examine some of the behavioral consequences seen in older individuals. Etiologies of the various stress-associated diseases during aging are not dealt with specifically, since that might entail a large chunk of geriatric medicine as well as an assumption that there is a direct link between stress and illness, a hypothesis that is not universally accepted (Watson & Pennebacker, 1989). Some of the biological phenomena associated with stress have been reviewed previously in the section on normative energy changes during aging. However, behavioral data were not discussed.

CLASSIFICATIONS AND MEASUREMENT

Classification

As is true of many behavioral constructs in the analysis of stress, we may use a variety of classificatory schemas based on the magnitude, quality, or temporal dimensions of the phenomenon. The latter include the duration of the stressor, the time after the stressor impacts on the person in whom the consequences—stress—appear, and the interposition of other stressors between the event and the measurement of the original event.

There are no widely accepted general behavioral taxonomies, and this also applies to stressors. Many studies and the resultant model incorporated data implying that chronic stressors interact or add to the existing stress (Fry, 1989b; Kanner et al., 1981; Pearlin et al., 1996; Russell & Cutrona, 1991). Even laboratory studies in which participants are required to perform simple tasks may involve an interaction of stressors. When a participant is experiencing stress at home, as a caretaker for a sick elderly person, for example, it may affect his or her laboratory performance. Usually, experimenters do not inquire about such extralaboratory stresses. Or the experience of a hassle from a traffic jam may be influenced by the chronic stress the person may be experiencing in his or her marriage.

H. Weiner (1992, pp. 36–37) uses three categories of events that induce stress: (1) natural occurrences and disasters (epidemics, snowstorms, tornadoes); (2) man-made disasters (deteriorating neighborhood, war); and (3) personal and individual experiences (bereavement, divorce, injury, retirement). These categories are descriptive, and they are primarily illustrations of the great variety of situations that can give rise to stresses. Some are expected, and a person can make preparations to respond to them, as in retirement, while others are unexpected, such as an earthquake; some are shared with other persons, as in a snowstorm during which social supports may be present, while others affect only one person at a given time.

Another classification based on the potential seriousness, both qualitative and temporal, of the situation was proposed by Chiriboga (1992). He differentiated (1) microlevel stressors (e.g., mislaying a social security check, being caught in a traffic jam); (2) mezzolevel stressors (e.g., divorce, bereavement), and 3) macrolevel stressors (e.g., war or economic recession). His classification relates to several other systems that have been discussed previously: microlevel stressors are similar to Lazarus and Folkman's (1984) concept of hassles; mezzolevel stressors correspond to the life events initially investigated by Holmes and Rahe (1967). Finally, it should be noted that in psychogerontological research, little attention has been given specifically to macrolevel stressors, though they have usually been investigated implicitly when cohort effects were analyzed. Studies such as those of Elder (1974) on the depression cohort did, however, examine macrolevel stressors. Moos and Swindle (199a) point out the importance of chronic long-term stressors, such as physical ailments or poverty that may frequently be at the root of the problems associated with life events, such as a sudden, acute health crisis.

Aged individuals, especially, are more likely to experience chronic rather than acute life events labeled as stressors. Wheaton (1996) combined temporal and quantitative dimensions in distinguishing six different types of stressors: (1) life events that usually are self-limiting; (2) chronic stressors; (3) daily hassles; (4) macro or systems stressors; (5) nonevents, when anticipated pleasant events do not happen; and (6) traumas, such as a major fire or sexual abuse during childhood. The main characteristic in the last category is the overwhelming impact of the event. There is a considerable overlap between the various schemas that have been proposed. The problem with all of these classifications is the difficulty of disaggregating various stressors. The absence of a satisfactory schema for classifying stressors makes generalizations very difficult and necessitates analyzing each type separately.

Measurement of Stressors

In general, we have relatively few problems in identifying biological stressors: There are normative data on environmental temperatures, noise levels, infectious agents, and sleep deprivation that commonly induce stress. In contrast, it is difficult to identify and measure psychosocial stressors, and the absence of a satisfactory classificatory system precludes the development of a meaningful metric. As in other areas of psychology, laboratory studies have been used as analogs of real-life stresses, but here, too, comparisons are tenuous. Requesting that a study participant perform a difficult task may be viewed as a stressor. However, at what level of difficulty does the task become a stressor?

Differences between various types of stressors, discussed previously, will lead to different methods of assessment, and the technique used reflects a certain theoretical orientation. An early but still widely used scale by Holmes and Rahe (1967), the Social Readjustment Rating Scale (SSRS), consisted of checklist of 43 various life events, such as death of a spouse, loss of a job, or marriage. The SSRS was standardized on a young population. Each event was weighted so that death of spouse was assigned 100 points, retirement 45, and so forth. The greater the number and importance of these life events, the latter determined from normative samples, presumably, the greater the degree of "stress." The total "stress" was based on the sum of the individual items. Several similar life-inventory scales were constructed later; some were even standardized on older people (Amster & Krauss, 1974; Plomin, Lichtenstein, Pedersen, McClearn, & Nesselroade, 1990). There have been numerous challenges to this approach. First, it is not practical to construct a list that includes most stressful life events, including, for example, previous abuses by a spouse or employer, or estrangement from a child; such an extensive questionnaire would exhaust the attention span of a responder. Second, the stress induced by the various items requiring readjustments is subject to cultural changes over time. For example, as the number of divorces has increased in our society, along with the expectation that this might occur, the stress induced by this event may have diminished. Clipp and Elder (1996) report that in one cross-sectional comparison of veterans of World War II, the Korean War, and the Vietnam War, there were significantly fewer cases of the posttraumatic stress disorder in the World War II group than in the later veteran groups. One possible explanation that the authors offer is that in previous generations, soldiers either would not admit having psychological disorders or the symptoms of stress were expressed somatically. Third, the context of the situation affects the experience of the stressor. The impact of fasting in order to reduce weight is different from fasting when a person has no food. Fourth, some of the items in the checklist of events that have been used to measure stress are confounded; for example, a physical illness is listed as a stressor, but it may be the consequence. Finally, individual events may not be discrete: Losing a job may lead to a divorce, or previous illnesses may be superimposed on more recent disabilities.

Turner and Wheaton (1995) reviewed the literature and included a bibliography of various life-event inventories, including several for older persons. An alternative technique is to use interviews that permit probing the severity of a specific event and including of unique stressors. Several standardized interview measures of life events have been developed (Wethington, Brown, & Kessler, 1995), but this technique is also subject to a variety of measurement problems.

While most life events recorded by checklists occur infrequently, the measurement of common, relatively minor, everyday stressors was developed by Lazarus and his students. Based on Lazarus's theory, it measures the *perceived* stressfulness associated with common everyday occurrences, hassles, and positive events or uplifts (Kanner *et al.*, 1981); the focus is on the perception or interpretation of an event. Death of a spouse receives a high stress score on the SRSS, but according to Lazarus, the amount of stress depends on the surviving spouse's perception of the event: The stress following the sudden death of a presumably healthy person is usually much greater than the passing of a chronically ill person who has been suffering for years.

The Hassles Scale consists of 117 items measuring commonly occurring, everyday annoyances such as as misplacing something, the arrival of unexpected company, or not having sufficient time for family. Items measuring uplifts include receiving compliments and a child showing some developmental progress. In an initial study with adults ages 45–64 years, DeLongis, Coyne, Dakof, Folkman, and Lazarus (1982) found that the Hassles Scale correlated significantly with self-ratings of overall health, somatic symptoms, and self-rated energy levels (being worn out at the end of the day or feeling lassitude), as well as a measure of major life events. The correlations, however, were modest, in the .2–.3 range. Numerous studies on various older populations have used some versions of the SSRS and the Hassles Scale or only one of these scales and related them/it to diverse measures of mental and/or physical health. It should be noted that the Hassles Scale and several related instruments were not standardized on older people. Landreville and Vezina (1992) obtained data from 200 community-dwelling volunteers ages 55 years and older on a revised version of the SSRS and a Hassles Scale similar to that used by Kanner *et al.* (1981), but items that physicians and psychologists rated as being possible symptoms of physical or psychological disabilities were not included in the scale. The participants also responded to a checklist of specific physical ailments, an overall assessment of their health and psychological well-being. In a multiple regression analysis, 49% of the variance of physical well-being was attributable to hassles, self-rated health, and limitations of activity. Life events over a 3-year period did not predict physical well-being. Psychological well-being was best predicted by daily hassles and age, and the correlation between frequency of daily hassles and life events was only .23. Most studies found that several variants of the SSRS and Hassles Scale are related to health, though the two types seem to measure different kinds of stress. The Hassles Scale seems to predict more labile indicators of stress (Aldwin, Levenson, Spiro, & Bosse, 1989). Beginning with the initial study by DeLongis *et al.* (1982), most researchers have reported, not surprisingly, that major life events influence daily hassles (Aldwin *et al.*, 1989; Chamberlain & Zika, 1990; Fry, 1989a), though as Landreville and Vezina (1992) reported, the correlations between the scales may be low; much depends on the specific contents of the scales. With refinements in the Hassles Scale and the use of older samples than in the original standardization study of Delongis *et al.* (1982), in which data from 45- to 64-year-old adults were used, the relationship between measures of hassles and life events was reported to be higher. For example, Aldwin *et al.*, (1989) reported an *r* of .43 between life events and hassles, Russell and Cutrona (1991) obtained an *r* of .54, and Fry (1989b), an *r* of .42. These represent modest relationships that seem to indicate the interaction of stressors (i.e., persons experiencing stress from life events are more likely to perceive hassles than those without major stressful life events). These findings support Pearlin *et al.*'s (1996) contention that stressors proliferate. It is also the application of the classical frustration–aggression hypothesis (Dollard, Doob, Miller, Mowrer, & Sears, 1939) that several aversive stimuli may have an additive effect. Finally, it is the "rediscovery" of the common-sense folk psychology wisdom that it is "the last straw that broke the camels back."

Most of the early stress research has been cross-sectional studies in which data were obtained on individuals who had experienced various major life events, such as retirement, residential relocation, hospitalization, or death in the immediate family. Lazarus and DeLongis (1983) reviewed briefly the conceptual problems of many of these studies. Aside from the difficulties that plague many cross-sectional studies, most of the research did not take into account the presence of small hassles that may exacerbate or interact with major life events, variations in coping styles, and more importantly, there were no data on neuroticism, which, according to Costa and McCrea (1990), can confound the measures of distress, the consequences of the stressor. Since data in a number of these studies were collected retrospectively, there was a reliance on the recall of the respondents. While the accuracy of factual questionnaire and interview data obtained from older community-dwelling residents in one study did not differ from that of younger respondents (Rodgers & Herzog, 1987), the information obtained did not deal with emotion-arousing items and events; we do not know whether there is interaction between age and the recall of emotion-arousing information. There is also a more serious methodological problem in cross-sectional studies that results from the more frequent reporting of stressful life events and daily hassles by persons who have high scores on tests of emotionality (Aldwin *et al.,* 1989). Do people who have high scores on measures of emotionality report or experience more symptoms of stress, or do stressful life events lead to greater emotionality?

Measurement of Stress Outcomes

Determining whether the consequences of stress are the result of biological or psychosocial stressors is frequently difficult. With acute, time-limited stressors, especially in the laboratory, we may employ a variety of standard biological or psychological tests ranging from measurement of hormones, CV indices, and immune indicators, to performance on a variety of standard psychological tests. With chronic stresses, we have an armamentarium of standard medical and clinical psychological instruments, the latter including self-report questionnaires. Other techniques that have been used include interviews, judgments of informants, and naturalistic observations (Lepore, 1995).

BIOLOGICAL EFFECTS

In Chapter 2, we reviewed various age-associated changes, primarily under normal conditions, in a number of biological systems that have been traditionally linked to behavior, including stressors. There have been some discrepancies in the results, probably due to the increased intra- and interindividual variabilities with age. We do not repeat here the previous material except for comments that may clarify some subsequent discussions of stress. With our primary emphasis on psychological stressors, we have to omit thermogenic, immune, and other important biological stressors.

ANS Studies of the Autonomic Nervous System in the Laboratory

Cannon (1915), in his Chapter 1 (pp. 1–2), specifically states that "biology has contributed much to clarify our ideas regarding the motives [*sic*] of human behavior." Later Cannon (cited by Shock, 1977), applied his concept of changes in homeostasis due to aging. The role of the visceral nerves (ANS) is treated almost from the beginning of his monograph. Measuring changes in ANS-innervated systems during mental work, *stress*, dates back to the early part of this century (Woodworth, 1938, pp. 257–297). The extent to which laboratory studies may serve as analogs of real-life stress is difficult to ascertain. Lacey (1967) and others have emphasized that ANS responses to a stimulus are fractionated; that is, different peripheral and central indices of ANS activity will not necessarily be correlated when the organism responds to different stimuli. Lacey (1967) and Lacey and Lacey (1970) originated the concept of "situational stereotypy," which implies that for different stimuli, the pattern of ANS responses will vary. Since with increasing age the different organs innervated by the ANS show differential pathology, situational stereotypy may be altered (Frolkis, 1977). Thus, the correlations between several ANS indices in different situations may be different for old compared to young individuals, and the correlations between ANS indices and performance measures in different situations may be affected by the age variable.

In the 1977 *Handbook of the Psychology of Aging,* Marsh and Thompson reviewed studies that attempted to compare ANS reactivity in young and old participants during the performance of various laboratory tasks. Different studies employed different peripheral indices of ANS activity. As mentioned earlier, the correlations between some peripheral indices of ANS are low. In most studies, older persons showed less ANS activity during the performance of the tasks than did younger persons. Eisdorfer (1967, 1968) and his colleagues, on the other hand, using the amount of free fatty acid in the blood, which can be used as an indicator of ANS activity, reported that older persons exhibit increased ANS activation, relating this finding to increased anxiety of older participants to laboratory tasks commonly performed by college students. According to Marsh and Thompson's review (1977), it has been difficult to replicate Eisdorfer's (1968) results; however, the characteristic of the participants, such as previous life experiences or present stressors, differences in the ANS measures, and task factors, may have contributed to the discrepancies in the findings.

Since the Marsh and Thompson (1977) review, several additional studies have appeared in which ANS measures were obtained during the performance of laboratory tasks. Furchtgott and Busemeyer (1979) found that heart rate (HR) changes during the performance of mental arithmetic problems were greater in young (ages 23–39 years) than in old (ages 60–87 years) individuals. Initial electrodermal response levels (EDR) were higher for young than for old participants, but during the performance of the task, there were no group differences. In a second task requiring free recall of 12 common words, the older individuals

showed a smaller increase in HR and EDR than did the younger participants; however, it took the older persons a longer time than the
younger persons to return to baseline levels after completion of the task.
It was also noted that the correlations between HR and EDR changes in
both tasks were very low, not statistically significant; thus, it is apparent that the two indices cannot be used interchangeably. But the HR and
EDR changes during the performance of the arithmetic task and recall
were more similar in young than in old participants, supporting Frolkis's (1977) theory, and suggesting that ANS activation across different
tasks, at least for the two types used in the study, is less similar in old
than in young persons. Smaller HR increases in older persons during
arithmetic calculations were also reported by Barnes, Raskind, Gumbrecht, and Halter (1982). In another study, Powell, Milligan, and
Furchtgott (1980) measured HR, BP, and EDR in young and older men
during reaction time (RT) and serial verbal learning tasks. There were
no significant HR changes in, group during the RT or the learning task.
The EDR changes were significantly lower during both tasks in the old
than in the young group; no significant BP changes occurred in either
age group during the RT performance. There were, however, BP age differences during serial learning tasks. Two different learning tasks were
used: in one, the stimuli were presented for 10 seconds each, a slow-
paced, easier task, while in the other the stimuli were presented for 4
seconds each, a faster-paced, more difficult task. Comparing systolic BP
(SBP) measured immediately before the learning performance with the
measurement after task completion showed that the changes on the
faster-paced, more difficult task were of the same magnitude in the two
age groups. However, on the easy task, the old group showed an increase in SBP from before to after task performance, while for the young
group there was a decrease in measurements from before to after performance. Diastolic BP (DBP) showed no performance-related changes.
In the old, but not in the young group, increases in SBP were related to
better learning performance, fewer trials to a criterion, and fewer errors
on the more difficult 10-second exposure task. As in the Furchtgott and
Busemeyer (1979) study, there were no significant correlations between
BP, HR, and EDR. It should also be noted that in this study, BP measurements were taken after the completion of the tasks, and the higher
SBP seen in the older group may have reflected a slower return to baseline. Another factor that differentiated the Furchtgott and Busemeyer
(1979) from the Powell *et al.* (1980) study was that in the former study,
the persons were primarily professionals or retired professionals who
had much experience as participants in similar studies, while in the latter study, the mean educational level was less than 12 years of com-

pleted schooling and the participants were laboratory-naive. Naliboff *et al.* (1991) tested older (ages 65+yrs) and younger women (ages 21–41 years) on arithmetic tasks in which they were either instructed ("stressed") to perform as fast as they could or were asked to perform under baseline conditions. The older participants showed lower HR and EDR responses and lower reactivity of natural killer (NK) lymphocytes to the stress condition. While the nature of the tasks, previous experiences with similar problems, and the indices used in the different studies varied, none of the studies supported Eisdorfer's hypothesis (1967) that cognitive performance deficits seen in the laboratory in older individuals are attributable to a large extent to increased anxiety, at least not to increases in HR, BP, or EDR.

In a series of studies, Faucheux and coworkers studied HR reactivity, catecholamine secretion, and behavioral indices of anxiety in older men. In an earlier study (Faucheux, Dupuis, Baulon, Lille, & Bourlièr, 1983), participants ages 51–55 years and 71–75 years were tested before, during, and after performance on visual and auditory memory tests, the Stroop colored word test, and a digit coding task. These data, basically, were similar to those of Furchtgott and Busemeyer (1979). In a later study, Faucheux, Lille, Baulon, Landau, *et al.* (1989) included women and extended the age range (18–73 years) in measuring HR and BP during and after the performance of several mental tasks such as visuospatial analysis of geometric figures and several arithmetic tasks. Again, HR reactivity was significantly lower in the older persons during the performance of these tasks, and recovery to the baseline was slower. Similar findings also occurred in measuring diastolic BP (DBP). Ditto, Miller, and Maurice (1987) tested women ages 17–28 years and 60–96 years while they were performing a mental arithmetic task and when they were exposed to anxiety and anger-inducing imagery. The older women showed a smaller rise in HR, but the BP changes were not affected by age. For the different tasks, the older women showed greater consistency in their BP and HR reactivity than the younger women. Similar results on age comparisons in ANS resposivity during mental tasks were also reported by Gintner, Hollandsworth, and Intrieri (1986).

Jennings, Nebes, and Yovetich (1990) obtained several CV measures during the maintenance of episodic memory for series of seven integers and in a visual RT task in 18 community-dwelling men ages 60–79 years and in 18 young male college students. Data were obtained on both the maintenance of memory and the RT task presented separately. Since it has been well established that on a 7-item serial memory task, age differences are small, a more difficult dual-task paradigm was also tested. Here, the presentation of the stimuli to be remembered were interspersed with a visual RT task. The stimuli to which the participant had to respond appeared randomly either before or after the presentation of integers that had to be maintained in memory; since both memory maintenance and RT performance require CV activation, the differences between the single and the more demanding dual task's allocation of peripheral CV resources were compared in young and old individuals. Good performance on both tasks resulted in monetary rewards whenever a predetermined level of performance was exceeded. During the dual-task procedure the rewards for the memory task were greater than for the RT task. Thus, it was hoped that the memory task would be the focus of attention rather than the RT task. On the single RT task, there was no difference between the young and old in the speed of responses, but on the single memory task, the proportion of correct responses was higher in the young than in the older participants. In the dual-task situation, RTs were significantly slower in the old than the young, but the proportion of recalled correct integers did not change from the single-task condition. The CV measures included HR, SBP, DBP, pulse transit times in the thumb and chest, pulse wave velocity (PWV), maximum SBP slope in the thumb and chest, and pulse amplitude on the chest. During the single-task performances, HR did not differ between young and old participants, but pulse transit time measured in both the thumb and the chest was shorter and PWV was longer in the older participants. During the dual-task tests, the older participants exhibited higher HR than did the young, presumably because of a greater memory load, but PWV did not produce any differential effects. The slope of the chest impedance measure was influenced more by memory load in the old. The authors hypothesized that the dual task required greater "resource allocation" for memory maintenance, inducing greater cardiac acceleration due to vagal inhibition and peripheral sympathetic activation in the old participants. This was verified for some of the indices (e.g., HR), but not for some of the other measures such as pulse transit time or PWV. In summary, the authors suggested that in aged individuals, the ability to maintain items in memory tends to decline and the organism compensates for this potential reduction by increasing CV activation, especially when the task demands are high, such as in a dual-task situation. A major difficulty with this study was that in the dual-task situation, the organism's physiological activation for the perceptual readiness needed for the RT task might have interfered with the physiological processes required for the maintenance of memory.

Levenson, Carstensen, Friesen, and Ekman (1991) asked participants in a laboratory to produce facial muscle configurations commonly found in various emotional states without telling them what each configuration represented. Next, they were asked to relive various situations that usually induce stress and emotions, such as death of a loved one, anticipating injury, or an unexpected event, while the participants' HR, EDR, finger temperature, and general somatic activity were recorded. At the conclusion, participants were also asked for self-reports of their emotional experiences during the experiment. Participants ages 18–30 and 70–83 years were compared; ANS patterns associated with somatic, emotion-specific activities in the older persons were similar to those found in the younger participants. However, the magnitude of the ANS changes was much smaller in the older sample, and somatic activity associated with fear was less in the older persons. The authors speculate that younger people respond with "flight" during fear, while older people "freeze." Older women reported stronger emotional experiences when reliving past emotional situations than did older men. While the "flight"–"freeze" change with age is plausible, a more parsimonious explanation for the smaller ANS reactivity is the usually observed lowered ANS reactivity in old persons (Faucheux *et al.*, 1983; Furchtgott & Busemeyer, 1979; Naliboff *et. al.*, 1991).

Data are available on a series of studies on HR and some on respiration changes by Swedish investigators. In one study, Molander and Bäckman (1989) measured HR and self-rated anxiety in young (ages 22–36 years) and middle-aged (ages 47–58 years) highly skilled miniature golf players in a laboratory containing a 10-hole course. Data were obtained during a training round and three competitive rounds arranged separately for the two age groups, with monetary awards for the three top players in both age groups. After completing half a round, five holes, of each game, players also rated their anxiety level, but no feedback was given about their HR. Overall, both age groups increased their HR and anxiety ratings from the training to the competition situation about equally. The performance data, however, show that the young group improved its performance from training to the competitive situation, while the trend for the older group was just the opposite. Unfortunately, no basal pretraining and precompetition HR data were presented. Molander and Bäckman also reported HR data obtained during the concentration phase for the first shot at each of the 10 holes, from 3 seconds before the start of concentration to 3 seconds after the end of this phase. The results indicated that during the concentration phases of the training period, the younger players decreased their HR, while the older players increased theirs. During competition, the younger players again showed large decreases in their HR, while the older players' HRs were flat. For the younger group, the decrements during the concentration phases were greater during competition than during training. Concentration times for the first shots for each hole (track) tended to be shorter for the older players, both during training and during competition. Since older persons require more time to return to a baseline level of HR, the shorter concentration times of the older players may have been exacerbated by a lack of recovery from the activity of the previous hole to the beginning of the concentration phase for the next hole. The HR changes were independent of respiratory changes during concentration. The authors hypothesize that older players show decrements in attentional activity, since it is usually assumed, at least in young persons, that attention to external stimuli produces HR reductions (Lacey & Lacey, 1970). The decreases in attention were the result of high arousal or anxiety, especially in the competitive situation, which was manifested by the older players in their higher scores and ratings of anxiety. It is noteworthy that there was no significant interaction between age and either HR or rated anxiety. The increases in HR and anxiety from the training sessions to competition were similar in the old and in the young.

In another ecologically realistic study during Swedish national competition tournaments (Bäckman & Molander, 1991), HR increases from training to competition were similar in the young and old players, as was rated anxiety. According to Molander and Bäckman, the rise in anxiety is an attempt by the older players to overcompensate for their perceived losses in cognitive abilities, by focusing less on external and more on internal cues. It is unfortunate that there were no initial HR data, which should be used as the baseline from which change scores could be computed. Also, however, an overarousal hypothesis might be tenable if we assume that the poorer performance of the older players, evident from their awareness of what their scores were, may have induced the higher anxieties in the older players. We should note that the mean age of the older group was only 55 years and the oldest player was 70. Did these persons perceive themselves to be able to play as well as they did at an earlier age (they were all highly skilled, "the best" players in their age group) and were they participants in an experiment in which they felt perhaps that they had to demonstrate that they have not "lost it" as yet? Such a hypothesis places the emphasis on a person's expectations and knowledge of outcomes as the source of high anxiety. The authors also noted that the older players had greater intra- and interindividual variabilities in HRs. These increases in variabilities are commonly found in older persons and reflect differences in health, experience, expectations, and other developmental changes that increase with age between individuals (Dannefer, 1988a, 1988b; Lipsitz, 1989). With small samples of 6 males per age group, now extended from 15 to

73 years, Molander and Bäckman (1994) again measured performance, HR, and self-rated anxiety during training and competition in a miniature golf laboratory. The age-related effects were similar to those reported previously; differences in HR were similar in 50–57 and 58–73 year age groups, and older performers had lower maximal values.

Several studies have examined the effects of life stresses on laboratory performance. Uchino, Kiecolt-Glaser, and Cacioppo (1992) measured CV changes in the laboratory in family caregivers of SDAT patients and in age-matched controls. The age range of both male and female participants was 30–84 years; for purposes of data analysis, the participants were split at the median age of 63.5 years. The older caregivers were mostly spouses of the patients, while the younger caregivers were mostly children. In the laboratory, each participant performed three brief, successive mental subtraction tasks; then, in a structured interview, social support data were also obtained. Older caregivers with high levels of social support showed typical decreases in HR reactivity from task to task, while the older participants with low social support showed increases indicative of a high level of arousal during the laboratory chores. SBP was also elevated in the older group with low social support. This study with a small sample size would indicate that social support may moderate the effects of laboratory stress on the cardiovascular functions in older individuals who are experiencing chronic stress as caregivers. As the authors noted, the difference in the kinship relationships of the younger and old caregivers may also have affected the result; an additional age-matched control group that did not include caregivers would have provided additional information pertaining to Pearlin *et al.*'s (1996) concept of primary and secondary stressors. Nevertheless, this study on the influence on laboratory performance of older people experiencing common, real-life chronic stress serves as a useful model for research on stress.

There have been several other studies of laboratory stressors in which the role of psychosocial factors in older SDAT caregivers was examined. Age was usually not a variable in these studies, since the caregivers typically were older spouses. We briefly note some of the findings: Vitaliano, Russo, Bailey, Young, and McCann (1993) used two laboratory tasks in measuring CV reactivity in older spousal SDAT caregivers and in matched controls; in one task, the participant had to give a 5-minute uninterrupted talk about the type of person his or her spouse was; this was assumed to be an emotion-arousing task. The other task was a digit symbol substitution task from the Wechsler Intelligence scale, a standard, age-sensitive cognitive task. The caregivers were more reactive than the controls only if they were hypertensives, and this manifested itself primarily in SBP reactivity in the emotionally arousing task. Recovery after the latter task was slower than after the cognitive task. Several psychological and sociological variables (e.g., anxiety, expression of anger, gender, and obesity) also contributed significantly to the variance in the recovery compared to the baselines on all CV variables. Interestingly, being a caregiver did not differentiate the groups in reactivity or recovery to baseline.

Conclusions

We discussed several diverse studies in which ANS data were obtained following exposure to various laboratory stressors, since it is frequently assumed that stress leads to disturbances of various internal organs innervated by the ANS. Granted, the stimuli in the laboratory may not have been perceived to be stressors by many of the participants in the experiments, but ethics puts a restraint on the kinds of studies we can conduct. Except for the early Eisdorfer studies (Marsh & Thompson, 1977), which lacked some important controls and could not be replicated, only Molander and Bäckman (1989, 1994) and Bäckman and Molander (1991) found increases in HR, the most widely used peripheral index, in laboratory studies, but they used motor tasks, which may produce a greater stress on the CV system than verbal tasks; all other studies reported decreased HR reactivity. Other peripheral ANS measures also have been reported either to show decreased reactivity in older persons or no differences compared to younger persons. It is plausible that older individuals exert less effort, a concept implying lower motivation or expectations (Mulder, 1986) in most laboratory studies. Examination of studies using different incentives in the laboratory or measuring the impacts of real environmental stressors may shed more light on the effects of age on stress. The Jennings *et al.* (1990) study also supports the theory that older individuals may not exhibit behavioral decrements in some situations, but with increased task difficulty or greater expectations of success, they exhibit increased cardiovascular activation to compensate for the usual behavioral and/or cognitive decrements.

The study by Uchino *et al.* (1992) seems to show that another factor, low social support in individuals experiencing chronic stress outside the laboratory, may affect HR responsivity during experiments. Though it may be difficult to determine the various nonlaboratory stressors the participant is experiencing at the time of the experiment, some effort could be made to obtain at least some information concerning such factors.

PSYCHOLOGICAL EFFECTS

In most psychological theories of stress, it is postulated that the consequences include changes in ongoing behavior or performance. Under naturalistic conditions, we frequently infer the presence of stress from behavioral changes, deviations from normative ongoing activities, without examining physiological indices. Can this be accomplished with laboratory stressors? To measure behavioral responses to stressors requires less elaborate instrumentation than for physiological changes and should, therefore, be more readily testable in the laboratory. Parenthetically, it is only for heuristic purposes and primarily on the basis of traditional methodological characteristics that we differentiate physiological and psychological indices.

Since performance changes with aging are affected by numerous cognitive, motor, and sensory factors, pragmatically, it is not easy to determine the roles that stress or motivation play in the analysis of most complex behaviors in the laboratory, where we cannot induce harm to a participant. Indeed, physiological indices, which we have reviewed previously, have been used to infer effort or motivation. At the present, cognitive theory predominates in the analysis of human experimental laboratory geropsychology. Salthouse (1991, pp. 182–184) states in his review that we have no "objective and direct methods for assessing motivation in cognitive testing situations," concluding that there is little evidence that lower levels of motivation of older adults are responsible for their relatively poor performance on cognitive tests; however, he does not specifically state that potential motivational changes do not contribute to performance deficits. Our analysis will be limited to studies in which there were psychological measures of older and younger persons who were subjected to similar types of psychological stressors. Before examining some ecologically valid "real-life" stressors (Chapter 10), we review the very few laboratory studies in which the experimenters induced conditions that presumably induced stress and in which both younger and older participants were tested.

Except for studies of attitudes that are the consequence of real-life experiences, the literature on stress and coping of older persons in laboratory situations is sparse. Ethical constraints place limits on laboratory studies of stress. Also, as noted, it is impossible to delimit quantitatively the magnitude of the task that constitutes determining what is a stressor. Lazarus, one of the major figures in modern research on stress, though beginning his studies in the laboratory, gradually began to deemphasize this approach in favor of field research because of the importance of the psychosocial setting that plays a major role in stress (Holroyd & Lazarus, 1982).

Several studies have attempted to induce stress by manipulating the significance of a task through instructions. Ross (1968) compared paired associate learning in college students and older adults (ages 65–75 years) using "neutral," "supportive," or "challenging" instructions. While this manipulation did not affect younger learners, the older ones did worse with the challenging instructions than with the neutral ones and performed best when supportive instructions were given. Similar, though not statistically significant, performance decrements with reproof were also reported by Lair and Moon (1972) on a digit symbol substitution task. In a simple letter cancellation task, however, Levendusky (1978) found that older persons (mean age 75 years) improved their performance after reproof compared to a "no comment" condition. The enhanced performance could be attributed to the informational value of reproof, since the participants did not know how well they were performing compared to the others prior to the feedback. Another explanation advanced by the author was that the negative feedback led to a more effective performance strategy. Finally, it should be pointed out that Levendusky measured performance in a motor task, and the other two studies involved more complex cognitive processes. Hill and Vandervoort (1992) found that free recall was adversely affected by state anxiety in older adults. Since no young adults were tested in this study, it was not possible to determine whether the effect of anxiety on recall is greater in old than in young persons. Deptula, Sing, and Pomara (1993) addressed this issue in their study. They measured free recall in 45 young (mean age 26 years) and 45 healthy older (mean age 67 years) persons who had self-rated their anxiety, depression, and withdrawal levels. For the young participants, there were no relationships between the affective states and recall performance. For the older persons, there were significant negative correlations between recall and the level of each of the self-rated affective measures. However, anxiety contributed only 8% of the variance, depression 12%, and withdrawal 30%. Since the measured affective states occur in many older individuals, it would seem important to ascertain them in studies in which younger and older individuals are compared. Both over- and underarousal have been invoked to account for decreases with age in the detection accuracy of tasks requiring sustained attention (McDowd & Birren, 1990), but in the experiments cited, there were no concomitant measures of arousal. Actually, a global explanatory concept of arousal has been subjected to increasing criticisms and a call for its abandonment (Neiss, 1988). Neiss prefers an analysis of different psychobiological states in response to different environmental threats or incentives. Every psychobiological state manifests itself in discrete cognitive, affective, and physiological responses. Neiss's approach does not differ markedly from Lazarus's emphasis on the role of social, psychological, and physiological, processes based on the individual's previous experiences (Holroyd & Lazarus, 1982). Such a strategy, however, leads to an abandonment of a general concept of stress, since there would be little communality between the various environmental conditions that give rise to a diversity of physiological and behavioral reactions.

In conclusion the few cited studies point out some of the problems in identifying psychological stressors in the laboratory: What type of task, under what conditions (instructions, incentives, significance for the participant), and for what personality type, does it become a stressor?

Social Support

There are a number of moderators that affect stress. One of the most frequently studied factors has been the presence of social support. Antonucci (1990), in her review of the field notes, states that "social support is a multifaceted concept with many determinants and consequences" (p. 205); she prefers the term "social relations" or social ties, which usually includes linkages with family and friends, and religious and other community organizations. However, the nature of the ties is usually not well specified (Burke, 1991). For some researchers, the concept is redundant, if social supports also includes the availability of resources or services provided by another person, since, by definition, the absence of resources is usually defined as a stressor (Antonovsky, 1990; Hobfoll, 1989; Kasl, 1992).

We address primarily the motivational factors in social support. Most of the research in this field has had an applied orientation in which the motivational basis of the need for receiving support was not examined. Antonucci (1990) noted the general ignorance concerning the role of social relationships in well-being and in buffering the effect of stressors. There is probably a multiplicity of motives that account for the different facets of social support. Some classifications of social supports are based on the motives that are being satisfied.

Classifications.   There have been several ways of classifying social support. Schwarzer and Leppin (1991) differentiate between cognitive and behavioral supports, with the former emphasizing the receiver's *perception* of social relationships, while the latter emphasizes the tangible receipt of support. The two indices are probably measuring different aspects of social support (Schwarzer & Leppin, 1991). Another common motivational classification is in terms of the type of support that is received: (1) in instrumental support, the recipient obtains assistance with chores, financial aid, and ADLs; (2) in expressive or emotional support, the person obtains self-esteem by feeling that somebody cares, and is being reassured; (3) informational support may help the person understand the sources of stress and develop coping strategies (Schwarzer & Leppin, 1991). Many support activities may simultaneously fit into all of these categories.

Previously, we saw that even in laboratory studies, a participant who experiences stress at home benefits from having social support (Uchino et al., 1992). Social support seems to be especially important for older individuals, since, in many instances, it prevents or reduces stress, while the absence of such supports can have opposite effects.

The large number and types of stressors combined with the various types of social support requires a match between resources and stress (Taylor & Aspinwall, 1996). Specifically, it has been suggested that in some uncontrollable stressful events, emotional support may be more beneficial than instrumental supports; for example, frequently, following the sudden death of a financially secure person's spouse, emotional support is probably the most helpful form of support. The example also illustrates the specificity of the needed support. At other times, the widowed person also needs instrumental and informational support. Thus, we see the difficulty in the design of studies that can be broadly applied.

Formal and Informal Sources.   In the construct of social support, there have also been differentiations made between informal sources of support, networks of family and close friends, and formal sources of support, such as social organizations. Krause (1990a) found that the latter were more effective in buffering the effects of stress measured in terms of health problems than were informal sources of support. The distinction between formal and informal sources of support may, however, hinge on the amount and quality of resources provided by the two types of sources, respectively. In a national study of 16,148 elderly in the United States, the substitution of formal for informal support was less apparent in black than in white families (Miner, 1995). In many instances, the formal sources of support do provide more resources and may make available better information than family or friends. Pearlin et al. (1996) also reported that emotional support does not help with caregivers' secondary stresses associated with job problems.

The extent to which there is a need for formal versus informal support depends on both cultural (Fry, 1996), including racial (Miner, 1995), and cohort (demographic) factors (Bengtson, Rosenthal, & Burton, 1990). In many nonindustrialized societies, certain family members (e.g., the oldest son or an unmarried daughter) tend to be obligated to be caregivers to older parents. Even in the United States, until about the middle of the twentieth century, it was not uncommon for older unmarried women to be parental caregivers. Changes in life expectancies, the ratio of of older to younger family members, and various social programs influence family caregiver relationships.

Some Studies with Large Samples.   The large number of variables that affect the influence of social support on stress outcomes requires that we focus on a few illustrations involving large samples. Most of the research with older populations has been on the stress resulting from caregiving (Pearlin *et al.*, 1996) or from experiencing illness. Chapter 10 reviews the stress experienced by older caregivers and discusses the role of social support on the stress experienced by an older person.

Haug, Breslau, and Folmar (1989), based on a 9-year longitudinal study of 647 older individuals, concluded that the availability of social resources plays a more significant role in survival than does self-assessed emotional or mental health, or cognitive skills measured on the Pfeiffer scale. Russell and Cutrona (1991), in another longitudinal study of 301 community-dwelling older adults, found that deficits in social support increased depression and the likelihood of experiencing daily hassles. In a 22-month longitudinal study of frail, Medicaid-eligible elderly (mean age 78 years), Mor-Barak, Miller, and Syme (1991) found that during the first 6 months of the study, social networks significantly affected self-rated health and buffered the undesirable effects of life events; however, later measurements did not produce statistically significant differences. Thus, social supports not only reduced for a short period the stress of life events, but they also had a direct effect on health. Because of the large sample size (the initial N was >3000, consisting of a heterogeneous group of elderly), the variance attributed to social support was small though still statistically significant. The authors do not explain the temporary nature of the benefits. Since the individuals were initially in poor health, over time, their conditions probably deteriorated and the benefits of social support could not compensate for the physical changes. In addition, Pearlin *et al.* (1996), on the basis of their own study, indicate that the duration of the maximum effect of social support during stress is an important variable.

Intergenerational Exchanges. Dowd's (1975) sociological exchange theory postulates that people behave in a manner that results
in maximum rewards and minimum costs. The person whose resources and contributions to a relationship exceed receipts should
gain power, while the recipient loses power. Since older people frequently receive more than they contribute, they should experience a
loss of power or prestige. According to this theory social supports
should diminish during aging. However, Antonucci (1991) modified
the exchange concept by the use of a life-span view of relationships,
assuming that people may have made "sufficient deposits" into their
"Support Banks" during their productive years so that they will have
a reserve from which to draw upon as they age (p. 179). For example, a
parent may spend a considerable amount of resources to educate a
child, placing a deposit in a "Support Bank," and in turn may receive
support from the child when he or she is old. The authors presented
some data on American (black and white) and French families that revealed preliminary but limited support for their theory of reciprocity.
The unequal availability of resources among the older parents and
their adult children complicated the analyses of exchanges; in addition, cultural, ethnic, and lifetime experiential factors lead to very
complex relationships.

Another possible mechanism that may play a role in the receipt of
support is altruism. Traditionally, psychology and sociology have favored egoism as the preponderant human motive (Batson, 1991, Chapter 3), and this is the basis for exchange theory. During the last several
decades, however, altruism has started to influence some social psychologists (Batson, 1991, Chapter 4), with a number of different models
proposed to account for its impact. For some theorists, altruism is based
on an intrinsic motive to achieve feelings of self-satisfaction; in another
approach, altruism reduces arousal by a person's not having to perceive
suffering in another person. Batson (1991, Chapter 12) concludes his
treatise by noting that, in most situations, it is difficult to separate ego-
istic from altruistic motives. In 1987–1988, Hogan, Eggebeen, and Clogg
(1993), as part of a stratified national survey, questioned 9,643 American adults about intergenerational exchanges. The latter included questions about caregiving, financial assistance, and advice. Exchanges
occurred in fewer than half of the families, with assistance occurring
primarily during ill health; the authors concluded that both exchange
and altruism can account for their data. Similarly, Silverstein and Litwak (1993), in a sample of 910 participants, measured adult children's
support of their parents. Not surprisingly, they reported that household
assistance depends on physical and social deficits and on geographic

factors, while social–emotional support is related to norms and personal affinity.

As part of a large-scale longitudinal study, Morgan, Schuster, and Butler (1991) obtained data from 513 community-residing adults, ranging in age from 57 to 103 years, on the total number of support exchanges each person sent and received. It was not until the age of 85 years that respondents reported receiving more support than they gave; this applied both to affective and instrumental supports. Interestingly, the age when the crossover occurred (i.e., when the older person received more support then he or she gave), was earlier for affective than instrumental supports. This study did not measure the amount of each exchange, only the frequency. The data do support the importance of differentiating the "old" population into such categories as "young-old" and "old-old."

Individual Differences.   We have previously referred to cultural factors in social supports, and this will also include gender differences (Antonucci, 1990). Aldwin (1994, pp. 139–140) and Sarason, Pierce, and Sarason (1994) discuss the effects of personality on social supports. In naturalistic studies, such as bereavement or health problems, it is difficult to separate the preexisting personality characteristics that induced the stress associated with an event from the social support or coping strategy of an individual. Finally, the perception of social support and well-being is to some extent mediated by genetic factors. Bergeman, Plomin, Pedersen, and McClearn (1991) assessed 424 Swedish twin pairs, ages 50–87 years, including identical and fraternal twins reared together or apart. They found that both genetic and nonshared environmental factors contributed about equally to the perception of the adequacy of social support. The same also applied to the relationship between perceived support and psychological well-being. This study confirms the commonsense notion that personality variables that affect perception of stress also influence the perception of social support.

Summary.   There is much evidence that certain types of social support prevent or ameliorate various types of stress. Just as the general construct of stress has numerous definitions, so does social support. Most frequently, social support is defined as the presence of social relationships or ties, and support may be in terms of the provision of various resources, emotional assistance, or provision of information. The importance of contextual factors almost precludes laboratory research, and it is very difficult to have meaningful studies on aging changes in support, though there have been a few longitudinal studies. In the latter, there were no controls for cohort or cultural change factors. In general, personality factors tend to confound the appearance of stress and the presence of social supports; most of the published research has been in specific naturalistic situations such as caregiving, bereavement, or illness.

Personal Control

Stress occurs whenever a person is blocked from achieving a goal or his or her state of equilibrium is disturbed. We have previously referred to the importance of LC in pain and health, a topic closely tied to stress, and we have reviewed the construct to some extent. Though there are major benefits from exercising control, there are also costs, since, at times, control may have what are regarded as undesirable consequences such as selfishness, cynicism, or materialism. There has been much research on the role of personal control in studies of stress: Older Adults experience decreased health, retirement, loss of a spouse, and other normative stresses that are usually associated with diminished ability to control one's activities; thus, this topic has been of major concern in gerontology.

Decreased control may affect emotional well-being, physical health, and coping with stress, and it may accelerate various decrements during aging. For Reich and Zautra (1991), the construct of control is transactional, just as is Lazarus's definition of stress; they found that belief in the ability to control one's life is influenced by such major life stressors as physical disability and even by small daily hassles. Thus, personal control is not a stable personality trait.

Primary and Secondary Control. Rothbaum, Weisz, and Snyder (1982) differentiated between two types of perceived control, primary and secondary. In primary control, there is an attempt to influence existing events by targeting the object or environment. In secondary control, the person may (1) identify with a powerful other who has primary control, (2) reinterpret the situation, or (3) change goals. Primary and secondary control are intertwined; usually, when primary control decreases, there is a tendency to adopt secondary controls, but secondary control is a heterogeneous category strongly dependent on culture. In Japan, for example, there is a proverb, "to win is to lose" (Azuma, 1984).

Aging. Aging has been associated in many, but not all studies, with decrements in actual and perceived personal control resulting from declines in biological and psychological abilities and from society's devaluation of the status of older persons. Heckhausen and Schulz (1993; 1995) presented a life-span theory of control, basically following the Rothbaum *et al.* (1982) classification of primary and secondary control. First, they emphasized the domain specificity of control. There are societal, age-graded opportunities and restrictions for certain behaviors. For example, an older person may have his or her pilot's license revoked, but many business establishments give discounts to older patrons As people age, there is a decrease in biological resources that requires increased secondary control, but primary control is still available in some domains. Sometimes secondary control may lead to greater primary control by the reinterpretation of the desired targets or the selection of more manageable goals. The transitions from primary to secondary control in various domains are difficult to specify; selection may require that only certain activities be pursued, while compensation may mean the greater use of technical aids or obtaining the assistance of other people.

Perceived loss of control in different domains may be related to societal expectations of the elder's activities (Gergen & Gergen, 1986). This may occur in institutional settings such as nursing homes or hospitals and even at home when the individual depends on home–health care services (Baltes & Wahl, 1992). Dependency behaviors are reinforced, while independent actions may interfere with the goals of the caregivers. This script was elaborated by Goffman (1961) in his study of mental hospitals; in the growing field of home–health care services, conflicts may arise between the desire for independence and the dependency supported by the caregiver. The normal declines in physical, psychological, and social functions, with the attendant losses in primary control in the elderly, may lead to depression in individuals who have difficulties in switching from primary to secondary control in a culture that overemphasizes the former.

Gatz and Karel (1993) surveyed LC in a 20-year study consisting of several cross-sectional (Ns = 1,331–2,044) and longitudinal studies (N = 560) of four generations of lower-middle-class Californians. There was an increase in internal control from 1971 to 1985, but the youngest participants in 1971 (grandchildren) and in 1991 (great-grandchildren) exhibited more external control. These data point out the need to consider both cohort and time of measurement effects, factors that have not been controlled in the great majority of studies.

Aldwin (1991) analyzed mailed-in questionnaire data from 228 respondents ages 18–78 years (mean 42 years) on the most stressful episodes they experienced during the previous month, their use of coping strategies, the perception of control of the event, and symptoms of depression. Age showed a low negative correlation with perceived control; at the same time, individuals who perceived that they were responsible for the occurrence of the stress-inducing episode were slightly less likely to use escapism, though the difference was not statistically significant. The betas in the multivariate analyses were significant, but most of the zero-order correlations of age with the other variables were less than .30. This study illustrates the complex relationships between stress, control, and coping strategies. Heterogeneity of the stressors contributes to low correlations and the use of efficient coping strategies, probably the result of experiences, may reduce the effects of low perceived control. Since this was a community-dwelling, self-selected group of respondents, the generality of the findings is uncertain. In a study of 127 nursing homes, 55 residential care facilities, and 62 congregate apartments, Timko and Moos (1989) found that the degree of policy choice and independence benefited primarily functionally able residents. For residents of poor functional ability, choice and independence were not related to adaptation.

Krause and Borawski-Clark (1994) obtained interview data from 1,103 persons with reference to eight social roles, including spouse, children, and friends, and the stressors encountered in these relationships. In addition, they measured global and domain-specific perceptions of control. Stressors in salient roles eroded feelings of global control, though the statistical relationship was small (beta = .08). At the same time, the presence of social support increased the feelings of control, presumably because the person's self-worth increased. These data point to the complex relationship between stress, social support, and personal control.

Aging brings about changes in life goals and concerns that can affect the control beliefs. Krause and Baker (1992), in an analysis of survey data of 819 older Canadians (mean 65 years), found that those who valued highly economic achievement reported a greater loss of feelings of general control than those for whom economic values were less important. The authors acknowledged several limitations of their analysis, including the absence of longitudinal data and the shortcomings in measuring personal control. They assumed that older individuals experience a decrease of their financial resources and an inability to recoup any losses, both reasonable assumptions that induce beliefs in decreased control. In Finland, Nurmi, Pulliainen, and Salmela-Aro (1992) obtained questionnaire data from Finnish participants measuring "hopes" and "fears," and ratings of each of these with reference to specific goals and concerns on a 4-point internality–externality scale.

Though there were 381 participants ages 19–71 years, only 34 presumably were older or retired persons. Older persons' control beliefs became more external in the areas of health, property, offspring, and the self. Unfortunately, the latter is not elucidated. The data are not surprising, for this, too, was a cross-sectional study with the various potential confounds in the interpretation of the results. In a Berlin sample of 49 older persons, mostly women, Baltes *et al.* (1990) recorded daily activities over a 6-month period and related them to functional health and personal control beliefs. Personal control correlated with the activities that occurred most frequently.

Some people opt for uncontrollability when faced with aversive choices. They do not want to take the blame for negative consequences of their decisions (Lazarus, 1991, p. 137). Also, at times, control may require excessive responsibilities, so that the costs of control may exceed the benefits, especially for older persons whose physiological or psychological functions are limited. This explanation is consonant with a laboratory study with college students (Wright, Brehm, Crutcher, Evans, & Jones, 1990) in which certain physiological and subjective indices of stress were relatively greater when control over aversive outcomes was moderate than when control was easy, relatively difficult, or impossible.

In addition to a generalized control factor, as measured by the Rotter or Levenson scales, the perceived degree of control occurs to a different extent in different behavioral domains (e.g., in health, finances, personal relationships, leisure activities, and intellectual behavior). People may perceive that they can exercise different amounts of control in different domains of life; this compartmentalization of control is especially significant for older people who show differential losses in functions (Dannefer, 1988a, 1988b) and, therefore, differential changes in control in various behavioral domains. Even the classification of health may be too broad when control is examined. It may be necessary to measure separately physician visits, hospitalizations, and drug usage, for example. Many investigators have taken into account this variability and have made specialized assessments of control of different functions.

Health problems, which are a common source of stress, were reviewed in Chapter 7. Some studies have reported that in later adulthood, financial strain can reduce the perception of personal control and have a strong impact on somatic symptoms (Krause & Baker, 1992; Krause, Jay, & Liang, 1991). The Krause *et al.* (1991) study was based on samples of over 1,500 respondents in both the United States and Japan. Contrary to the authors' expectations, they found similar relationships between financial strain and feelings of control and self-worth in the two cultures, perhaps a reflection of the westernization of modern

Japan. In three studies of college students and elderly adults (age ranges 60–94 years), Lachman (1986) found that in domain-specific scales measuring control in health or intellectual behavior, older persons were more external than were younger individuals, while a generalized scale showed nò age effects. The data also showed that the domain-specific scales were better predictors of behavioral outcomes for older persons than for college students. Such an outcome would tend to indicate that for the elderly, perceived control varies in different behavioral domains. Since Lachman only tested health and intelligence, however, the latter probably of little interest to the elderly, her findings may have been affected by her choice of the control measures used, though these data may also support the frequent finding that aging is associated with a narrowing of one's focus of interest. Lachman acknowledges that predictability of outcomes of LC measures depends on using scales that tap domains relevant to the interests of the subjects.

Control and Responsibility. While control has been endowed with beneficial consequences, it also carries with it *responsibility* for the outcomes of action. We have noted previously that faced with aversive choices, some people do not want to take the blame for negative consequences of their decisions (Lazarus, 1991, p. 137). If control leads to a reduction of stress, all is well; however, if the behavior that is controlled by the actor leads to failure, the initial stress may be exacerbated by the burden of culpability (Shaver, 1992). The concept of attribution of responsibility has been further dissected into (1) the responsibility for the problem (causation) and (2) the responsibility for its solution (Brickman, Rabinowitz, Karuza, Coates, *et al.,* 1982). While, for some individuals, there may be a symmetry between a belief in the responsibility or nonresponsibility of experiencing a problem and its solution, for others, the attribution for the causation and its solution are discrepant. A person may feel that he or she caused the problem but may not feel responsible for its solution; in another situation, a person may feel responsible for solving a problem, though he or she may not feel responsible for causing it. The concept of personal responsibility is somewhat similar to the construct of LC (Weiner, 1992, pp. 211–220). However, Rotter's LC is linked closely to expectancies, whereas personal responsibility for the attribution of the cause of a problem does not imply an expectancy. Furthermore, LC is assumed to be a personality characteristic that is presumably stable through adulthood.

Brickman and colleagues' (1982) conceptualization of responsibility in terms of attribution of control, in which the cause of a problem and its amelioration are separated, has led to several interesting studies.

In four related studies with small Ns (20–54 per study), Karuza, Zevon, Gleason, Karuza, and Nash (1990) compared attributions of responsibility of college students and adults participating in senior citizens centers or in Meals on Wheels programs. In all four studies, the participants were given questionnaires to assess their perceived responsibility for the cause and the solution of "general problems" in life. In Study 1, the elderly, compared to the college students, were less likely to attribute to themselves responsibility either for the cause or the solution of problems, the usual medical model. Similarly, the enlightenment model, in which the person is responsible for the cause of the problem but not for solving it, was selected more frequently by the elderly, while a larger number of college students chose the moral model, in which the individual is responsible for his or her problem, as well as for solving it. In Study 2, data were obtained from Meals on Wheels program participants as well as from professionals and paraprofessional. As might have been expected, the providers chose more frequently an enlightenment model (i.e., the person is responsible for the cause of the problem but not for the solution). In Study 3, data were obtained from young, middle-aged, and elderly volunteer helpers; compared to the young or middle-aged, the elderly expressed a significantly lower preference for the compensatory model (i.e., that they were not responsible for the cause of the problem but should be responsible for the solution). As in the first study, a larger percentage of elderly and middle-aged persons chose the medical model. In Study 4, the participants responded to problems pertaining to a broken leg and to depression. For depression, the elderly chose the medical model less frequently than for the problem associated with a broken leg, though for the young, the nature of the problem did not seem to affect preferences. Although the medical model is not necessarily the most adaptive, the convergent preferences for this model by the four different samples of elderly pose a societal dilemma. If these findings can be substantiated, the choice creates difficulties in the efforts to teach older citizens to adopt healthy lifestyles and ultimately will lead to increased burdens in providing care.

Ray, Raciti, and MacLean (1992) presented 110 retirement-community residents with two sets of vignettes: Half of the participants received a set labeled as representing a medical problem experienced by an older person, and the other half were given an identical set labeled as a psychological problem; the participants were asked to imagine that they were faced with these symptoms. Perception of the problem as either medical or psychological significantly affected attribution of responsibility: Of those who received the psychological label on the vignettes, 65% subscribed to a moral model (i.e., that they themselves were responsible for the problem), whereas only 29% of those who received the medical labels subscribed to this model. In contrast, of those who received the medical labels, only 7% subscribed to a moral model and 20% to the medical model. The compensatory model (i.e., the participants are not responsible for the cause of the problem, but are responsible for its solution) was chosen by 51% of those given the medical-labeled vignettes but by only 28% of those who received the psychological label. Contrary to expectations, those receiving the medically labeled vignettes chose a compensatory rather than a medical model, but those with a psychological vignette did select the moral model. Also, regardless of how they attributed responsibility, 79% of participants indicated that they would seek help. This may be related to the low socioeconomic level characteristic of the group. Of those who received the psychological vignette, the most frequent (45%) choice of help was from their social network rather than from helping professionals. Thus, this study supports the frequently reported observation that earlier cohorts are hesitant to seek help from mental health professionals (Schaie & Willis, 1991, pp. 514–517). Aldwin (1992), in a survey of 238 men and women ages 18–78 years, found that older respondents were less likely to claim responsibility for their health problems and assumes that older people tend to avoid self-blame and guilt feelings.

Summary. Modern Western societies are imbued with the belief that a person should exercise personal control of his or her activities. Aging is associated with various losses in health, physical strength, finances, and other resources, which tend to restrict a person's control in many contexts of the environment. Stress ensues from any blockage of a desired goal or interference with ongoing activities or the normal state of an organism. Exercising personal control should moderate stress, but not all stressors are amenable to the exercise of control. This is most apparent in natural disasters. Two types of personal control have been proposed: Primary control occurs when the person exerts direct influence on the environment, and secondary control occurs when the person depends on powerful others or the situation is reinterpreted.

The contextual basis of stress means that personal control varies from situation to situation. Since human motivation is not limited to the satisfaction of biological needs, expectations and perceptions of mastery, accomplishment, and cognizance are also important; all of these attributes depend on personal control. The locus of the reinforcements for various activities may be attributed either to internal or to external factors, and such attributions may be global or specific for various activities.

In aging, the decrements in primary control are replaced by secondary control. The significant role of culture in the experience of stress requires that cohort and time-of-measurement factors be included in studies of control, but there have been few such efforts. There is a scarcity of even longitudinal studies on control; thus, most of our information is on age differences. Typically, older people tend to be more external in their control beliefs. In many important situations, older people opt for less control, since this relieves them of responsibilities and reduces their culpability.

CONCLUSIONS

In this lengthy chapter, changes in stress with aging were reviewed. One of the foremost modern students of this topic, Selye, postulated that aging is a stressor, a disturbance of the normal equilibrium that then leads to stress, the consequence of the disequilibrium. Many of our cultural stereotypes reinforce this notion. This has led to much effort, frequently, to an exclusion of other interests in gerontology, to analyze the stress aspects of aging and to ignore the growth or positive changes occurring during the later stages of life. Some of the material presented in this chapter just as appropriately could have been included in the following chapter on coping. The two constructs are isomorphic, but to make the material less unwieldy, we separated them into two chapters.

The initial difficulty in the analysis of this topic pertains to the definition and/or theory of stress in general, not specifically within the context of aging. Many of the major controversies in the approaches to the foundational aspects of psychological theories (e.g., behaviorism vs. cognition, transactionalism vs. structuralism, reductionism vs. dualism) are to a large extent mirrored in the problems encountered in dealing with stress. Several major psychological theories were briefly presented. One of the two most common paradigms uses Selye's stressor as a stimulus and stress as a response. The other, championed by Lazarus, is a model of *psychological* stress which is neither an input, stimulus, nor is it the person's reaction, but rather it is the person–environment relationship, which depends on the individual's motivations and cognitions when the person perceives a threat, challenge, or potential harm. Also, there is much evidence that a given stress begets other stresses.

Stress, at least for those not adhering to a transactional model, has been analyzed in terms of both its biological and psychological consequences. Since Selye's time, we have known that the hypothalamic–

pituitary–adrenocortical (HPA) system plays a major role in the organism's response to stressors. In the elderly, it is believed that the HPA system functions near to a threshold level, and some investigators have reported that plasma levels of corticosteroids are elevated. This would imply that older persons are more likely to experience stress than are younger ones when the equilibrium is disturbed. The HPA is closely linked to the activities of several other physiological systems; for example, the reactivity of the CV system and other organs innervated by the ANS decreases with age, but the changes depend on the health status of the person. This produces a decrease in homeostasis of several components of the system during aging and increased intra- and interindividual variabilities in responses to high-level stressors. Finally, recovery to a baseline is slower and this may then produce a relatively long cycle of imbalance in which new environmental disturbances are superimposed on the still-unresolved previous disequilibria. In addition to neuroendocrine vulnerability, the immune system may also be affected. A higher incidence of various illnesses, broadly defined as stressors, and the prevalence of depression, lead to a proliferation of stresses. These findings tend to lend support to a transactional view, as proposed by Lazarus.

Though there are limitations in the amount of stress that can be induced in a laboratory setting, there have been several studies measuring concurrently ANS responses and performance on several learning and psychomotor tasks; the assumption here is that these tasks induce stress. Performance decrements were observed primarily when the tasks were demanding, but in several studies, increased CV activation was observed, presumably to compensate for normal perceptual, motor, or cognitive decrements. Threats or anxiety in laboratory situations had a greater adverse effect on older than younger participants.

Much of our information on stress must depend on field observations. Some of the data are reviewed in subsequent chapters. Stresses result both from simple daily hassles, such as misplacing an object, and from more serious life events, such as loss of a spouse. A major source of stress in older individuals is the presence of various diseases, many of which are chronic conditions. Finally, on the macrolevel, conditions such as economic recession will also induce stresses.

The relative contribution of personality characteristics in the genesis of stress is a focus of much debate and research. It reflects the diverse theoretical positions of the investigators. For Costa and McCrea (1990), stress is a reflection of an individual's personality, as in neuroticism, and they advocate using objective measures of stressors such as the loss of spouse. On the other hand, in (Lazarus's 1993) transactional approach, personality may be either the antecedent or the consequent variable of stress, where the latter depends on the environmental context that produces different responses to the presumed stressors.

The presence of social supports, a multifaceted concept, reduces stress and is especially important in attenuating the effects of illness, a major source of stress in older populations. Social support may be viewed as a resource, and loss of resources induces stress. The old-old, the most vulnerable age group, are most likely to benefit from social supports.

Another factor in the appearance of stress is personal control. In Western societies, control is an important motive and its loss associated with various disabilities afflicting older persons leads to stress. Perceived control is associated with the perception of competence and well-being. There may be both a general perception of control and domain-specific controls pertaining to intellectual competence or health. There is some tentative evidence that domain-specific control is more important for older people than for younger individuals, reflecting a narrowing of interests in older persons. This is especially important in gerontology. Another related concept affecting stress is the perception of responsibility for both the occurrence of a condition and the alleviation of the stress produced by the problem. Compared to young people, in some simulation studies, older people were less likely to attribute to themselves responsibilities for the cause and solution of medical problems. Such studies point to the importance of cultural and cohort factors associated with control and responsibility for the solution of various problems encountered in life.

The large number of variables that determine the consequences of stressors usually means that any specific factor makes only a small contribution to the total variance. The need for large samples to obtain data that have any statistical validity creates practical difficulties for most investigators.

CHAPTER 9

Coping

INTRODUCTION

Development of the Construct

Aldwin (1994) observed that "contemporary American culture has become nearly obsessed with stress and how to cope with it" (p. 71). Modern technology has raised our hopes that most adversities of life have easy and rapid solutions. The various self-help books and media programs on stress and what to do about it attest to the importance of this concept and attempts to cope. Much of applied psychology, especially the fields of clinical and counseling psychology, consists of efforts to enhance an individual's coping responses. The ascriptor term *coping* did not appear in the index of *Psychological Abstracts* until the mid-1960s, and it was not included in the 1983 *Encyclopedic Dictionary of Psychology* (Harre & Lamb, 1983). However, interest in coping, or at least the usage of the term, has grown rapidly, so that in the 1994 index of *Psychological Abstracts,* there were over 400 references under the ascriptor term *coping behavior.* This growth parallels the increase in the articles on stress, since in most models, coping is the organism's response to stress in the attempt to control, avoid, or prevent emotional distress (Pearlin & Schooler, 1978). In a review of performance and aging, the well-known gerontologist Welford (1992) states that the "problems for older people in coping both individually and on a social scale . . . are probably the greatest challenge at present to applied psychology in relation to aging and will become more urgent as the proportion of old people in the population increases" (p. 191). The contextual nature of coping means, however, that many events that usually affect an older person, such as widowhood, various chronic diseases, or financial losses, all involve coping. Unless the author used the term *coping* in his article, it did not appear under that ascriptor in *Psy-*

chological Abstracts; it is therefore difficult to determine the size of the literature pertaining to this topic.

In the social sciences, though the term *coping* is of relatively recent origin, its modern antecedents may be traced back to two separate concepts. One of these is the Darwinian evolutionary construct of *adaptation* or adjustment, which first appeared in the middle of the nineteenth century (Leahey, 1991, p. 116), and the other is *defense mechanism,* introduced by Sigmund Freud in 1894 (A. Freud, 1946) to describe the ego's struggle against painful or unendurable ideas or affects. Various defense mechanisms such as repression, projection, regression, or sublimation develop in an attempt to reduce anxiety. Perusal of *Psychological Abstracts* indicates that until the 1950s, the hegemony of behaviorism in U.S. psychology until the 1950s resulted in minimal usages of the construct of defense: Between 1927 and 1950, only 10 articles in English were indexed under the ascriptor "defense mechanisms," and all of them were either published in psychoanalytic journals, or they were book and review articles in which there was a reference to defense mechanisms. However, during this period and later on, too, *adjustment* was the commonly used construct. In several volumes of *Psychological Abstracts* in the 1960s, coping was cross-indexed with adjustment.

Previously, we raised the thorny issue of separating physical or physiological and psychological stressors, and this difficulty also plagues the analysis of coping. Various diseases and deteriorations of the sensory and motor systems are the common lot of older people. Examination of these changes is in the domain of geriatrics, and well beyond the scope of this volume; simultaneously, numerous psychosocial stressors frequently interact, such as the loss of a spouse affecting finances, or conflicts with an adult child affecting a marriage. We analyze coping mainly in response to some psychosocial stressors, while recognizing the interdependence of physiological and psychosocial stressors.

For the sociologist Aneshensel (1992), coping and social stress are isomorphic constructs, since social support, a coping factor, attenuates social stress. Lazarus (1993) and other psychologists have proposed similar models for psychological stress and coping: If a person's relationship with the environment is changed by the coping responses, the appraisal of stress will also change. Thus, much of the material that was discussed in the chapter on stress could equally be part of a chapter on coping.

Definitions

A broad definition of coping implies that the description of almost every facet of the existence of older persons is an appropriate topic for the investigator who assumes that aging per se induces stress in the organism, which then requires coping. Thus, coping implies that the individual needs to adjust to the changing internal and external circumstances that induce stress. Some have also used the construct *adaptation,* a term borrowed from biologists, but for most psychologists the latter refers primarily to reflexes or physiological changes that occur during stress. Lazarus (1991, p. 7), however, entitled his book *Emotion and Adaptation* to emphasize the point that the constructs cannot be separated. Since life is a continuous flux of internal and external conditions, an examination of the coping or adjustments to the frequent changes in the environment can be investigated at almost every instance of a person's existence. It is a dynamic, continuously fluctuating process, but all activities do not necessarily lead to successful adaptations. Some psychologists attempt to differentiate between coping, adaptation, and emotional responses; Aldwin (1994, pp. 81–83) includes in the concept of adaptation not only coping but also "mastery" and "defenses." We have previously commented on the possibility of personal growth that may follow exposure to a stressor; thus, all learning or problem solving involves adaptations to present or future environmental challenges. According to Aldwin, many everyday, routine habits, such as toiletry, are adaptations to living in a society. However, there are many situations that straddle everyday habits and *anticipatory coping;* brushing your teeth every day, for example, prevents the development of dental problems. Most common habits forestall stresses that may create coping problems. Aldwin also uses the example of automobile driving. The novice experiences stress the first time he or she drives on a freeway, but gradually, as the person continues this routine, the stress disappears. Of course, driving in heavy traffic on a foggy morning will induce stress even in experienced drivers. Similarly, many emotional responses, such as vocalizing in response to stepping on a sharp nail, should not be considered coping responses, but here, again, in many situations, there are no sharp boundaries between coping and emotional responsivity. Hearing about an injury to a loved one may initially induce an outburst of tears; continued crying may then serve as a coping response.

While admitting that there are numerous coping mechanisms, McCrea and Costa (1986) ultimately relate them to their personality theory in which neuroticism, extroversion, and openness to experiences are the determiners of coping as well as well-being. In two studies with well-educated older samples (Ns = 255 and 151, respectively), self-rated, spouse-rated, and peer-rated personality characteristics all seemed to correlate with coping effectiveness; thus, coping may be viewed as another facet of well-being.

Later Costa, Somerfield, and McCrea (1996) again emphasized the continuity between routine problem solving or adaptation and coping. The distinction between the terms is clear when we compare major stressors with less serious ones. For example, stress resulting from losing a social security check can be easily remedied and represents problem solving or adaptation. On the other hand, being told by a physician that a diagnostic test has revealed the presence of a serious disease or experiencing the unexpected death of a spouse is likely to be perceived as a serious stressor that requires coping. The blurring of distinctions between stresses and normal adaptations in everyday activities also implies that there are as many ways of coping as there are techniques for problem solving. The continual difficult quest in psychology for a taxonomy of learning and problem solving means that there are no simple solutions in an analysis of the responses to serious stressors.

In Chapter 8, we referred to daily hassles, life events, and chronic strains. Each of these requires coping, but the strategies will vary. Kaplan (1996) muses that, in a sense, everyone is continually under stress because the environment makes constant demands on the individual. This may require that a person arbitrarily decide the starting point of stress that begets an unsolvable problem.

Shaver (1992) prefers the descriptive term *stress management* to *coping.* The term *management* more commonly incorporates preparation, responses, and dealing with chronic residues of acute stressor episodes, while coping, according to some investigators, may involve helplessness or no reactivity, or avoidance (Chiriboga, 1992). However, since the term *stress management* is used less frequently than *coping* in the literature, we use the latter term, while being aware of Shaver's criticisms.

COPING STYLES AND STRATEGIES

Theories

The earlier popularity of psychoanalytic theory among many mental health professionals warrants first a brief reference to Erikson's (1963) developmental theory, which states that the challenges during the various stages of life can result in different outcomes depending on the person's ability to manage the stresses. Midlife, according to Erikson, is the period of "generativity,"and those who cannot cope with the demands at this stage will stagnate. During the last stage of life, late adulthood, people search for ego integrity; those who cannot cope with the vicissitudes of aging experience despair. Though many clinical observations may be interpreted as supporting the broad outline of Erikson's theory, most recent research has focused on more specific approaches to coping.

Lazarus (1991, p. 129), in his relational theory of motivation and emotion, incorporated many ideas formulated by several social-cognitive theorists, including Bandura (1991). According to Bandura, people's actions (motivations) are guided by anticipation of the consequences, and this determines the goals that they set for themselves. Human behavior is regulated by one's perceived self-efficacy in achieving personal goals. Perceived ability to control potentially challenging or threatening events is a major coping mechanism. For Bandura, anxiety results from perceived low self-efficacy in responding to anticipated events. Avoidant behavior and anxiety arousal result from a person's belief that he or she will not be able to cope with the situation. Bandura seems to exclude avoidance as an effective coping mechanism. Under some circumstances, however, Lazarus (p. 412) believes that denial, repression, and other similar defense mechanisms that include avoidance may be effective coping styles.

Lazarus (1991, pp. 112–115) defines coping as "a cognitive and behavioral effort to manage specific external and internal demands (or conflicts between them) that are appraised as taxing or exceeding the resources of the person." We have previously discussed Antonovsky's (1990) theory of generalized resistance resources (GRRs); stresses and difficulties in coping are the result of not possessing adequate general resources.

Coping can be either an activity that ameliorates an emotional distress, labeled problem-focused or behavior-focused coping, or a process in which the only change is the way the person–environment relationship is perceived or thought about, without affecting any behavior. The latter is frequently labeled as emotion-focused coping. For example, a person may expect to be in a situation that in the past has been unpleasant. He or she may act to avoid the place where distress occurred, a form of problem-focused coping. Alternatively, the person may reinterpret the situation, a form of cognitive coping, and the previously experienced anxiety, shame, or other emotions will be removed or lessened. Lazarus admits that his definition of coping creates some redundancy between the concepts of appraisal and cognitive coping. Coping is highly contextual, and for purposes of broad generalization, personal coping styles or traits need to be downplayed. Lazarus (1991, p. 405) also uses the construct inappropriate coping; for example, a person uses alcohol or tobacco in threatening situations, and the behavior leads to illness. Of course, alcohol and tobacco may temporarily reduce anxiety, an immediate coping response, but in the long run, it is a deleterious option. The example illustrates an important temporal factor that complicates the analysis of many stress and coping phenomena: short-term coping is not equivalent with the long-term achievement of a desirable outcome. Indeed, the concept of foresight associated with efficacy or mastery implies the ability to achieve long-term rather than short-term goals.

Chiriboga (1992) raises the issue, also encountered in the definition of stress, whether coping refers to behaviors that alleviate a stressful situation, to a personality characteristic, to a defense mechanism, or to some combination of some of the above. Chiriboga's essay illustrates some of the confusion. "At the most general level, the word 'coping' can refer to any activity aimed at reducing distress, or only to those behaviors and qualities associated with the actual alleviation of the distress" (p. 39). Thus, coping may be either a cognitive or a behavioral activity that alleviates or reduces distress. But in describing the results of his own research, he refers to seven coping styles, or strategies of coping, one of which is "noncoping." There can be several interpretations of the latter strategy. One would be the absence of any responses to a stress, in which case the concept of coping, at least in the short run, is superfluous. On the other hand, noncoping may also refer to responses that are ineffective or maladaptive in removing or at least alleviating the stress. In the latter instance, a better classification would be in terms of the relative effectiveness of various coping styles, both in terms of short- and/or long-term benefits. In Chiriboga's classification of coping, the styles, aside from noncoping, are related, though not hierarchically, to the degree to which various aspects of stress are alleviated.

Holahan *et al.* (1996) postulate four basic coping strategies: (1) cognitive approach, (2) cognitive avoidance, (3) behavioral approach, and (4) behavioral avoidance. In addition, they propose two different subtypes within each category, such as (a) logical analysis or positive reappraisal within the cognitive approach category and (b) seeking guidance and support or taking a problem-solving action within the behavioral approach category. It is not obvious how the subcategories differ from each other. In essence, their theory is similar to those of Lazarus (1991) and Chiriboga (1992). The most common functional categorization that has been proposed by many researchers is, namely, (1) management of the problem, problem solving, or problem-focused coping and (2) emotion-focused or cognitive coping, when a person reinterprets the threat or challenge (Folkman, 1991). In many events, both types of strategies may occur simultaneously. A person may reappraise the problem—cognitive coping—and also change his or her actions—problem-solving coping.

The diverse biological and psychosocial consequences of stress probably precludes the development of a simple hierarchical schema for classifying coping styles. If coping is synonymous with adaptation, then responses that are maladaptive should not be labeled coping. Some behaviors usually labeled as coping responses in situations that are assumed to be stress-inducing may actually represent learning of novel person–environment contingencies. A very broad definition of coping would encompass the whole domain of learning, the most thoroughly researched area in psychology.

Assessment Problems

The diverse theoretical orientations of the researchers, and thus definitions, also affect assessments. There are several factors that create difficulties in analyzing coping: According to Beehr and McGrath (1996), stress and coping are heavily value-laden, which underscores the need to analyze the differences in the motive of the individual, though in practice this occurs very infrequently. We have already noted that social stress and coping are isomorphic; thus, we have expectations that certain frequently occurring events are social stressors that require a coping response. Furthermore, the temporal feature of the consequences of the stressor affects the evaluation of the coping response. Finally, the issue of person versus situation also affects classification and measurement.

Previously, we described some broad types of coping mechanism or styles based on several theoretical models. In addition, there have been more detailed descriptions of coping behaviors that may be subsumed within the broad categories. Pearlin and Schooler (1978) identified 17 separate coping styles, but many of them are applicable only to specific circumstances such as parenting or marriage. In her review, Folkman (1991) identified between 8 and 28 different patterns proposed by different investigators. Zeidner and Saklofske (1996) name eight different criteria that have been used in the assessment of coping outcomes; these include reduction of physiological reactions, reduction of psychological distress, social functioning, returning to prestress activities, maintenance of self-esteem, and the perception of others who interact with the person (e.g., children, spouses, or friends). These criteria cover the spectrum from biological to sociological methods; the relationships between various measures have not been investigated. They may depend on numerous contextual factors; in addition, an individual frequently experiences multiple stressors simultaneously in different contexts. Since stress may interfere with a person's repertoire of normal adaptive responses in many domains, there is a further complication in the assessment.

Schwarzer and Schwarzer (1996) reviewed several current coping inventories. They were critical of the lack of attention to the goals that an individual may have in the pursuit of various coping strategies at different times and in different situations. In many instruments, the respondent is given hypothetical scenarios, but such a strategy may identify dispositional strategies that may have limited validity for real-life events. Asking people to recall real-life stresses involves problems of recall, and recall may be contaminated by the experiences that occurred after the event.

Personality

In his clinical practice, S. Freud observed diverse defense mechanisms in different patients. According to A. Freud (1946, pp. 35–36), people develop permanent defensive operations in dealing with stressful or traumatic situations. In Chapter 7 on health, we indicated that psychosomatic medicine, which grew out of Freudian theory, attempted to classify people on the basis of the pathologies that they developed in different organ systems in responses to stress. In this approach, it was assumed that a person tends to rely on a restricted repertoire of defense mechanisms that then lead to a search of individual coping styles.

In the Anglo-American tradition, the search has been for behaviorally based personality constructs as determiners of coping responses. Costa *et al.* (1996) and Hewitt and Flett (1996) reviewed a large number of studies that related coping behavior to personality characteristics: Not only are coping responses affected by personality, but also the perception of the stressor, as we noted in Chapter 8, is a function of personality. Much research has been devoted to the roles of optimism–pessimism, (LC), and indices based on Costa and McCrea's NEO Personality Inventory (1985a) (measuring neuroticism, extroversion, and openness, and other similar personality constructs that have been postulated in the development of stress and the associated coping responses). Yet Hewitt and Flett (1996) believe that not enough attention has been given to certain important personality variables such as attributional style or dependency. Their commentary reflects the compexity of the construct of personality.

The Context

As in other domains of psychology, some researchers in coping emphasize the dominant role of personality, while others prefer to look for the context in which the stressor occurs; it is the person–situation debate that has recently characterized personality research (Parker & Endler, 1996). The context-driven basis of coping is apparent from a perusal of the *Psychological Abstracts* references to stress and coping in the elderly. Almost all of them are to specific, applied problems, responses to persistent hardships commonly experienced by older people. In Chapter 10, we briefly review some research on bereavement and on caregiving, in which the constructs of stress and coping are used interchangeably, as has been the common practice in much applied work. There is a large body of literature on how older persons who are experiencing the usual aging changes in sensory abilities and other physiological disabilities cope with these normative symptoms of aging. There are also numerous reports on coping with various common illnesses such as arthritis, cancer, and cardiovascular diseases that afflict the elderly, and on coping with the existing psychosocial and economic conditions affecting many older persons in our society. In many instances, older people experience simultaneously many stressors (e.g., caring for an ill spouse, suffering from arthritis, and having financial problems). Taylor and Aspinwall (1996) emphasize that for different stressors, effective coping strategies vary, and it is necessary to match available coping strategies and resources with the features of a stressful event. For example, avoidant strategies are not very effective in coping with chronic illness or many family-related stresses, though the latter may be reduced by problem-focused coping. Furthermore, preexisting stressors, including daily hassles, influence the perceived stress and the available coping strategies.

We discussed earlier the contextual factors in research on stress, illustrated by Dura and Kielcolt-Glaser's (1990) observation that volunteers in caregiving research represent a biased sample. Similarly, Chiriboga (1992) cited Baum's concern that people who have recently experienced a catastrophic event are unlikely to participate in research projects. Conversely, some people are eager to participate in research on coping, since they believe it will be a source of social support and an opportunity for satisfactory social relationships. Research on coping depends primarily on field studies with distinct samples of participants possessing numerous characteristics that are difficult to assess; thus, the results of many field studies have limited generality.

Social Supports

As in the development of stress, social support is critical in coping. In many situations, the appearance of social stressors is associated with a lack of social support; for example, an older person who has a close relationship with a financially well-off child may never experience economic hardships. A married older person with a healthy spouse is more likely to cope with health problems than a widowed individual. Pierce, Sarason, and Sarason (1996) conceive of social support as a multifaceted construct. It includes features of personality, personal relationships, and social structures, and these factors are interrelated. The age-associated changes in personal relationships and membership in social organizations will therefore also influence coping. The old-old, the most vulnerable age-group, benefit most from social supports.

Life Transitions and Cultural Changes

D. Gutmann (1977, 1992) provided several example of different coping behaviors of the elderly in various preindustrialized and modernized societies. Among other observations, in various societies, he noted gender-associated aging changes in coping mechanisms related to the differential functions performed by men and women during the different stages of life. The cultural factors are analogous to cohort effects, a construct that currently is preferred by gerontologists. We have previously pointed to some cohort changes in what are considered nonnormative events that induce stress. The stress associated with divorce, or with many health problems that in the past were considered to be incurable, currently leads to coping behaviors that are at variance with previous practices.

Traditionally, stage theories of development and personality, such as Erickson's (1963), have focused on adaptations during those periods in life that in our society typically result in major changes in abilities, habits, status, social relationships, or cultural norms for responsibilities and privileges. Life stages are sometimes referred to as transitions that may engender a crisis that leads to adaptation or coping (Schaie & Willis, 1991, pp. 71–74); aging produces important motivational–emotional transitions (Lazarus, 1991, p. 346), and these transitions are especially stressful when they do not occur at a cohort's normative time of the life course (e.g., forced retirement at the age of 55 years or divorce at the age of 60 years). In many Western societies, there has been a lengthening of the normative time frames for various life transitions (O'Rand, 1996). Sociologists have been applying the constructs social stress and coping to ongoing role strains rather than to unexpected events (Aneshensel, 1992; Cohler, 1991). Most life transitions are expectable and ongoing for some length of time, implying that social stresses are normal phenomena occurring during certain periods in life.

Important to the growing interest in coping are the rapid cultural innovations occurring in Western societies. The changes are especially difficult for older people who, during a lifetime, have acquired many potent habits that may be inappropriate and difficult to modify during the later periods of their life. Recent cohorts have more education, which includes information about age-associated changes and potential ways of coping with some of the disabilities of old age.

Motivation and Coping

In Chapter 8, we defined stress as a disturbance in homeodynamics; coping is an attempt to rectify the disequlibrium. An analysis of coping therefore requires an understanding of the person's motives. Lazarus (1993) emphasizes the need to pay more attention to the motivational implications of coping, because how a person copes in a given situation depends on his or her goals in that circumstance. Maes, Leventhal, and de Ridder (1996) use the example of the cardiac patient who is well enough to go to work but believes that it is more important to spend time with his family. These authors bemoan the lack of attention paid to one's life goals in most models of coping; Lazarus noted this shortcoming in his own research (1991, p. 115), as have most other coping studies. We should note, however, that stress may induce profound changes in life goals. The unexpected need to become a caregiver to one's spouse may affect a person's motivation. Since, in most instances, we do not have information about an individual's motivation prior to the occurrence of a stress, it is difficult, if not impossible, to determine changes.

We have also stressed the role of personality in coping. Following Murray (1938), we may consider motives as the fundamental units of personality that determine the significance of goals. Thus, an analysis of personality factors will also be a measure of some motivational variables. Realistically, however, this is a difficult task, since a major stressor may affect a person's life goals. Non-normative events (e.g., the physical limitations following a serious automobile accident) may alter a person's personality and life goals.

THE AGE FACTOR

There have been several recent reviews of the confusing literature on age differences in coping. As was to be expected from Lazarus's model, in her review of age differences in coping strategies, Folkman (1991) found that there were very wide ranges of strategies that people use in any given encounter. None of the studies she cited had been longitudinal, and most of the research was based on only one or two samples of a person's coping processes in specific contexts. However, if Lazarus and his colleagues are correct that stress and coping are context-specific, then attempts to arrive at generalizations and classifications should be difficult. In her review, Folkman found that in several studies, no differences occurred in coping strategies or in problem-solving versus emotion-focused processes when younger and older adults were compared. But several investigators did find that older adults used fewer fantasy or escape strategies, and some researchers also reported that younger adults used more information-seeking strategies, more confrontational styles, more emotional expressions, and less acceptance of responsibility. It seems that these differences are probably cohort effects, a manifestation of the cultural changes in our society: We are living in the information age and it may be incorporated into coping strategies; information seeking and planful problem solving, reported in one study in Folkman's review (1991), are related to increased educational attainment in younger cohorts; confrontation, increased emotional expression, and less acceptance of responsibility for one's actions probably represent generational changes that are similar to the observations in sequential studies of personality, when several cohorts were followed longitudinally (Schaie & Willis, 1991, pp. 290–294). Folkman (1991) also cautions that the discrepancies in the findings on coping may represent primarily contextual differences. For example, family-associated stresses for younger adults usually involve children at home, whereas, for older persons, this is a rare occurrence. Aldwin (1994, pp. 234–239) came to the tentative conclusion that older people may learn to focus on context-specific strategies in which a reappraisal of the situation may reduce the stress. She refers to this as transformational coping that is energy-efficient.

Though she does not mention it, Aldwin's conclusion is similar to that of Brandstädter and Renner (1992), who attribute the lack of significant age differences in coping styles in most studies to some theoretical deficiencies, hypothesizing that aging is associated with changes in coping strategies. Based on cross-sectional data, they found that young adults exhibit personal preferences for active–tenacious goal pursuits in solving problems, while older individuals have more passive–accommodative tendencies, resulting in flexible goal adjustments. The latter consists of reinterpreting initially aversive situations and relinquishing the pursuit of blocked goals. Brandstädter and Renner (1990) developed two 15-item scales: Tenacious Goal Pursuit and Flexible Goal Adjustment. They administered these scales, as well as a German adaptation of Levenson's scales of generalized control beliefs and several instruments to measure life satisfaction and other personality variables to 890 Germans ages 34–63 years. The results tended to support their hypotheses: With aging, though their oldest participants can be labeled middle-aged, there was a gradual shift from assimilative to accommodative modes of coping, and scores on both scales were positively correlated with internal control beliefs, life satisfaction, and low levels of depression. At every age level, males scored higher on the Tenacious Goal Pursuit Scale than did females, but on the Flexible Goal Adjustment Scale, for some cohorts, but not for all, women had higher scores than men. The results led Brandstädter and Renner to conclude that the increase in uncontrollable events during aging leads to a dominance of accommodative over assimilative modes of coping, and that for successful aging it is necessary to emphasize accommodative rather than active assimilative modes of coping. Examples of Tenacious Goal Pursuit Scale items are include "The harder a goal is to achieve, the more desirable it becomes to me" and "If I run into problems, I usually double my effort." Examples of Flexible Goal Adjustment Scale items include "I can adapt quite easily to changes in a situation" and "Even if everything goes wrong, I can still find something positive about the situation." These scales were related to the perceived distance and change toward 17 personally valued developmental goals. The Brandstädter and Renner (1990) constructs are somewhat similar to Weisz's (1982) differentiation of primary and secondary control; when assimilative tendencies—primary control—become ineffective, accommodative tendencies develop. This distinction differs from Weisz's construct of secondary control in that they are not deliberately chosen strategies.

Based on some preliminary data, Heckhausen and Schulz (1995) dispute Brandstädter and Renner's contention that tenacious goal pursuits decrease during aging, though they do postulate, as do Brandstädter and Renner (1992), that flexibility in coping strategies does increase during aging and that it is associated with selectivity. Heckhausen and Schulz (1995) also admit that the stability of control is domain-dependent. It is apparent that control and coping will vary from context to context and the instruments used in the assessments affect the interpretation of the changes.

Strack and Feifel (1996) concluded that the relationship between aging and coping is too complex to arrive at any definitive conclusions. Neither an age-graded developmental nor a contextual model is adequate. Ruth and Coleman (1996) complain that'in coping research, most efforts have been directed toward the so-called internal stable personality traits, and little attention has been given to factors that change during the life span, such as values, goals, motives, and attitudes. Analysis of purpose and meaningfulness in life have received short shrift. Perhaps the difficulties in the studies of these phenomena have contributed to their neglect in gerontology.

Analytical studies on age differences are difficult. The changes in most domains of behavior during different stages of life will also lead to changes in coping strategies, such as cognitive attempts to counter stresses (Folkman, 1991). Since aging is typically associated with various social-role transitions and actual or perceived decrements in motor, sensory, and cognitive abilities, we can expect that the older person must make lifestyle adjustments, and these may be viewed as changes in coping styles. The older person also has accumulated experiences that should affect coping; habits or learning style are continuously modified in response to changing environmental demands. In addition, resources that influence coping, such as social supports or finances, also will affect the perception of stress and coping. Of necessity, we limit our inquiries primarily to some age-associated differences in coping strategies of healthy older people, keeping in mind the conceptual difficulties in obtaining meaningful data in this area. While much has been written about coping in older individuals who have various illnesses and handicaps, to review this literature would require separate sections dealing with almost every disability occurring in the elderly. We examine a few recent studies that have been devoted to measuring coping styles in the elderly. Chapter 10 is devoted to an examination of stress and coping in two frequently occurring life events during the later stages of life.

McCrea (1982) obtained data from several hundred individuals ages 24–91 years who had experienced various stressors during the past year. Their modes of coping response were factor-analyzed, yielding 28 coping mechanisms; differences between young and old respondents were largely a function of the types of stresses that were experienced. Similarly, in a study by Keefe and Williams (1990), no age differences could be discerned in the coping strategies and their effectiveness in chronic pain sufferers, supporting McCrea's theory. Chiriboga (1992), in a study of a random sample of divorced men and women ranging in age from 20 to the mid-70s, identified seven coping styles, including one labeled noncoping. Again, contrary to expectations, no age differences were observed.

Aldwin (1992) obtained survey data from 238 men and women ages 18 to 78 years on stress and coping. Her focus was on two coping strategies: (1) instrumental action, a problem-focused strategy; and (2) escapism. She also obtained health data and the attribution of responsibility for their problems. Older respondents used escapism strategies less frequently, but they also were likely to disclaim responsibility for their problem. While at first glance this seems inconsistent, Aldwin assumes that self-blame and guilt feelings tend to be avoided by older people; thus, they deny of responsibility for many of their health problems. This is a case of positive illusions or optimism, which has been found to be helpful in the analysis of stress and coping (Seligman, 1991). Also, older people can benefit from their previous experiences with similar health problems, and this may be an example of wisdom.

In a prospective study of 81 independently living elderly (age range 65–91 years), Smith, Patterson, and Grant (1990) found that coping styles in life events predicted psychological disturbances but not self-reported physical disturbances 4 months later. The changes were associated with avoidant or escapist responses. However, the psychological symptoms during the follow-up period were related to the initial observations; thus, coping styles were a function of the personality characteristic of the individual, supporting McCrea and Costa's (1986) theory and findings. Also, the 4-month observation period may have been too short to observe major changes, and the individuals may have been unable to detect small physiological changes affecting health.

Roberto (1992) examined coping strategies after hip fractures in 101 community-dwelling older women ages 65–94 years. As others have reported, a wide variety of coping strategies was employed by the participants, but "seeking social support" was the most commonly taken action. Use of several emotion-focused strategies was related to poorer functional recovery. The author acknowledges the limitations of her study: The information was obtained retrospectively, it was cross-sectional, and there were no data on women who did not wish to participate or those who did not survive from the onset of the injury to recovery. This study illustrates the isomorphism between stress and coping.

Diehl, Coyle, and Labouvie-Vief (1996) administered a battery of scales measuring coping and defense mechanisms, ego level, and verbal ability to a stratified sample of 400 community-dwelling participants ranging in age from 10 to 87 years. Older adults reported that they tended to use "more mature" coping and defense strategies that involved a reappraisal of conflict-inducing situations via a reduction of the perceived conflict and lowered impulsivity; women at all ages also tended to use strategies that reduced conflicts. At all ages, such strategies are related to higher verbal abilities. The data refute the stereotype of the old person who reverts to child-like behavior. The authors acknowledge the limitations of this cross-sectional study. Since it has been posited that today's young people grew up in a more violent world in which aggression is more acceptable, cohort and time-of-observation factors need to be considered. The data tend to support Brandstädter and Renner's theory (1990) of age-associated accommodation.

WISDOM AND RELIGION

Another concept related to mastery and, therefore, to coping is wisdom. *Psychological Abstracts* through 1992 had not used the ascriptor "wisdom." Empirical research on this ancient religious and philosophical concept that had been associated with aging did not start until the 1970s (Clayton & Birren, 1980). Wisdom is a multidimensional construct that frequently includes complex cognitive processing, values, and coping (Aldwin & Levenson, 1994). Achenbaum and Orwoll (1991) posited three dimensions of wisdom: affective, cognitive, and conative, the old Aristotelian triarchy. In each of these domains wisdom can occur in intrapersonal, interpersonal, and transpersonal functions; thus the authors proposed nine categories of wisdom. Baltes, Smith, and Staudinger (1992) define wisdom as the availability of good judgment and advice about important but uncertain matters of life, including its finitude. Such knowledge—wisdom—considers fundamental pragmatics of life in the context of societal changes and also includes the ability to cope. The multidimensionality of the concept creates assessment difficulties in the measurement of developmental sequences. Age-associated deficits in the cognitive dimension may be compensated for by decreased arousal and accommodative changes in goals. The latter may lead an older person to accept more diverse goal objects (Schaie & Willis, 1996, p. 396). In short, a strategy that minimizes confrontation may be labeled wisdom.

Staudinger and Baltes (1996) found that people in the 45- to 70-year age range show greater wisdom than those in the 20- to 44-year age range, although the observed difference was small and context-dependent. Antonovsky (1990) also included knowledge as an important variable determining GRR, which prevents or reduces stress. Similarly, for Hobfoll (1989), knowledge is a resource whose presence protects a person from the development of stress. While the two latter theorists do not use the concept of wisdom, it seems that it applies also to their models.

Consideration of wisdom with its value component leads to an examination of another coping mechanism available to older people, namely, religion. Religious behavior is only infrequently mentioned in the psychological literature (Vande Kemp, 1996), for though religious values and activities influence many individuals, there has been a tendency in Western psychology to neglect this aspect of our experience. There have been several recent reviews on religious coping (Koenig, 1994; McFadden, 1996; Pargament, 1996; Worthington, Kurusu, McCollogh, & Sandage, 1996), but the coverage in the various reviews is selective and only McFadden (1996) specifically includes older people. A major difficulty in this field is the definition and measurement of religious activities and beliefs (McFadden, 1996).

Practically all of the reported research has been cross-sectional or short-term longitudinal studies. Since religious beliefs and the role of religion in people's lives have been changing during the post–World War II period (Hoge, 1996), comparing people who represent various cohorts neglects much relevant information. Most of the reported findings show that various indicators of religiousness are related to coping or adjustment to crisis (Pargament, 1996). It is less clear what aspect of religion is most important for effective coping, but there are some data that have addressed this issue: Allport and Ross (1967) differentiated two types of religious orientation or motivation: (1) an extrinsic orientation where people use religious activities because they satisfy other interests (e.g., social relationships), and (2) an intrinsic orientation where the religious activities per se are the motivation. At times, the two motives are difficult to distinguish; a person may initially attend religious services for social motives, but this may lead to an intrinsic need to satisfy *spirituality* or to obtain a religious uplift. Vallerand, O'Connor, and Hamel (1995) further subdivided extrinsic motivation into (1) self-determined and (2) non-self-determined. There is a fine line in this differentiation; extrinsic religious motivation may be of little benefit in coping with stressors, but intrinsic motivation may be beneficial, and there is little evidence that the latter has adverse effects (Worthington *et al.,* 1996). On the other hand, O'Connor and Vallerand (1990), in interviews of 176 French Canadian nursing home residents, found no difference in the inverse correlations between self-determined extrinsic and intrinsic religious motivation, respectively, and depression, but religious amotivation correlated highly with depression. In a review of several empirical studies Pargament (1996) found a clear relationship between general indicators of religiousness and religious coping and adjustment to crisis. Koenig (1994) presented data on the relationship between religious coping and several indices of physical and mental health, developing a scale measuring religious beliefs and activities in a cross-sectional study of 1,011 male veterans, ages 20–39 years and 65+ years, admitted to a hospital for various medical conditions. The data were collected in Durham, North Carolina (southern United States), and the sample included an overrepresentation of members of conservative Protestant denominations. In addition to initial cross-sectional analyses, data were obtained over a 16-month period on 306 participants who were readmitted to the hospital a second time. There was a high prevalence of religious coping in the older men, and decreasing physical health was associated with more religious coping. Religious copers were more likely to be married, have high levels of social support, be less depressed (whether self-rated or investigator-rated), have lower cognitive impairment, and lower alcohol use. In another study of 1,299 community-residing adults, men and women, ages 60+ years, there was no evidence that religious activities and beliefs affected anxiety. The cross-sectional data do not permit us to determine the roles of beliefs and religious practices of the individual prior to onset of the crisis. How does religiousness change as a function of age and various stressors?

CONCLUSIONS

Though the concept of coping did not appear in psychology until relatively recently, the terms *adjustment* and *defense mechanisms* can be traced back to the beginnings of modern psychology. As with stress, there are controversies concerning the definition of coping: Does it refer to behaviors that alleviate a stressful situation, to a personality characteristic, or to a defense mechanism? The latter may consist of behaviors or cognitive activities in the presence of some unconscious conflicts; coping behaviors may be either problem-solving activities or avoidance. The cognitive activity is a reappraisal of the situation to reduce the perception of stress. The latter has been referred to as emotion-focused coping. In many situations, both types of coping may occur.

Psychologists have identified numerous coping styles. The theoretical orientation of a scholar will influence the classification of these styles, and the variety of instruments that have been employed by investigators makes comparisons between studies very difficult. Coping or adjustments a person makes in response to stresses or changing environments can be invoked to explain most situations facing an individual. For many scholars, stress and coping are isomorphic. Shaver and others actually use the term *stress management*. In general, the context and cultural factors—including cohort effects—influence coping styles. It is therefore unlikely that we can arrive at generalized principles of coping, because personality and motivational variables, life goals, are critical in the choices of coping strategies. Coping is value-laden, but few investigators have examined the motives or life goals of the coper. In the absence of data prior to the occurrence of a major stressor, this is a difficult task, since experiencing stress may affect the person's motives.

Aging is associated with social losses, ill health, and various declining perceptual, motor, and cognitive abilities. Coping is therefore of great importance in the analysis of the life of an older person. For many sociologists and some psychologists, life transitions such as retirement or widowhood in the later years are the major sources of social stress that entail coping; thus, the construct is applied primarily to anticipated long-term changes rather than to unexpected events. There is much information on coping with loss of a spouse, caregiving chores, and specific disabilities such as declining visual abilities, arthritis, and hip fractures.

Almost all of the research has been cross-sectional, which limits the analysis of aging changes and the generality of the findings. Many, but not all investigators have reported that older persons use fewer fantasy or escape strategies, and conversely, younger adults use more information-seeking and confrontational strategies. The latter probably represents cohort and/or education factors. According to Brandstädter and Renner (1992) and Aldwin (1994), coping as reappraisal seen in older persons is an accommodative or energy-conservation strategy. For several health-related stresses, it has been reported that older persons use denial of responsibility as a coping mechanism. However, optimum coping strategies vary for different stressor, and as an individual's abilities decline, social supports play an increasingly important role.

Brandstädter and Renner introduced two constructs, tenacious goal pursuits and flexible goal adjustment, to differentiate coping in the young and the old. Older individuals are more likely to use flexible goal adjustments as coping mechanisms, making accommodations to fit their diminishing abilities when they feel that they can no longer engage in tenacious goal pursuits.

There has been recent interest in wisdom, traditionally associated with maturity, and in religious activities and beliefs as important cop-

ing factors. Both of these are multidimensional concepts that are difficult to measure. According to Baltes, certain types of life experiences
lead to wisdom-related knowledge. Whether they become more important with age has not been ascertained, since most studies these phenomena have been cross-sectional. Similarly, enhanced coping has been
found in older persons who have strong, intrinsic religious motivation.
Here, too, all of the data are cross-sectional, and the role of the cohort
factor is not known.

CHAPTER 10

Ecological Studies of Stress and Coping

INTRODUCTION

In the chapters on stress and coping, we emphasized the importance of the context and the difficulties in generalizing from laboratory research or from one field study to another in which a different stressor was encountered. First, we already have noted some of the inherent methodological problems in field studies of stress and aging. We usually do not have data on the individual prior to the experience of the stressor. Second, for many life events, it is not possible to compare young and old persons, either because a stressful life event commonly occurs only during a certain stage of life (e.g., unemployment in the young and retirement in the old) or the event has a different meaning or consequence for persons of different ages, as do divorce or death of a spouse. Third, older people are more likely to experience chronic stressors that may by exacerbated by other, more recent acute stressors. For example, in addition to her own chronic health condition, a wife may be burdened by a newer need to be a caregiver to her husband. Elder, George, and Shanahan (1996) allude to the paucity of data on the impact of chronic stressors on more recent burdens. While there have been studies in which the effects of a life event for a young and old person were compared, invariably, conclusions were drawn from separate studies in which young individuals were observed in a different context from that applied to older persons. Also, the impact of an event depends on the person's previous experiences with similar stressors, as well as cohort and time-of-measurement factors.

MEASUREMENT

Assessing Stressors

Several scales were developed that covered stress-inducing events likely to affect primarily older persons. Zautra *et al.* (1994) reviewed 13 such scales. Potentially, the most significant events affecting the lives of older people include (1) social losses resulting from the death or institutionalization of a spouse; (2) illnesses; (3) role changes, such as retirement; (4) caregiving; and (5) changes in the pattern of everyday activities associated with normal age-associated sensory and motor limitations. In the summary of their review Zautra *et al.* noted that different instruments have been developed to answer a variety of research questions. Some deal only with major life events, while others focus on daily stressors or hassles. Chronic stresses or strains are more difficult to assess, and most of the more reliable instruments are domain-specific (Herbert & Cohen, 1996). In addition to standardized scales, Zautra *et al.* (1994) also recommend the use of idiographic, personal biographical narratives in studies of the lives of older adults. In the chapter on stress, we referred to the influence of daily hassles and uplifts in triggering or ameliorating stress, influences that frequently are not included in many standard stress scales. The idiographic approaches may include descriptions of unique, rarely occurring events that would unduly inflate standardized scales so that they would be burdensome for most test takers. We make a brief reference to this method in Chapter 11.

Measuring Coping

The limitations of laboratory studies of stress and the presumed greater ecological validity of field studies have resulted in a relatively voluminous literature on the psychological manifestations of stress and the coping mechanisms employed by younger and older individuals in diverse real-life settings. In Chapter 8, we reviewed some of the Molander and Bäckman studies (1989, 1994) of heart rate (HR) patterns of young and old miniature golf players, an uncommon stressor for most people. Some of the data were collected in the laboratory, and some at local and national tournaments. Thus, such research can be classified as either a laboratory study or a field study. Another illustration of the occasional artificiality of separating laboratory and field studies was the Uchino *et al.* (1992) investigation in which older individuals who were caretakers of Alzheimer patients were compared with noncaretakers during the performance of a laboratory task. This study points significantly toward the potential contribution(s) of stresses that occur outside the laboratory affecting performance in the laboratory. Time constraints and the absence of appropriate assessment instruments typically mean that investigators do not collect such data from their participants in experiments. Also, most laboratory studies deal with short-term stressors that are probably of lesser significance than some of the life events we now review: In this chapter, we examine field studies in which the investigator had no, or little, opportunity to design or control the parameters that are of major significance in the analysis of stress and coping. Data can be obtained only from volunteer participants representing very heterogeneous populations.

The broad impacts of most major life events have been studied per se, not necessarily as an attempt to understand the role of stress or coping mechanisms in general. Most of the reports are attempts to provide guidance to an afflicted individual. There is much literature on such specific stressors as the effects of involuntary retirement (Quinn & Burkhauser, 1990), death of spouse (McCrea & Costa, 1988; Norris & Murrell, 1987; Parkes, 1987), and other major life events. Indeed, many of the applied problems in gerontology, such as relocation, institutionalization, specific illnesses, and responses to natural disasters, may be regarded as stressors and thus be appropriate subjects for the analyses of coping responses. To the extent that much of psychopathology deals with the consequences of exposure to stressors, inquiries in the broad field of gerontological mental health also fall into the domain of stress studies. We briefly review two frequently major stressors that have been receiving much attention in gerontology.

CAREGIVING

Scope of the Problem

The prolongation of life expectancies in most Western societies has increased the likelihood that a person, especially a woman, will be a caregiver for an older relative (Moen, Robison, & Fields, 1994). It has been estimated that at the present in the United States, there are between 2.4 and 3.1 million caregivers just for older dementia cases (Schulz, O'Brien, Bookwala, & Fleissner, 1995). The estimate does not include caregivers for other common disabilities of the elderly or the increasing incidence of caregiving for an adult handicapped child. Noninstitutional caregiving in our society is most frequently performed by a spouse, usually by the wife rather than the husband, since women live longer and men tend to marry younger women (Gatz, Bengtson, & Blum, 1990). Most of the caretakers are elderly. After a spouse, children—most frequently, daughters—are unpaid caregivers. Furthermore, according to Brody (1985), for the middle-aged and the young-old, parent care is currently a normative stress in our society, though Brady does not consider some psychological benefits that may accrue to the caregiver, such as self-actualization or repayment of obligations. Adult children are more likely to care for a mother than a father (Miller, McFall, & Montgomery, 1991), which is probably related to normal demographic factors in our society and to the closer relationships between a mother and child. With the increasing incidence of divorce and child rearing by single mothers, caregiving by children for their mothers rather than fathers is bound to grow.

The societal implications of noninstitutional caregiving have produced one of the most prolific research areas in gerontology (Lawton, Moss, Kleban, Glicksman, & Rovine, 1991). Between January 1, 1990 and June 30, 1996, *Psychological Abstracts* had over 1,100 items listed under the "ascriptor" caregiving. This does not even include many references in allied fields, such as economics, medicine, nursing, public health, and social work. Pearlin *et al.* (1996) have emphasized that caregiving induces "stress proliferation" whereby other stressors arise from the caregiving process; thus, some of the ramifications of caregiving stress are probably not even referenced under caregiving in literature indices. Much of the research has focused specifically on Alzheimer-type dementia (SDAT) caregiving, since it encompasses the largest number of disease-specific studies.

Models of Caregiving

A construct of caregiver perception of *burden* was introduced into the gerontological literature by Zarit, Reeves, and Bach-Peterson (1980). The caregiving burden is especially acute in Western cultures that emphasize independence and personal growth. Thus, the burden may affect employment, finances, leisure time, privacy, household routines, and place constraints on several aspects of normative living patterns. This is in accord with Pearlin's view of stress proliferation (Pearlin *et al.,* 1996).

Examination of caregiving stress is difficult. Pearlin, Mullan, Semple, and Skaff (1990) presented a model of STAD caregiving and the stress process, which, just for the background and context factors, en-

compassed numerous SES characteristics (age of caregiver and care recipient; economic resources of care recipient and caregiver; education,
ethnicity, and employment status of caregiver), caregiving history, family and network composition, and availability of social services. Then,
there are numerous primary stressor indices, such as cognitive status of
the care recipient, behavior problems, and relational variables. Next,
Pearlin *et al.* (1990) refer to secondary stressors, such as economic problems and family conflicts that ensue from the primary stressor(s). Finally, personality variables of the caregiver, social supports, and coping
strategies also affect the stress outcome. They admit that caregiving
stress is a multifaceted process in which a change in one component
can influence several others, and that their model is only "an heuristic
device rather than as a literal reflection of realities" (p. 591). These complex relationships create analytical problems for the investigator.

Gatz *et al.* (1990) developed a conceptual framework in which the
stressor, appraisal, and mediators determine the outcome. Figure 10.1 is
a somewhat modified form of their model.

Lawton *et al.* (1991) emphasize that both the burden and the satisfaction from the caregiving activity need to be taken into account. They
presented a model that included (1) the characteristics of the recipient,
such as demographic variables, severity of the impairment, and amount
of required caregiving assistance; (2) relationship of caregiver to recipient; (3) demographics of caregiver; (4) social resources; (5) self-rated
health; and (6) self-perception of caregiving burden, including satisfaction from caregiving and psychological well-being. The major differ-

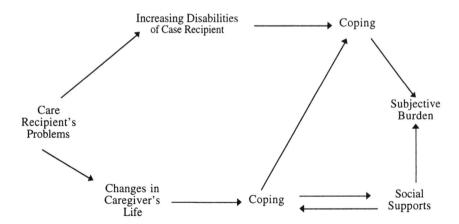

Figure 10.1.   Caregiver's stress and coping (Based on Gatz *et al.,* 1990).

ence between the Lawton *et al.* (1991) and Pearlin *et al.* (1990) studies is the emphasis by the former on appraisal of the situation, whereas Pearlin's background in sociology leads to more concern for the various objective structural factors (i.e., SES and network composition). Lawton *et al.* (1991) tested their model by performing separate path analyses of spouse and child caregivers; personality characteristics of the caregiver were not considered. In 557 spouse or child caregivers (mean age 60 years), most of the observed relationships were not unexpected except perhaps for the following: Satisfaction from the caregiving activity was unrelated to self-evaluated health; increasing impairment of recipient decreased caregiving satisfaction for children, but not for spouses. While data on age were recorded, they did not appear in the analysis. Based on their model, the significance of this study is the inclusion of not only the negative aspects of caregiving, but also the positive affective benefits that may occur and may lessen the burden, especially for spouses. The satisfaction may be related to the intrinsic motivation of helping another person, and it is more likely to occur in the early stages of caregiving (Stoller & Pugliesi, 1989).

The problem of predicting caregiver stress is even more complex than that presented by the Pearlin *et al.* (1990), Gatz *et al.* (1990), and Lawton *et al.* (1991) models. The perceived or "objective" burden depends on the activities that the caregiver must perform. First, it might be possible to relate the measures on the Activities of Daily Living Scale (ADL) with some indices of perceived burden. But not all ADLs are equally burdensome: Preparing a meal may be less burdensome for some caregivers than giving a bath. Second, during a long period of caregiving, the ADLs usually change. An even more important caveat in most caregiving studies is the use of convenience samples. Volunteers for such studies are more likely to be individuals who are experiencing much stress and who seek social support by participating in support groups from which study participants are frequently obtained.

Braithwaite (1992, 1996), in her analysis of the caregiving burden literature, places an emphasis on the interruption of certain common needs, normal everyday activities in our society that are faced by the caregiver. Some of these are similar to those seen during other life experiences, such as taking care of an infant. Braithwaite (1996) also includes in her model other factors that are frequently overlooked in many interpretations of caregiving, such as the awareness that deterioration is occurring in the care recipient, the unpredictability of the changes, and the lack of choices available to many caregivers who typically experience a multiplicity of losses. For the author, caregiving burden is a subjective phenomenon depending on the appraisal of the caregiver, and she follows Lazarus's (1990a) position in assuming that caregiving burden is a mediator between environmental stressors and the stress reaction. Her approach is also similar to that of Lawton *et al.* (1991), who emphasize appraisal and reappraisal of the perceived threat and the available coping mechanisms. This approach contrasts somewhat with the Pearlin *et al.* (1990) model, which places greater emphasis on several objective variables. However, in both models personality of caregiver is taken into account. Parenthetically, in a small sample, Hooker, Frazier, and Monahan (1994) found that the spouse's personality accounted for 60% of the variance in dementia caregivers who used emotion-focused coping, but only 15% of the variance in problem-focused coping.

Moos and Swindle (1990a, 1990b) developed an inventory of eight domains of chronic life stressors. Specific negative life events, such the death of a loved one or retirement, exert their major influence by affecting chronic strains and resources. Conversely, the long-term strains influence the stress resulting from negative life events; thus, there is a transactional relationship between chronic strains and negative life events. The authors use the term "stressful life circumstances" to refer to a series of long-term strains in which an individual finds him- or herself, such as chronic illness, financial hardships, or persistent family problems.

In contrast to the emphasis on the detrimental features of caregiving, investigators have also begun to examine some of the benefits that may occur. (Kramer, 1997a, 1997b) has reviewed the literature and analyzed 29 such studies. She believes that social science in general has been focusing too frequently on dysfunctions, and this seems to be especially true in gerontology, where the assumption has been that older people's lives are full of burdens. Also, society is more willing to support studies that demonstrate burdens rather than benefits. This is exemplified by many of the stereotypes of the aged (Barrow, 1996, p. 29). Broadly speaking, for Kramer, gains consist of an increase in life satisfaction associated with caregiving. For some older individuals, especially spouses, caregiving is an important motive that fulfills their meaning of life. In Chapter 12, we review the purpose and meaning of life.

In an extended summary, Kramer (1997a) raises a number of methodological issues in caregiving research. According to Kramer, in many reports, (1) definitions are not clear; (2) convenience samples are used; (3) there are numerous confounds; (4) there are limited data on the psychometric characteristics of the instruments; and (5) the variety of caregiving tasks and recipient characteristics are not specified. The shortcomings apply not only to gains but also to measures of strain. In Kramer's review, there are no references to studies in which only strains but no gains were reported. In the latter studies, were there gains that were not measured, or were none found? In addition, the definition of strain and gain are complex. Dorfman, Holmes, and Berlin (1996), in a study of caregiver wives of U.S. veterans, also found that caregivers' satisfaction was related to their appraisal of self-efficacy and social support, variables more strongly related to satisfaction and to the perception of burden than were the background and context variables. It was also significant that caregiver burden and satisfaction were not polar opposites on the same continuum.

Outcomes

Zarit *et al.* (1980) developed a self-report scale that measures the perception of burden of family members who are the primary caregivers of community-residing demented elderly. The authors were primarily concerned with psychological distress rather than "objective" health changes. Though their instrument is still used, it has been amplified over the years by several others (Deimling, 1994). Burdens may be domain-specific or a global composite index may be determined. Domain specific definitions of burden have been used to measure different aspects of caregiving stress (Zarit & Teri, 1992). Some of the discrepancies in the definitions are due to the different models of stress used by investigators or by the inclusion of adaptation processes. Also, some investigators have restricted the construct burden to the caregiver's perception, while others have included objective measurements of stress (Miller *et al.*, 1991; Vitaliano, Russo, Young, Teri, & Maiuro, 1991). But it is difficult to separate "objective" from "subjective" measures, as we have previously indicated: Reports of pain or lack of sleep, unless the person is being observed in a sleep laboratory, are frequently assumed to be objective indices of stress, yet they do depend on self-reports. As with other aspects of stress, personality of the caregiver affects perception of stress and the mental and physical health consequences. Many of the instruments, however, do not pay sufficient attention to the coping resources of the caregiver (Deimling, 1994). After her analysis of previous studies, Kramer (1997b) presents a model that includes the care recipient's characteristics, the various caregiver characteristics, including some motivational factors (attitudes, effort), and the availability of resources. These background and context variables are important in the appraisal of role gains and role strains.

Schulz, Visintainer, and Williamson (1990) reviewed 34 studies that had data on physical and/or psychiatric morbidity of caregivers of older individuals. In all studies, stress with psychological and/or physical symptoms was reported, with depression being the most common consequence. A follow-up review by Schulz et al. (1995) covered 41 studies between 1989 and 1995. Their conclusions did not differ much from the 1990 review (Schulz et al., 1995). Depression again surfaced as the most common outcome of caregiving stress. The evidence for physical morbidity was more equivocal and usually associated with depression and lack of perceived social support. In three studies, older caretakers reported more psychiatric symptoms, but in five others, there was no apparent relationship; in the other 33 studies, age was not examined or reported. These reviews are of great assistance in the assessment of the field.

In both of these reviews (Schulz et al., 1990, 1995), the authors were concerned about the heavy reliance on self-reports with a variety of instruments that make comparisons across studies difficult. They stressed the importance of obtaining more objective measures, especially of physical health symptoms. Scharlach, Runkle, Midanik, and Soghikian (1994) also questioned the lack of representativeness in many studies of caregiving stress, because the more depressed caregivers are unlikely to volunteer for studies. This issue, however, can be raised in conjuction with many gerontological studies, as well as with research in many other fields of the biological and social sciences. Dura and Kiecolt-Glaser (1990) compared caregivers interviewed at home with those willing to travel to a university clinic (taxi fare was provided), and in a second study, respite care users who were willing to participate in the study were compared with those who refused. Caregivers interviewed at home tended to be more depressed than those who came to the clinic; an analysis of respite care users revealed that those who did not participate in studies provided care for more impaired patients. Even these limited studies show the problems encountered in attempting to obtain representative samples in gerontological research. Schultz et al. (1990) also emphasized the need for prospective studies, since cross-sectional studies are more likely to assess or neglect to include other concomitant stressors. The latter factor also points to the importance of a large number of moderating or intervening variables that affect the health–stress relationship and require multivariate statistical analyses. Also, Schulz et al. (1995) pleaded for the greater use of standardized assessment tools and emphasized the need for longitudinal studies, where the transition from noncaregiving to caregiving roles might elucidate the impact of stress on the medical and psychological status of the caregivers. At present, we have no good data on how the caregivers functioned prior to the onset of the caregiving burden.

In a stratified random sample from a health maintenance organization in California, Scharlach *et al.* (1994) obtained questionnaire data from 628 caregivers and 6,599 controls, all aged 50+ years, on headaches, backaches, insomnia, and gastrointestinal disturbances. Though the caregivers reported more symptoms typically associated with stress, examination of the number of outpatient visits to medical or psychiatric clinics showed no differences between the groups. Several interpretations of these data are possible; while the number of clinic visits is an objective datum, the motivations for such visits are varied.

A variable that is not often measured is the previous health history of the caregiver. Russo, Vitaliano, Brewer, Katon, and Becker (1995) investigated the lifetime history of mental disorders in 82 SDAT spousal caregivers and in demographically matched controls. The incidence of major depressions and/or general anxiety disorders in persons who had previously received such diagnoses tended to reappear after they became caregivers. The authors propose that psychiatric responses to stressors such as caregiving are an individual characteristic. At the same time, they also caution that study participants may have been a self-selected group that had psychiatric problems in the past.

Motivation

Not many investigators have explicitly mentioned the motivational factors in caregiving. What are some of the motives? Kramer's model (1997a, 1997b) does include a motivational variable, but she found that most studies have been atheoretical. However, there have been some investigations in which references have been made to social exchange theory, role theory, work motivation, or religious beliefs. Social exchange theory hypothesizes that the caregiver has an expectation of receiving some material, social, or psychological benefits. We may also include Antonucci's (1990) hypothesis that caregiving is payment for previous benefits given to the caregiver. Implicit in this approach is also the human need for companionship, seldom referred to by investigators; role theory assumes that the caregiver will enhance his or her social esteem; work motivation theory may lead to the perception of heightened competence; religious motivation may be based on the perceived commitment "until death do us part" (Koenig, 1994, p. 376). Several of the theoretical models may be subsumed under the construct of intrinsic motivation in which extrinsic rewards are at a minimum, especially in the case of dementia caregivers. According to Farran (1997), caregiving appears to be analogous to altruistic behavior or an existential philosophy of life (Chapter 12), but at present, the various motivational models are difficult to fit into most existing paradigms of stress and coping because there are usually several motives that may lead to caregiving. Also, as mentioned in the discussion of health behaviors, there is considerable overlap between the various theories.

In one of the few studies in which there was an attempt to analyze the motivation of caregiving daughters, Litvin, Albert, Brody, and Hoffman (1995) asked their participants to rank-order the relative priorities of their responsibilities. Never-married coresiding daughters rated caregiving as their highest priority; many had left their jobs for this chore and had few competing demands. We may also assume that for many, the parent(s) served as a very important confidant. Finally, it should also be noted that Pearlin *et al.* (1990) emphasize that in caregiving, the importance of several motivational variables may change over time; societal attitudes and the availability of various public and private assistance programs limit the predictability of caregiving stress from a set of earlier measurements. Caregiver stress cannot be viewed as an "event or a unitary phenomenon."

Spousal Factor and Age of Caregiver

Spouse as Caregiver. The spousal factor is frequently confounded with the age of the caregiver. The relationship of a spouse who is a caregiver, usually more similar in age to that of the recipient, is very different from that of a child caregiver. Chappell (1990) reviews some of the differences between caregivers who are spouses and those who are children. In addition to the age factor, spouses tend to have a closer relationship. They usually coreside with the patient, they may find many physical chores too burdensome, and they are more likely to worry over the potential of major disabilities or death of the elder spouse. Children sometimes resent having to take care of a parent, and they are more likely to be employed or have other family responsibilities than are spouses. Since wives are more likely to be a younger spouse than are husbands, in many studies, women report experiencing greater stress than do men (Barusch & Spaid, 1989; Hinrichsen, 1991). Also, in most past and current studies, wives belonged to cohorts in which many financial management decisions and access to assets were controlled by the husband. When he became disabled, the wife perceived a greater burden than when the situation was reversed, though in succeeding cohorts, this differential may disappear. Finally, it is possible that women are more caring and more affected by the disability of a loved one than men, although in some studies, husbands reported a significantly greater burden than did wives (Jutras & Veilleux, 1991). The authors hypothesized that husband caregivers were more likely to have had a reduction in their professional activities prior to becoming a caregiver than did wives. Also, one may assume that husbands were less familiar with many everyday household and caretaking chores than were their wives; among many previous cohorts in our society, many husbands seldom, if ever, cooked or did the laundry. Related to the author's attributions of stressors was the observation of a lowered perceived burden of unemployed, including retired, caregivers. It is apparent that a very large number of factors influence caregiving burdens. Gatz *et al.* (1990) noted that spouses are more vulnerable to caregiving stressors than are other family members. Since spouses are more likely to live together, are more interdependent, have suffered losses of joint social and affectionate exchanges, and ultimately are older than children, it is difficult to tease out the family relationship role from that of age and numerous other factors that also may affect the degree of stress.

Age. Ideally, one would like to examine the role of age in caregiving-induced stress by comparing experiences of older and younger caregivers who are burdened with similar care recipients. Such comparisons, however, are difficult to obtain. Though, theoretically, age can be a variable in analyzing caregiver stress, in practice, it is confounded with a host of other variables such as the relationship of the caregiver to the recipient, or health of the caregiver, many of which influence the development of stress. Younger spousal caregivers may be more resentful of having to perform caregiving chores.

Fitting, Rabins, Lucas, and Eastham (1986) reported that younger spousal caregivers of older dementia patients showed more deviations on the MMPI than older caregivers; the authors interpreted this as a sign of more loneliness, resentment, and greater responsibilities experienced by the younger caretakers. This study is a good illustration of the difficulties of attempting to dissociate age from other variables that determine stress. Their findings were later confirmed by Barusch and Spaid (1989). In a sample of 126 family caregivers, mean age 57 years, Killeen (1990) also found a correlation of −.26 between age and perception of stress. Her explanation was that younger caregivers had multiple roles and the older caregivers had learned how to cope with adversity. She also emphasized the intrusion of caregiving on free time, and this has a greater impact on young than old caregivers. Compared to many other studies, her sample of caregivers was relatively young and heterogeneous, as can be inferred from a *SD* of 14, with the mean of only 57 years. In a 2-year longitudinal study of depression in SDAT caregivers, most of them spouses or adult daughters with a mean age of 58 years, caregiver age was not a significant variable in either baseline or follow-up depression symptomatology (Schulz & Williamson, 1991). The importance of an age factor may be related to a finding by Kramer (1993) on satisfaction of caregivers wives that is related to the marital history and the prior relationships in the marriage. In a study of 72 dyads, duration of marriage correlated with the perception of a lesser burden; similarly, those who were married more than once, and those who had a poor prior marital relationship experienced more depression. Kramer speculates that this may be a cohort effect; in the past, many people believed that marriage is a commitment associated with certain obligations. Vitaliano *et al.* (1991) used a two-wave design to study 95 spousal caregivers and the SDAT care recipients, with an initial assessment and a 15- to 18-month follow-up. Only dyads in which the care recipient showed progressive cognitive or functional deterioration during the second assessment were included in the data analysis. This exclusion, combined with dyads in which death or divorce occurred, or whose members moved, left 79 participants for the analysis of caregiver burden. Mean age was 71 years for care recipients and 67 years for caregivers. While the level of functioning of the care recipient, caregiver personality, physical health, and the availability of social resources predicted follow-up caregiver burden, age was not a significant factor; it was probably embedded in some of the other significant predictors, and the age difference may have been too small for statistically significant effects. Interestingly, at the initial baseline assessment, age of the caregiver showed a negative correlation with caregiver vulnerability (i.e., older caregivers were less vulnerable). Fitting *et al.* (1986) and Barusch and Spaid (1989) have reported that many younger spouses may have felt resentment or vulnerability at having to be a caregiver. The expectation for being a caregiver is more stressful at a younger age, or the severity of the problem of younger patients is greater. However, as was previously noted in assessing the burden at the 15- to 18-month follow-up, age was not a factor. It is possible that the caregivers adapted to their caregiving chores. In their study of 527 family-member caregivers of SDAT patients, Skaff and Pearlin (1992) using structured interviews, found that the chores resulted in a "loss of self." Both younger adult children and younger spouses experienced a greater loss than did the older spouses. It is expected that younger persons would perceive caregiving as a greater interference with other goals at their stage of life, while older caregivers would perceive it as being normative. However, the total amount of variance in loss of self that could be accounted for was small. The finding that younger caretakers experience more burden fits the Fitting *et al.* (1986) and Vitaliano *et al.* (1991) studies. Pearlin *et al.* (1990) previously acknowledged the complexity of their model, which uses a large number of variables to predict the stress-induced outcomes, many of which are not interrelated. Furthermore, they also emphasize that the variables may change over time with the changes in societal attitudes and the availability of various public and private assistance programs, which may limit the predictability of caregiving stress in a given set of measurements at a specific time. Caregiver stress is not be viewed as an "event or a unitary phenomenon."

Schulz *et al.* (1995), in their review, found that in only eight out of 41 studies was age reported as a factor in caregiver distress, and in only three of them was there a negative correlation between age and psychological distress, while five studies found no relationship. In two of the three reports that found a relationship, spouses were compared with adult children; since there are numerous differences between spouses and children, mentioned previously, it is difficult to determine how age was affected by the various correlates. None of the studies found any significant correlation between physical health and age. Dorfman *et al.* (1996) reported that older spouses and those who gave care for a longer period actually experienced less burden. They ascribed this to the fewer outside demands expected of the older spouses and/or to a habituation factor. Talkington-Boyer and Snyder (1994) also found that older caregivers of SDAT patients reported more satisfaction in their activities.

In a broad critique of the caregiving literature, Abel (1990) deplored the quantitative approach in the analysis of caregiving and advocated instead a qualitative, open-ended interview approach. She believes that we are dealing with complex interpersonal relationships, not all of which are necessarily stressful. Since the majority of caregivers are women, she makes frequent references to feminist social science and the need for policies that are more favorable for women and domestic caretakers who are usually at the bottom of the economic ladder.

Social Support

Much of the previously reviewed general effects of social support on stress and coping apply also to caregiving. Most commonly, social supports moderate the experience of stress. We have already referred to the Uchino *et al.* (1992) study in which SDAT patient caregivers who had social support showed lower cardiovascular stress reactivity in a laboratory study than comparably aged adults who did not have much social support. In the Vitaliano *et al.* (1991) study, social resources interacted with a personality variable, anger, as one of the strongest predictors of caregiving burdens over a relatively extended time period. In this study, short-term prospective analysis demonstrated that not all baseline assessment variables are equally important in predicting continuous stress effects. Dorfman *et al.* (1996) noted that the number of visits and phone calls by family or friends had little effect on caregiver satisfaction or strain. Pearlin *et al.* (1996) found that formal instrumental supports by paid help or agencies are most helpful in reducing the burden of daily functional dependencies such as grooming and cooking. However, informal support—family and friends—tends to be more useful in managing behavioral problems such as emotional outbursts. These studies point to the complexity of the concept of social support.

SUMMARY

Caregiving is a common stressor that affects many older people in our society. Among the inherent difficulties in examining this area is the motivation of the study participants. Many of them expect therapeutic benefits from taking part in the research. The theories and variables such as personal control, social support, personality, and health status discussed in Chapter 10 on stress and coping need to be considered also in the analysis of caregiving. Since men in our society have a shorter life expectancy and tend to marry younger women, most commonly it is the wife who has to care for her ailing husband.

While many negative life events tend to decrease with age, caregiving is a chronic stressor for older people, and many stressors interact. Since many of the elderly also experience physical problems or financial hardships, caregiving stress may exacerbate the effects of other stressors.

Not only does caregiving induce burdens, but it may also produce benefits. Some caregivers receive satisfaction from the activity, either in terms of extrinsic reinforcers or the intrinsic motivation of helping others. Practically, it is not feasible to do a cost–benefit analysis of burdens versus rewards, and this relationship may change during various caregiving stages. It would be very difficult to construct valid psychometric instruments that measure the various nuances of burdens and benefits; there is also some evidence that benefits and burdens are not on a continuum.

The authors of a complex sociological model (Pearlin *et al.*, 1990) involving numerous objective indicators warn that they are presenting only a heuristic device that will have to be modified as data accumulate and as culture changes. Such caution and many caveats in the analysis of caregiving-induced stress also apply to other frequently encountered stressors. Psychological modelers (Braithewaite, 1996; Gatz *et al.*, 1990; Lawton *et al.*, 1991) place more emphasis on the perceptions of the caregiver than on objective indices, and the difficulties of disentangling objective from perceptual measures are present in many areas of gerontology.

While we have a few data on longitudinal changes measured over a span of a few years, as we have repeatedly noted, there is an absence of sequential information that separates the role of cohort from that of age in the perception of stress. Social supports and other factors that moderate stress are also critical in caregiving. It should be apparent that the analysis of stress in older persons is probably even more difficult than in younger age groups because of increased intra- and interindividual variabilities.

BEREAVEMENT

Introduction and Definitions

Caregiving is often related to bereavement since the two frequently follow each other. In many instances, it is an ongoing process, though it has not been always treated as such in studies of bereavement-induced stress (Bass, Bowman, & Noelker, 1991). *Bereavement* is the loss of a loved one, usually a family member, by death. *Grief* is the emotional response to the loss, and *mourning* consists of the actions of expressing grief (Stroebe, Stroebe, & Hansson, 1993). Mourning practices are cultural phenomena affected by numerous societal factors, and they tend to change over time.

Pearlin *et al.* (1990) have proposed that stressors interact and that different stressors may produce a chronic stress context; thus, caregiving stress may turn into bereavement-induced stress. Bereavement may be not only a stressor, but also be associated with feelings of relief when a long period of caregiving is terminated by death of the recipient, or other positive emotions may occur when interpersonal conflicts were present prior to bereavement (Arbuckle & deVries, 1995). In the United States, over 50% of all women over the age of 65 years have been widowed at least once (Barrow, 1996, p. 96).

Motivation and Coping

The irrevocable biological and psychosocial losses associated with bereavement induce stress with which the person attempts to cope. There has been limited research on effective coping mechanisms (Stroebe, Hansson, & Stroebe, 1993). The large number of factors affecting bereavement precludes a determination of an optimum coping mechanism. However, in spousal bereavement in the elderly, according to Lund, Casserta, and Dimond (1993), the best predictors of coping are the personal resources of the elderly. This includes psychosocial resources, such as social support, education, and health, as well as physical resources. This approach is consistent with the previously discussed resources hypotheses of stress proposed by Antonovsky (1979) and Hobfoll (1989).

Cultural Differences

Stroebe, Gergen, Gergen, and Stroebe (1992) note that the significance of bereavement is a function of culture. In some societies, death of a loved one results in long-lasting, profound grief, while in other cultures the untoward psychological consequences are minimal. According to Rosenblatt (1993) white Anglo-Saxon Protestant Americans tend to "psychologize" their emotional pain, maintaining self-control and suffering in silence. On the other hand, many ethnic groups in the United States somatize theirs and are more likely to show overt emotional responses of grief.

Measurement

The stress associated with bereavement is difficult to measure. Grief is a normal emotional phenomenon, but it is such an individualized process that we cannot specify its characteristics or delimit its duration (Shuchter & Zisook, 1993). As a stressor, bereavement may induce adverse biological and/or psychological changes common to many other disequilibrating conditions. In addition, various social and economic problems may ensue from the loss of a loved one. At times, bereavement may also have positive consequences, growth or adaptation, though these occur less frequently in older persons. As with other stressors, bereavement is moderated by numerous intra- and interpersonal factors. Though there have been attempts to classify stages and duration of grief, they seem to lack validity. Wortman and Silver (1989) reviewed the literature on coping with loss. The assumption that, at least in our society, bereavement inevitably induces distress or depression is a myth. Similarly, the need to "work through" grief is not supported by research. Since most studies of the bereaved take place some interval after death, people tend to recall things to fit their beliefs. In the section on caregiving, we referred to Kramer's review (1997a) of some the benefits to the caregiver that may ensue; similar positive consequences, though probably less frequently, may also occur in bereavement. These are, however, difficult to evaluate.

In addition to some of the major difficulties in many studies of aging, such as the cohort effect and the cultural milieu at the time of observation, there are some specific obstacles that apply primarily to bereavement:

1. In many published studies, the initial observations or measurements occurred at varying time intervals after the death of the loved one. The number of bereaved individuals accessible to an investigator at approximately the same time, even if the time frame is measured in weeks, is limited. Also, it is unethical to approach a family member immediately after the loss takes place. What is a "decent" interval? This and similar issues were discussed by Parkes (1995) in his ethics guidelines for working with the bereaved.

2. In some instances, death occurrs after a lengthy period of coma or extreme incapacitation, as in dementias. The bereaved may have been a long-term caregiver. Can we use the date on a death certificate as the zero point for the time interval?

3. In many studies, we do not have any baseline data on the prebereavement physical and psychological status of a person. What is the appropriate time before bereavement to obtain a baseline, since, in many instances, the deceased had been ill for some period before death?

4. In some studies, there have been attempts to differentiate between expected and unexpected losses. When the deceased is older, this categorization becomes more difficult.

5. Some older persons are so affected by the loss of their loved one that they are unavailable for studies because of their distress and/or because they had to relocate to receive needed assistance with their everyday activities. Conversely, some bereaved feel that an expert interviewer may act as an therapist who may help in "working through" the grief. There are very few studies in which the investigator mentions the refusal rate of those who had been approached.

6. When and how often should the bereaved be studied in a longitudinal study? During long time intervals, various events will confound the bereavement consequences. In several studies, it has been found

that the immediate effects of bereavement are different from the long-term ones (Sanders, 1993; Stroebe & Stroebe, 1993).

7. Though classification in terms of spousal, parental, or child bereavement is common, not many studies take into account the long-term social relationships between the bereaved and the deceased. We noted previously that the duration of marriage and the quality of relationships affect the perceived burden of spousal caregivers (Kramer, 1997a, b). Retrospectively, the closeness of the relationship is more difficult to assess, since it is assumed that people are reluctant "to speak ill of the dead."

Despite some of these problems, we can obtain useful information. Some of the difficulties in obtaining needed data are not limited to bereavement, for in most other ecological studies of stress, many similar, knotty issues arise. Each of them contain specific variables that are unique to a particular stressor.

Social Support

In Chapters 8–10 on stress and coping, we reviewed the important role of social supports. This factor is especially important in bereavement, since social isolation is a frequent consequence of widowhood. Several studies have shown that living with others, greater family ties, or even having telephone contact with others reduces mortality of older persons (Stroebe & Stroebe, 1993). Though in these studies there were no nonwidowed controls, whether we have here main effects or interactions, we can assume that social support is a contributing factor.

We differentiated instrumental (economic resources, assistance with everyday activities) from emotional support. Another categorization is in terms of externally evaluated versus perceived support. Others also add informational support to these categories. Stylianos and Vachon (1993) reviewed the role of social support in bereavement, and Lopata (1993) examined social support of urban U.S. widows, mainly in Chicago ethnic neighborhoods; Lopata concluded that in the past, the family served as the primary source of both instrumental and emotional supports, but with widowhood, some of the supports weakened and some women became socially isolated and economically destitute. The growth of opportunities for women in the labor market has improved their financial resources and led to some social supports outside the family. At the same time, the decrease in lineal kin size and the greater mobility in our society that often distances children and other family members from the bereaved has reduced certain potential sources; these societal changes have increased the heterogeneity of social supports and the consequences of widowhood. Stylianos and Vachon (1993) emphasize the multidimensional nature of social support and the necessity to fit the needs of the recipient with the nature, amount, and timing of the support. Attempts to provide support may be perceived as stressors; that is, the recipient tends to feel that he or she is incompetent, and some activities may have both positive and negative consequences. The reviewers also refer to studies in which some personality variables of the bereaved, such as self-esteem or sociability, influence the perception and elicitation of social support. However, personality variables also affect the perception of distress after bereavement (Sanders, 1993). Though social support may be affected by personality factors, George (1996a) believes that, in general, social support has robust effects on health, and this may be applicable also to the stress following bereavement.

Aging

As in caregiving, there are a number of factors embedded in the question of age. The most frequent loss for an older person is a spouse. However, with the increases in life expectancy, older individuals may also experience the loss of a parent, or even a child. Death of a spouse or child may also mean loss of a caregiver or confidant, and financial deprivation. Thus, examination of the consequences of the death of a loved one may involve a variety of losses. Most of the studies have been cross-sectional, with the attendant problems of interpretation of the effects.

As a stressor, bereavement induces physiological and/or psychological morbidity common to many other disequilibrating conditions. In addition, various social and economic problems may ensue. We have also noted that stress, in general, is moderated by numerous intra- and interpersonal factors. Social support and personal control, discussed in Chapters 8–10 on stress and coping, also affect bereavement. The Stroebe, Stroebe, and Hansson (1993) *Handbook of Bereavement* refers to a very large number of studies of these factors; for illustrative purposes, a few studies, some covered in the *Handbook,* and some more recent ones, are reviewed.

Physical and Mental Health

Only for heuristic purposes do we differentiate physical health and psychological distress. Psychological stressors usually also induce physical health problems and some of these may be of long duration and may even be irreversible. The weakened immune system then subjects the person to greater vulnerability to various stressors. Much research has been devoted to changes in health after bereavement; since, usually, we do not have prebereavement health information, most studies are mainly comparisons of bereaved and nonbereaved persons matched on a number of demographic variables. There are only a few anecdotal and clinical reports relating prebereavement health problems to bereavement morbidity (Sanders, 1993). Pearlin *et al.*'s (1996) stress proliferation hypothesis predicts increasing health problems in ill persons after bereavement. Later, we review mortality data following bereavement.

Many studies have found poorer physical health in the bereaved, but the heterogeneity of the groups with numerous confounding factors does not lend itself to simple generalizations. Adjustment to bereavement is a multifactorial process in which there are no simple relationships between health and psychosocial measures (Stroebe, Hansson, & Stroebe, 1993). A major factor is the time after the loss that the data are collected. Most studies of bereavement difficulties have produced skewed data; nevertheless, in many instances the consequences may be profound.

In a prospective study of 63 adults over the age of 55 years, Norris and Murrell (1987) compared persons who reported loss of a spouse, parent, or child with 383 demographically matched controls. From 18 months before the death to the time of death, psychological distress increased, and this was followed by a decrease, so that 12 months later, distress was lower than it had been 18 months prior to the loss. On the other hand, there were no self-reported health effects during the entire 30-month duration of the study. The authors hypothesized that distress is probably more pronounced, in general, prior to the death of a family member and immediately after the event than it is 6 or 12 months following the loss. Age did not contribute to the variance in this sample. However, Bass and Bowman (1990) noted that Norris and Murrell did not obtain data on whether the bereaved were involved in the care of the deceased person during the illness preceding death. In their own small sample, as a part of a larger study over several years, Bass and Bowman collected face-to-face interview data on spouses and adult children who were caregivers of their chronically ill family members, all of whom were impaired by more than one disease condition. While bereavement added to the distress induced by caregiving, no mention was made of the age variable, perhaps because the sample was small. In addition, for the caregiver, caregiving may have attained important motivational values that were lost by the death of the loved one. Finally,

guilt feelings, engendered by a belief that inadequate care may have hastened the death, could have reduced any relief from distress. In a follow-up report, Bass *et al.* (1991) found that support to the care recipient
from other kin or professionals prior to the death helps them in the adjustment to bereavement. Surprisingly, support to the surviving caregiver during bereavement may actually hinder adjustment. Again, these
data must be interpreted cautiously since the sample size was small.

Based on a study of 350 widows and widowers and 126 demographically matched controls, Shuchter and Zisook (1993) recorded numerous grief responses over a 13-month period. The most frequent
responses were crying, expressions of disbelief about the loss, feelings
of loneliness, difficulties in concentration and decision making, anger,
anxiety, and guilt. Depression was the most frequent mental health
problem, and about one-fourth of the study participants also reported
physical health problems. However, there were no objective data on
participants' health prior to bereavement. The bereaved also used a variety of coping mechanisms: Comparing the data at 2-months and 13
months, some large changes were observed. At the initial period of testing, 29% reported being sad or downhearted and 27% were tense or
keyed up. By 13 months, the two measures decreased to 16% and 15%,
respectively. On the other hand, irritability increased from 11% to 45%
during the two testing periods. Relationships with relatives and friends
did not change, nor did self-identity during the study.

McCrea and Costa, (1988), in a 10-year follow-up of participants in
the National Health and Nutrition Examination, also found that widows
and widowers showed little difference compared with a control group
in self-rated health, activities of daily living, social network size, extroversion, openness to experience, psychological well-being, or depression. The various factors that were discussed in the measurement
section could not be controlled in this survey. Perkins and Harris (1990)
used National Opinion Survey Research data collected between 1978
and 1985 on the effect of the death of an adult family member on self-
rated health of the survivors. For a 5-year period following bereavement, only middle-aged adults (ages 40–59 years) reported significant
health problems. Neither young adults nor those ages 60–79 years reported that bereavement had affected their health status, even though
many of them actually experienced multiple incidents of bereavement.
Most likely, older adults expect to be affected by deaths in the family.

The importance of the past personal history of dysphoria influences psychological distress after bereavement. In a study involving
four periodic face-to-face interviews for 25 months, Hays, Kasl, and Jacobs (1994) followed 494 persons ages 44–80 years who had been ad-

mitted to a hospital for severe illness or surgery. Of these, 154 became bereaved and the others served as controls. Those with a history of dysphoria were more likely to exhibit elevated levels of dysphoric symptoms, general anxiety, and hopelessness/helplessness. They also had smaller social networks and felt immediately after bereavement that they had little support, but this dissipated with time. The authors admit that the sample size was small and the age range was large. In another study from the same group (Mendes de Leon, Kasl, & Jacobs, 1994) of 139 community-residing widows ages 65–99 years, depression remained elevated for a longer time period in the young-old (65–74 years) group than in the older ones.

In a national probability sample, Arbuckle and deVries (1995) compared 41 adult bereaved parents and 143 bereaved spouses with 407 nonbereaved adults. The median age of the bereaved parent was 71 years and for the bereaved spouse, 73 years. Data were obtained 2–15 years after the loss on measures of personal functioning in terms of perceived health, depression, self-efficacy, life satisfaction, and future orientation. Gender, education, income, and duration of bereavement had modest influences on personal functioning. Women tended to be more affected by the bereavement than men. In the cohort that was studied, many women depended on their spouses for financial support. Education appeared to be the strongest covariate. Surprisingly, unexpectancy of the loss was not a factor; the latter finding is contrary to that reported by Moss, Moss, Rubenstein, and Resch (1993), who measured grief in a small sample of women who lost their mothers. However, Arbuckle and DeVries (1995) did not specifically measure grief as did Moss *et al.* (1993), and they obtained some of the measurements 2 years after the loss, by which time grief may have dissipated. One important factor frequently overlooked in bereavement studies is personality correlates of the bereaved. In most previous reviews, age per se was not found to induce increased vulnerability in the bereaved (Lund *et al.,* 1993; Sanders, 1993; Stroebe & Stroebe, 1993).

Mortality

Much data had been collected on mortality after conjugal bereavement. Stroebe and Stroebe (1993) in their review, found an excess mortality in most studies across cultures; widowers seem to be more vulnerable, especially during the first months after the loss. Unexpectedly, the younger bereaved tend to be affected more. The authors discuss numerous hypotheses to account for the findings.

SUMMARY

To summarize the research on what is frequently considered one of the most serious stressors in our society—bereavement, it appears that for many older individuals, age is not a significant contributor to the distress experienced following the loss of a loved one. Expectancies for such events and previous encounters with deaths among family and friends would seem to play a major role in alleviating the distress. For many older community-dwelling individuals, coping mechanisms are not necessarily adversely affected by age. A major factor seems to be the availability of both personal and physical resources. Since bereavement frequently is part of a cascade of several diverse stressors, it is difficult to arrive at broad generalizations, and with the large number of potential responses to stress, it is problematic to make quantitative comparisons between young and old persons who experience what may appear to be similar environmental burdens or stressors. However, it is safe to conclude that older persons may have fewer options in responding to stress.

CHAPTER 11

The Self

INTRODUCTION

Most human activities encompass components that are based on both biological and social motives, and the two are intricately related. In all of the previously reviewed topics we made references to cohort and cultural factors. Almost by definition, the influence of these factors is more pronounced in social than in biological motivation. Many motives change as people experience a lifetime of sundry events, especially in modern societies where there is a rapid cultural flux. The increasing mobility of people and the variety of experiences associated with the diversity of environments lead to increases in intra- and interindividual variabilities as people age, which tends to limit the generality of specific research results in social more than in biological motivation in gerontology. Also, the impact is greater in older than in younger individuals, thus; the results of simple cross-sectional studies are inadequate, and we need at least longitudinal investigations and, ideally, sequential designs (Schaie & Willis, 1996, Chapter 5)—a combination of longitudinal and several cross-sectional studies. Yet logistical problems have limited the use of the latter designs. Since much research in gerontology, as in many social sciences, is focused on immediate applications, there is less concern with broad generalizations.

Some psychologists have cast doubts on the possibility of integrating the biological and social areas of psychology (Koch, 1976, 1993). Since the concept of motivation is applied both to predominantly biologically and socially determined antecedents, we review some of the social motives that have attracted the attention of investigators in gerontology. Ours cannot be an exhaustive analysis of all social motives, since in the absence of accepted reliable behavioral taxonomies, it is impossible to arrive at any groupings that will satisfy various theorists. As

Geen (1991) has observed, the scope of social motivation and the emphasis given to it by psychologists cannot be circumscribed.

THE SELF AND SOCIAL MOTIVATION

Hilgard (1987, pp. 367–368), in his history of American psychology, perceived two trends in social motivation: In one direction the analysis hinges around the self-concept, and in the other, the emphasis is on social relations. The two are, of course, intertwined. It seems appropriate, therefore, to begin a review of social motivation with the self, since this concept pervades all of social and much of biological motivation. In the 1880s, although James, Dewey, and their contemporaries freely used the term self-concept (Allport, 1943), it gradually disappeared from large segments of American academic psychology with the rise of behaviorism (Hilgard, 1987, p. 506). In the 1930s, the Gestalt psychologist Lewin and the impact of Freudian theory on American academic psychology ushered in the reemergence of cognitive concepts, followed in the 1950s by a veritable boom in cognitive psychology, with a renewed interest in the self. In every one of the six chapters in Volume 38 of the *Nebraska Symposium on Motivation* (Dienstbier, 1991), there are references to the self. Between 1987 and 1993, over 36,000 articles with the ascriptor "self" appeared in *Psychological Abstracts*, and in 961 of them, there is a cross-reference to the elderly. The large volume of research in which the self-concept is used requires that we restrict ourselves to issues of importance to motivation in relatively healthy older persons.

SOME DEFINITIONAL PROBLEMS

James (1890, pp. 292–294) divided the self into a material self (the body), a social self, and a spiritual self. The self engenders self-feelings and actions leading to self-preservation, a motivational concept. James cited the old joke about the self, in which it consists of my body, my soul, and my clothes, since people identify themselves not only with their bodies but also with their material possessions. Many individuals buy certain model cars to express their self-concepts; other persons identify themselves by the house in which they live, the clothes they wear, and the restaurants they patronize. James (1890) discussed separately *self-estimation, self-feelings,* and *self-seeking,* as well as conflicts of the different selves. In a more recent exposition, Kuhl (1994) postulates that any mental state or process, whether a belief, a desire, or a feeling, can be described as part of the *self*. The belief in the ability to control events is *self-efficacy; self-esteem* refers to positive self-related emotions. Other investigators have favored an Aristotelian tripartite division of the self into (1) a cognitive dimension, or the self-concept, which includes the sum total of the beliefs about the self; (2) an evaluative dimension, or self-esteem, which concerns how one feels about the various aspects of the self; and (3) a conative (motivational) component, implying action orientation (George, 1990).

The use of the term *selves* rather than *the self* refers to different domains or contexts of knowledge structures and motivations (e.g., family relationships, health, play, or friendships). People's motives and behaviors can assume very different contexts in their family or on a job; the meek boss may be a tyrant at home. In the review of personal control, we have already noted that LCs, characteristics of the selves, are domain-specific to some extent. This does not mean that they are completely orthogonal, but that measurements of some indices of the self do not apply to other contexts.

According to Banaji and Prentice (1994), the self-motives can be classified into two sets, namely, those that have self-knowledge as a goal, and those that have self-enhancement as a goal. Self-knowledge incorporates the motivation to assess one's traits and abilities that are important in predicting and controlling the environment, while self-enhancement may be related to some need for achievement (pleasure?) and self-protection (pain avoidance?). Some psychologists also add the motive for self-improvement (Novick, Cauce, & Grove, 1996). It seems, however, that the various sets are interrelated: Self-improvement usually leads to self-enhancement or to self-protection. For Deci and Ryan (1991) the processes of the self are primarily motivational. For example, persons who judge themselves as weak or inadequate will have different goals from those who perceive themselves as strong or adequate. The learned helplessness seen in some older persons is a manifestation of such self-perceptions. Conversely, those elderly who feel strong or adequate will continue to remain active even when "objective" physical indices suggest that normal age decrements have occurred.

We may view the self, or more appropriately our selves, as a bridge in our understanding of the relationships of biological and social motivation. People must eat to survive, but their food preferences are an expression of their selves. Not only have there been diverse usages of the construct incorporating the term *self,* other terms, in which *self* is not spelled out—such as, ego, personality, consciousness, and mind—frequently refer to similar constructs (Levin, 1992).

In imitating the physicists' reference to a "particle zoo," a metaphor applied to the tremendous increase in the number of new particles that has been put forth, Tesser, Martin, and Cornell (1996) coined the term *self-defense zoo.* They pointed to the large variety of conceptions of self-defense processes that have been proposed for the maintenance of self-esteem. Curiously, these reviewers did not make a reference to Branstädter and Renner's (1992) construct of flexible goal adjustment, the ability to change one's goals, which is important in the life of older individuals Tesser *et al.* (1996) do mention, however, task substitution as a self-defense mechanism, and Kernis (1995) noted the multifaceted nature of self-esteem, viewed as a defensive or as a "growth oriented" process. Also, self-esteem may be conceptualized as a trait or as a state. A similar complexity seems to be applicable to self-efficacy or competence. Novick *et al.* (1996) admit that investigators in this field are engaged "in a search of an elusive construct." Bracken (1996), in his summary of the contributions in *The Handbook of Self-Concept,* bemoaned the absence of any agreements pertaining to this field, and Hattie and Marsh (1996) also note that the proliferation of many related self-terms leads to confusion. This profusion of constructs has led to the production of numerous instruments in a variety of contexts, all purportedly measuring several dimensions of the self. In addition, there is a large empirical literature that has examined LC, expectancies, level of aspiration, and other terms related, but not necessarily identical, to any specific self-constructs.

Self-mechanisms are an important part of personality, another concept that is difficult to define. This is not surprising, since, for many theorists, the two refer to the same construct. Personality and the self are critical in the interaction of a person with others. Our conceptions of our selves begin in early life, when the mother influences the behavior of the infant. The term *selfish,* for example, is a description of a personality that includes an index of self-esteem, self-enhancement, relationships to other persons, and other positive characteristics. A person's preferences, values, self-definitions, and other personality characteristics constantly reflect the contributions of other individuals. Self-conceptions are influenced by previously established motivations and, additionally, as people interact with others, their self-conceptions and motivations are affected. Thus we have here a superordinate equilibratory feedback or homeostatic mechanism (Appley, 1991). Figure 11.1 is a simplified version of Markus and Herzog's (1992) self-concept model.

In this model, various antecedents, such as life events, employment, and education, bear upon the past, present, and future selves. These selves then determine self-esteem, well-being, and choices of activities. Almost all facets of human existence that involve some aspect of motivation include some self-mechanism.

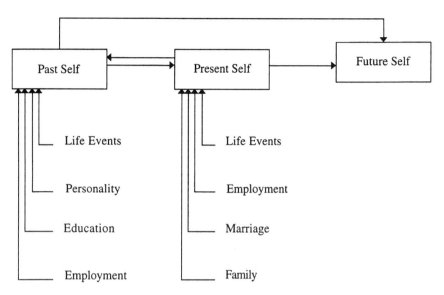

Figure 11.1.   Relationships of past, present, and future selves (Markus & Herzog, 1992).

Not everybody accepts the importance of assessing the self-concept. In a review of mostly studies of children and young adults, Berndt and Burgy (1996) are not sure about the value of measuring self-concepts. Hattie and Marsh (1996) observe that there has been little research to demonstrate the significance of the self-concept in predicting many types of behavior. Not surprisingly, the emphasis on the self-concept is culturally determined, and the current determiners may not be of much value in the future. D. Gutmann (1977) observed that narcissism or egocentrism has been increasing with urbanization. In most instances, self-concept measures have been used post hoc to explain behavior. Markus and Herzog (1992) state that possible selves are "elements of the self-concept that can easily assume a new form" (p. 118). Such fluidity creates measurement problems.

AGING

Theories: Stability or Change?

Much has been written about stability and change of various aspects of the self and/or personality during adulthood. Heatherton and Weinberger (1994) edited a book devoted to the latter topic. For our purposes, the primary focus is on the motivational aspects of the self or personality, since some definitions include several cognitive and other dimensions in which the motivational component is less explicit. Some contributors to the Heatherton and Weinberger (1994) volume championed stability, while others presented strong arguments for change. In an analysis of the divergent viewpoints, Pervin (1994c) referred to similar, previous useless debates on the related issues of nature versus nurture and person versus situation. There are numerous difficulties in attempting to clarify the problem of stability:

1. Definitions used by various investigators and the instruments employed are not uniform.
2. How large a difference can be tolerated before we abandon the concept of stability?
3. Sometimes the terms *continuity* or *development* are introduced, and it is not clear how these relate to stability. Development by definition implies change.
4. There are numerous dimensions of personality or selves even within a specific theoretical system.
5. The intervals between measurements and the ages at the time of measurement are not specified. Are the time intervals in determining stability the same at various chronological ages? Common sense would lead us to believe that a 2-year interval at the age of 4 years is different from the same interval at the age of 70 years.
6. What is the impact of various life experiences at various ages? *Success* or *competence* may have a different meaning at the age of 30 years than that at the age of 60 years. Collins (1996) reviewed the options for representing change over time.

Some psychologists postulate that the self is relatively conservative (Banaji & Prentice, 1994). Individuals want to justify and protect their past and present conceptions and evaluations of the self, which should lead to stability of self-evaluations. People frequently reconstruct their own life histories to present a unified representation of the self; however, the nature of stability may not be applicable to the various dimensions of the self. Pervin (1994a, 1994b) believes that affects are more stable than cognitions, and that behaviors are least resistant to change. Self-ratings show smaller changes than do those made by a laboratory observer, but this is to be expected if behaviors are less stable than affects. Group data are more stable than growth curve analyses. Finally, it should be noted that people tend to seek environments that support stability, since changes may induce stress. In his concluding comments on the various presentations in the monograph on the stability of personality, Weinberger (Heatherton & Weinberger, 1994), a clinical psychologist, relates some of the research to the practice of psychotherapy, which, almost by definition, is an attempt to achieve certain changes. Thus, persons who seek counseling, who read the currently very popular self-help books, or even listen to radio or watch television may be attempting to change some aspect of their personality. Many of Weinberger's comments echo those made by Pervin (1994c). Weinberger stresses the work of those who emphasize a person's search for meaning, which requires a continuous effort throughout life to change. This viewpoint was elaborated by McAdams (1994), who believes that the traits that tend to be the basis for postulating stability of personality do not tap into the *core* facets of human functioning; such core concerns are primarily descriptions of motives and goals of what people want at various periods of life, and these are difficult to capture in standardized questionnaires. A person's goals tend to change during different periods of life. McAdams favors the use of narratives, a life-story model, to interpret this approach to the self. Certain significant episodes in a person's life are bound to produce changes. He admits that there are practically no data that have examined age-associated changes using this approach. We review some related material on the meaning of life in Chapter 12. Stability is supported in certain environments. In a community with a large number of older individuals, a person may become aware that her or his age-associated changes are not unique. Indeed, the comparison with other members of the cohort may increase one's self-concept.

Role Changes

Sociologists, emphasize the importance of a person's role in society. Usually, role changes or life events, such as retirement, grandparenthood, widowhood, or a major physical disability, can affect the self-concept and thereby provide an opportunity for reorienting one's motives. Many of these changes are age structured; that is, they typically occur at a specific age or limited time interval, such as retirement. Though the normative "time clocks" in our society have been changing to some extent (O'Rand, 1996), many still persist, with only minor shifts in the age of their occurrence. In many Western societies in which occupation or work-related status is the focus of a person's self-identity, retirement requires a profound change of the self. For some high-status positions this change is difficult; in the United States, even after retirement, a judge or a senator is still referred to as "Judge or "Senator." The adult individual whose major motives are not associated with employment will be affected much less than the person for whom work is the primary motivation in life. The salience of the self-concept also changes with age, such as that of the parent, who during aging experiences a role reversal and its potential for stress. In Chapters 8, 9, and 10 on stress and coping, we discussed the importance of life events and life transitions as sources of stress that may require coping and reconceptualization of one's self. Expectancies are important. Non-normative life events are likely to produce dramatic changes in the self-concept than expected or normative events; for example, for many people in the United States, forced retirement is more stressful at the age of 55 years than when it occurs at a later age.

Both Pervin (1994b, c) and Weinberger (1994) would like to see more longitudinal studies, though neither author grapples with the logistics of such studies. Most of the published longitudinal data are based on small samples of relatively more affluent, more educated, and healthy older people (Schaie & Willis, 1991, p. 247). With the public's increasing awareness of the importance of research, we may see more data based on "less privileged" individuals.

Models of Change

With the aforementioned caveats, we briefly refer to a few models that have been proposed to account for the aging changes of the self. In Chapter 9 on coping, we discussed Brandstädter and coworkers' analysis of coping mechanisms (Brandstädter & Renner, 1990; Brandstädter & Greve 1994a; 1994b), in which they postulated that aging is associated with a gradual shift from assimilative to accommodative goal strategies. In accommodation, the perception of personal goals is altered. In addition, the authors also introduced a concept of *immunization* whereby information processing is biased to mitigate self-discrepant evidence that reduces negative feedback about the self. In this model, goal salience changes during the life span, with persons who have several goals in life finding it easier to shift to alternative options. Also, persons whose self-percepts include high self-efficacy would find it more difficult to accommodate.

A slightly different theory was proposed by Heckhausen and Schulz (1995), for whom aging results in an increasing reliance on secondary control. When primary control becomes weaker because of sensory, motor, or other losses, people resort to secondary control by using cognitive adaptations, such as changes in goals or the use of social comparisons with other older persons. However, secondary control is less efficacious than primary control; regardless of age, primary control is more desirable. Though some investigators relate some self-concept domains to self-efficacy and/or personal control, the empirical bases for these relationships are weak (Novick *et al.*, 1996). Nevertheless, we present data in which self-efficacy was used to evaluate the self-concept. Heckhausen and Schulz (1995) downplay Brandstädter and Renner's (1990) emphasis on the decreases in active goal pursuits. It appears that the differences in the two theories depend on definitions and the measuring instruments. In addition, secondary control is a heterogeneous category that is culturally determined (Azuma, 1984).

Baltes and Baltes (1990) proposed a theory of selective optimization and compensation whereby people who encounter losses select from their available life goals and focus on those that are particularly relevant for them. This may entail enhanced effort on the goals that are retained. It is not clear to what extent the Brandstädter and Greve (1994a) model differs from that of Baltes and Baltes (1990).

Dixon and Bäckman (1995) have attempted to integrate the various forms of adjustment or compensation for the normal aging losses that have been proposed by gerontologists. Though there seems to be a similarity between the various models that we have described, each seems to be applicable primarily to a specific behavioral domain. The specificity reflects the general problem seen in attempts to unify and classify the phenomena studied by psychologists.

Previous Reviews

The 1985 *Handbook of the Psychology of Aging* included a comprehensive review of age-associated changes of the self (Bengtson, Reedy, & Gordon, 1985). The studies were categorized separately for (1) the cognitive components measuring the self-concept or corresponding personality scales, (2) self-esteem, and (3) studies of the conative (motivational) component of self-conception. In the summary tables of research on the cognitive components of self-conception, 38 studies were listed, but only 12 were longitudinal and/or sequential, and of these, only three involved measurements over a 15-year period or longer, and only two obtained data on persons older than 65 years All of the latter were based on personality scales. A variety of instruments was used, which, in addition to specific self-concept and standard personality indices, included variables measuring body image, role membership, self-efficacy, locus of control, and social responsibility. It is difficult to draw specific conclusions from such a mélange and the small number of longitudinal studies of older individuals. In their summary Bengtson *et al.* indicate that most correlational studies have found stability during adulthood, but findings based on mean levels were inconsistent and subjective perceptions of the self (using open-ended questions) tended to show more changes than standard personality measures. Since most of the data were either cross-sectional or covered only a relative short portion of adulthood, the contributions of cohort membership and social/cultural trends cannot be ascertained.

All 17 studies of self-esteem were based on cross-sectional data. They reported either no age differences or higher self-esteem in older cohorts. In one study in which there was a negative correlation between age (range 60–92 years) and self-esteem, there was also a positive correlation between health and self-esteem. These findings point to the importance of health in self-perception.

Seven studies, six longitudinal, measuring the conative component of self-conception, were based on clinical ratings by trained examiners. However, of these, only four obtained data on people older than 55 years. Three were based on adults initially studied as children, adolescents, or mothers in Oakland and Berkeley, California. The participants in these studies were a selected group whose average IQ and socioeconomic status were higher than those of the general population (Haan, Millsap, & Hartka, 1986). Again, mean-score analyses tended to show greater changes than did correlations, though the latter were low. Personality dimensions reflecting cognitive style, anxiety, and energy–outgoingness were relatively more stable. These findings are parallel to the child development literature, which reports that those dimensions of the self that reflect constitutional or temperamental factors are relatively stable, whereas "content-oriented" dimensions, such as values, interests, and attitudes, are less stable. Of course, it is not easy to separate some of these dimensions. Also, there seem to be gender differences in stability. The older participants all experienced the Great Depression and World War II, and these major societal events and the associated situational factors probably influenced some of the self-conceptions of these cohorts.

Later, Markus and Herzog (1992) again analyzed the role of the self-concept in aging, though their conclusions were based primarily on studies of age differences, and they did not consider the potential cohort and time of measurement changes. For the authors, the self-concept provides an integrative framework for research on aging, and it is the key concept for achieving successful aging. Similarly, the responses to

the various stressors accompanying aging depend on the person's perceptions of self-efficacy. According to Markus and Herzog, self-efficacy
is related to the role of control, which was discussed in the analysis of
stress. Control suggests that the person has a high degree of self-efficacy.
There is a positive relationship between self-efficacy beliefs and self-
reports of competence (Willis, 1992).

It is apparent that the self is implied in a large number of human
motivational constructs. As Bengtson *et al.* (1985) previously noted, the
stability of self-perceptions during aging is still in dispute, but even
those investigators who believe that changes occur attribute them to potent social–environmental factors (George, 1990) or to major decrements
in health that override long-established habits and attitude. The
changes are most apparent in response to so-called non-normative influences (Schaie & Willis, 1991, p. 26), and the effects vary from domain
to domain. Judgment of normativeness is heavily laden with cultural
factors. More commonly, the changes in self-perception are subtle
(Markus & Herzog, 1992), occurring gradually as we age. The case study
of Brim's father (1988) is a good example of the slow changes in one's
goals. After retirement as a college professor, he bought a large tract of
land on which he developed an orchard. Initially, he did all of the work
himself, but as his physical abilities began to diminish, he hired help.
Then, he gradually reduced his goals to the maintenance of a garden
near his house; finally, he only tended a small flower bed in a window.
The issue with the self-concept is analogous to the general question
about the stability of personality during aging. Since the self is a major
component of personality, we cannot separate changes in the self from
changes in other dimensions of personality. We can, however, examine
the components that are affected by age. George (1990) believes that
self-consistency and self-esteem motives tend to counteract the effects
of environmental changes threatening the stability of self-conceptions.

Some Recent Studies

The self was implied in the context of several previous topics in
which personality influenced motivation. Here, we present some recent
studies in which older individuals' self-conceptions, motives, goals, or
values were measured. The very large body of literature in this area
means that emphasis is given to reports with large samples or those that
raise interesting issues.

Rapkin and Fischer (1992a) obtained questionnaire data from 179
members of an RSVP group, a federally sponsored community volunteer

organization for people over the age of 60 years. A factor analysis yielded 10 factors, with the first three labeled Achievement, Maintenance of Social Values, and Disengagement. Age did not influence these factors, and the authors speculated that they represent enduring personality characteristics. However, their age range was restricted. Another finding was the emergence of an Energetic Lifestyle factor, representing items measuring a desire for greater stimulation and challenge. This factor was related to good health and being married. Since these were individuals who volunteered for community activity, this result is less surprising than the authors' assertion than the results were unexpected. Also, some older persons reported a desire to achieve new roles and to maintain certain previous ones, while seeking at the same time to disengage from others. The various goals tended to be determined independently. As the authors cautioned, this was a relatively healthy community-residing sample that was actively involved with volunteer work in the community. Another aspect of this study attempted to relate life satisfaction to the expressed personal goals (Rapkin & Fischer, 1992b); both general well-being and domain-specific measures were obtained, as well as recent and past major life events (e.g., death of spouse, serious illness, crime victimization). In addition to the factor analysis described previously, Rapkin and Fischer also subjected the data on personal goals to a cluster analysis to consider combined or synergistic effects of goals. The results indicated that life satisfaction can be associated with a variety of personal goals. In this group, past losses were not related to global satisfaction scores—probably a reflection of the ability of these individuals to accommodate their goals to the losses. Presumably, those who could not make satisfactory accommodations dropped out of the RSVP or did not return the questionnaires. The health status of the 56% of individuals who did not return the surveys was not determined. Since, even among the survey respondents, recent life events and health were negatively related to life satisfaction, presumably, many of the non-respondents had such negative experiences.

Lapierre, Bouffard, and Bastin (1993), in examining motivations of older Canadians, analyzed from a sentence-completion test 15,020 aspirations reported by 708 participants. They found that goals related to the self, such as health or self-preservation, were most frequently mentioned. The second most frequently mentioned goal category was contact with others (e.g., stay with my wife for a long time, see my friend, help my daughter). This study illustrates both the variety of the domains in which the self manifests itself and the interactions of the various selves. In interviews of a stratified sample of 1,103 older persons, Krause and Borawski-Clark (1994) found that social support raises self-esteem and the perception of control in salient social domains (e.g., as husband, parent, or friend). This study emphasizes the need to determine the salience of the social domain in which social support occurs. Labouvie-Vief, Chiodo, Goguen, *et al.* (1995), in a cross-sectional study from a representative U.S. midwestern suburban sample, obtained projective and "objective" self-representation data from 149 participants ages 11–85 years; self-representation scores peaked in middle-age (46–59 years), representing a more differentiated inward orientation that is less influenced by the environment. This peak corresponds to Erikson's (1963) construct of generativity. The authors acknowledge that they could not differentiate aging from cohort factors or changes in self-disclosure; also, considering the age range that was covered, the sample size was small.

In a German study of changes in a group of 70- to 103-year-olds, Smith and Baltes (1993) obtained cross-sectional data on the self-concept. Age differences were small up to the age of about 85 years, and they were less than interindividual differences in the various age groups. Heidrich (1994), in a study of 149 community-dwelling "advantaged" women ages 61–93 years, who were tested twice over a 2-year period, found that positive relationships with others was the most important dimension of the ideal self. Autonomy, which according to Erikson (1963) plays an important role in development, was less important than personal growth, purpose in life, or social relationships. There was stability of the scores over the 2-year interval.

In a longitudinal study measuring six aspects of personality over a 30- or 40-year time span beginning at the age of 18 years, Jones and Meredith (1996) obtained data on self-confidence. There was a progressive increase on this factor but the measurement did not cover "older" participants, and, again, the age and cohort factor could not be isolated in this cohort that experienced the Depression and World War II.

THE TEMPORAL FACTOR: PAST, PRESENT, AND FUTURE SELVES

Working within a cognitive framework, Markus and Nurius (1986) introduced the construct of possible selves, the types of selves one likes to be or is afraid of becoming in the future. Cantor and Zirkel (1990) referred to cognitive-motivational units in which individuals reveal something about their pasts and/or their future desires. These units represent the person's perceptions of past, present, and future life goals as shaped by his or her memories, abstractions, or organizational schemas with various temporal foci in which activities occur. A person may believe that

"I used to be a good mother," "I am in good health," or "I would like to play golf after retirement." The three examples represent three different activity or motivational domains with three different temporal foci. The possible or future selves also provide an evaluative and interpretative context for the present self. A discrepancy between the desired possible self and the present self energizes the individual for action; up to a certain level, the greater the discrepancy, the stronger the motivation to change the present self. Aging leads to changes in possible selves, usually with a decrease in the total number of possible selves. As we indicated before, aging narrows the focus of one's activities in general.

Ryff (1991) gave six structured self-report scales to 308 individuals divided into young, middle-aged, and older adults (mean age 74 years). The scales included measures of self-acceptance, relations with others, autonomy, environmental mastery, purpose in life, and personal growth. Respondents were asked to describe their present self, past self, ideal self, and future self. Young and middle-aged adults saw considerable improvements from the past to the present self on all dimensions of well-being, while older persons indicated stability from the past to the present. Young and middle-aged persons also saw continued gains in the future on most scales, while the oldest group foresaw declines on most measures but reported a closer fit between their actual and ideal self-ratings. The pessimistic view of the future by the oldest group puzzled the author; however, realistically, this is not unexpected, since the stereotypes of old age in our society are primarily negative, and most elderly do suffer some losses.

In a cross-sectional interview study of 30 middle-aged and 30 older women (mean 70 years), Bearon (1989) found differences in the wishes and hopes of the two groups: Health was more salient for the older than the middle-aged group, while material well-being was more frequently cited as important by the middle-aged group. Maintaining the status quo was more important and seeking positive change less important for the older women. In this cross-sectional study with small samples, the role of the cohort could not be determined; nevertheless, it is apparent that there are qualitative differences in the sources of satisfaction between middle- and old-aged women. Similar results from both men and women were obtained by Cross and Markus (1991), though in their study, the family domain received somewhat less attention. In a commentary on the latter report, Baltes and Carstensen (1991) pointed out the importance of the possible selves for successful aging.

Hooker (1992) also found that for older adults, health-related possible selves are much more important than they are for college students. Overall, the number of hoped-for and feared selves was larger in college students. According to Hooker and Kaus (1994) the health-related possible selves develop in midlife (approximately fourth or fifth decade); the data for these conclusions were obtained cross-sectionally and may reflect our present culture's emphasis on health maintenance. Though the data were not conclusive, there was a tendency to see health-related possible selves associated with higher health-behavior scores. From a different theoretical perspective, Holahan's (1988) study of Terman's gifted older adults also found that life goals or purpose are important for health and well-being. Since she, unlike Markus and Cross (1991), did not categorize her domains—for example, there was no specific reference to family activities—her data are not directly comparable to those mentioned earlier, but she also reported that activities are important for health and well-being. In addition to the possible selves, past selves, of course, also play an important role (Markus & Herzog, 1992); a person's past affects his or her present as well as future selves, but recollections of the past may be rewritten by one's current goals. Markus and Herzog cite as an example one older person's past self: "I never had the means to do much traveling. As I see it now this is not important. I was able to educate my children who are now successful, and that is more important than seeing foreign countries." Many older individuals have a large repertoire of experiences in certain domains that may enhance their selves, commonly referred to as wisdom (Markus & Herzog, 1992).

In a cross-sectional study of 1,256 Germans ages 54–78 years, Brandstädter, Wentura, and Greve (1993) used self-ratings of actual and desired selves. Both actual and desired selves increased between the ages of 54 and 65 years, and this was followed by decrements; the actual and desired selves showed parallel aging changes, as did retrospective and prospective perceived gains and losses for the same age periods. The authors interpret this to mean that persons accommodate their expected losses by adjusting their expectations. This produces few age-associated discrepancies between actual and desired selves, and it provides little support for changes in subjective well-being in healthy older individuals. The data are used as evidence to bolster Brandstädter and Renner's (1990) theory of flexible goal adjustment during aging.

CONCLUSIONS

The self plays a key role in social motivation. For some psychologists, the processes of the self are primarily motivational. There have been numerous ways of defining and classifying the self, or, more appropriately, the selves. Any mental state or process such as a belief, desire, or feeling can be described as part of the self, and it is frequently difficult to differentiate various dimensions of the self from personality, consciousness, and related concepts. The multifaceted nature of the self varies in different life domains, such as health, family, or leisure activities. A person can also describe his or her self-conceptions in terms of the past, present, and future. The latter has been referred to as possible selves, whereby the individual expresses hopes and wishes—goals—for the future. For many older people, the most frequent possible selves pertain to health, activities, and relations with others. Past conceptions influence the present and future selves, and those whose past selves did not attain expected goals may have low life satisfaction in later years.

It is difficult to determine the stability of the self during adulthood because there are no criteria for specifying changes, many of which are subtle and gradual. If we use the concept of development, we are implying change. In general, self-conceptions that are most closely related to temperament, such as sociability, competence, and anxiety, tend to remain consistent in the absence of major non-normative events. Different personality types show different patterns of changes following stresses and life transitions. Wherever individual-difference factors affect motivation in various behavioral domains, the self needs to be considered; thus, there are references to the self in a number of other topics that are being reviewed. Older people tend to have actual selves that are closer to the ideal self than do younger people. Some older persons may reconstruct the past so that, in retrospect, perceived goals have been altered.

Older persons who have had many experiences may have more diverse and complex selves in some domains than younger individuals. This may be the basis of wisdom, which is considered to be an attribute of old age. In general, however, older persons have fewer possible selves associated with diminished sensory, motor, and social abilities than do younger individuals. The self is to a large extent determined by social interactions; therefore, it is influenced by the environment. Thus, the importance of cohort and time-of-measurement factors reduces the value of cross-sectional studies, the simplest and most commonly used designs in human gerontology. The few longitudinal studies of the conative self from childhood and adolescence to adulthood have not produced consistent results.

At present, the empirical literature limits the conclusions that can be drawn about aging changes of selves, yet several dimensions of the self are the major components of motivation and life satisfaction. Ultimately, we may assume that positive self-conceptions are the basis for *successful* aging.

CHAPTER 12

Purpose or Meaning of Life

THE CONSTRUCT

In the previous chapter, our discussion of the self was largely based on its mainstream quantitative treatment in academic psychology. A somewhat different approach to the self has come from philosophy, namely, existentialism, which actually represents several related systems.

Existentialism, as developed by the philosopher Dilthey (1833–1911), stressed the individual historicity of human beings in contrast to the mechanistic natural sciences approach favored by most psychologists in the early part of this century, when the discipline attempted to establish its independence from philosophy. Psychologists were searching for relatively immutable causal relationships and reinforcers in the universe. According to many existentialists, people search for purposes and meanings in life. Consciousness includes values and goals, which necessitate respect for an individual's autonomy (Brennan, 1994, p. 296). Related to existentialism is phenomenology, a method that emphasizes the unity of immediate experiences of activity or events, in contrast to the approach in the classical sciences of physics and chemistry, which seeks to determine the fundamental elements of objects that need not be active or experienced. For Brentano (1838–1917), one of the early modern proponents of phenomenology, physics deals with mediate experiences—we do not perceive molecules, electrons, or subatomic particles, while psychology deals with immediate experience—ideating, judging, wishing, feeling, and other psychological phenomena (Boring, 1950, pp. 359–361). Currently in psychology, existentialism and phenomenology are closely related (Brennan, 1994, pp. 303–304) and the existential–phenomenological movement has influenced a diverse group of American social, clinical, and personality psychologists such as G. Allport, Maslow, Rogers, and R. May.

The general phenomenological–existential approach has been applied to studies of the social aspects of gerontology. Kenyon (1988) and Moody (1988) reviewed some existential theories of aging, mainly as they can be used in the analysis of social and intellectual developments. Kenyon (1988) is critical of several scientific studies of aging that did not sufficiently account for "personal existence," or the self, and assumption of human nature. It seems appropriate to review, therefore, this "third force movement" in psychology, the first being represented by traditional experimental psychology and the second by Freud (Brennan, 1994, Chapter 17), as part of the role of the self in the motivation of older people. Kenyon (1996), in an introduction to the use of autobiography in gerontology, presents some of the theoretical issues concerning the importance of personal meaning in aging. We know ourselves, as revealed in an autobiography or life story, but this knowledge is constantly changing; furthermore, life stories may be based on public or private stories, family stories, or cultural stories. In older persons, the past may be reconstructed to serve the present. The various accounts of an individual's life stories at various times are not necessarily coherent; thus, according to the phenomenological approach, the question of stability versus continuity of personality or the self over the life span may not be relevant. A variety of qualitative methods are applicable to the analysis of life stories or the life course (Hendricks, 1996; Marshall, 1996). Datan, Rodeheaver, and Hughes (1987), in a review of the diverse methodologies that have been used in studies of life-span development, reflected on some of the fundamental discrepancies among the findings, with traditional psychometric approaches of personality contrasted with those using idiographic or descriptive techniques. Birren and Lanum (1991) note that it is easier to focus scientific investigations on areas farthest removed from those considered parts of human nature. This observation can be further extended to apply to psychology. Studies of overt behaviors and extrinsic reinforcers are easier to assess than are altruism, spirituality, virtue, meaning of life, and other similar abstract constructs. Thus, twentieth-century psychology has largely ignored such aspects of human existence. Kagan (1996) has raised a similar complaint in the context of studies of child development that had little to say about a moral sense.

While the construct, *meaning of life,* has arisen from existentialism or phenomenology, some psychologists have applied to it techniques that fit more mainstream psychological methodologies. We focus primarily on the studies of the latter genre. Our approach is analogous to Rychlak's (1993) advocacy of theoretical complementarity, physical and psychological dualism, but it still insists on a unified methodology. The material that follows could have been incorporated in the previous chapter, since meaning or purpose of life is embedded in an individual's motives and some of these studies were reviewed previously. In this chapter, we focus on research in which the construct of meaning has been explicit; it will become apparent that there has been much cross-fertilization of constructs as well as experimental methods. We briefly present first the approach of some representatives of this movement, especially those who influenced gerontological research.

MODERN EXPOSITORS

Frankl

Though he has received little attention in American psychology (Schultz, 1977, p. 117), the Austrian psychiatrist Frankl (1962, 1967) has had considerable influence on studies of motivation in older persons. In an autobiography, Frankl (1962) described his 3-year experience in Auschwitz and other Nazi concentration camps and how he managed to survive despite the dehumanizing brutalities and a lack of basic biological necessities. He attributes his survival to (1) freedom of the will and (2) a "will to meaning" or "meaning of life"; by freedom of the will, he meant that he was able to view the situation from his own perspective rather than from that of his tormentors. By "will to meaning" and "meaning of life" he meant that he described his search for a transcendent purpose for his existence. For Frankl, these are the major factors of human motivation. During his ordeals in the concentration camps, he kept thinking about the future instead of abandoning all hope in an environment that provided no external tangible reinforcements for a purpose to live: "It didn't really matter what we expected from life, but rather what life expected from us" (p. 77). Those who had lost their sense of purpose perished. For Frankl, "life" is not something vague, but the tasks that a person should perform are very concrete. It was such an attitude that kept him alive, even when it involved great suffering. Of course, the meaning of life differs from person to person, and it changes for the same individual from time to time. For Frankl, meaning must be extracted from the existing situation, though it may be horrible. Each individual must discover his or her own purpose by commitment to others, transcending the self. The will to meaning is not equivalent to Freud's pleasure principle or Adler's will to power (Frankl, 1967, pp. 5–6). Pleasure occurs when the will to meaning is obtained, and power is a means to an end. While biological homeostasis is essential, for

Frankl (1962, p. 42), it cannot be the ultimate aim of life; even if a person should satisfy all of his or her biological needs, he or she would still be experiencing an existential vacuum. A lack of purpose in life is a neurosis. This is a problem in Western societies for many older people, whose previous major motivations in life were to perform well in an occupation and to raise a family. Once these tasks have been completed, they lack a purpose for living.

While philosophers have pondered the question of meaning since ancient times, Frankl's post–World War II writings have provided an impetus to social scientists to tackle the problem and to create objective techniques for its measurements. Several empirical tests of Frankl's ideas were developed, and some of them were combined with other related constructs, for example, life satisfaction and, personal relationships (Harlow & Newcomb, 1990).

Maddi

In the *Nebraska Symposium on Motivation,* Maddi (1970) claimed that the search for meaning is the "ultimate problem" of human motivational psychology. Adults cannot escape the question of which activities in terms of family, job, or recreation are worth pursuing. Which reinforcements are meaningful? In existential psychology, each decision and action a person takes creates meaning; personal choices are thus meaningful, and the individual is responsible for them (Maddi, 1970). Kenyon (1996), however, believes it is not always easy to separate events for which an individual is responsible from those that occur accidentally. To what extent are people responsible for the health problems that afflict them in old age? According to Maddi, present functioning is influenced by future goals. Death anxiety, which appears even in adolescence, and various gross social upheavals precipitate existential questions. For Maddi, many problems in psychopathology revolve around the search for meaning: Apathy, boredom, nihilism, and depression are symptoms of existential sickness. Sometimes the incessant need to search for dramatic causes may also be a manifestation of this sickness.

Klinger

Writing "in the tradition of scientific psychology," Klinger (1977, p. 4) constructed a theory of motivation that emphasizes a person's feeling that life is meaningful. For Klinger, meaningfulness is akin to *purpose.*

In an open-ended questionnaire, 138 college students were asked what contributed to the meaningfulness of their lives; having friends, family, religious faith, and education were among the most frequently reported items. Klinger (p. 10) also notes that we cannot infer what is meaningful for someone by knowing his or her objective circumstances cɔ ɔy observing behaviors. Aging for some people is described by Klinger (pp. 226–234) as a stage of life in which few activities that younger people enjoy, such as romantic love, work, and positions of power, make their lives meaningful. While the loss of some of these incentives in the elderly is inevitable, others can be attributed to our social system, in which older persons are considered dispensable.

Reker and Wong

Reker and Wong (1988) reviewed some of the psychological literature on personal meaning and proposed a theory of personal meaning or the meaning of life for an individual within the context of gerontology, acknowledging their debt to Frankl (1967) and Maddi (1970). Their fundamental postulate is that every individual is motivated to seek and find personal meaning in existence (p. 222). They view personal meaning as a multidimensional construct with at least three related components— cognitive, affective, and motivational, the classical triarchy of the self. Their motivational component refers to an individual's value systems that guide, direct, and energize activities and determine goals. Reker and Wong define personal meaning as the "cognizance of order, coherence, and purpose in one's existence" (p. 221). Though they make no references to Antonovsky (1990) and his sense of coherence (SOC) construct, which he posits as an important buffer in stress, Reker and Wong's definition is very similar. The importance of order and purpose was also Maddi's (1970) criterion of meaning. As did previous writers, Reker and Wong (1988) admit that some values a person holds may be conflicting with some of these factors arising from sociohistorical events that impact on previously established values. During his concentration camp experiences, Frankl (1962) thought about the importance of a future orientation, though meaning must be discovered from the existing circumstances even when the latter are horrible. Compared to the period of Frankl's development of his thinking, Reker and Wong (1988) wrote during a period of normal world conditions and placed less emphasis on the future orientation, championing an integration of the past, present, and future. They cite others who recommend that one's present and future meanings should depend on the review and evaluation of the past. Aging persons who experience losses of physical or mental abilities, or economic and other social resources, must reconstruct their values and meanings. However, the importance of a future-time perspective for the motivation of older persons has been emphasized by a number of gerontologists (Lapierre *et al.*, 1993). Reker and Wong use Erikson's (1963) and Bühler's (1962) concepts of increasing integration of personal meaning during normal—or to use a currently popular term, "successful"—aging (Ryff, 1989a). The approach to death also raises existential issues related to religion; Reker and Wong (1988) cite studies that indicate religion is positively related to older persons' finding meaning and life satisfaction. They also reviewed both qualitative and quantitative methods applicable to the measurement of personal meaning.

Baumeister

Baumeister (1991) postulates that people have *needs for meaning* (p. 11). These include the concepts of purpose, value, efficacy, and self-worth: Purposes are specific goals and their fulfillments; goals are external to the individual, while fulfillments are intrinsic purposes. Baumeister (pp. 33–34) admits that the two categories are not always discrete; values are justifications, and efficacy implies control over events. Finally, self-worth enables people to feel they have positive values that lead to feelings of a sense of superiority in some aspect of life. Baumeister (p. 44) realizes that self-worth and value may overlap. Aging is associated with losses of control and efficacy, and older persons need to replace many previous goals with new ones (pp. 42, 320, 323). As does Klinger (1977), Baumeister implicates social factors in the devaluation of the role of older people in modern societies (pp. 105, 154).

RELATIONSHIP TO OTHER CONSTRUCTS

The sense of meaning or purpose can be related to several other constructs that we have discussed previously. Rothbaum *et al.* (1982) relate Frankl's (1967) construct of will to meaning or purpose to secondary control in which the situation is reinterpreted. Such control is especially important for older persons when primary control is not attainable because of diminshed biological, psychological, or social resources, and the environmental situation appears to be hopeless. They cite laboratory studies in which children who fail on a task may resort to an interpretive secondary control. In many situations, achieving meaning in lieu of attempting to exert primary control may be adaptive, since the person may focus on the development of skills that will later lead to primary control.

Brandstädter and Renner's (1992) construct of accommodation can also be subsumed under the construct of meaning of life. Finally, Erikson's (1963) stages of life describe the changes in motivation at various points in the life span.

EMPIRICAL STUDIES

The lack of agreed-upon definitions of personal meaning has resulted in a number of studies in which this construct has been measured very differently. This is not surprising, if Maddi's (1970) ascription of "search for meaning" as the ultimate human motive has any validity. We began our monograph emphasizing the diversity of views about motivation; thus, in attempting to define personal meaning, or the "basic" human motive, we are bound to discover great variations in definitions. Several investigators developed their own scales to measure meaning in life or purpose, while others used existing scales that were originally devised to measure related constructs. We briefly review some of the studies in which data were collected on older populations, primarily those in which comparisons were made also with data from younger participants.

One of the earliest attempts operationally to test Frankl's ideas (note that he never claimed that he had a "theory" of meaning or purpose) was by Crumbaugh and Maholick (1964), who developed a 22-item (later reduced to 20 items) Purpose in Life (PIL) attitude scale, which was initially used to test some of Frankl's ideas in different populations. It has "lately" gained popularity and has been applied in studies of alcoholism, suicide, depression, and drug abuse (Harlow & Newcomb, 1990; Reker & Wong, 1988). While the PIL correlates highly with some measures of depression, it may also reflect an existential, vacuum-like construct (Dyck, 1987). However, according to Klinger (1977, p. 347) the PIL test, in addition to measuring meaningfulness, also includes items that measure some of its consequences, such as depression.

Reker, Peacock, and Wong (1987) developed a 46-item Life Attitude Profile (LAP) scale consisting of seven dimensions measuring (1) life purpose (LP), (2) existential vacuum (EV), (3) life control (LC), (4) death acceptance (DA), (5) will to meaning (WM), (6) goal seeking (GS), and (7) future meaning (FM). In a study of 150 men and 150 women ranging in age from 16 to 75+ years, they administered the LAP and a 14-item well-being scale, which included measures of both psychological and physical well-being. GS and FM exhibited a linear decline with age; EV showed a U-shaped relationship with age, with the young adults and the oldest group (75+) scoring the highest on this dimension; DA and LP increased linearly with age, while LC and WM were similar at all ages. Combining data for all ages, FM, LP, and LC showed positive correlation with perceived physical and psychological well-being, while lack of meaning and purpose in life and DA were negatively correlated with well-being. Analysis of LAP and well-being data indicated that the relationships between these measures varied during different stages of life. The desire to achieve new goals and the anticipation of a meaningful future showed the most dramatic declines with age. The increased EV in the oldest-old probably reflects the low status of this age group in our society. The authors caution the readers that this was a cross-sectional study that did not take into account the sociohistorical changes experienced by the participants. Also, there were no objective data on physical health. This was a correlational study that could not determine whether well-being, physical and/or psychological, enhances a sense of meaning or purpose, or whether causality is in the other direction. Related to the last issue, the sources of meaning or purpose were not investigated. Later Reker (1994) again reported that PIL scores increase with age in healthy successful elderly.

Ryff (1989a) constructed a six-dimensional scale of psychological well-being. One of the six scales was labeled PIL. This scale as well as other previously employed self-rating scales of affect balance, life satisfaction, morale, LC, and depression were administered to young, middle-aged, and older adults ($N = 80$ for the oldest, mean age 75 years). The latter group was highly educated, healthy, and financially well off. The PIL items correlated between .60 and .33 with the other previously used scales of well-being. The new scale of well-being was then factor analyzed: The PIL items had a moderate loading on Factor 1, (.41) labeled general well-being by Ryff, but they had a higher loading on Factor 2 (.71) labeled self-acceptance. Other items on this factor with high loadings measured personal growth (PG) and positive relations (PR) with others. The results fit some of Frankl's (1967) notions. PIL items showed an inverted U-shaped relationship with age, with the middle-aged group having the highest scores and the old group the lowest. This factor accounted for 51% of the variance. On Factor 3, labeled environmental mastery (EM), PIL items had a loading of less than .40. Some of the data agree with some of those reported by Reker et al. (1987), who found that EV was the lowest in their middle-age group and highest among the old and young participants. But Reker et al. (1987) and Reker (1994) also found that PIL increases with age, a discrepancy that may reflect differences in the scale items or sample characteristics. Using a structured interview format, Ryff (1989b) obtained data from 59 middle-aged (mean age 52 years) and 102 older (average age 73.5 years) community-residing adults. The middle-aged respondents stressed the importance of self-confidence, self-acceptance, and self-knowledge, while the older participants cited acceptance of the inevitable aging-associated declines. Both groups reported that family was the most important factor in their lives. While the middle-aged respondents focused next on jobs, the older ones placed health as the next important factor.

Ryff and Essex (1992) again used Ryff's scale (1989a) and found that after residential relocation, PIL, EM, and PR accounted for most of the variance of psychological well-being. As they caution, this correlational study could not determine the direction of causality. Did individuals showing the positive psychological characteristics relocate, or did those who adjusted to relocation interpret their relocation favorably? In other words, the perceptions may be either the antecedents or the consequences of relocation. Ideally, pre- and postrelocation data would have been desirable, as well as some measures other than self-reports, such as behavioral observations, measures of physical health, or peer reports. With a later sample Ryff and Keyes (1995) essentially replicated the previous findings.

Baum and Stewart (1990) obtained data from 185 volunteers ages 17–96 years on the amount and origins of most meaningful events in a person's life. A total of 708 life events was categorized. The most frequently mentioned category for men was work, and for women, love and marriage. Most meaningful events occurred between the ages of 25 and 43 years, and the types of meaningful experiences were similar in old and young respondents. The extent to which widely held social stereotypes influenced responses of older individuals could not be ascertained. A longitudinal study, a difficult undertaking, might provide some clues. In a New Zealand sample of 155 people aged 60+ (mean 69 years), Zika and Chamberlain (1992) correlated responses on three instruments, each measuring psychological well-being, life satisfaction, and psychological distress, with three different measures of meaning in life, including the PIL test and Antonovsky's (1979) SOC. The correlations among the three life-meaning scales ranged between .62 and .84. Thus, the three instruments measured a similar construct. The correlations among each of the life-meaning scales and the three instruments assessing life satisfaction ranged from .79 to .60, for psychological distress, from −. 63 to −.36, and for psychological well-being, from .77 to .56. The PIL showed the highest correlations between the life-meaning and the well-being measures. Alpha coefficients demonstrated high levels of internal consistency for all measures. The life-meaning measures were negatively related to anxiety, depression, and emotional control, and positively related to emotional ties and general positive affect. Overall, the study suggests that psychological well-being and meaning-of-life measures overlap. Just as in the Reker *et al.* (1987) study, the direction of causality and the sources of meaning were not determined. In older individuals with an accumulation of life experiences, this may be a difficult task. In the Lapierre *et al.* (1993) study, transcendental goals (e.g., religious aspirations, or having a good death) increased with age. With a smaller sample of 55- to 89-year-olds in the Netherlands, however, Smits, Deeg, and Bosscher (1995) were unable to support the Zika and Chamberlain (1992) findings.

Ruth and Öberg (1995) asked 37 urban Finns, ages 73–83 years and living alone, to tell them their life histories. The interviews, which lasted 4–16 hours, were analyzed to understand how sociohistorical and personal factors influenced the development and maintenance of "a way of life." Though six general patterns were discerned, they ranged from a life of misery ("a bitter life") to happiness ("a sweet life"). Childhood, economic conditions, a spouse, health, urbanization, and historical events all influenced satisfaction in old age. A comparison of elderly Jewish immigrants in Cleveland, Ohio, and in Leeds, England, in the 1970s, who received similar assistance from their children, demonstrated the role of early family experiences and the children's lifestyles on parent–child interactions late in life (Francis, 1984, pp. 75–76). Simply analyzing current circumstances of older people is unsatisfactory. These studies cast doubts on cross-sectional studies that do not probe the life history of a person.

DePaola and Ebersole (1995) evaluated a brief open-ended question—"What is the strongest meaning of your life right now?"—in 53 nursing-home residents (mean age 81 years), in 36 community-residing elderly (mean age 76 years), and in adults over the age of 30 years. The respondents could also indicate that nothing is meaningful. In all three groups, relationships were mentioned most frequently as the most important factor. Health came in second in the elderly community group, but pleasure was named more frequently in the nursing-home group. Thus, even in nursing homes, life is not meaningless.

CONCLUSIONS

Existentialism, a philosophical concept regarding the search for meaning and purpose in life, also influenced psychosocial gerontology. Recently, investigators have begun to rely again on methodologies of self-reports and autobiographical techniques in their studies of goals and purposes. In Western societies, since old age is considered to be a phase of decline in the human life span, questions arise about the motivations or purpose of the elderly in continuing to remain active. Several new instruments were developed to measure constructs based primarily on the writings of Frankl, who stressed the "will to meaning." Attempts have also been made to relate them to other constructs previously investigated, such as life satisfaction, morale, happiness, personal control, future orientation, and positive affect. In several studies, it has been demonstrated that some of these constructs overlap, which is to be expected in a field where definitions abound, and, consequently, the instruments do not have the psychometric characteristics that we usually associate with more traditional measurements in psychology. This has also led to somewhat discrepant findings in different studies. At the same time, this effort has revealed the shortcomings of research in personality, in which little attention has been given to the individual life histories of the study participants. Furthermore, during development, persons continuously seems to adjust and change their perception of the meaning of life. This creates problems for a *strong* stability theory, though, for purposes of prediction, stability is preferable.

While there are numerous antecedents affecting the self and the perceived meaning and purpose of life, in most instances, health, finances, family, other sources of companionship, and religion are major contributors. Currently, successful aging, encompassing most of these constructs, is a popular term in both the scientific and lay literatures. Maddi views the construct of meaning as the "ultimate human motive."

CHAPTER 13

Social Relationships

INTRODUCTION

In Chapter 11, reference was made to Hilgard's (1987) observation that one of the major thrusts in studies of social motivation has been the analysis of social relations. We have also indicated previously that B. Weiner (1992, p. 363) believes that a theory of human motivation must be able to account for affiliative goals. The present topic is of major significance in gerontology, for many older persons would be hard pressed to manage without the assistance of others. Such dependencies have led to the proposition that organisms have a need for what has been variously called attachment, social contact, or social relationships. The whole discipline of sociology is based on the assumption that social interactions are an essential part of human existence. The need to belong manifests itself already in most animal species; from the earliest period of human evolutionary development, mating, subsistence, and protection required the presence of more than one person. The "lone wolf" is a common pejorative metaphor.

We have reviewed the influence of social support, the role of other people in the prevention or reduction of stress and mortality. Similarly, health behaviors are also facilitated by social support. Here, we are primarily concerned with age-associated changes in social contacts, affiliation, social relations, social ties, attachments, friendships, and other related constructs that describe social interactions between people who are kin or friends. Some of the findings on the self, reviewed in the previous chapter, are applicable also to the analysis of social relationships.

Definitions

Though there is a growing literature in this field, Antonucci (1990; 1991) and Berscheid (1994) have noted that there has not been a unified framework for this research that has emanated from diverse disciplines such as psychology, sociology, anthropology, social work, nursing, epidemiology, and so on. Currently, Western societies are mobile, and changes in family and other kin relationships have complicated the analysis (Blieszner & Adams, 1992, p. 3). The latter can be attributed to increases in divorce and remarriage rates, single-parent families, diverse stepfamily models, and other less traditional family forms. There is a lack of agreement on the definitions of most constructs pertaining to social relationships (Schwarzer & Leppin, 1991); yet in the analysis of several topics in gerontology, an understanding of social relationships is critical. While many interactions are close or intimate, people also experience numerous casual contacts in their daily lives, such as those that occur between a telephone operator and a caller, a salesperson and a customer, or a bank teller and a depositor. Occasionally, it is difficult to separate casual from close contacts: Clergy and their congregants may be engaged in a variety of contacts, some very casual and others more close; a long-time client of a beauty salon may develop close contacts with a beautician, who may provide the client with social support such as advice or even catharsis. Similar relationships may occur among bartenders, patrons, and other service providers in our society, fragmented by specialists, and there is widespread use of crises telephone hot lines, where strangers reveal their intimate feelings and concerns to an anonymous person.

Wood (1989) distinguishes between interactions and relationships: for her, interactions are the observable, specific social episodes that occur in a given context, whereas relationships are the cognitions a person has about interactions. Relationships are abstract, decontextualized categories. Wood illustrates her distinction with studies in which measures of family visits, interactions, did not affect feelings of loneliness, since, presumably, the latter is a function of a relationship rather than merely the frequency of contacts. Also, she points out that one cannot always ask persons directly to rate their interactions on some scale of closeness. It would seem that she applies her concept of relationships to what others have labeled close interactions; however, as we have noted, the constructs are not uniformly defined; thus, boundaries between close and casual interactions are fuzzy. Duck and Montgomery (1991), in their introduction to a volume on studies of interpersonal interactions, emphasize that "objectivity in interaction research is impossible"

(p. 12). Different measures that have been used in this field reflect the varied theoretical assumptions of the investigators. For instance, self-report data can differ from those obtained from outside observers or a participant in a relationship, and cognitive, affective, and behavioral data may lead to divergent results. Wills (1991) believes that an important variable in social relationships is the perception of dependability; the assumption in the construct "high emotional support" is that the person will be available when the need arises and that such support is more likely to come from family than from friends (Felton & Berry, 1992). However, since people have numerous motives, it is difficult to determine the contribution that various members of one's network can make when "a need arises." In some studies, it has been reported that among older people, friends are more commonly relied on for active leisure, but family members are more dependable as sources of contact, security, and social support (Larson, Mannell, & Zuzanek, 1986). Also, given today's complex family forms, studies often do not contain a careful analysis of the kinship and closeness relationships.

Schwarzer and Leppin (1991) attempted to synthesize a taxonomy of social relationships based on previous usages. They cite House *et al.*'s (1988) three relationships constructs: (1) "social integration," which refers to the quantity of social relationships, the size of the networks, and the frequency of contacts, all of which can be measured "objectively" and require only minimal perceptions by the receiver; (2) "social network structure," defined as a set of relational properties such as reciprocity, durability, sex composition, or homogeneity, which also require minimum cognitive demands from an individual, though more than in social integration; and (3) "relational content," comprising social support, control, social demands, and conflict. Schwarzer and Leppin (1991) believe that this sociological analysis does not emphasize sufficiently the psychological functions, mainly the benefits of social relationships in what has been broadly subsumed under the concept of social support, except perhaps in the relational content category. Cognitive factors such as perception of support or expectations are minimally present in the House *et al.* (1988) system. Schwarzer and Leppin (1991) propose a taxonomy of three types of social relationships: (1) a sociological network analysis like that of House *et al.*, described earlier; (2) a *cognitive social support* analysis in which expectations and the evaluation of the amount of support are determined; (3) a behavioral *social support* category that in times of need provides the mobilization (a coping strategy), actual receipt, and evaluation of emotional, instrumental, and/or material support(s). Figure 13.1 is based on Schwarzer and Leppin's three approaches to measuring social interaction and social support.

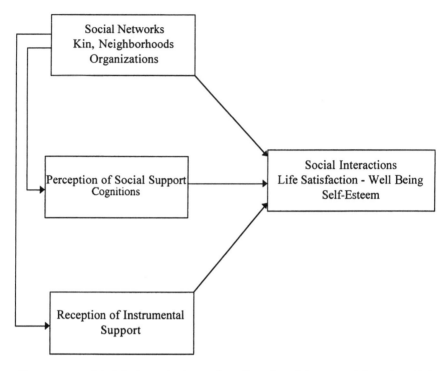

Figure 13.1.   Model of social relationships (based on Schwarzer & Leppin, 1991).

Data for a sociological network analysis are suitable for large-scale demographic studies, since there is little need for cognitive evaluations, and there are logistic problems in obtaining detailed interviews in large samples. On the other hand, the Schwarzer and Leppin (1991) model requires measures of recipients' expectations and evaluations of received support. The expectancies are anticipatory, whereas behavioral supports are retrospective (p. 439). The authors present a transactional model influenced by Lazarus's theory (1991), and since there are continued transactions between individuals in social relationships, data analyses can become complex. It is not surprising, therefore, that Schwarzer and Leppin (1991) acknowledge that the intercorrelations even within the three approaches to measuring social support have been very low in studies where this was attempted. In addition, presumably, there is a lack of uniformity in the definitions and/or measurements of the constructs. The interests of investigators from different disciplinary backgrounds and the availability of research resources usually determine the taxonomy used in various studies; in epidemiology, for example, social network structures can be readily ascertained and such data are important for policy planning in a population. In contrast, in clinical psychology, the focus is more likely to be on cognitive social support as it affects an individual. Schwarzer and Leppin cite studies in which perceived and received support are almost unrelated. They also believe that cognitive social supports are a function of personality predispositions, more so than are social integration and behavioral support. Thus, in contrast to younger adults, in older people with perceptual and/or memory deficits, there may be even lower correlations between perceptions of cognitive social support and other measures of support. On the other hand, it is possible that the experiences of older people could lead to better evaluations of expectations.

THEORETICAL PERSPECTIVES

Troll (1980), in an introduction to a section on interpersonal relationships in a monograph on some psychological issues of aging, observed that most of the research in this area had been atheoretical, mainly descriptive and pragmatic. Broad psychosocial theories of aging that are primarily based on motivation, such as disengagement, activity, continuity, and exchange, have also been applied to social contacts. There have been additional theories specifically addressing interpersonal relationships. We review some of these theories, though not all of them specifically address aging changes.

THEORIES

An Intrinsic Motive for Contact or Attachment

Baumeister and Leary (1995) reviewed the modern history of this topic. Fairbairn, Harlow, Bowlby, and others (Ryan, 1993) have championed the presence of an intrinsic motive for attachment or close contacts in the young infant in addition to the instrumental motives for the satisfaction of other needs. For survival, the infant requires the protection and care of a caretaker; by extension, it has been assumed that this motive persists and also occurs in more mature organisms (Belsky & Cassidy, 1994), though some have questioned the evidence for the continuity of this behavior (Duck, 1994; Hendrick & Hendrick, 1994). The problem may hinge on the definition of attachment. While the need for some organismic attachments may be intrinsic, especially during infancy and early childhood, there is also much evidence that extrinsic reinforcements and other variables in socialization are crucial in the formation of social relationships. The benefits of extrinsic rewards in the maintenance of social relationships persist beyond the periods of early development. Accordingly, friendships and other social ties result from "mutually satisfactory interactions" (Geen, Beatty, & Arkin, 1984, p. 329). Of course, not all social interactions are satisfactory, but the frequency of those that have positive consequences in the elderly far exceeds those that are negative (Rook, 1990). Negative social relationships induce stress, a topic that was reviewed previously (Chapter 8). Here, we discuss only the satisfactory consequences. Though they do not use the construct attachment, the Schwarzer and Leppin (1991) model deals with attachment, but it is to a large extent applicable primarily to periods of stress. Perhaps attachments are most needed and most apparent during such circumstances. The construct of social support that reduces stress is an example of extrinsic motivation for attachments.

Many studies of friendships in older adults (Blieszner & Adams, 1992, pp. 79–85) imply reciprocal exchanges and social supports. As mentioned previously, intrinsic and extrinsic motives are difficult to separate. In addition to being instrumental for obtaining many nonsocial necessities for survival in our complex world, it has been postulated that people also have needs that can be satisfied only by interpersonal relationships, or affiliations such as self-esteem, approval, or self-evaluation (Schachter, 1959, p. 2). Many motives for affiliation have characteristics pertaining to both nonsocial and social goals, such as acquisition of information, which may be instrumental for reaching nonsocial survival needs and also satisfies the social needs of self-esteem or prestige. In the first instance, affiliation is a means for achieving a goal, and in the second, it represents the goal itself. This apparent duality illustrates the quandary in attempts to separate intrinsic from extrinsic motives. Pragmatically, the extent to which the need for affiliation is intrinsic or based on instrumental nonsocial needs cannot be easily determined, and the differentiation may not be important. An older person may have an intrinsic or a social need to be with others, but friends may also provide information that is nonsocial and valuable in enhancing health. Thus, there have been no attempts to address any age-associated changes of the intrinsic need.

Social Exchange

In contrast to the previously discussed approaches based on an intrinsic or "instinctive" need for attachment, several sociologists, including Homans (1961), proposed a social exchange theory according to which social interactions are guided by the expected rewards minus the costs that accrue from the relationship. In our discussion of social support as a moderator of stress, we presented Dowd's (1975) application of exchange theory to that construct. Since older people in our society are supposed to have fewer tangible and/or intellectual resources that they can provide to others, it is unlikely that they will be sought out for social interaction.

There are several difficulties with a broad exchange theory, since there are a variety of resources that may be exchanged. Foa (1993) proposed a theory that does differentiate between the outcomes of exchanges of various types of resources: A person giving love to another may perceive that she has not lost any love and has the same amount still available, but giving another person $100 will mean that the giver will be $100 poorer (Hinde, 1993). Parents who provide nurturance and information to their young children do not necessarily expect to receive the same resources in return as they age.

Similar objections may also be raised with respect to reinforcement theory. There have been numerous definitions of reinforcement, ranging from drive reduction to expectancies–values. Related to this problem is the evidence that many behaviors are intrinsically motivated with no obvious external reinforcers. To illustrate just one study that is difficult to reconcile with a simple application of exchange theory, Morgan *et al.* (1991) found that in community-residing adults, on average, the total number of support exchanges with kin provided by older adults exceeded those they received until about the age of 85 years. In evolutionary psychology, it is assumed that helping younger kin is reciprocal altruism (Buss, 1996), but anthropologists emphasize the cultural transformation of biological kinship, and this includes the assistance provided to older relatives (Fry, 1996). Thus, a test of exchange theory is contextually and probably also observer-driven.

As part of the construct of social support, Jackson, Antonucci, and Gibson (1990) modified the exchange theory. According to them, during a lifetime, older people amass or "bank" contacts and support during their younger years, which they can then apply for in later adulthood when their resources become depleted. Antonucci (1991) coupled the "bank" construct of exchanges with a life-span convoy model of social relations: Convoy connotes protection; as people mature they develop relatively stable and enduring social relations that are usually protective, though at times they may be harmful. The "banked" supports are perceived as sources of future assistance. Earlier in history, in many societies and to some extent even in ours, having children was viewed as the major source of future support. For example, a parent may spend a considerable amount of resources to educate a child, placing a deposit in a "Support Bank," and in turn may receive support from the child when he or she is old. Jackson *et al.* (1990) presented some data on American (black and white) and French families that revealed limited but preliminary support for their theory of reciprocity. However, the convoy model does not incorporate social contacts within the older age cohort. Older people do develop friendships and provide assistance to members of their cohort though no "banking transactions" occurred earlier. Antonucci's concept also has difficulties in explaining some relationships between mothers and adult children who do not provide much support, yet close relationships continue (Talbott, 1990). According to Blau (1964), love relationships cannot be equated with other exchanges. Foa's resource theory (1993) extended this approach by showing that various other resources are also not interchangeable. Jones and Vaughan (1990) found that even among elderly friends, social exchanges are not salient issues in friendship satisfactions.

Social relations have cumulative influences on the individual; there is a hierarchy of social relations, so that some are more salient and significant than others. Parent–child relationships are usually closer than those between siblings, and both kinds are more important and enduring than friendships. Though Antonucci (1991) does not specifically indicate the mechanisms or motivational basis of the relationships, her exchange and convoy model assumes that it is based on the continuation of the infant's bonding with the mother. During development, this generalizes to family and friends. However, a distinction can be made between attachment and social support (Barnas, Pollina, & Cummings, 1991; Carstensen, 1992, 1993): Attachment figures are always members of a social support network, but not all members of the latter are necessarily attachment figures who could effectively contribute to a sense of security. Attachment in this approach is viewed as an intrinsic need, whereas support is the extrinsic motive for providing instrumental assistance for achieving various goals. Finally, the criticisms leveled against exchange theory apply also to some extent to Antonucci's modification—specifically, to her "banking" aspects, which assumes that it is necessary to have reinforcers available to receive contacts. Here, too, evolutionary concepts do not fit into the model.

Disengagement–Activity–Continuity

Probably the best-known theory of contact that has had a major influence on gerontology was developed by sociologists Cumming and

Henry (1961). Though the original empirical support for their theory was inadequate, they proposed that it is normative and expected that older people progressively withdraw and disengage from social contacts and that society in turn also seeks to disengage from the elderly. The theory is rooted in the biological phenomenon of a gradual deterioration of various bodily systems during aging that leads to inactivity and isolation from others. From an evolutionary viewpoint, a withdrawal of the older cohort is the optimum condition for the succession of generations. Cumming and Henry based their conclusion on a cross-sectional study of 200 healthy, Kansas City adults ages 50+ years. Those older than 75 years reported significantly fewer social activities than those ages 50–54 years To some extent, then, this theory describes the consequences of biological deterioration.

In contrast, activity theory negates the inevitable declines with age. Havighurst (1952), influenced by the Chicago school of functional psychology (Boring, 1950, pp. 552–553), put forth an activity theory according to which optimum aging is associated with the maintenance of activity even in later stages of life. While decreases in social contacts are bound to occur when sensory and motor capacities diminish, complete disengagement occurs only when the individual becomes grossly incapacitated during the last stages of life.

Neugarten and associates (1964) formulated a continuity theory that straddles disengagement and activity. According to Neugarten, social activities are determined by a complex relationship between various predispositions, biological and social changes, and environmental factors. While some types of contacts decrease with age, others may actually increase. Disengagement, activity, and continuity are general motivational theories applicable not only to social contacts but also to all behavior during aging. It is therefore difficult to separate the analysis of social relationships from other behavioral changes. It is interesting that all three theories—disengagement, activity, and continuity—are based on different interpretations of the evolutionary theory of adjustment championed by the Chicago school of functional psychology. Also, as noted in the analysis of the development versus stability of personality in adulthood, at what point is it appropriate to assume that activity changes to disengagement?

Socioemotional Selectivity

Carstensen (1992, 1993) developed a socioemotional selectivity theory (SST) to account for the motivation for social contacts across the life span. For her, social contacts are not equivalent to support; decreased contacts with age do not necessarily imply decreased support. Thus, she addresses a different issue than does Antonucci (1991) in her exchange convoy model. Carstensen integrated much previous work, theoretical and empirical, in developing her theory, using as her starting point Schachter's (1959) theory positing numerous goals for affiliation or contact. Aside from the instrumental benefits of contacts that facilitate the acquisition of the necessary commodities for everyday existence, such as food or shelter, contacts also satisfy many psychological goals, some pertaining to obtaining or verifying information, others related to the self, such as approval or comparison with other members of a cohort. As already noted, in many instances, we cannot separate the various types of goals.

Carstensen (1992, 1993) placed the noninstrumental psychological goals into several categories. First, interpersonal contacts are necessary for obtaining information. For the young child, interpersonal contacts are the sine qua non for learning about the world. By the time that people become adults, they have acquired a storehouse of information and have also learned how to obtain additional information without the benefit of many contacts with others; as people age, this need is presumably reduced, and people can be more selective in their choice of contacts. Second, young people need interpersonal contacts to develop a self-concept, for only by comparing oneself with others is it possible to develop a reliable self-concept. During adulthood, the self-concept becomes well integrated and stable, and tends to be maintained into late adulthood as long as a person is in good health (Schaie & Willis, 1991, pp. 283–284). Because heterogeneity increases with age, comparisons with a large group of others may actually become less meaningful; thus, selectivity of social contacts is essential. Third, emotions are intimately associated with social behaviors. Children are easily emotionally aroused by a variety of social stimuli, but as people become adults, they become competent in regulating their emotional arousal.

There is some dispute about the ability of older people to maintain control of their emotional arousal, though some recent evidence actually indicates some decrease in arousability, as previously reviewed. Carstensen believes that in some situations, older people are less able to control their emotions than are younger people because of some cognitive deficits; still, the degree of arousal may be lower in many situations. Carstensen argues that since many social contacts entail energy expenditures that may be costly to an older person, it is more economical to be selective in one's contacts. While there may be fewer social contacts as people age, those that do occur tend to be more meaningful, share more intimacy, and be more supportive. In commenting on Carstensen's theory, Ryan (1993) notes that it is not apparent why emotional salience of social contacts should increase with age. Do social contacts in the elderly satisfy needs other than those that occur in young people?

Synopsis

The theories are not mutually exclusive, and each may profitably be applied to some aspects of social contacts. No studies have attempted to compare the theories, and probably the variety of contexts in which social contacts occur makes it difficult to make comparisons. Hazan and Shaver (1994) noted that we lack a comprehensive theory of close relationships in general, not just in gerontology. The role of culture may be, however, even more important in studies of aging since older people experience more sociocultural transformations than do the young. We present some recent work on social relations in older individuals, though most of the studies were cross-sectional and descriptive.

ISOLATION AND LONELINESS

Definitions

Studies related to contact have frequently been framed in terms of its low levels or absence, namely, social isolation and/or loneliness. In many penal systems, isolation and solitary confinement are among the harshest punishments that may be imposed. Social isolation is a multidimensional construct, since there are numerous factors which contribute to it. There are some differences between social and emotional isolation (Chappell & Badger, 1989; Wills, 1991): Loneliness corresponds to emotional isolation, while social isolation is a physical or externally determined variable. This differentiation is somewhat analogous to that posited between interactions and relationships (Wood, 1989) or casual and close contacts. Loneliness results from an absence of close contacts or relationships; for example, an older person may live in a rural setting far removed from other persons and be socially isolated, yet not feel lonely or emotionally isolated because of the easy access by telephone to kinfolk or friends. Conversely, a person may be in an institution, even sharing a bedroom with another resident, and still feel emotionally isolated and lonely, yet not be socially isolated. Personality characteristics contribute to the perception of emotional isolation. Some people have a greater need for close contacts than do others. Furthermore, American culture, with its emphasis on privacy and control, may contribute to social isolation (Rubinstein, Kilbride, & Nagy, 1992). To study interactions is easier than studying relationships; an observer can measure interactions, but relationships require a self-report by a person concerning the cognitions or emotions involved in an interaction. Similarly, there is a distinction between attachment and dependency; a man might be dependent on a caregiver who may be an employee but not feel attached to her. On the other hand, while he does not receive care from a daughter, he might feel attached to her. In the past, many autobiographies and diaries have described a sense of isolation or solitude during the later stages of life (Lowenthal & Robinson, 1976). Modern, easily accessible transportation and communication systems such as the telephone, fax machine, and interactive computer network systems tend to reduce one form of social isolation and perhaps also feelings of loneliness. Lifeline emergency alarm systems are available in many places, though some elderly are unwilling to accept this new technological device (Monk, 1988). Many older persons still feel intimidated and confused by modern communication technologies, and some feel that it intrudes on their privacy. Yet in spite of telephones and visits, some elderly still feel separated from family (Fry, 1996).

Some Data

There are no good data to determine the changes in family contacts for our older population, though some investigators claim that, overall, the incidence of social isolation among older people is less today than what has been commonly assumed in familiar stereotypes (Kaufman & Adams, 1987; Monk, 1988). Social relationships are related to culture, which changes over time. Mullins and Tucker (1992) found differences in the feelings of isolation in large samples ($N > 1,000$ per group) of older English- and French-speaking Canadians who were seasonal migrants in Florida. While the two groups differed in the number of children, types of residence, age, and other factors, culture may also have had an influence. It was difficult to ascertain the contributions of the ethnic–cultural difference and other factors as the basis for the reported discrepancy; however, the study does point to the difficulties in studying feelings of isolation. Similarly, cohort and time of observation play important roles in the formation of friendships (Blieszner & Adams, 1992, p. 26). Also, in older people, marital status (widowhood), frailty or poor physical/mental health, and low SES tend to be common correlates of isolation and loneliness (Delisle, 1988; Wenger, Davies, Shahtahmasebi, & Scott, 1996). Though there are some differences among studies in the contributions of the variables that are reported to affect loneliness (cf. Mullins & Mushel, 1992), presumably the results of different measurement scales and populations tested, there is a considerable agreement among the reports. However, several studies found that there are positive correlations among living alone, social isolation, and feelings of loneliness (Delisle, 1988). A major shortcoming of research in this area is with definitions. Contrary to the accepted wisdom, in a recent standardization of a frequently used measure of loneliness (UCLA Loneliness Scale—Version 3), Russell (1996) reported that older people had the lowest scores on that scale. Can those results be attributed to sampling?

Attempts to ameliorate the negative effects of loneliness were tried by Heller, Thompson, Trueba, Hogg, et al. (1991), who designed an intervention study aimed at developing peer-support dyads via telephone contacts in a community of low-income elderly women living alone. As a group, those who completed the study did not show improved mental health, as measured by a morale, depression, and loneliness scales. Those who maintained contact tended to have similar demographic characteristics (age, education, income, marital status, presence of children), similar activity levels (frequency of church and club attendance), and similar social-competence levels. In summary, this study indicates that it is difficult to graft friendships using only telephone contacts in the elderly who are isolated.

In a study on the experience of loneliness, Mullins and Mushel (1992) and Mullins, Smith, Colquitt, and Mushel (1996) collected questionnaire data from 700+ older adults (mean age 75 years) whose self-rated health was fair to good. Loneliness was inversely related to the number of friends, poor self-rated health, and being male. In their restricted age range, age was not a significant factor, nor was the relationship with spouses and children. Contact with family or friends, rather than emotional closeness, was more significant. The lack of influence of spousal relationships was surprising, but since these were individuals who participated in group activities and therefore interacted frequently with others, the sample may not have been representative of an older population. Also, the absence of questions on other social activities, such as church or other group participations, further limits the generalizability of the data. Also, those who indicated loneliness may have experienced a lack of contacts in the situation in which the data were collected. Steinbach (1992) also found that "talking with relatives or friends" reduced the probability of institutionalization and/or mortality in 5,151 older people when age, self-rated health, number of activities of daily living, and gender were controlled. Living with a spouse did not have a protective effect on mortality, a finding contrary to many others in the field. Steinbach speculates that in her study, the contributions of relatives and friends may have reduced the usual impact of the spouse. Also, the chronicity of various health problems was not included in her design, and she admits that the complexity of the variables in this area will require additional replications.

FACTORS AFFECTING CLOSE CONTACTS

Numerous psychosocial variables affect close contacts. As Blieszner and Adams (1992) have noted, the context in which the contact occurs is critical. In some reports, demographic information is available on the effects of cohort, health, household composition, gender, SES, education, marital status, and several other variables. Blieszner and Adams also cite studies showing that reciprocity and similarity tend to be more important for older women than for men. The studies probably reflect cohorts in which widowed women were more dependent on friends than were men, and the latter were less likely to be living without a spouse (Palmore, 1981, p. 76). In addition to easily measurable demographic variables, we may also add personality factors such as sociability or extroversion, which serve as important motives for contact (Kogan, 1990; Russell, 1996). Unfortunately, there is little convergence in the various approaches to personality as influential factors in affecting contact; the multiplicity of goals sought through contacts is bound to affect the importance of various parameters of this behavior.

Adams and Blieszner (1994), in their development of a framework for studies of friendships, deplored the sparsity of longitudinal research. In the same article, however, they also characterized friendship as a constantly evolving relationship. If we are searching for a dynamic pattern, then longitudinal studies would be problematic. According to the authors, changes are especially prominent during life-course transitions, and since age is associated with many such transitions (e.g., retirement, loss of spouse, or residential relocation), longitudinal research would be very difficult.

Types and Relationships and Nature of Activities

Baltes *et al.* (1990), in a time-budget study of the daily activities of 60 older Berliners, found that they spent their time mainly in activities that do not involve other people, such as housework, shopping, dressing, and eating. Some of the activities that may be considered nonsocial in the United States can involve social contacts in other cultures: in Berlin, shopping, for example, may involve social contacts with the butcher, baker, and chatting with friends in the store. Even visiting a medical clinical may satisfy social contacts. This study illustrates the difficulty in categorizing instrumental nonsocial from social goals.

In a cross-sectional study of 156 community-dwelling and institutionalized older adults ages 70–104 years in Berlin, Lang and Carstensen (1994) found that the number of members of social networks decreased with age. However, the number of very close relationships showed only a slight, not statistically significant, decrement with age. Those with nuclear family members who tended to be younger and lived in the community felt more socially embedded than those without family ties. The latter, however, compensated for the lack of nuclear family members by having more friends and distant kin serving as intimates. Since these people tended to be older and institutionalized, they were in greater need for instrumental support. The authors did separate in their analysis the community-dwelling from the institutionalized participants. Overall, the data supported Carstensen's SST (1992): Even though the total number of social network decreases, close relationships are maintained into very old age.

Benefits of Relationships

The effects of meaningful contacts, such as those with a confidant or companion, are more important for morale or well-being than the total number of casual contacts (Chappell & Badger, 1989; O'Connor, 1995; Palmore, 1981, p. 61). The quality of the relationships seems to be more important in contact with friends than with family (O'Connor, 1995). "Quality," however, is difficult to measure; a number of factors may play a role here: (1) People may feel that they have an obligation to maintain family contacts; (2) in a major emergency, family members may be more likely to respond; (3) family contacts may benefit not only the older individual, but also other kin. Wills (1991) reported that size of social networks does not correlate highly with measures of emotional support. Similar findings based on a large sample ($N = 1,071$) were also reported by Mullins, Mushel, Cook, and Smith (1994). However, Gupta and Korte (1994), in an interview study of 100 single (widowed, divorced, separated) noninstitutionalized elderly (mean age 77 years), found that peer groups and confidants had similar effects on perceived well-being. Apparently, different persons are needed to achieve different goals. For elderly singles, friends are needed to satisfy social needs that are not always met by confidants. These studies emphasize the necessity of separating contact and social support, as was suggested by Carstensen (1993).

Older friends serve as an important source of companionship and social support (Blieszner & Adams, 1992, pp. 82–85), especially when kin are no longer available. In their study of 708 elderly Canadians, Lapierre *et al.* (1993) measured the participants' motivational goal objects using a sentence-completion test. While 18% of the responses referred to contact, only 1% of these was coded as intimate contact. The largest percentage (8%) of the contacts was coded as altruistic, and the remaining responses pertained to family, friends, support, or consideration from others. There was probably a certain degree of overlap between the categories. While the desire for contact, in general, increased with age in this elderly group, intimate and altruistic contacts were inversely related to age; thus, the need for contact seemed to have been related to the assistance that older people have in their everyday activities. The desire for contact was higher in women, those living at home, and those without a spouse, all indicators related to the need for instrumental support.

Holahan (1988), in her 1982 questionnaire study of the Terman gifted (ages 65–75 years), obtained three factors of 11 life goals deemed important by this relatively advantaged group. The second factor was labeled involvement, and "having many pleasant relationships," followed by "enjoying intimacy with others," had the highest loading on this factor. Rapkin and Fischer (1992a, 1992b) in their study of personal goals of older adults, also found that maintenance of friendships and kin relationships was rated as very important for life satisfaction.

Barnas *et al.* (1991), in a small sample of older women ($N = 48$), found that 94% had a secure attachment with at least one adult child, but the quality varied across children for women who had more than one child. However, attachment relations were more significant in coping with everyday rather than major stressors, and the less secure mothers had more rather than fewer coping responses. The authors raise several possible explanations to account for their findings. Aside from problems with the validity of the measurement instruments, does a person who had insecure attachments to children gradually acquire coping mechanisms?

Previously, we referred to Heidrich's (1994) study of community-dwelling advantaged women ages 61–93 years, in which positive relationships with others were the most important dimension of the ideal self. Autonomy, which according to Erikson (1963) plays an important role in development, was less important than personal growth, purpose in life, or social relationships. In the same vein, we also described a study by DePaola and Ebersole (1995), who found in nursing home and in community-residing elderly, as well as in adults over the age of 30 years, that relationships were mentioned most frequently as the most meaningful factor in their lives.

A Long-Term Longitudinal Study

Save for the Terman follow-up (Holahan, 1988), we have reviewed were cross-sectional or short-term longitudinal studies in which several important variables were confounded. There have been very few longitudinal studies; two of these were multidisciplinary, conducted at Duke University from 1961 to 1976, based on noninstitutionalized elderly. In Study 1, 268 persons ages 60 years and older were periodically tested as long as they survived, but for a maximum of 21 years, at which time there were data available for only 41 participants. In Study 2, an initial sample of 502 persons ages 46–72 years was followed for a maximum of 6 years, with social data at the last testing available on 375 participants. In both studies, there were slow but steady declines in the means of total social activities with age (Palmore, 1981, pp. 49–54). These changes represented mean group data and there were considerable within-group and between-cohort variations. Many of the participants reported no changes with age, and some even exhibited increased social activities. In both longitudinal studies, there was evidence of strong continuity of social activities (i.e., those active at the initiation of the study tended to maintain their activity). There was little change in attendance at club meetings, and attendance at church meetings even showed increases in some cohorts. In general, declines did not appear in the latter until after the seventies. The total number of people in a person's social network tended to remain constant. Though the number of friends decreased somewhat, this was balanced by an increase in the number of contacts with relatives outside the household. Self-rated health and physical functioning, number of people in household, gender, marital status, having children, education, income, and occupation were related to social activities.

CONCLUSIONS

All of the social sciences study interactions or relationships between people, but there is little agreement on the definitions in this area. Observable social interactions differ from interpersonal relationships, the latter implying emotional closeness or attachment. However, the boundaries between these two types of contact are fuzzy; a low level or absence of contacts leads to social isolation, while a lack of close contacts produces loneliness. While modern transportation and communication devices can reduce social isolation, we have no long-term data. In general, there are positive correlations between social isolation and loneliness, which then may lead to mental health problems. Some of the studies on relationships overlap with those that examined the self, and culture and/or cohort are critical factors in this field.

Though most research in this field has been descriptive and atheoretical, there have been several theories attempting to account for age-associated changes. In addition to an intrinsic motive for contact, which is presumably maintained throughout life and is difficult to divorce from many extrinsic motives, several broad social psychological theories have been proposed. Social exchange theory, based on postulates of classical economic theory of utilitarianism or behavioristic reinforcement theories, assumes that contacts decrease in modern societies because older persons have little power or few reinforcers to attract younger individuals. This theory can be criticized for its dependence on reinforcement, a construct that is difficult to define. Helping relationships, as postulated by exchange theory, are culturally determined. Antonucci modified the original exchange theory by assuming that people can bank their exchanges earlier in life for use later on. Also, people develop with others relatively stable and enduring protective relationships that may be called upon as the need arises. Her theory may be more appropriately applied to social support phenomena than to attachment.

Disengagement theory, based on the biological phenomenon of decline, has been applied to social contacts; its major tenet is that as people age, they are forced to reduce contacts with the environment because of declines in physical capacities, and this also has evolutionary value for the succession of cohorts. An opposing theory claims that activity that also includes contacts is the desirable goal for optimum aging. Finally, a continuity theory, which straddles the two approaches, emphasizes a complex relationship between previous habits, biological and social changes, and existing environmental factors. Since these theories are stated very broadly and encompass much of the behavior, and not just contacts, of older individuals, empirical data available in different contexts may be cited in support of all three theories. It is also very difficult to define continuity.

Carstensen proposed a socioemotional selectivity theory according to which older people have less need for contact with others since they already have a well-developed, stable self-concept that does not require comparisons with other people. Furthermore, since, in many situations, social contacts may induce emotional arousal that may be more difficult to handle or more costly for older persons, they will reduce their total number of contacts, selecting only those that are emotionally more salient.

There have been relative few studies to compare specific theories. A number of psychosocial variables, such as marital status, gender, health, SES, and others, have been found to affect close contacts; cohort and ethnocultural factors are very important. Since the motivation for close contact may vary from situation to situation, the context in which this behavior occurs needs to be considered. Finally, contacts may satisfy numerous instrumental goals that change as the person ages. The large number of variables poses problems for investigators who wish to arrive at broad generalizations. There have been, however, studies that targeted specific populations. Most commonly, friends are more likely to satisfy the need for companionship, while family members are called upon for instrumental support. Only two investigators have reported longitudinal data, and one of these spanned only ages 17–52 years; in the latter, there were few changes between the ages of about 30–52 years. The two other longitudinal studies, one following individuals from the age of 60 years until the person could remain as a participant, but for a maximum of 21 years, and a second one for 6 years, reported few age-associated changes in contact that were independent of the context. There was a very large heterogeneity in the observed changes, with some persons reporting increases in contacts, others decreases, and some no changes. Health, economics, and other common decrements associated with aging are bound to affect contacts. In several studies, it was found that social relationships are the most meaningful activities for many adults. Most of the studies have been based almost exclusively on self-report data. Occasionally, investigators compared their findings with data from similar studies with younger adults.

The number of friends tends to decrease during aging, but contact with family remains stable or even increases. The latter may be associated with the increase in one's family network with age; however, the overall number of intimate contacts may show decrements. These data support Carstensen's socioemotional selectivity during aging. Feelings of loneliness are related to health and SES, and attempts to graft friendships in isolated, lonely individuals are difficult. There have been no systematic analyses of aging changes in friendships or other forms of contact.

CHAPTER 14

Achievement Motivation

THE CONSTRUCT

Introduction

One of the most thoroughly studied social motives, albeit mostly with younger populations, is achievement. In several general theories of human motivation (Atkinson, 1964; Heckhausen, 1967; McClelland, 1961; B. Weiner, 1992), achievement motivation plays a central role. According to B. Weiner (1992, p. 179), " Achievement theory, in contrast to the conceptions of Freud, Hull, and Lewin, has focused upon the role of individual differences in achievement needs in attempting to understand motivational processes." Though our interest in this monograph is on changes during aging, it also seems appropriate to examine briefly this motive. While achievement is probably of lesser importance during aging, both Kausler (1990) and Filipp (1996) in their chapters, respectively, in the two latest editions of the *Handbook of the Psychology of Aging,* included this topic in the chapters on motivation. Both authors reviewed primarily the role of achievement motivation in the laboratory performance of cognitive tasks. Filipp laments the absence of data in other settings. Even the few recent studies that she did review were mainly on the desire for control, or self-efficacy, and anxiety, factors that may be only indirectly related to the need for achievement.

Historical Development

In 1938, Murray presented a theory of personality based on the person's *needs* or *drives.* Reading his monograph, it is apparent that he was influenced to some extent by behaviorism, the then-dominant approach to psychology in America. For Murray, needs have an energetic and a directional or selective aspect—traditional definitions of motivation. However, as a clinician, he was influenced primarily by psychoanalysis. He postulated that introspection will reveal a person's needs or desires and that some of them may be unconscious. Needs and desires are two aspects of "the same thing" (p. 64); they can manifest themselves in fantasy, for desires may be expressions of some wishes that are not realistic. Murray divided needs into primary viscerogenic (biological) and secondary psychogenic ones, identifying some 28 needs in the latter category. Many of them interact and/or a given activity may represent the expression of several needs; for example, a person running for public office may have needs for achievement, dominance, or affiliation. Murray used the letter n to label needs (e.g., $nAch$ represents the need for achievement). To reveal covert (inhibited) and unconscious (partially repressed) needs, he believed it was necessary to resort to thematic constructions—fantasy techniques. Murray developed a widely used thematic apperception test (TAT) in which a person is asked to interpret a series of pictures of ambiguous social situations. The test was based on Freud's technique of free association.

Though there have been studies of a number of Murray's needs, $nAch$ has generated by far the most effort, especially by McClelland (1992), Atkinson (1992), and their associates. The interest in $nAch$, with its implications for potential practical applications to productivity, is understandable in Western societies in which, according to the sociologist Max Weber (1958), the work ethic leads to an emphasis on acquisition rather than only on biological needs as a major source of human motivation. Several hundred studies have correlated $nAch$ with various measures of performance on various laboratory tests, school achievement, job performance, child-rearing practices, leadership effectiveness, and even economic growth in different countries (McClelland & Winter, 1969). Recent studies, however, have found no relationship between meaures of self-attributed achievement and economic development (Jackman & Miller, 1996). Understandably, studies with older adults on $nAch$ have been less common since they are not enrolled in schools, involved in the world of work or in similar endeavors. The prevailing attitude in the Western world has been that old age is a period of disengagement that does not lead to much achievement motivation.

Beginning in the 1950s, a few new projective tests and several objective tests of achievement motivation began to appear (Fineman, 1977). Most of them were easier to administer and to score than the TAT; it was expected that they would be more reliable than the TAT. Entwistle (1972) found that the reliability (internal consistency) of the TAT was low, rarely exceeding .40. In his review of 23 different tests, each purporting to measure achievement, Fineman (1977) found that they do not appear to measure the same construct; the correlations between the TAT and questionnaire measures of achievement motivation were virtually zero. Furthermore, almost all of the tests have been standardized on student populations, and their face validity (examination of the test by experts) can be very low for nonstudent populations. This criticism is especially relevant in the context of gerontological studies. McClelland *et al.* (1989) responded to the various critics by pointing out that the questionnaire responses represent self-attributed achievement (*sanAch*), part of the self-concept, which expresses conscious, immediate, specific goal-directed motives, often reflecting social norms. On the other hand, *nAch* represents broad implicit motives that sustain gross behavioral tendencies over longer time periods; they measure dispositions rather than temporary arousal states. Spangler (1992) used meta-analyses of 105 randomly selected research articles to examine the validity of both TAT and of questionnaire measures of *nAch,* and his analyses supported McClelland's distinctions between implicit TAT and explicit questionnaire measures of achievement motivation. The different techniques seem to be measuring different phenomena, even though they are both referred to as indices of achievement motivation. Spangler (1992), in his analyses, did not use data based on Spence and Helmreich's (1983) conception that achievement motivation is a cluster of interacting factors rather than a single unitary construct. Each presumably reflects relatively enduring dispositional tendencies. Previously, McClelland *et al.* (1989) also ignored the Spence and Helmreich (1983) research program. The latter relied on questionnaire data; thus, their emphasis was on what McClelland *et al.* (1989) postulated as explicit motivation with social incentives. However, Spence and Helmreich (1983) believed that much of their research measured intrinsic achievement motivation. An important finding of this work was the presence of interactions of extrinsic and intrinsic motives. This conclusion is not different from McClelland *et al.*'s (1989) hypothesis that various motives and incentives interact, and this was also a finding in Spangler's (1992) meta-analyses.

Cultural Factors and Methodology

The importance of cultural changes in the strength of various social motives was observed by Veroff, Reuman, and Feld (1984), who, in national surveys of need achievement with large representative samples (Ns 1,363 and 1,208, respectively), found inconsistencies between findings in 1957 and 1976. Stevens and Truss (1985) measured 15 personality traits with the Edwards Personal Preference Schedule, a questionnaire based on Murray's theory of manifest needs, with a sample of college students in the late 1950s and with another sample in 1978. Over the approximately 20-year period, there were differences in the mean scores of college student, including decrements for both male students in Achievement and increases in Affiliation, Abasement, and Nurturance; females decreased in scores on Deference and Order, and increased on Achievement, Autonomy, Aggression, and Heterosexuality. Thus, simple comparisons of either cross-sectional or longitudinal studies of the same individuals do not take into account cultural changes.

The controversy surrounding measurement of aging changes in achievement motivation relates to a broad fundamental issue in the measurement of personality, cognition, and motivation, and this is more relevant in analyzing old age than other stages of life. There is an abundance of debate concerning appropriate methodologies and theories for studying motivational changes. Some of the differences in studies of changes early in development are discussed by Ryan (1993). With people experiencing a lifetime of diverse experiences, the intrusion of additional factors amplifies the difficulties: Many social motives interact; the motive to achieve may be associated with a motive to be affiliated with others, to exert power, or to be intimate. McClelland (1992), in the context of his research on measuring motives based on imaginary story contents, found that, using his classificatory schema, many of the motives overlapped. He prefers the concept of specific motivational configurations, which consists of combinations of motives that are related to certain behavioral activities. The combinations are not necessarily additive, and they may change during different stages of adulthood. Since we lack longitudinal data, not much is known about the stability of the patterns; thus, it is difficult to extrapolate findings obtained earlier in life to later adulthood (Hooker, 1992). In several chapters (e.g., 1, 7, 8, 9, 10, 11, 13), we have already discussed the relationships between motivation and personality. There have been several longitudinal studies of traits (Kogan, 1990) whose purpose was to determine stability of personality during adulthood. These and other studies raise questions about the relationship of various trait measurements, a classical topic in personality and motivational variables (Kogan, 1990). The boundaries between motivation and personality are amorphous. However, it seems unwise to equate the constructs of trait and motive, at least when standard psychometric instruments are used to measure traits. Though some motives may be central to some traits, the connection of some traits, such as abilities (intelligence, finger dexterity) or physique to specific goals and motives is limited (Read, Jones, & Miller, 1990). There has been much work devoted to changes in interests and activities associated with aging. While motivation is one major determiner of activity, incentives, abilities—both physical and mental, habits and health status also play key roles in a person's behavior. The constraints of physical, psychological, and social losses during aging require a shift from tenacious goal pursuits to accommodative goal adjustments (Brandstädter & Renner, 1990). Unless an investigator examines motivation within the context of a specific activity, it is not possible to delineate the factor(s) accounting for the changes. How does aging affect overall striving or achievement?

SOME DATA ON OLDER POPULATIONS

Currently, jobs or employment in which achievement motivation is important are much less central in the lives of most older people in Western societies than in the past (Ryff, 1989a). Various savings and social programs in industrialized countries provide at least minimum wherewithal for older people. Most of the earlier research on achievement motivation was based on student populations, individuals preparing for the world of work; thus, there has been little interest in studies of achievement of older persons. The few instances where data have been collected on seniors' achievement motivation constituted a minor aspect of broader investigations of the lives of older people. In a cross-sectional study of 1,366 men and women, Veroff, Atkinson, Feld, and Gurin (1960) found that *nAch* assessed with TAT cards showed tendencies for declines with age in both men and women, but their categorization of the participants' ages into decades and the presentation of only percentages of high scores makes it difficult to determine the shape of the age curve. The authors admit that they did not control for cohort effects and age biases in the pictures they used, and none of the pictures in the cards represented an older person; the authors acknowledge the need for better data on age changes. In another cross-sectional study of traits in 296 men and women ages 22–90 years, Costa and McCrea (1988) were unable to find a statistically significant correlation between age and achievement motivation ($r = .09$), though for several other traits (e.g., aggression or play), significant relationships with age were recorded. Parenthetically, they did find a significant positive correlation between education and a measure of achievement, indicating a need to control for this factor. According to McClelland *et al.* (1992), however, this study measured *sanAch* rather than *nAch*. Also, the sample measured highly educated individuals who probably were high on *nAch* throughout their lifetimes.

Using the data previously published by Veroff *et al.* (1960), as well as another sample of 1,208 respondents from the same cohorts, but not the same participants, Veroff *et al.* (1984) compared the data collected in 1957 with those obtained in 1976; the most important finding was the inconsistency in relative motive strengths between the 1957 participants and those in 1976 among some of the cohorts, though a few did show stability on some motives. Women's achievement and affiliation motives declined at the older ages, but the achievement motives were higher in 1976 than they were in 1957. The authors attribute the changes over the 20-year period to the increase in employment and status of women in the workforce. Achievement also dropped with age for men beginning in middle-adulthood, but the data were similar for the 1957 and the 1976 samples. In the 1980s, Mellinger and Erdwins (1985) compared groups of young adult women (mean age 34 years), midlife groups (mean ages 46–48 years), and older groups (mean ages 66–70 years). At each age level, there were groups of homemakers, married career women, and single career women. In the younger and midlife age levels, there were also groups of students. Older women showed less achievement motivation and had a greater need for affiliation than the young or middle-aged groups.

As part of a study on cautiousness, Okun and Di Vesta (1976) developed a questionnaire to assess *nAch* in a small sample of young (ages 18–30 years) and older (ages 60–76 years) adults. Supporting the Veroff *et al.* (1960) findings, there was an inverse correlation between *nAch* and age; as expected, they also reported that older adults had lower levels of aspiration and greater cautiousness, but the relationships between the latter variables and *nAch* were not tested specifically, probably because the sample sizes were small. More recently, in two samples of participants (*N*s 169 and 104, respectively) ranging in age from 16 to 67 years, Mehrabian and Blum (1996) also found small but statistically inverse relationship between age and achievement orientation, with the correlations higher for men than for women. The authors relate this finding to the lower trait of dominance in older persons.

Information about achievement motivation is also available from studies that were not specifically focused on this motive. In Chapters 11 and 12, we discussed the self and the meaning of life. For many people, achievement is an important goal that is also the *raison d'être* for all motives. In most of the studies that were reviewed in Chapters 11 and 12, achievement, at least the way it is measured in younger populations, plays a minor role in the life of older persons.

Holahan (1988) analyzed the relationships of life goals to activity participation, health, and psychological well-being in the 65- to 75-

year-olds who were participants in the Terman Study of the gifted initiated in 1922; these individuals have been part of the longest continuous study of psychological factors of the human life cycle. They were highly educated, and most of them had been financially and occupationally successful; many of them had received recognition by society for their achievements. Of 879 mailed questionnaires, 814 were returned to the investigator and 681 were used in this study. The mean age of the 336 men and 345 women was 70 years, and 87% of the men and 54% of the women were married at the time of the survey; only 3.6% of the men and 7.8% of the women were never married. Also, 38% of the men and 15% of the women still worked more than 20 hours per week. These demographic data are cited to emphasize the uniqueness of this population. The participants were asked to check the importance of various goals or purposes for their lives and the data were subjected to a factor analysis that produced three goal scales: Autonomy, Achievement Motivation, and Involvement. The participants were also asked to indicate their involvement in a list of activities, their health status, and their psychological well-being. Scores on all three goal scales correlated significantly with health, especially Autonomy and Achievement Motivation, and psychological well-being correlated with Involvement and Achievement Motivation. A path analysis indicated that the relationship of life goals to health and psychological well-being is mediated by participation in activities. Autonomy was less highly related to activity than were scores on Involvement and Achievement Motivation. The lesser contribution of Autonomy to health and psychological well-being may reflect the measures used in the questionnaire. On the factor Autonomy, the highest loadings were contributed by items "to remain independent," "to be financially secure," and "to remain healthy." Ryan (1993) emphasized that autonomy is not independence, though in common usage, the two terms are equated and frequently may be related. For Ryan, *independence* refers to not relying on others to satisfy one's needs, while *autonomy* implies a sense of volition. According to Ryan, a person can be dependent in a relationship but not necessarily lack autonomy. Physical disabilities may affect older people's independence, yet they may have a choice in the activities they pursue. Thus, Holahan's (1988) Autonomy factor was most likely Independence, which may relate less to health and psychological well-being than items that presumably would have measured Autonomy. Perhaps other items in the questionnaire may have produced factors that might have dissociated independence from autonomy. Heckhausen and Krueger (1993), in a study of German adults ages 60–80 years, found that with the normal age-associated declines, many functions of self-enhancement, an aspect of achievement motivation, became salient in some adaptations to losses. Compared to younger persons, of course, the domains in which self-enhancement occured were different; the data were based on a rating of 100 adjectives, and the relationships between the responses and actual behavior cold not be ascertained.

Lapierre *et al.* (1993) used a sentence-completion technique to obtain data on goal aspirations from 704 low-SES French Canadian participants ages 64–90 years. About half were community-dwelling and the other half resided in institutions. Of the 15,020 responses classified into 10 content categories, the least frequent references were to exploration and possessions. The exploration category included responses implying *gains,* such as information or knowledge, but only 1.7% of the responses referred to such gains. Possessions included references to *acquisitions* of money, material wealth, items of comfort, and only 0.7% of the responses were in this category. Even if we assume that achievement consists of explorations and acquisitions, goals typically associated in younger persons with achievement motivation, only 2.4% of the responses from these elderly were achievement aspirations. In this sample of low-SES Canadians, achievement motivation was practically nonexistent. The institutionalized participants did not differ from the individuals living at home except that the former mentioned more frequently religious aspirations and having a good death.

CONCLUSIONS

One of the most widely studied social motives has been achievement. B. Weiner (1992), in the final comments in his textbook on human motivation, states that any adequate theory of motivation must be able to account for achievement strivings and affiliative goals, presumably the two dominant sources of motivation in our culture. Schooling, followed by an occupation in which achievement motivation plays a significant role, absorbs a significant time of a person's life from childhood to the beginning of old age; these stages of life have provided the major impetus for studies on achievement, mainly with students, the most accessible population in psychological studies. The last period of life, on the other hand, is usually retirement, during which achievement is of minor significance. According to Erikson and others, this is the time of life when people look back and reflect on their past achievements; thus, the last period of life has produced few studies on achievement. The common stereotype of the aged is that they are amotivational.

The concept of achievement is not simple. In an applied setting, achievement may refer to the need for advancement in an organization, having high work standards, or receiving recognition from one's peers. The correlations between the various indices tend to be low. As with most human motives, achievement may be intertwined with a variety of other motives, such as power, dominance, autonomy, affiliation, or altruism.

Even with younger people, most of the studies have been cross-sectional. In the few studies in which there were older participants, researchers have found either decrements in achievement motivation or no changes, with the latter findings coming mainly from studies of more educated participants. Also, even with younger individuals—middle-aged or young adults, there are pronounced time-of-observation and cohort effects. Achievement motivation, using diverse self-rating questionnaires or interviews, is greatly influenced by the prevailing ethos during the person's formative years. What these factors are, or the critical developmental period, cannot be specified at the present, nor do we know how various developmental influences interact with the cultural milieu at the time that the data are collected. These factors have not been teased out thus far. The more educated and occupationally successful individuals tend to maintain their achievement motive to a greater extent than those with less education. These findings support to some extent the hypothesis that during adulthood, personality tends to be relatively stable.

Finally, little attention has been paid to the satisfaction that older parents or other close relatives receive from the achievement of their offspring or kin. Various theories of motivation may be invoked here: In the absence of any data, social exchange theory and its extension, Antonucci's exchange convoy model, Erikson's generativity construct, or a midlevel evolutionary theory model (Buss, 1996), all may seem appropriate. Perhaps satisfactions obtained from the successes of one's offspring may be only quantitatively different from the rewards that a person perceives when a favorite sports team wins. The efforts to experience achievements in individuals or groups with which one has strong bonds may represent *vicarious* achievement.

CHAPTER 15

Leisure

INTRODUCTION

Definitions and History

It seems appropriate to conclude our monograph with a review of leisure, which encompasses a variety of activities involving numerous overlapping motives. As with most constructs in the behavioral and social sciences, the definition of leisure is closely associated with the theory espoused by the user (Ajzen, 1991). In many instances, however, researchers depend on the "commonsense" usage of the term (Kelly, 1992), so that leisure is defined as nonobligated time or time left over from work that is necessary to tend to biological needs; the terms *leisure* and *recreation* are frequently used synonymously (Driver, Brown, & Peterson, 1991). Most current theories can be traced back to earlier speculations (Mitchell & Mason, 1934, Chapter 3). Gordon, Gaitz, and Scott (1976), in tracing the history of leisure, note that Aristotle differentiated leisure from relaxation; leisure for him was not instrumental in preparation for work, as might be the case with relaxation, but it had intrinsic values that afforded the individual the opportunity to become virtuous, which then leads to happiness. In this conception, virtue may be equivalent to what has later been referred to as *serious leisure* (Stebbins, 1992, p. 5). Aristotle did not consider amusement a form of leisure, since it only produces temporary pleasures and relief from drudgery. Later, Lord Kames, an eighteenth-century English nobleman and philosopher, defined play as "an occupation engaged in for recreation rather than for business or from necessity" (cited by Mitchell & Mason, 1934, p. 52).

After retirement from work, there is usually more time available for one's favored nonobligatory activities. To a certain extent, this topic may shed light on motives that are not constrained by work and family responsibilities. Many human activities involve a multiplicity of motives, and leisure is closely intertwined with several of those that were discussed previously. Much leisure time is spent in social interactions; for example, in Chapter 13 on social relationships, there were several references to friendships, indicating that for many older people, friends tend to be more important for leisure activities than for social support. However, many people also engage in leisure activities in anticipation of obtaining some social support from friends in cases of need (Coleman & Iso-Ahola, 1993). Thus, a substantial part of leisure can be incorporated in the examination of social relationships. In Chapter 7 on health, there were references to the motivation for exercise, an important feature in many types of leisure. Similarly, certain aspects of eating, drinking, and most sexual behaviors also entail leisure.

Riley (1992), in her analysis of the optimization of the potentials for the aged in the twenty-first century, places leisure activities near the top of her priorities. But neither in the literature on motivation nor in other areas of psychology has enough attention been given to this facet of life, save in child development, in which there have been numerous studies of play. Since young children have little, if any, obligated time, most of their activities may be subsumed under play or leisure. However, leisure has attracted much interest in a variety of disciplines other than psychology, mainly in sociology, but also in economics, anthropology, political science, theology, and philosophy, and its applications have permeated social work, architecture, recreation, business, city planning, and related fields (Kaplan, 1961). While psychological investigations of work and commerce began early in this century (Leahey, 1991, pp. 224–225), the motivation for these activities was believed to be critical, since work and commerce are associated with behaviors that are essential for survival, while it was assumed that leisure was not needed. Gordon *et al.* (1976), in their introduction to leisure, refer to the Christian doctrine in which "work" and "good works" are "moral and spiritual imperatives," while leisure is primarily a time for rest preparing the person for work. This is also denoted by the term *recreation*. Hockey and James (1993, p. 136) refer to Western societies as "work societies," which shape not only the economic lives of their inhabitants but also the cultural values. Thus, these societies have been much more willing to support research on work than on leisure. However, values in Western societies have been changing, and that fact has in many instances reduced the rigid dichotomy between work and leisure. A person may have been making quilts at home as a hobby; her neighbors admire her workmanship, which then leads to quilting as a business. Older professional golfers have their own tour in which prize monies approach those distributed to younger players. The difficulty of separating work and leisure is of special significance in gerontology (Cutler & Hendricks, 1990), for many people retire from work, voluntarily or involuntarily, even though they are still capable of holding many positions in the job market. What should older people do to occupy their time?

Current Status

Studies of leisure are frequently part of a broader analysis of time allocation during the course of a day or other temporal units. The total available free time for most adults in technologically developed countries has been growing; the number of hours working on a job has been decreasing, and the introduction of a variety of labor-saving devices is reducing the time spent on preparing and maintaining everyday essentials for living that pertain to shelter, meals, and clothing. In many instances, advances in transportation, communications (word-processors, phones), health care, and other necessary activities of daily living are lengthening the time available for leisure. In Western cultures, free time and vacations have become "needs" (Cross, 1993, pp. 204–205).

The importance of leisure for the elderly population has caught the attention of the general public and business. Retirement-living housing advertisements, many based on consumer surveys, stress the availability of diverse leisure activities as a major attraction of their locales. Ekerdt (1986) traces the present belief that activity, in general, is beneficial to the older individual—the so-called "busy ethic"—to the older notion of the "work ethic," to which we referred previously. The current, busy ethic is supported by the efforts of the retirement–leisure industry, with its stress on the importance of engaging in "meaningful" activities by channeling retirees into developed mainstream leisure activities such as playing golf or participating in community theater. Typically, these commercial enterprises do not mention the similar benefits derived from walking or writing memoirs, which do not require special expensive facilities. Many states and localities, especially those with mild climates, are making strenuous efforts to attract older people to relocate. In addition, many leisure-oriented industries such as travel and publishing have established separate departments focusing on older consumers. The hospitality industry—restaurants and hotels—offers special discounts to older patrons. Organizations for older citizens, such as Senior Citizens Centers, emphasize the availability of leisure facilities as a significant asset of their programs. We even have leisure counselors who advise clients how to spend leisure time. Nurmi (1992), in a study of Finnish students and government employees, distributed an open-ended questionnaire to determine expressed life goals. He found that for those ages 55–64 years, the major goals included health, retirement, travel, the self (unspecified), children, and leisure activities. The latter were more important for men than for women. Presumably, in this cohort, men were more likely to have been employed full-time, whereas women were occupied with household chores that were less likely to change much during later adulthood. Since leisure is multi-faceted, some activities so classified show increases with age; others diminish either in the intensity or time spent in participation, and some stay level. Furthermore, the increased heterogeneity of older populations makes group comparisons somewhat dubious. At the same time, leisure may be viewed as a problem for some individuals who are so work-oriented as to believe they will have nothing to do to occupy their time after retirement (Stebbins, 1992, p. 127).

The increasing amounts of nonobligated time in the lives of the elderly in modern societies are not necessarily free of problems. In the past, we saw in the media, and in real life, older people sitting on park benches and feeding pigeons or spending time on the town square and whittling. More recently, in large urban areas, we find them congregating in the halls of shopping malls, the modern equivalent of the town square or rural general store and just sitting or occasionally chatting with other retirees; this has been dubbed malingering (Graham, Graham, & MacLean, 1991). In another, less complimentary portrayal, the elderly lounge in a nursing home dining–recreation room and stare at television screens. Juxtaposed to what some observers perceive to be gloomy scenarios, we also see advertisement of older people spending much of their time on golf courses or enjoying the amenities aboard luxury cruise ships. These diverse, popular, and to some extent, veridical, representations of a substantial segment of older peoples' frequent leisure activities point to a heterogeneous domain of behaviors classified as leisure. Such images also lead to opposing stereotypes of pitiable impoverished elderly versus the greedy old rich.

THEORIES

We briefly present some current psychological and sociological theories of leisure that influenced some relevant research. None of these was specifically developed in the context of the life span. Developing a broad theory of leisure applicable to both younger and older adults may be especially difficult, since many of the factors in such a theory (e.g., family relationships or the meaning of work), are not comparable across the life span (Anderson, 1959). In addition, the continuous cultural changes play a major role in the significance of various aspects of obligatory and discretionary times.

Kaplan

Rather than providing a narrow definition, Kaplan (1961) assumed that leisure encompasses six "elements," including (1) an antithesis to work for compensation; (2) pleasant expectations; (3) a minimum of social obligations; (4) a perception of freedom; (5) a close relationship to cultural values; and (6) an activity related to play. Culture or cultural activities are not defined. How does listening to a symphony on a tape or on television differ from watching a made-for-television drama or a sitcom? Kaplan's background is apparent in his definition of leisure. Nevertheless, his is a contemporary cognitive approach to leisure that depends on the perception of the person's use of time. He wrote during the period in which modern cognitive psychology began to emerge, and his negative "elements" of nonwork and minimum social obligations make it difficult to categorize leisure, including the separation of sundry nonwork "obligatory" from "nonobligatory" activities in general. Is playing golf with a business client leisure? How shall we classify attendance at a church picnic or volunteering at a hospital? Where do we place sundry lobbying activities on behalf of a political candidate?

Csikszentmihalyi

Influenced by current trends in motivation, Csikszentmihalyi (1975; Csikszentmihalyi & Kleiber, 1991; Csikszentmihalyi & Rathunde, 1993), one of the few psychologists who applied his theory also to leisure, believes that there is no distinction between obligatory and discretionary time. For him, the experience of enjoyment during the performance of any activity is associated with intrinsic motivation; a person continues to engage in such an activity without consideration of extrinsic rewards. When the task demands for which the goals are clear exceed slightly one's competence and the person is completely enveloped in the activity, a feeling of "flow" emerges and the person has a sense of personal control. The activity tends to become "autotelic"— worth doing for its own sake (Csikszentmihalyi & Rathunde, 1993). The autotelic activities do not include satisfying innate "biological" motives such as eating or sexual behavior, which are also pleasurable, and neither does watching television or being entertained at a sports event produce flow. The concept of flow denotes action involving the expenditure of energy and directionality, the classical connotations of motives. Flow is an emergent characteristic of a person who is deeply immersed in the performance of certain tasks. Though many leisure activities provide enjoyment, flow or self-actualization is not always present, and in real life, this is frequently the case, for instance, in listening to a comic in a nightclub or watching most television programs (Csikszentmihalyi & Kleiber, 1991). Some individuals equate leisure with the absence of effort and exertion of skills. Such an attitude runs counter to what Csikszentmihalyi advocates as the optimum form of leisure. Many leisure activities involve both intrinsic and extrinsic motivation, such as playing tennis in a tournament in which the winner receives a trophy or taking photographs, which are then shown to friends who admire the artistry and thereby enhance the self-esteem of the photographer. Flow has been measured using interviews, questionnaires, and the experience-sampling method (ESM) in which an electronic pager periodically or aperiodically directs the person to record in a diary information about ongoing activities, contents of thought, companionships, effort, and intensity of mood. The data are then analyzed in terms of skills and perceived challenges in various activities. If skill and challenge are both high, the person experiences flow; if skill is high and challenge is low, boredom prevails; if challenge is high and skill is low, anxiety is present. Flow provides a person with what Maslow (1973) called a peak experience that leads to self-actualization (Csikszentmihalyi & Kleiber, 1991), which entails full use and exploration of one's talents and capacities. Just as stress depends on the individual's response to a given stimulus, flow cannot be predicted in advance from the nature of the activity. More importantly, Csikszentmihalyi does not specify what kinds of motivation maintain autotelic action (Ryan, 1993). How do environmental contexts provide appropriate challenges? Experiencing flow is not necessarily associated with activities approved by society, for a person may experience it during acts of violence or gambling. Csikszentmihaly's approach harks back to a much earlier, "simpler," and frequently idealized era in history when many farmers, artisans, artists, physicians, scientists, and others could presumably spend much of their time in pursuits that were intrinsically enjoyable and there were few external constraints on their activities. Even today, there are some older people whose hobbies are cabinetmaking or quilting, activities that provide both intrinsic and extrinsic rewards. However, an analysis of work or leisure activities in our society would probably reveal that not many older, or even younger persons, frequently experience flow.

Lawton

Lawton (1985) developed an ecological cognitive model of activities in which he relates a person's hedonic tone (pleasure, interest, satisfaction, or mood) to the relationship between personal competence and "activity demands" denoted by the physical energy expenditures and physical stimulus characteristics of a task. According to Lawton, any performance may involve intrinsic, extrinsic, or a combination of both types of motives; this approach applies not only to leisure but also to all activities, including obligatory as well as discretionary functions, a dichotomy favored by Lawton. At the same time, he finds it difficult to differentiate leisure from work, since intrinsic motivation and "self-realization," presumably the same constructs as self-actualization, can also occur during work. What may be viewed by society or another person as work may be perceived by the individual as nonobligatory, intrinsically motivated activity.

In an elaboration of his model, Lawton (1993) formulated a tridimensional approach to leisure based on his review of many empirical studies. His first category, labeled *experiential*, consists primarily of activities in which intrinsic motivation predominates. It includes activities in which the person seeks solitude, emotional satisfaction from the activity itself, relaxation, or catharsis. The second category, labeled *developmental,* consists of intellectual challenges, skill development, releases of surplus energy, self-actualization, and health activities. The latter activities, in addition to an intrinsic motive, also include an instrumental component that may be of potential use in the future; activities in this category seem to fit Csikszentmihaly's theory. The third category, labeled *social,* includes social interactions, social status, and volunteering. Lawton admits that these categories are not based exclusively on studies with older persons and that the analysis of specific leisure activities may reveal that they may be placed simultaneously into more than one category. We have previously discussed the multiplicity of motives associated with the performance of various leisure activities.

Stebbins

The sociologist Stebbins (1992, pp. 3–5) adopted Parker's (1982) time-budget continuum of five categories of daily activities: (1) working time or subsistence time; (2) work-related time (e.g., traveling to work, "grooming" for work, entertaining clients); (3) time for satisfying physiological needs (e.g., sleeping, preparing meals, or eating); (4) nonwork obligations, semileisure (e.g., visiting family, taking care of pets, political activities); (5) uncommitted time, leisure. The first four categories correspond to Lawton's obligatory functions. Stebbins further differentiated between *serious leisure,* during which the person makes an effort to find self-fulfillment and enhance his or her identity, and *casual leisure,* such as taking a nap, watching a soap opera on television, or going to a picnic. Stebbins's definition of serious leisure is similar to Kaplan's (1961) definition of leisure in general, and both approaches can be traced to Aristotle. Gordon *et al.* (1976) also spoke of leisure as a discretionary, personal, expressive activity in which meanings are more important than instrumental themes that lead to later gratification. There is also a certain resemblance between Stebbins's (1992, p. 112) definition of serious leisure and Csikszenthmihalyi's (1975) experience of flow. In both constructs, commitment and effort are present.

Losier, Bourque, and Vallerand

Losier, Bourque, and Vallerand (1993) posited a motivational model of leisure based on Deci and Ryan's (1991) self-determination theory. Beginning with Harlow, Harlow, and Meyer (1950), who first introduced the concept of intrinsic motivation in their studies of puzzle solving in monkeys (leisure activity?), much of the subsequent research in this area involved play, games, and similar activities that may be labeled leisure (Deci & Ryan, 1985). Thus, many current models of leisure are based on the theories developed to account for intrinsic motivation. In a study of 102 French-speaking Canadians, both men and women (mean age 74 years; mean educational level 8.4 years), Losier *et al.* (1993) tested their model of self-determined or intrinsically motivated leisure activities. They borrowed Deci and Ryan's classification (1985, pp. 40–42), which varies in the degree of perceived self-determination, using those based on (1) intrinsic motivation, (2) extrinsic motivation, and (3) amotivation. The latter consists of actions that do not represent well-organized goals (e.g., passivity, or disorganized activity, sometimes referred to as helplessness). Extrinsic motivation can be further subdivided as self-determined and non-self-determined. In many instances, the availability of extrinsic rewards can permit the individual to determine his or her action, while in other circumstances the person has no choice. But Deci and Ryan (1991) did not distinguish between two categories of extrinsic motivation; rather, they proposed a continuum of perceived control that ranges from the traditional, intrinsically based motivation with no extrinsic rewards, to situations in which extrinsic rewards are present. The person may have a range from full to no control in the choice to act and to achieve rewards. Degree of self-determined motivation determines the level of satisfaction and amount of participation in a specific leisure activity. Though in the Losier *et al.* study a path analysis indicated that motivation accounted for 32% of the variance of leisure participation, this still leaves a large amount of the variance that can be attributed to several other factors. Unfortunately, the repertoire of activities constituting leisure was not presented. If leisure is an expression of time spent on nonobligatory (i.e., self-determined activity), then no other outcome could have occurred.

Synopsis

The difficulties in categorizing time spent in diverse activities have led Csikszentmihalyi (1975), Lawton (1985, 1993), and Cutler and Hendricks (1990), among others, to minimize the dichotomy between work and leisure. It is the person's perception that imbues any given activity with the meaning of work or leisure. An activity, mainly one labeled serious leisure by Stebbins, may be considered work by some people and leisure by others. Similarly, Driver *et al.* (1991) believe that no specific behaviors can be called leisure. To frame it in modern motivational terminology, leisure is any activity that is intrinsically rewarding, not controlled by external rewards; the individual is free to engage in it, and it is not essential for basic biological functioning. Some have attempted to associate leisure behavior with motives labeled curiosity, exploration, novelty, or changes in routine. The latter constructs themselves are too ill-defined and do not provide a suitable anchor for the concept of leisure; also, they would exclude from leisure such activities as chatting with a spouse or child. However, there is much evidence that intrinsic and extrinsic motives, obligatory and nonobligatory activities, frequently interact (Geen *et al.,* 1984, pp. 278–288). It is apparent that Parker's (1982), Stebbins's (1992), or any other classificatory schema cannot be applied rigidly. A person preparing the family dinner, Stebbins's category 3, who enjoys cooking, may spend much leisure time in the kitchen. It is an obligatory activity to prepare food, but he or she engages in leisure activities in baking bread and pastries or in arranging fancy *hors d'oeuvres.* Such an effort meets Stebbins's criterion for serious leisure since it requires expenditures of energy and fiscal resources that lead to personal fulfillment and enhanced identity. Similarly, Csikszentmihalyi (1975) does not differentiate between the extrinsic and intrinsic motives that are present during many activities; for him, it is not meaningful to categorize activities into work and leisure.

Driver *et al.* (1991), Cutler and Hendricks (1990), and Burrus-Bammel and Bammel (1985) deplore the lack of theories, but they attribute it to the paucity of research devoted to this field. In a thoughtful critique on a series of conferences on leisure and aging, Anderson (1961) wondered whether it is possible to arrive at a theory of leisure, "a tidy model which makes possible the testing of a series of interlocking generalizations derived from a key principle" (p. 428). Anderson observed that Kaplan's (1961) "elements" were poorly defined, and if they are unique to each person, depending on the individual's perception and interpretation of the activity, it is unlikely that anything beyond a descriptive account, limited to a given cultural framework at a certain time in history, can ever be achieved. The complexity in analyzing leisure is not too different from the problems in other areas of human activity, and the generality of research is the quintessential problem in much of current psychology. Anderson hoped for a development of solid minihypotheses that could be tested and suggested studies in different environments in which, presumably, with "various types of motivation," it might be possible to discover generalizations that might have broad applications. The problem with such a proposal may be difficult to reconcile with a frequent definition of leisure, namely, intrinsic motivation or the absence of externally manipulated incentives. Intrinsic motivation does not lend itself to the manipulation of motives. It has been shown that the introduction of external rewards may reduce the strength of intrinsic motivation (Geen *et al.*, 1984, pp. 306–307).

THE ROLE OF MOTIVATION AND
ITS ASSESSMENT

Attribution of Motives

In the previous section on the definitions of leisure, it was apparent that implicit or intrinsic motives are frequently the basis for defining some activities as leisure. Among those who called attention to the importance of motivation in describing leisure activities of the elderly was Lawton (1985). He emphasized the need to examine not only the personality characteristics and experiences of the individual, but also the social context. The meaning of the activity or motivation as part of the person's total time-budget and personal goals, as well as his or her satisfaction, must be considered. In their definitions, Csikszentmihalyi

(1975), Gordon *et al.* (1976), Kaplan (1961), Lawton (1985), and Stebbins (1992), among others, implicitly assume certain motivational variable, but several of the definitions are so broad that there may be numercus motives or values underlying this group of behaviors. For example, in Gordon *et al.*'s (1976) classification of leisure, there is a considerable overlap of motives involved in diverse activities. Travel, which is classified as developmental, may also involve socialization when a person is part of a tour group, and such an activity may be altruistic or even extrinsically motivated when one takes grandchildren on a trip. As another example, there seems to be some lack of consistency between Gordon *et al.*'s conceptualization of leisure that excludes the individual's relation to an institution and includes the authors' listing of organizational participation as a developmental form of leisure. This apparent contradiction illustrates the difficulty in defining the motives involved in the behaviors that constitute the domain of leisure. A person working for an organization may be required to participate in a political demonstration or may benefit if the candidate is victorious, but another individual may be intrinsically motivated to contribute resources to an office seeker in the absence of any tangible benefits to be derived from the candidate's victory. The latter's expressed agenda or viewpoints may be consonant with those of a constituent. Thus, the intention to engage in a certain activity is a key, though this may not be always easy to ascertain, or even apparent to the participant. There are many potential determinants of similar nonobligated activities, especially the more complex ones, such as performing in a community theater or being active in a local Senior Citizens center. A given activity may simultaneously satisfy several motives. Our previous reference to travel and Ajzen's (1991) example of a woman who goes camping with her family points to the complexity of analyzing motivation. Among the various factors initiating travel, we may first consider the potential for increasing family solidarity on the trip; second, camping may bring her closer to nature, a current normative belief in our society for which the motivation is probably very complex; third, the woman may also consider the possible developmental benefits of the trip for her children. Ajzen also notes that many leisure activities involve both objective goals, such as improved cardiovascular fitness and acquiring new friends, and subjective goals, such as a sense of achievement, increased life satisfaction, and reduced anxiety. The benefits of leisure activities may be examined from both the perspectives of an individual as well as from that of society. The latter focuses on the role of recreation in group cohesion, cultural creativity, or social innovation.

In the previously reviewed study by Rapkin and Fischer (1992b) of 179 RSVP members (mean age 73 years), the expressed motives for participating in the program—volunteer work—were meeting new people and striving toward self-fulfillment in leisure. Since these were individuals who volunteered for RSVP, the results were not surprising. It is frequently assumed that leisure and activities associated with sociability are closely related; aside from a sense of achievement, it is apparent that the motivation for leisure includes a variety of social motives.

Mannell (1993) gathered data from 92 retired older adults of both genders over a 1-week period using Csikszentmihalyi's ESM (Csikszentmihalyi & Rathunde, 1993). Contrary to Csikszentmihalyi's theory, he found that flow was experienced to a greater extent in freely chosen extrinsically motivated than in freely chosen intrinsically motivated activities. The extrinsically motivated activities involved a sense of commitment or obligation, primarily family/home care, volunteer activities, and active leisure, which was not present in the intrinsically motivated activities Mannell (1993) relates these commitments to Stebbins's (1992) construct of serious leisure. However, the uncommitted activities included a large amount of passive leisure, such as watching television or reading a book, constituting over 50% of all activities. Those participants who experienced more flow (i.e., had more committed activities) experienced greater life satisfaction. Does this study suggest that serious leisure in our culture needs some extrinsic rewards or recognition?

Assessment

Intertwined with the analysis of motives are certain assessment issues. Gordon *et al.* (1976) mentioned several problems associated with time-budget studies. Among these were the following: The categories are not mutually exclusive (e.g., several motives may be involved in shopping); the categories are either too general or too specific; time sampling methods restricted to a few days may miss rare and important events, such as the wedding of a grandchild; there is no theoretical rationale for the specific formulation of a category. To these, we can add the problem of the reliability of some of the questionnaires.

Lawton (1985) criticizes unidimensional systems of leisure as well as those that lack any subjective measures of the participants' affect. This complicates the analysis of the motivations for any given activity, more so in leisure, in which there are more kinds of intrinsic rewards and fewer constraints than in most work situations. For Mobily, Lemke, and Gisin (1991) a leisure repertoire consists of activities capable of producing perceptions of competence and psychological comfort, an approach not much different from Ajzen's (1991), Lawton's (1985, 1993) or Csikszentmihalyi's (1975). They admit that psychological comfort is difficult to operationalize, but so are several other affective characteristics proposed by others.

Though it might appear that Tinsley, Teaff, Colby, and Kaufman's (1985) research does not have a motivational basis, their emphasis on social relationships in terms of the disengagement–activity continuum implicitly assumes a motivational construct (i.e., approach–avoidance). They analyzed activity data from 1,649 respondents in a national convenience sample, ages 55–75 years. Respondents were asked to complete a paragraph about leisure, and the six clusters of activities found in this young-old sample were labeled companionship, compensation, temporary disengagement, comfortable solitude, expressive solitude, and expressive services, respectively. This taxonomy is based on social relationships, in contrast to the Gordon *et al.* (1976) system that emphasizes intensity of expressive involvement. Tinsley *et al.* (1985) did not separate, for example, games and sports involving group activities from playing bingo or watching a basketball game. Similarly, in Cluster 3, they included reading as well as collecting stamps. The sole dimension in the Gordon *et al.* classification is degree of expressiveness, while Tinsley *et al.* limited themselves to social relationships and degree of disengagement.

Work attitudes and habits, and thus motives, also spill over to leisure time (Kirkcaldy & Cooper, 1992; Parker, 1982, pp. 140–142). For some people, there is generalization from work to leisure activities, like the proverbial sailor who goes boating while on shore leave; for others, off-work activities are compensations for work time, like those attributed to Roosevelt Grier, a well-known professional football player who engaged in needlework in his spare time.

For our present theme, it is noteworthy that in an edited volume on the benefits of leisure, Ajzen (1991) points out that in studies of leisure, there is frequently a lack of concern with people's motivation to engage in various activities. The choice may be at times related to the benefits, or extrinsic motivation, to be derived from a specific activity; for example, the motivation for choosing physical exercise as a form of leisure may be associated with the desire for health maintenance. Crafting cabinets in one's basement may produce furniture that may have commercial value. Even volunteering may lead to public recognition that may satisfy a variety of social motives. Since Ajzen also believes that many leisure activities may simultaneously satisfy several goals, the diversity of available goals and methods for achieving them makes it problematic whether any empirically derived theories can be developed.

In short, it is apparent that different taxonomies of leisure are based on diverse motivational conceptions. Some are based on the intensity of expressive involvement (Csikszentmihalyi, 1975; Gordon et al., 1976). This approach bears some similarity to psychological analyses of arousal induced by novelty or curiosity (Berlyne, 1960). Others have applied classical sociological theories of disengagement–activity–continuity (Tinsley et al., 1985). Some psychological theories (Mobily et al., 1991) have focused on the psychosocial construct of an intrinsic need for competence, as proposed by White (1959) and Bandura (1991), or in Deci and Ryan's (1991) theory of self-determination, which is a modification of White's theory. The theory of Losier et al. (1993) is an example of the latter. While motivational factors are either explicitly or implicitly present in the most studies to which we referred, the diversity of methodologies makes it impractical to draw comparisons.

THE LIFE COURSE

Recently, in most industrialized as well as other societies, retirement has been occurring at progressively earlier ages, and simultaneously, longevity has been increasing (Quinn & Burkhauser, 1990). All of these factors have brought about more free or nonobligated time for older people to pursue leisure activities. In addition, the rising economic status of retirees (Easterlin, 1996) provides them with more choices for leisure activities.

Many studies have reported that the total time devoted to leisure and self-expressive activities increases with age in healthy adults (Gordon et al., 1976). Tokarski (1993) reported that in 1986, in West Germany, retired people averaged 9.7 hours of daily free time after subtracting time for sleeping, eating, cleaning, housework, and other essential chores. Similar data have been reported for Great Britain (Argyle, 1992, p. 104). In a study of men in England, Long (1989) compared the percentages of time spent on different common activities before and after retirement. He found that percentages increased on personal care and domestic activities, leisure at home, and leisure away from home. Domestic activities can be performed more leisurely and may extend to doing tasks personally that prior to retirement would have been neglected or done commercially. For example, the percentage of time devoted to meals and snacks increased from 9.5% before retirement to 13.2% after retirement. Similarly, cleaning, decorating, and domestic repairs jumped from 0.7%

to 4.7%, an almost sevenfold increase. Visiting friends or relatives and shopping also showed increases. A microanalysis of the various daily chores may reveal that some of them may be considered leisure activities; some people enjoy shopping or cooking. These may then be classified as leisure activities for those individuals, while for others they may be chores. However, it should also be noted that in the Long study, the men had spent most of their adult lives working in an era when many of their wives were not employed, and the husbands were probably performing few domestic chores; then, with retirement, they probably took on more domestic responsibilities. With the increased employment of women, the percentages of time for men and women may now be more similar. All in all, it is safe to assume that the time devoted to leisure activities after retirement does not necessarily fill all of the time devoted to work prior to retirement. There are many activities that previously had to be neglected, done hastily, or relied on commercial assistance that can now be performed more leisurely, and the person may find satisfaction in this work. The occasional plaint of a retiree, "How did I ever have time to work?" expresses this feeling. While the validity of time-budget studies of specific activities based on interviews or diaries may be questioned (Niemi, 1993), other types of information tend to support the increasing role of leisure in the aged. Nieswiadomy and Rubin (1995) analyzed changes in data collected by the U.S. Bureau of Labor Statistics Consumer Expenditure Survey of a national sample of retirees. Between 1972 and 1973 and 1986 and 1987, the percentage of retirees' income spent on leisure doubled.

To place the study of leisure during late adulthood into a developmental framework, Gordon (Gordon *et al.*, 1976) relied on Erikson's theory to propose stages of ideal life-cycle activities for urban middle-class Americans in the latter half of the twentieth century. Leisure is viewed as one of the diverse components of life's developmental sequence. During each stage, there are value dilemmas between needs for security and challenge. In retirement, the dilemma is between meaningful integration and autonomy, both difficult constructs. Figure 15.1, based on Gordon *et al.*'s (1976) classification of leisure activities, is in terms of the intensity of expressive involvement.

This system illustrates the problems discussed previously in attempting to classify leisure. For example, Gordon *et al.* eliminated from their system participation in large-scale public-service activities, such as political demonstrations, religious ceremonials, or university inaugurations, that primarily involve a person's relationship to an institution, activities that are, however, usually discretionary and freely chosen. Nor do they include volunteer work in their schema. Cutler and

Intensity of Expressive Involvement	Very High	SEXUAL TRANSCENDENCE Examples: Sexual activities, highly competitive games
	Medium High	CREATIVE ACTIVITIES
	Medium	DEVELOPMENTAL Examples: Travel, serious reading
	Medium Low	DIVERSIONS Examples: Hobbies, light reading
	Very Low	Relaxation

Figure 15.1.   Various forms of leisure activities classified according to intensity of expressive involvement (based on Gordon *et al.,* 1970).

Hendricks (1990) point to the importance of the context, such as cohort, culture, gender, personal resources, health, residence, social support—all of which determine the degree of leisure participation at various ages or stages of the life course.

Riley (1994) advocated an age-integrated model of the life course in which some aspects of education, work, and leisure are distributed throughout the life span. There is some evidence that during the past century, there has been a trend to reduce specific age-differentiated activities; for example, youth is not solely devoted to education, midlife to work, and old age to leisure (O'Rand, 1996). For some persons, midlife and old age are also devoted to education, and leisure frequently occupies much time of those in midlife. The loosening of the normative life-course stages has also resulted in increased heterogeneity of activities within each cohort (O'Rand, 1996); however, on the whole, most activities, even in Western societies, still follow an age-differentiated model.

Numerous health, family, economic resources, and other environmental factors can affect leisure activities of older people. A survey of the literature led Gordon *et al.* (1976) to the conclusion that with increasing age, there is a decrease in the range of leisure activities, and that sedentary and homebound forms tend to predominate. The authors also presented data based on their interviews of 1,441 persons ages 20 to 94 years; age-associated decrements were reported for all categories except for solitary activities after the age of 75 years. Between the ages of 65 and 74 years, there was an increase in television viewing, cultural consumption (listening to music, going to art galleries), and home embellishment. Age-associated gender differences were also noted. Some of these could be expected. For example, women reported decreases in cooking after the age of 45 years, while men showed increases in this activity after the age of 30 years.

Starting in 1968, Lowenthal and her coworkers (Chiriboga & Pierce, 1993), as a part of a longitudinal study of life transitions, interviewed 50–60 persons per age group of lower middle-class or blue-collar San Franciscans. Five interviews were conducted periodically with each participant over a 12-year period. For the last contact, 78% of the original sample was available. In addition to an activity checklist, data were collected on several measures of perceived stress, self-rated health, and some personality variables. With reference to the activity data, a cluster analysis produced an optimum differentiation. Cluster 1 consisted of individuals high in various maintenance activities (cooking, household chores), sports, and social activities, but low on contemplative and solitary activities (walking, praying); they labeled this a "simple pleasure" group. In Cluster 2 were individuals low in social as well as in contemplative and maintenance activities; they were labeled "minimalist." Cluster 3 consisted of individuals high in solitary, maintenance, and outdoor activities, and they were called "creatively engaged." Cluster 4 consisted of a small group of individuals labeled "socially focused." Cluster 5 persons were high on sports, social activities, contemplative activities, and solitary activities, and they were labeled "vigorously engaged." This group represented the youngest participants. Sports included both participation as well as being a spectator. Social activities included items such as travel, picnicking, eating out, and going to the movies. Contemplative activities included walking, praying, daydreaming, and writing. Younger participants were more involved in all categories of activities except housework. Older participants watched more television and rested more. For those who experienced little stress during the period from the baseline measurements to the first 5-year follow-up, all activity measures tended to be stable. On the other hand, high-stress experiences affected the stability of several measures, especially social and outdoor activities. Overall, the clusters are difficult to order on one or even on several singular dimensions, and they tend to support Lawton's (1985) conception of the multidimensionality of leisure. No data were presented for the longer follow-up periods. The authors speculate that leisure activities may predispose an individual to different stress experiences. The relatively small sample sizes limit the generalizations that can be made. Hutchinson (1994) conducted 3,072 observations of various activities in Chicago public parks, involving about 18,000 people and encompassing the whole age range from childhood to late adulthood. Not unexpectedly, the types of activities seen, such as jogging, bicycling, and talking to others, followed age-associated decrements in strenuous physical exertion as well as gender differences. Stanley and Freysinger (1995), in a questionnaire study of people who were initially ages 50–59 years, and who were retested again 16 years later, found that age and health had a greater effect on leisure in men than in women and that changes were less apparent in women. Since, in our society, at least in the past, more men engaged in strenuous physical activities than did women, the data were not unexpected. Verbrugge, Gruber-Baldini, and Fozard (1996), in a questionnaire study of 1,816 men and women between 1958 and 1992, found that longitudinal data mirrored information obtained in cross-sectional studies.

SOME DETERMINANTS OF LEISURE

We have previously indicated that there are no broad general theories or definitions of leisure. It is difficult, therefore, to specify the important variables associated with the changes that occur in various kinds of leisure during aging aside from the obvious ones that result from normal physical decrements.

Previous Life Experiences

We have noted already that the late-life cycle is a continuation of previously acquired habits, and many researchers have emphasized a life-course analysis of the use of time. Havighurst (1952), in his analysis of adjustments in U.S. society, listed the development of adult leisure activities as a task or motive for middle-age (pp. 86–87). For later adulthood, new leisure activities are also desirable (pp. 92–96). Havighurst described normative expectations in mid-twentieth-century America. More recently, Cutler and Hendricks (1990) also emphasized the need to take a life-course perspective, since leisure activities in older persons usually represent continuations of activities that are similar to those they performed at younger ages; the young, avid reader or music lover will continue these pursuits during his or her life. There are, of course, some unavoidable qualitative and quantitative modifications. Going beyond leisure to other aspects of life, the same theme was more recently emphasized by Atchley (1993) in his continuity theory, which stresses the consistency or coherence of patterns of activity through adulthood. Individuals have a strong motivation to continue well-established habits, and this includes leisure activities. Such continuities lead to predictability, which reduces the probability of stress experiences that may be harmful to older people. A person who earlier in life developed competence in some form of artistic performance or sports will continue to pursue this activity into later maturity until physical impairments interfere with the performance. For example, Anna, a retired professor of studio art, volunteered to teach painting in a senior citizens center. Cousins (1996), in a study of 337 women ages 70–98 years, found that among the best predictors of exercise in this group was the encouragement that these women received to engage in sports while they were children. This does not mean, however, that older people cannot develop new interests, and some of the latter are frequently similar to earlier leisure activities; when older persons can no longer play basketball or tennis, they may learn line-dancing. There are also older individuals who develop new interests that are unrelated to their previous leisure. For example, some well-known successful people (e.g., Winston Churchill, Dwight Eisenhower, Grandma Moses), began painting at a fairly advanced age.

Culture and Cohort

There have been some studies examining the role of culturoethnic factors in leisure (Crandall & Thompson, 1978; Riddick and Stewart, 1994). In many of them, however, SES, health, and life satisfaction are confounding variables. Allen and Ching-Sang (1990) interviewed 30 noninstitutionalized, retired African American women ages 65+ years (mean 75) in Florida; during their working years, they were employed as domestics, factory workers, beauticians, nurses, and in similar jobs. Ten of the 30 did not attend school past the sixth grade, and only one completed 1 year of college. They valued their freedom from having to work as a luxury that they did not enjoy previously. Most defined leisure in the context of helping others, especially through church activities in which all of the women participated. Thus, even taking care of a disabled husband was considered to be a leisure activity. More commonly, caretaking of a spouse is considered to be a barrier to leisure time (Moss, Lawton, Kleban, & Duhamel, 1993).

The time devoted to leisure varies substantially from locale to locale. Moss and Lawton (1982) obtained time-budget data from 535 noninstitutionalized older persons in Philadelphia, Pennsylvania, 59% of whom were women. The sample consisted of four groups: (1) independent community dwellers, (2) independent public housing occupants, (3) recipients of in-home services, and (4) people on an institutionaliza- tion waiting list. The first group spent an average of 37% of the waking day on obligatory activities, and the second, 27%. The differences be- tween the two groups were accounted for mainly by a greater amount of yard and housework required of the community-residing compared to the public-housing group. On the other hand, Baltes *et al.* (1990), in their sample of elderly—mostly women—in Berlin, Germany, found that 61% of their waking day hours was spent on obligatory activities such as self- care, housecleaning, cooking, shopping, medical treatments, and nap- ping. About 13% was spent on mental activities (e.g., reading, writing, cultural activities). Nine percent was devoted to media consumption (television, radio), 9% to socializing, 5% to physical activities, and the rest to volunteer and religious activities. Functional health and personal control were important determiners of time allocation. It would seem that in this German sample, the elderly spent much more time on oblig- atory activities than comparable U.S. samples. Unfortunately, Baltes *et al.* did not separate the different aspects of obligatory activities, pre- cluding specific comparisons with the Philadelphia samples. One can speculate about differences in time required for shopping, houseclean- ing, and other necessary activities of daily living between the two coun- tries. For a number of years, the average U.S. household probably contained more labor-saving devices, such as dishwashers, garbage dis- posals, microwave ovens, and electric juice extractors, than what was available in Berlin at the time of the study. Classification of some of the activities in the two studies may also have been different. More impor- tantly, similar activities may have served different purposes in the two samples; in some instances, shopping in Berlin may have provided more opportunities to chat with the baker, a friend, than does shopping in a U.S. supermarket. Yet all of these activities might have been classified as obligatory in both the Berlin and the Philadelphia samples.

Cutler and Hendricks (1990) cite studies showing that the value at- tached to leisure was less in cohorts who grew up during periods of eco- nomic hardships, and there are currently differences between native and foreign-born elderly in the United States. In one study (Tokarski, 1993), it was reported that the amount of social contacts per week in those older than 65 years was more than twice as much in the Nether- lands than in the United States. What these differences reflect may be attributed to several factors: First, they may represent to some extent the diverse definitions of leisure; if, for example, volunteer activities, reli- gious functions, or extended family responsibilities are considered as part of obligated rather than free time, then many older persons who grew up during times of economic hardships or in other cultures may have little or no free time, as commonly conceptualized in our culture, even after they have retired from a paid occupation; some elderly may not be motivated to participate in what are frequently considered to be leisure activities. Second, housing patterns are important determiners of social contact; the American emphasis on privacy probably leads to residential patterns that reduce social contacts. If the Netherlands sample consisted of elderly who lived in communal housing, more common in many Western European countries than in the United States, or with relatives, they were more likely to have social contacts than did the U.S. sample. Third, U.S. elderly probably spend more time viewing television. Fourth, in the Netherlands, there may be more members of the extended family with whom older people socialize.

The cohort and/or age effect on cultural activities was investigated by Koland (1994) in three intrafamilial generations in Vienna, Austria. Preferences for cultural activities (e.g., music, literature, television, movies, dancing, and the theater) varied from generation to generation, and as expected, the differences between the first and second generation were less than those between the second and third generation. This finding reflects the global impact of modern communications technology.

One study of malingering (Graham *et al.,* 1991) in Canada surveyed 300 male and female participants ranging in age from 65 to 80+ years. There was an age x gender interaction in the frequency of malingering; it was most prevalent among men over 80 years and least prevalent for women ages 75–79 years. Thus, even for an activity that requires minimal motor or sensory exertions, age and gender were important factors. Those with the least education exhibited the highest frequency of malingering, presumably because it requires few financial, mental, and physical resources. Number of contacts with relatives and friends was inversely related to this behavior. Shopping malls provided a convenient outlet for socializing for those with few relatives or friends.

These studies indicate that culture, cohort, gender, and experiential factors are important in leisure studies. Only minimal generalizations can be made from cross-sectional data or even from simple longitudinal designs. This complexity has probably discouraged investigators from analyzing an important facet of the daily life activities of older persons.

Health

Of the large number of variables that affects leisure, health, including mobility, is by far the most important one (Burrus-Bammel & Bammel, 1985; Lawton, Moss, & Fulcomer, 1987). Arthritis, the most prevalent chronic disease in the elderly (Schaie & Willis, 1996, p. 437), limits many types of leisure activities common in younger populations. Similar constraints are also associated with other frequent chronic diseases of older persons. Many studies have also reported that with increasing age, there is a direct relationship between degree of satisfaction with leisure and life satisfaction (Cutler & Hendricks, 1990). However, this relationship may be spurious; since leisure activities are associated with good health and the former is also directly related to life satisfaction, both indices may be primarily reflecting a health variable(s). In the Lowenthal study (Chiriboga & Peirce, 1993), the decrements in some leisure activities encountered by older individuals in a 5-year longitudinal study following exposure to relatively high degrees of stress may have been associated to some extent to health problems.

It seems essential that leisure studies take into account the health status of the participant and at the least separate the young-old from the old-old in any analysis, yet the health factor is frequently overlooked. For example, Gordon *et al.* (1976) described the results of structured interviews in 1969, obtained from 1,441 residents of Houston varying in age from 20 to 94 years. While data on age and mental health were reported, there was no reference to physical health.

Mobily, Lemke, Ostiguy, Woodard, *et al.* (1993), in a study of 125 elders of both genders (mean age 69 years), administered a scale of intrinsic motivation (Wessinger) and then obtained data on the frequency of various exercise activities that have cardiovascular benefits (walking, bicycling, swimming) and/or musculoskeletal benefits (calisthenics, gardening, weight training). They also recorded information on self-perceived health. There was no significant correlation between the scores on an intrinsic motivation scale and the amount of exercise. There are several possible interpretations of these findings; the scale may have low validity, the sample size was too small, or that there may be no relationship between exercising and intrinsic motivation. Since exercising is generally believed to have health benefits, this activity may not be intrinsically motivated, at least in terms of the Wessinger scale. People are told by their health professionals or family to exercise, and this becomes an obligatory activity.

Socioeconomic Status and Some Other Variables

It is trivial to say that many leisure activities require financial resources. Vacation travel is expensive, as is playing golf, or eating in many restaurants. Higher SES increases participation in various leisure activities (Burrus-Bammel & Bammel, 1985; Cutler & Hendricks, 1990).

SES also affects education and occupational history, and these also have an impact on leisure habits. Other important factors, aside from those mentioned previously, are gender, personality, and family composition (Burrus-Bammel, & Bammel, 1985; Hutchinson, 1994; Stanley & Freysinger, 1995). Several of these factors are confounded and/or they interact. Gender differences, in general, tend to be smaller than they were in the past (O'Rand, 1996). There are no data that specifically compare historical changes of the gender factor in leisure activities.

Lawton (1994) correlated leisure activities with personality or affective measures in 826 Elderhostel participants (mean age 69 years) using a previously developed scale from his laboratory (Lawton, Kleban, Rajagopal, & Dean, 1992). He controlled statistically for education (mean educational level 15.6 years) and self-rated health. People who were high in surgency (energetic), sensation seeking, and who expected fewer age-associated changes tended to participate more frequently in leisure activities. To some extent, these factors are similar to what may be described as extroversion. Emotional control, moodiness, and emotional maturity (expressing fewer worries) were unrelated to leisure activities. However, the activities surveyed were primarily overtly observable social behaviors. Solitary walking or book reading were not included. Even so, the affect variables accounted only for modest amounts of variance for the different activities. Also, this was a cross-sectional study of relatively well-educated elderly. The importance of the congruence between personality and leisure activities has been reported for younger employed professionals (Melamed, Meir, & Samson, 1995).

ADULT EDUCATION

A leisure activity that has been thriving recently is adult education for seniors (Schaie & Willis, 1996, pp. 355–356). It fits Riley's (1992) notion of an integrated lifetime model of activities. Many educational institutions provide this service gratis or at a reduced cost to older persons. Hobbies, recreation, or personal development are the most common goals. These choices further support the importance of leisure in the life of older persons. Most of the enrollees are relatively well-educated elderly (Pearce, 1991; Schaie & Willis 1996, p. 356), and this again fits with the notion that previous activities tend to be maintained through the life course.

The extent to which older people participate in educational activities is difficult to ascertain. According to one report from Germany, only about 1–3% of those over 65 years are enrolled in formal educational courses (Karl, 1991). A 1980 unpublished survey of colleges and universities in South Carolina by the author also found that the enrollment was less than 1% of the age cohort. However, aside from formal enrollment in established educational institutions, there are numerous other educational opportunities specifically organized for the elderly: The Elderhostel programs, held mainly on college campuses, offer seniors various short-term educational courses inexpensively in an informal atmosphere (Schaie & Willis, 1996, pp. 357–358). For many participants, attendance at an Elderhostel combines education with other leisure activities such as travel, socialization, or planning for retirement migration. Many senior centers and social organizations offer a variety of courses, usually taught by professional educators, covering such diverse topics as foreign languages, computer literacy, writing autobiographies, history, and numerous immediately applicable skills. In the United States, Shepherd's Centers, a national organization, provides educational programs in many churches. In most instances, it is difficult to separate the contributions of social motivation from the motivation to acquire competence. In addition, how can we assess the educational components resulting from reading, radio, television, or internet browsing? Activity surveys do not differentiate between pulp fiction and scholarly books. Similarly, most published time-budget data of television viewing by the elderly do not take into account the nature of the programs; in the United States, the *active improvement* component of watching soap operas is probably different from that derived from watching the History, Discovery, C-SPAN, other educationally oriented channels, as well some programs on the major networks. There have been some recent attempts to examine this factor. Riggs (1996) in an ethnographic study using interviews, focus groups, and observations of television viewing in a relatively affluent retirement community, found that many individuals were taking advatage of this medium to continue their involvement in intellectual pursuits. Modern computer technology, readily available at home, such as the Internet and e-mail, can further enhance educational activities of older persons who may find it bothersome to travel to an educational center.

AMENITY MIGRATION

If in retirement, leisure is viewed as a functional equivalent of work for younger people (Cutler & Hendricks, 1990), some retirees will seek environments that maximize leisure opportunities, just as younger individuals seeking work tend to move to locations where there are jobs.

Wiseman (1980) developed a behavioral theory to account for the migration of older individuals, positing three types of motivation for migration: The first is "amenity migration," when relatively well-off, educated, healthy, younger retirees seek environments that have pleasant climates and provide leisure opportunities; most of these locales are also associated with greater opportunities for outdoor recreation. The second source of motivation for migration is assistance, when the elderly person moves to a location near kin or friends who can provide needed support; some move to all-elderly retirement, but these tend to be less healthy older persons who have few relatives and to communities that offer a spectrum from independent living to nursing-home care (Silverstein & Zablotsky, 1996). The third motivation is return migration, when people move back to the area in which they grew up or lived for a long time; this may be in many instances related to the second type in that there may be kin or friends in the previous location to provide assistance or social support, and the local culture may be more congenial with their early established habits. In this chapter on leisure, we therefore focus only on amenity migration.

Haas and Serow (1993) extended Wiseman's motivational model by adding also a push factor in migration, in which not only the attractiveness of the new location, a *pull* factor, is an incentive, but also the aversiveness, a *push* factor, of the current location. In their study, climate was the most important push factor, followed by urban problems, and then economics (cost of living, property taxes). The large number of elderly in-migrants in the Sunbelt states represents mainly amenity migrants. However, even the construct of amenity migration in most studies does not separate the contributions of climate, economics, leisure opportunities, neighborhood (the presence of others from the same age cohort with perhaps similar values and life experiences), and other components of amenity. We may assume, however, that climate is closely related to increased opportunities for leisure. In the winter, even many younger people living in Northern states fly south to play golf. In cold blustery climates, outdoor recreational activities are usually limited to skiing and similar sports that are unsuitable for most older individuals. Real estate developers have capitalized on the desire of seniors to migrate from the areas in which they were employed, which has led to the development of retirement communities described as "American Originals" (Streib, 1993). Most of the developers stress the availability of recreational/leisure opportunities, especially for the "young-old" retirees. In his review of retirement communities, Streib notes that a major consideration in decisions to relocate to a retirement community is the availability of pleasant and rewarding leisure activities in close proximity to residents' homes. In one such community of only 2,000 residents, over 100 diverse leisure activities were scheduled. In a small sample of Sun City, Arizona, residents, an amenity-rich retirement community designed for active retirees, Gober and Zonn (1983) found that, next to climate, the availability of recreational facilities was the most important factor in the decision to relocate. Of course, other factors also contributed to that decision; the Sun City residents were a self-selected group of relatively healthy and economically comfortable retirees.

Haas and Serow (1993) conducted a telephone survey of older adults near retirement age who had moved to western North Carolina (WNC), an area with the highest mountains east of the Mississippi. Data were analyzed from 586 households, a larger sample than that found in most comparable studies. The occupants ranged in age from 40 to 90 years, were mostly married, and were economically well-off. They were highly educated; 30% possessed a postbaccalaureate degree, and an additional 55% had a bachelor's degree or some college education. Only about 44% of their annual income was derived from Social Security. The important factors that attracted them to WNC, in descending order, were scenic beauty, climate, recreational opportunities, cultural amenities, tax rate, and cost of living. Scenic beauty, in most instances, is associated with numerous leisure activities such as hiking, picknicking, or just admiring the scenery. Working individuals often spend vacations in such areas; they become acquainted with the various benefits, including recreation, available in that locale, and this serves as a major pull factor. In a neighboring state, data were available from a 1990 survey of a sample of 436 residential/retirement-community residents and 551 military retirees in South Carolina (College of Business Administration, University of South Carolina, 1991). This also was a well-educated, relatively affluent population. In the nonmilitary sample, 31% had a postbaccalaureate education, and 46% had a bachelor's degree or had attended college. In the military retiree group, 18% had postbaccalaureate education, and 62% had a bachelor's degree or had attended college. No data on specific annual incomes were obtained, but in the community–retiree group, only 33% of income came from Social Security and 23% from private pensions, while 39% was derived from investments and 6% from business and other sources. In the military retiree group, 53% of the income came from military benefits and Social Security. In the community group, climate, health care availability, several economic factors (cost of living, taxes), and closeness of relatives and friends were rated as more important factors in selecting a retirement location than were recreational/leisure activities. The ratings of the military retirees were similar, except that they also ranked closeness to a military base as an additional factor that was more important than recreation/leisure activities. Presumably, closeness to military medical facilities was an important factor.

Some of the discrepancies between the WNC and the SC samples may be attributed to differences in the methodology used in the data collection; WNC survey questions were asked over the telephone, while in the SC study, respondents had to rate a limited number of items on a mail-questionnaire. It is possible that the SC group tacitly assumed that the favorable climate provided more opportunities for recreation that they did not have to mention separately. Also, in the WNC sample, recreation was not mentioned as frequently as a push factor that caused the migrants to relocate; perhaps the respondents compensated for that by mentioning it more frequently as a pull factor. The SC survey did not inquire about push factors. Both samples consisted of self-selected migrants who chose the areas in which they relocated in terms of their interests, which, of course, varied. Nevertheless, leisure opportunities were considered as a factor in both groups and only their relative importance was different in the two samples. Cuba and Longino (1991) interviewed 149 migrants in Cape Cod, Massachusetts. Here, too, the availability of leisure activities was rated as very important, together with scenic beauty, climate, and economic conditions. The published data do not permit an analysis of the relative significance of each factor. Jackson and Day (1993) surveyed all counties in the United States that had a larger percentage of military retirees than the national average. Most of the counties in which older retirees relocated had mild winter temperatures and/or a coastal water access location, important amenity factors with a recreational component. It is apparent that the growth of amenity migrations and the attendant development of retirement communities attest to the significance of leisure in the lives of the economically advantaged healthy elderly.

VOLUNTEERING

Definitions

In the Introduction, we referred to leisure as time devoted to nonobligatory activities. Also, for many gerontologists, the role of leisure for the elderly is equivalent to that of work at younger ages. In our analysis of theories of leisure, we emphasized that it is difficult to subscribe to a simple dichotomy of work or obligated time and leisure or nonobligated time. This dilemma also applies to volunteering, for many kinds of volunteer activities do not fit into a simple schema. Stebbins (1996) asserts that volunteering is invariably, or frequently, a form of serious leisure, though the latter itself is an amorphous concept. It may satisfy several motives, such as helping others, helping oneself, or a combination of motives. For Mannell (1993), volunteering is a freely chosen committed activity based on intrinsic motivation that requires expenditures of energy and foregoing some short-term pleasures from less demanding activities. In contrast, Kleiber and Ray (1993) raise the issue of whether volunteering is a form of leisure. According to them, volunteers usually do not consider this activity to be leisure.

In their reviews of the literature, Fischer, Mueller, and Cooper (1991), as well as Cnaan, Handy, and Wadsworth (1996), emphasize that there are no definitions, boundaries, or standards for voluntary labor; some apply the concept only to activities performed under the sponsorship of an organization, but others include informal services, such as driving a disabled person to his or her physician or taking care of a neighbor's pet. In informal services, it is difficult to draw the line between helping a neighbor and one's distant or even close kin when the latter may be an obligatory activity.

The nature of volunteer activities is also very diverse. It may include serving as a trustee of a senior center, as an usher in a church, or visiting the sick in a hospital, stuffing envelopes during a political campaign, or distributing food in a homeless shelter. Many activities labeled as voluntary are actually obligatory. A young person who applies for college may volunteer to tutor handicapped youngsters, since such activities may be used as a criterion in admission decisions. In some high schools, volunteering is part of the graduation requirement. People with strong intrinsic, religion-oriented motives may consider volunteer activity an obligation.

On the basis of their review, Cnaan *et al.* (1996) posited several dimensions—or more accurately, criteria—of voluntary activities. A slightly modified version of this model includes the following dimensions: (1) free choice; (2) no, or only nominal remuneration, such as a free lunch during the volunteering period; (3) formal or informal structure (i.e., activity in an established organization vs. helping a neighbor); (4) the intent to provide assistance; (5) the nature of the beneficiary (i.e., family member, friend, the community).

Motivation

An analysis of various definitions of volunteering reveals that several different motives may play a role. According to Okun (1994), the motives for volunteering may include (1) expression of deeply held beliefs; (2) enhancement of one's social networks; (3) the need to feel appreciated and enhance self-esteem; (4) gaining a greater understanding of the world; and (5) career-related benefits. Clary, Snyder, and Stukas (1996) developed the Volunteer Functions Inventory (VFI). The authors were interested in measuring the motivations for volunteering; in a stratified national survey of 2,671 persons, a factor analysis produced six scales: (1) Values (altruism or humanitarianism); (2) Career; (3) Understanding; (4) Socialization; (5) Self-Enhancement; and (6) Protection. The motives varied for different venues of activities such as human services, religious organizations, and politics. Overall, values tended to be the most important motive, but the authors admit that the complex nature of motives and various behaviors precludes simple generalizations. The level of education and the values of the person were the best predictors of volunteering. It is apparent that Okun (1994) and Clary *et al.* (1996) arrived at very similar conclusions. Most of the proposed motives are complex and it is difficult to dissociate them.

We have previously discussed the self as one of the major social motives. Volunteering may be associated with group accomplishment, an important social goal; on the other hand, much volunteer work (note the usage of the term *work*) may be based on *altruism,* or "the right thing to do," but this introduces another complex concept (Batson, 1991): Does altruism satisfy an intrinsic motive or does it reduce an aversive arousal caused by witnessing another person's suffering (pp. 44–46)? One factor in the Clary *et al.* (1996) VFI scale is "protection." In Chapter 8, we referred to altruism, which is frequently the basis of social support.

Midlarsky and Kahana (1994, pp. 39–40) stretch the definition of altruism by resorting to the concept of degrees of altruism; it seems that they are acknowledging that there are numerous motives, difficult to disentangle, that may be the basis for altruism. As we noted, in addition to altruism, there are numerous other motives that are important for some individuals who participate in volunteer activities. Fischer *et al.* (1991) acknowledge that the absence of payment as a criterion of voluntarism is an inadequate measure. A volunteer who reads to residents in a nursing home may receive a free lunch while there, may become educated about some health problems, or a family member may receive preferred admission to the home. Can these benefits be considered remunerations?

Aging

There have been a number of studies of age effects on volunteering, though most of them have been cross-sectional, with no control for cultural changes. In 1975, Harris and associates (cited by Midlarsky & Kahana, 1994, pp. 134–135) found that 22% of elderly are engaged in some organized volunteer activities. In 1991, in a national telephone survey of 962 respondents ages 60 years or older, Marriott Senior Living Services found that over 41% had participated in some form of volunteer work during the past year, though, on the average, they contributed to it less than 1 hour per week. In the 65- to 69 and 70- to 74-year age groups, the percentages were 46 and 45, respectively, but even in the 80+ group, the percentage of volunteers was still 27. Another study reported that volunteer participation in the United States tends to show peaks in the mid-30s to mid-40s, followed by relatively constant levels up to the mid-70s, when, presumably, disabilities reduce the ability to provide services (Harootyan & Vorek, 1994). The same authors also reported that the percentage of retired persons who participated in volunteer activities was not higher than percentages among those employed full-time. Since most senior volunteers devote less than 1 hour per week to this activity (Marriot Living Services, 1991; Okun, 1994), for most retirees, volunteering cannot be assumed to be a substitute for work. Chambre (1984) reported that the presumed role loss following retirement does not lead to volunteer activities; persons who did volunteering in midlife tended to continue it after retirement, but those without such activities during the working years did not begin to do so after retirement.

Midlarsky and Kahana (1994) reviewed helping and volunteering in later life within the context of altruism, and they also presented data from some of their naturalistic studies. They found that most people reported that their helping behavior did not decrease with age unless illness, lack of adequate transportation, or finances interfered (p. 227). Kincade *et al.* (1996) in a stratified national survey, interviewed 3,485 Medicare recipients over age 65 years; one-third were providing assistance to a spouse, about 20% did organized volunteer work, 16% provided child care, and 40% listened to problems of other people and/or offered advice. These data did not include such activities as transporting a neighbor or friend to a physician, feeding a neighbor's pet, visiting sick friends, helping with household or car repairs, and numerous other nonreimbursed activities that might be considered voluntary. This study illustrates the problem in circumscribing volunteer work. Factors that enhanced volunteering included being a woman, being younger, having better self-reported health, and having a higher level of education. The latter factor is probably confounded with higher SES. Contrary to expectation, there was no difference between rural and urban residents.

Midlarsky and Kahana (1994, p. 233) ascribe altruistic behavior of older people to a greater need to find meaning in their life. We reviewed this topic in Chapter 12. The authors deplored the paucity of research data on this important facet of an older person's life; lest we be too optimistic, more research data are unlikely to provide greater insight on the relationship between altruism and the meaning of life. The diversity of definitions of what constitutes volunteering and the multiplicity of motives that influence these activities present huge challenges to the researcher. As culture changes, so does society's need for various types of volunteering

CONCLUSIONS

Today, in most industrialized societies, older people retire from work, and this provides them with opportunities to pursue other activities. Though leisure activities are very important in the life course of healthy older adults, occupying perhaps a considerable portion of their waking hours, relatively little effort has been devoted to leisure by psychologists, though other social scientists have been studying it more diligently. In the past, it has been assumed that leisure is not as significant for well-being as is work; more recently, however, in Western societies, it has become a "need" at every stage of life. Leisure consists of multifaceted behaviors, frequently defined as nonwork or nonobligatory activity, and it encompasses numerous motives. Some psychologists define leisure as activity that has intrinsic motivation and is thus primarily self-determined and internally controlled. But most activities at all stages of life, including work, have both intrinsic and extrinsic motivational components. Similarly, the distinction between obligatory and nonobligatory activities is not always easy to establish. Obligatory domestic chores may include both leisure and nonleisure aspects. Exercising also is frequently based on intrinsic as well as extrinsic motives for maintenance and enhancement of health. In most theories of leisure, motivation is either explicit or implicit.

Leisure should be considered a part of the total matrix of activities in which a person is daily engaged. Most studies find positive correlations between satisfaction with leisure and general life satisfaction, but the causal sequences, if any, cannot be determined. The multiple motivations for leisure activities are greatly influenced by the culture and change with birth cohorts, as we saw in comparing data obtained in the United States and in several Western European countries. In the United States, some data have reported differences between native and foreign-born elderly. Similarly, individuals who experienced economic hardships in their youth have different interests from those without such life experiences. Such findings tend to indicate that patterns of leisure activities developed earlier in life persist into the later years.

Ongoing stresses also affect leisure activities. Structurally oriented sociologists have provided descriptive data, primarily on the quantity of various activities classified as leisure. There have been several different classificatory schemas proposed by investigators. Health, as are almost all activities occurring in late adulthood, is a prepotent factor in the quantity, quality, and choice of leisure. Finances, education, family responsibilities such as caregiving for a spouse, living arrangements, and the availability of leisure facilities are among the factors influencing leisure participation. With increasing educational levels in the population, increased access to advertisements and media presentations of the "good life," and an overall rise in the standard of living in industrialized societies, various leisure activities are perceived as important needs.

Amenity migration for climate and recreational opportunities influences many young-old in our present US society to relocate. Others change residences within a locality or affiliate with organizations that provide enhanced leisure activities. Havighurst has suggested that in middle adulthood, people should adjust their leisure activities to fit the onset of normal biological and psychosocial changes associated with the later stages of life; it is not clear to what extent Havighurst's proposal is contrary to a continuity theory or whether it consists only of a small modification of previously established habits. Reliable longitudinal data on the continuity of leisure are lacking, and considering the numerous interacting factors that play important roles, this is not surprising. At the present, there are no satisfactory psychological theories to account for leisure, and the complexity of what may be defined as leisure activity is unlikely to lead to such a theory in the near future.

Finally, we have also briefly examined volunteering—activities that are labeled serious leisure by some. Here, too, investigators have described a large variety of activities based on numerous motives, and some have introduced the concept of altruism, an intrinsic motive to help others and to find meaning in life, which further confounds an already complex topic. In short, it is difficult to provide a brief summary of volunteering, an important aspect in the life of many people.

CHAPTER 16

Epilogue

The widespread dissemination of information spawned by the modern communications revolution has also affected the growing segment of the population labeled "old." No longer is the average person in Western society satisfied with accepting his or her fate, with all the pleasures and many vicissitudes that in the past have characterized aging; instead, there is a search for successful or optimum aging. Sometimes this has also been referred to as an attempt to enjoy a high quality of life. What is the basis for achieving such a desirable state, and what are the motives and goals that produce such well-being?

As in most biological and social sciences, we are plagued by problems of definitions that are exacerbated in cross-disciplinary studies such as gerontology. Though much effort has been devoted to the analyses of the concepts of motivation, well-being, quality of life, and even aging, there have been few attempts to integrate this work with the empirical literature, and the definitions are frequently context-specific. To be pragmatic, and to be able to achieve the goal of covering some of the highlights of the findings on the well-being of our older population, we adopted a somewhat loose, commonsense approach in defining the concepts in this area.

Though no elaborate studies are necessary to show that many goals and the consequent activities of an octogenarian differ from those of a young adult, such a crude analysis is inadequate for a better understanding of human motives and goals in the later part of life. The latter involves knowing many facets of a person's activities and beliefs, and this is such a formidable task at any age that many psychologists, especially those concerned with the basic principles of the field, have either eschewed the concept of motivation or have ignored it in their research. Yet in many applied areas, whether education, psychotherapy, or sales, the concept of motivation has been promoted as a key to achieving numerous specific goals. The activation and direction of behavior commonly used in the definition of motivation depends on both certain biological essentials for survival and many learned patterns of behavior that are greatly influenced by the prevailing culture. To study motivation, it is therefore necessary to analyze both biological and psychosocial mechanisms. Aging is associated with many, more or less, inevitable biological losses even in persons considered to be "healthy"; the limitations are especially noticeable in the speed and strength of the behavioral, sensory, and muscular activities frequently used as indices of many motives.

We tried to simplify our review by focusing primarily on the research with relatively healthy older individuals. To inquire about the motivation of the elderly who have severe physical and mental limitations would require an understanding of various aspects of geriatrics, with a separate treatment devoted to each individual disease. In Western societies, it is often assumed that most old people have major disabilities that need to be addressed. As in other areas of the biological and social sciences, the public is more willing to support research on applied problems than on basic science. A well-known gerontologist attached the label "Alzheimerization" to the current research efforts in gerontology, and while much is written about the problems of older people afflicted with cancer, dementia, and other severely disabling conditions, the majority of those over the age of 65 years describe their health as "good" or "excellent." Even at more advanced ages, a large percentage of the elderly have relatively few functional limitations.

We began our review with a brief look at the energetic or metabolic changes accompanying aging. Starting in early adulthood, there are many more or less inevitable biological losses, even in persons considered to be "healthy." Many of the biological limitations of aged persons are most pronounced when the organism must perform rapidly or with a great expenditure of energy, and the age-associated deficits are especially large when environmental disequilibria require an excess of energy expenditure to return to a normal state. Diseases and other stressors therefore affect older persons more than they do the younger ones. Much of this research has been in the context of health and stress; the latter replacing the traditional concept of adjustment, previously favored by psychologists. Many stressors in modern, rapidly changing societies are psychosocial disequilibria resulting from unexpected events or unfulfilled desires; in increasingly complex environments, the variety of stressors also becomes more numerous and generalizations are more difficult, yet modernization also produces a search for successful aging that implies the attenuation and absence of stress. Not surprisingly, much of the research on stress and aging has been in the context of stressors that are commonly associated with aging, such as health problems, caregiving, or bereavement. We have therefore devoted more space to this topic than to other aspects of motivation. Simultaneously, many of the so-called biological motives that have been traditionally studied in the analysis of motivation, such as sleeping, eating, drinking, or sexual activities, are affected only to a small extent in healthy older persons. Many of the age-associated changes in these domains can be attributed to a large extent to psychosocial factors, primarily previously acquired habits that are currently inappropriate, financial losses, or changes in interpersonal relationships.

Human motivation does not depend primarily on biological mechanisms: An understanding of psychosocial environmental factors is essential, and this creates major difficulties in psychological gerontology. Since the environment is in constant flux, both early and later experiences will influence an older person's motives. The effort to tease out the contributions of the various environmental contexts or experiences is a Herculean task. With increasing age, the person accumulates experiences, all of which have the potential to influence behavior; thus, studies in gerontology are much more difficult than those of earlier stages of life. Even a "simple" longitudinal study in which the same cohort is followed over a lifetime has been a rarity in psychogerontology. In the few studies where this was accomplished, the samples consisted of very select individuals, usually the more educated, who were willing to devote time to help science. We are not certain if other cohorts with different lifetime experiences would manifest similar changes in motivation. The inevitable diversity of lifetime experiences also leads to large intra- and interindividual variabilities that require large study samples, with the attendant logistics problems that lead some investigators to abandon more traditional psychological experimental methods and to concentrate on idiographic or case-study methodologies. Generalizations based on such a methodology are much more formidable than those based on standard nomothetic techniques. However, there have been also attempts to blend various research techniques.

There is much evidence that various motivational changes during aging are a function of the individual's personality, another contentious construct. Some investigators actually define personality in terms of a pattern of motives; a pattern implies that most complex behaviors depend on a multiplicity of motives, and some of them may change as a person ages, while others stay constant. To understand and predict behavior such as interpersonal relationships, it would seem essential that there be a certain stability of adult personality; otherwise, life would resemble a Dr. Jekyll-and-Mr. Hyde situation in which interactions would be unpredictable. Several theorists strongly support continuity. Most of the exceptions to continuity occur when a person experiences *non-normative* events, but continuity and non-normativity are difficult to define. How large a difference can be tolerated without violating the concept of stability? Societal norms change, and the globalization of information and increasing cross-national migrations affect norms or expectations. Not too long ago, a divorce in middle or late adulthood was non-normative, but today, it is much less so. Culture changes during a long lifetime, and this will influence the perception of stress or non-normativity. A large number of psychosocial variables affects personality, which may then influence physiological mechanisms and ultimately result in health consequences. The importance of the context in studies of motivation, stress, and ethical issues, with the use of analogs, precludes the use of controlled laboratory studies; furthermore, many events are unique to later life, and that limits generalizations based on younger populations. Retirement, relocation because of disabilities, or loss of a spouse do not occur frequently in young adulthood, and in the rare cases when they do happen, their meaning is very different from that affecting an older person. In most instances, we have little information on the previous experiences of the older adult.

To the extent that motivational factors are controlled, studies of cognitive and perceptual phenomena during aging are also affected by cultural changes, but most likely to a lesser degree than are those in motivation. Values and beliefs, fundamental aspects of culture, are critical factors in understanding psychosocial motives. In many Western societies, from early childhood on, we emphasize the need for people to exert control over their activities, but in many other cultures, this seems to be less important, or the definition of control merely implies that events are not unexpected.

In most laboratory studies of age-associated changes of learning, memory, or perception, the motivation of the participants is not determined, but we saw that the stresses resulting from the home environment may influence the laboratory performance of an older person. Most laboratory studies depend on convenience samples, and it is cumbersome to inquire about the motivation of the participant and the various stressors that currently affect him or her in the experiment. While, in many studies, participants are asked about their physical health, or are even examined to some extent it, it is extremely rare that there is any effort to inquire about stresses and mental health problems unless the symptoms are obvious.

Perusal of the social motives shows their dependence on health, but otherwise, at the present time, it is difficult to discern close relationships between the various social and biological motives. This would seem to provide support for psychologists such as Koch (1993), who believe that there is no unified science of psychology. It depends, however, on the degree of generalizations that we are seeking. For example, one of the major, frequently seen, age-associated changes in social motivation is a narrowing of the focus in social interactions, a reduction in the number of individuals with whom older people maintain contacts, which is analogous to the biological phenomenon of reduction of activity that occurs during aging. Thus, there are some parallels between social and biological motivation, but the underlying mechanisms are complex.

Examination of reviews and textbooks in psychogerontology reveals attempts to transfer the study of problems important in the life of younger adults, such as achievement-related motivation, to older populations, though some of these seem to have little relevance in later life. In this domain, Erikson's concept of generativity during midlife, followed by integrity in later adulthood, was developed at a time when few individuals survived in good health to late adulthood, but at present, many older adults are still involved in abetting the success of their midlife adult children and younger grandchildren. There has been little psychological research on this aspect of late adulthood, though economists and other social scientists have examined financial transfers between generations. Similarly, activities such as amenity migrations and leisure, important in the life of older persons, are underresearched by psychologists, though it is sometimes assumed that such activities frequently are equivalent to work in earlier adulthood. We have briefly reviewed a few of these less traditional topics in psychogerontology in the hope of encouraging additional work in this domain.

Numerous conceptual and methodological questions were raised in this review. Much that has been written on aging deals with the various complex problems of living encountered by the elderly. There is no succinct answer to the question, "What is successful aging"? Botwinick (1984, pp. 87-89) referred to three very broad, fuzzy factors of health, adequate financial resources, and having a confidant, but none of these factors can be quantified, and they vary as a function of cohort, culture, and other contextual factors.

I do not want to conclude on a pessimistic tone, as evidenced by the introduction of the concept of successful aging in the beginning of this epilogue. It seems appropriate, therefore, to quote from the earliest

American book in psychogerontology, written by the first president of the American Psychological Association, G. Stanley Hall (*Senescence*, 1922, p. 327): "For myself, I frankly confess that the longer I live the more I want to keep doing so." The author was 78 years old when this was published, at a time when only 1.4% of the United States population was age 75+ years (U.S. Bureau of the Census, 1996).

References

Abel, E. K. (1990). Informal care for the disabled elderly: A critique of recent literature. *Research on Aging, 12,* 139–157.

Achenbaum, W. A., & Orwoll, L. (1991). Becoming wise: A psychogerontological interpretation of The Book of Job. *International Journal of Aging and Human Development, 32,* 21–39.

Adams, R. G., & Blieszner, R. (1994). An integrative conceptual framework for friendship research. *Journal of Social and Personal Relationships, 11,* 63–184.

Adelman, R. C. (1995). The Alzheimerization of aging. *Gerontologist, 35,* 526–532.

Adler, N., & Mathews, K. (1994). Health psychology: Why do some people get sick and some stay well? *Annual Review of Psychology, 45,* 229–259.

Ajzen, I. (1991). Benefits of leisure: A social psychological perspective. In B. L. Driver, P. J. Brown, & G. L. Peterson (Eds.), *Benefits of leisure* (pp. 411–417). State College, PA: Venture.

Ajzen, I. (1996). The social psychology of decision making. In E. T. Higgins & A. W. Kruglanski (Eds.), *Social psychology: Handbook of basic principles* (pp. 297–325). New York: Guilford.

Aldwin, C. M. (1991). Does age affect the stress and coping process? Implications of age differences in perceived control. *Journals of Gerontology, 46,* P174–P180.

Aldwin, C. M. (1992). Aging, coping, and efficacy: Theoretical framework for examining coping in life-span developmental context. In M. A. Wykle, E. Kahana, & J. Kowal (Eds.), *Stress and health among the elderly* (pp. 96–113). New York: Springer.

Aldwin, C. M. (1994). *Stress, coping, and development: An integrative perspective.* New York: Guilford.

Aldwin, C. M., & Levenson, M. R. (1994). Aging and personality assessment. *Annual Review of Gerontology, 14,* 182–209.

Aldwin, C. M., Levenson, M. R., Spiro, A., & Bosse, R. (1989). Does emotionality predict stress? Findings from the normative aging study. *Journal of Personality and Social Psychology, 56,* 618–624.

Allee, W. C. (1951). *Cooperation among animals with human implications* (2nd ed.). New York: Schuman.

Allen, K. R., & Ching-Sang, V. (1990). A lifetime of work: The context and meanings of leisure for aging black women. *Gerontologist, 30,* 734–740.

Allport, G. W. (1943). The ego in contemporary psychology. *Psychological Review, 50,* 451–478.

Allport, G. W. (1947). Scientific models and human morals. *Psychological Review, 54,* 182–192.

Allport, G. W., & Ross, J. M. (1967). Personal religious orientation and prejudice. *Journal of Personality and Social Psychology, 5,* 432–443.

American Psychiatric Association. (1994). *Diagnostic and statistical manual of mental disorders* (4th ed.). Washington, DC: Author.

American Psychological Association. (1993).*Vitality for life: Psychological research for productive aging.* Washington, DC: Author.

Amster, L. E., & Krauss, H. H. (1974). The relationship between life crises and mental deterioration in old age. *International Journal of Aging and Human Development, 5,* 51–55.

Andersen, R. (1968). *A behavioral model of families' use of health services.* Chicago: Center for Health Administration Studies, University of Chicago.

Andersen, R. M. (1995). Revisiting the behavioral model and access to medical care: Does it matter? *Journal of Health and Social Behavior, 36,* 1–10.

Anderson, J. E. (1959). The use of time and energy. In J. E. Birren (Ed.), *Handbook of aging and the individual* (pp. 769–796). Chicago: University of Chicago Press.

Anderson, J. E. (1961). Comments. In R. W. Kleemeier (Ed.), *Aging and leisure: A research perspective into the meaningful use of time* (pp. 428–432). New York: Oxford University Press.

Andres, R., & Tobin, J. D. (1977). Endocrine systems. In C. E. Finch, & L. Hayflick (Eds.), *Handbook of the biology of aging* (pp. 357–378). New York: Van Nostrand Reinhold.

Aneshensel, C. S. (1992). Social stress: Theory and research. *Annual Review of Sociology, 18,* 15–38.

Angulo, J. F. (1988). Foodways, ideology and aging: A developmental dilemma. *American Behavioral Scientist, 32,* 41–49.

Antonovsky, A. (1979). *Health. stress, and coping.* San Francisco: Jossey-Bass.

Antonovsky, A. (1987). *Unraveling the mystery of health: How people manage stress and stay well.* San Francisco: Jossey-Bass.

Antonovsky, A. (1990). Personality and health: Testing the sense of coherence model. In H. S. Friedman (Ed.), *Personality and disease* (pp. 155–177). New York: Wiley.

Antonovsky, H., Sadowsky, M., & Maoz, B. (1990). Sexual activity of aging men and women: An Israeli study. *Behavior, Health, and Aging, 1,* 151–161.

Antonucci, T. C. (1990). Social supports and social relationships. In R. H. Binstock & L. K. George (Eds.), *Handbook of aging and the social sciences* (pp. 205–226). San Diego: Academic Press.

Antonucci, T. C. (1991). Attachment, social support, and coping with negative life events in mature adulthood. In E. M. Cummings, A. L. Greene, & K. H.

Karraker (Eds.), *Life-span developmental psychology: Perspectives on stress and coping* (pp. 261–276). Hillsdale, NJ: Erlbaum.

Appley, M. H. (1991). Motivation, equilibration, and stress. *Nebraska Symposium on Motivation, 38*, 1–67.

Appley, M. H., & Trumbull, R. (1967). *Psychological stress: Issues in research.* New York: Appleton-Century-Crofts.

Arbuckle, N. W., & deVries, B. (1995). The long-term effects of later life spousal and parental bereavement on personal functioning. *Gerontologist, 35,* 637–647.

Argyle, M. (1992). *The social psychology of everyday life.* London: Routledge.

Arling, G. (1985). Interaction effects in a multivariate model of physician visits by older people. *Medical Care, 23,* 361–371.

Atchley, R. C. (1993). Continuity theory and the evolution of activity in later adulthood. In J. R. Kelly (Ed.), *Activity and aging: Staying involved in later life* (pp. 5–16). Newbury Park, CA: Sage.

Atkinson, J. W. (1964). *Introduction to motivation.* New York: Van Nostrand.

Atkinson, J. W. (1992). Motivational deteminants of thematic apperception. In C. P. Smith, J. W. Atkinson, D. C. McClelland, & J. Veroff (Eds.), *Motivation and personality: Handbook of thematic content analysis* (pp. 21–48). New York: Cambridge University Press.

Ausman, L. M., & Russell, R. M. (1990). Nutrition and aging. In E. L. Schneider & J. W. Rowe (Eds.), *Handbook of the biology of aging* (3rd ed, pp. 384–406). San Diego: Academic Press.

Azuma, H. (1984). Secondary control as a heterogeneous category. *American Psychologist, 39,* 970–971.

Bäckman, L., & Molander, B. (1991). On the generalizability of the age-related decline in coping with high-arousal conditions in a precision sport: Replication and extension. *Journals of Gerontology, 46,* P79–P81.

Bakan, D. (1968). *Disease, pain and sacrifice: Toward a psychology of suffering.* Chicago: University of Chicago Press.

Ballieux, R. E. (1992). Bidirectioal communication between the brain and the immune system. *European Journal of Clinical Investigation, 22*(Suppl. 1), 6–9.

Baltes, M. M., & Carstensen L. L. (1991). "Possible selves across the life span": Comment. *Human Development, 34,* 256–260.

Baltes, M. M., & Wahl, H. W. (1992). The dependency–support script in institutions: Generalization to community settings. *Psychology and Aging, 7,* 409–418.

Baltes, M. M., Wahl, H. M., & Schmid-Furstoss, U. (1990). The daily life of elderly Germans: Activity patterns, personal control, and functional health. *Journals of Gerontology, 45,* P173–P179.

Baltes, P. B. (1987). Theoretical propositions of life-span developmental psychology: On the dynamics between growth and decline. *Developmental Psychology, 23,* 611–626.

Baltes, P. B., & Baltes, M. M. (1990). Psychological perspectives on successful aging: The model of selective optimization with compensation. In P. B.

Baltes & M. M. Baltes (Eds.), *Successful aging: Perspectives from the behavioral sciences* (pp. 1–34). New York: Cambridge University Press.

Baltes, P. B., Smith, J., & Staudinger, U. M. (1992). Wisdom and successful aging. *Nebraska Symposium on Motivation, 39,* 123–168.

Baltes, P. B., & Willis, S. L. (1977). Toward psychological theories of aging and development. In J. E. Birren, & K. W. Schaie (Eds.), *Handbook of the psychology of aging* (pp. 128–154). New York: Van Nostrand Reinhold.

Banaji, M. R., & Prentice, D. A. (1994). The self in social contexts. *Annual Review of Psychology, 45,* 297–332.

Bandura, A. (1977). Self-efficacy: Toward a unifying theory of behavioral change. *Psychological Review, 84,* 191–215.

Bandura, A. (1991). Self-regulation of motivation through anticipatory and self-reactive mechanisms. *Nebraska Symposium on Motivation, 38,* 69–164.

Barker, R. G., & Wright, H. F. (1951). *One boy's day: A specimen record of behavior.* New York: Harper.

Barnas, M. V., Pollina, L., & Cummings, E. M. (1991). Life-span attachment and socioemotional functioning in adult women. *Genetic, Social, and General Psychology Monographs, 117,* 175–202.

Barnes, R. F., Raskind, M., Gumbrecht, G., & Halter, J. B. (1982). The effects of age on the plasma catecholamine response to mental stress in man. *Journal of Clinical Endocrinology and Metabolism, 54,* 64–69.

Barrow, G. M. (1992). *Aging, the individual and society* (5th ed.). St. Paul, MN: West.

Barrow, G. M. (1996). *Aging, the individual and society* (6th ed.). St. Paul, MN: West.

Bartley, S. H., & Chute E. (1947). *Fatigue and impairment in man.* New York: McGraw-Hill.

Bartley, S. H. (1981). IV. Fatigue. *Perceptual and Motor Skills, 53,* 958.

Bartoshuk, L. M. (1990). Chemosensory alterations and cancer therapies. *National Cancer Institute, 9,* 179–184.

Bartoshuk, L., & Duffy, V. (1995). Taste and smell. In E. J. Massoro (Ed), *Handbook of physiology: Section 11. Aging* (pp. 363–375). New York: Oxford University Press.

Bartoshuk, L. M., & Weiffenbach, J. M. (1990). Chemical senses and aging. In E. L. Schneider & J. W. Rowe (Eds.), *Handbook of the biology of aging* (3rd ed., pp. 429–443). San Diego: Academic Press.

Barusch, A. S., & Spaid, W. M. (1989). Gender differences in caregiving: Why do wives report greater burden? *Gerontologist, 29,* 667–676.

Bass, D. M., & Bowman, K. (1990). The transition from caregiving to bereavement: The relationship of care-related strain and adjustment to death. *Gerontologist, 30,* 35–42.

Bass, D. M., Bowman, K., & Noelker, L. S. (1991). The influence of caregiving and bereavement support on adjusting to an older relative's death. *Gerontologist, 31,* 32–42.

Batson, C. D. (1991). *The altruism question: Toward a social-psychological answer.* Hillsdale, NJ: Erlbaum.

Baum, S. K., & Stewart, R. B., Jr. (1990). Sources of meaning through the lifespan. *Psychological Reports, 67,* 3–14.

Baumeister, R. F. (1991). *Meanings of life.* New York: Guilford.

Baumeister, R. F., & Leary, M. R. (1995). The need to belong: Desire for interpersonal attachment as a fundamental human motivation. *Psychological Bulletin, 117,* 497–529.

Beach, F. A. (1956). Characteristics of masculine "sex drive." *Nebraska Symposium on Motivation, 4,* 1–32.

Bearon, L. B. (1989). No great expectations: The underpinnings of life satsfaction for older women. *Gerontologist, 29,* 772–778.

Beehr, T. A., & McGrath, J. E. (1996). The methodology of research on coping: Conceptual, strategic, and operational-level issues. In M. Zeidner & N. S. Endler (Eds.), *Handbook of coping: Theory, research, and applications* (pp. 65–82). New York: Wiley.

Belsky, J., & Cassidy, J. (1994). Attachment and close relationships: An individual-difference perspective. *Psychological Inquiry, 5,* 27–30.

Bem, S. (1995). Motivation, cognition and action. In I. Lubek, R.van Hezewijk, G. Peterson, & C. W. Tolman (Eds.), *Trends and issues in theoretical psychology* (pp. 226–232). New York: Springer.

Benca, R. M., Obermeyer, W. H., Thisted, R. A., & Gillin, J. C. (1992). Sleep and psychiatric disorders: A meta-analysis. *Archives of General Psychiatry, 49,* 651–668.

Bengtson, V. L., Reedy, M. N., & Gordon, C. (1985). Aging and self-conceptions: Personality processes and social contexts. In J. E. Birren & K. W. Schaie (Eds.), *Handbook of the psychology of aging* (2nd ed., pp. 544–593). New York: Van Nostrand.

Bengtson, V. L., Rosenthal, C., & Burton, L. (1996). Paradoxes of family and aging. In R. H. Binstock & L. K. George (Eds.), *Handbook of aging and the social sciences* (4th ed., pp. 253–282). San Diego: Academic Press.

Bergeman, C. S., Plomin, R., Pedersen, N. L., & McClearn, G. E. (1991). Genetic mediation of the relationship between social support and psychological well-being. *Psychology and Aging, 6,* 640–646.

Bergner, M., & Rothman, M. L. (1987). Health-status measures: An overview and guide for selection. *Annual Review of Public Health, 8,* 191–210.

Berkanovic, E., & Hurwicz, M.-L. (1992). Illness episodes, physician visits, and depressive symptoms. *Journal of Aging and Health, 4,* 331–348.

Berkman, L. F. (1988). The changing and heterogeneous nature of aging and longevity: A social biomedical perspective. *Annual Review of Gerontology and Geriatrics, 8,* 37–68.

Berlyne, D. E. (1960). *Conflict, arousal, and curiosity.* New York: McGraw-Hill.

Berndt, T. J. & Burgy, L. (1996). Social self-concept. In B. A. Bracken (Ed.), *Handbook of self-concept: Developmental, social, and clinical considerations* (pp. 171–209). New York: Wiley.

Berry, D. T. R., & Webb, W. B. (1985). Sleep and cognitive functions in normal older adults. *Journal of Gerontology, 40,* 331–335.

Berscheid, E. (1994). Interpersonal relationships. *Annual Review of Psychology, 45,* 79–129.

Betts, N. M. (1988). Nutritional perspectives and aging. *American Behavioral Scientist, 32,* 17–30.

Birren, J. E., & Bengtson, V. L. (Eds.). (1988). *Emergent theories of aging.* New York: Springer.

Birren, J. E., & Birren, B, A. (1990). The concepts, models, and history of the psychology of aging. In J. E. Birren & K. W. Schaie (Eds.), *Handbook of the psychology of aging* (3rd ed., pp. 3–20). San Diego: Academic Press.

Birren, J. E., & Cunningham, W. (1985). Research on the psychology of aging: Principles, concepts, and theory. In J. E. Birren & K. W. Schaie (Eds.), *Handbook of the psychology of aging* (2nd ed., pp. 3–34). New York: Van Nostrand Reinhold.

Birren J. E., & Lanum, J. C. (1991). Metaphors of psychology and aging. In G. M. Kenyon, J. E. Birren, & J. J. F. Schroots (Eds.), *Metaphors of aging in science and the humanities* (pp. 103–129). New York: Springer.

Birren, J. E., & J. J. Schroots (1996). History, concepts, and theory in the psychology of aging. In J. E. Birren & K W. Schaie (Eds.), *Handbook of the psychology of aging* (4th ed., pp. 3–23). San Diego: Academic Press.

Birren, J. E., Sloane, R. B., Cohen, G. D., Hoyman, N. R., *et al.* (Eds.). (1992). *Handbook of mental health and aging* (2nd ed.). San Diego: Academic Press.

Blau, P. M. (1964). *Exchange and power in social life.* New York: Wiley.

Blazer, D. (1996). Geriatric psychiatry. In R. E. Hales, & S. C. Yudofsky (Eds.), *Synopsis of psychiatry* (pp. 1307–1321). Washington, DC: American Psychiatric Press.

Blazer, D. G., Hays, J. C., & Foley, D. J. (1995). Sleep complaints of older adults: A racial comparison. *Journals of Gerontology Series A, 50A,* M280–M284.

Bleecker, M. L., Bolla-Wilson, K., Agnew, J., & Meyers, D. A. (1987). Simple visual reaction time: Sex and age differences. *Developmental Neuropsychology, 3,* 165–172.

Blieszner, R., & Adams, R. G. (1992). *Adult friendship.* Newbury Park, CA: Sage.

Bliwise, D. L. (1993). Sleep in normal aging and dementia. *Sleep, 16,* 40–81.

Bliwise, D. L., Carskadon, M. A., Seidel, W. F., Nekich, J. C., *et al.* (1991). MSLT-defined sleepiness and neuropsychological test performance do not correlate in the elderly. *Neurobiology of Aging, 12,* 463–468.

Blumenthal, J. A., Emery, C. F., Madden, D. J., George, L. K., *et al.* (1989). Cardiovascular and behavioral effects of aerobic exercise training in healthy older men and women. *Journals of Gerontology, 44,* M147–157.

Borg, G. (1977). *Physical work and effort.* Oxford, UK: Pergamon Press.

Borg, G. (1982). Psychophysical bases of perceived exertion. *Medicine and Science in Sports and Exercise, 14,* 377–381.

Borg, G., & Linderholm, H. (1967). Perceived exertion and pulse rate during exercise in various age groups. *Acta Medica Scandinavica, 182*(Suppl. 472), 194–206.

Boring, E. G. (1950). *A history of experimental psychology* (2nd ed.). New York: Appleton–Century–Crofts.

Botwinick, J. (1984). *Aging and behavior* (3rd ed.). New York: Springer.

Botwinick, J., & Schock, N. W. (1952). Age differences in performance decrement with continuous work. *Journal of Gerontology, 7,* 41–46.

Bracken, B. A. (1996). Clinical applications of a context-dependent, multidimensional model of self-concept. In B. A. Bracken (Ed.), *Handbook of self-concept: Developmental, social and clinical considerations* (pp. 463–503). New York: Wiley.

Braithwaite, V. (1992). Caregiving burden: Making the concept scientifically useful and policy relevant. *Research on Aging, 14,* 3–27.

Braithwaite, V. (1996). Between stressors and outcomes. Can we simplify caregiving process variables? *Gerontologist, 36,* 42–53.

Brandstädter, J., & Greve, W. (1994a). The aging self: Stabilizing and protective processes. *Developmental Review, 14,* 52–80.

Brandstädter, J. & Greve, W. (1994b). Explaining the resilience of the aging self: Reply to Carstensen and Freund. *Developmental Review, 14,* 93–102.

Brandstädter, J., & Renner, G. (1990). Tenacious goal pursuit and flexible goal adjustment: Explication and age-related analysis of assimilative and accommodative strategies of coping. *Psychology and Aging, 5,* 58–67.

Brandstädter, J., & Renner, G. (1992). Coping with discrepancies between aspirations and achievements in adult development: A dual process model. In L. Montada, S. H. Filipp, & M. J. Lerner (Eds.), *Life crises and experiences of loss in adulthood* (pp. 301–319). Hillsdale, NJ: Erlbaum.

Brandstädter, J., Wentura, D., & Greve, W. (1993). Adaptive resources of the aging self: Outlines of an emergent perspective. *International Journal of Behavioral Development, 16,* 323–349.

Brennan, J. F. (1994). *History and systems of psychology* (3rd ed.). Englewood Cliffs, NJ: Prentice Hall.

Bretscheider, J. G., & McCoy. N. L. (1988). Sexual interest in healthy 80- to 102-year-olds. *Archives of Sexual Behavior, 17,* 109–129.

Brickman, P., Rabinowitz, V. C., Karuza, J., Coats, D., *et al.* (1982). Models of helping and coping. *American Psychologist, 37,* 368–394.

Brim, O. G. (1988, September). Losing and winning. *Psychology Today, 22,* 48–52.

Broadbent, D. E. (1979). Is a fatigue test now possible? *Ergonomics, 22,* 1277–1290.

Brody, E. M. (1985). Parent care as a normative stress. *Gerontologist, 25,* 19–29.

Brody, E. M., & Kleban, M. H. (1983). Day-to-day mental and physical health symptoms of older people: A report on health logs. *Gerontologist, 23,* 75–85.

Buck, R. (1988). *Human motivation and emotion* (2nd ed.). New York: Wiley.

Bühler, C. M. (1962). *Values in psychotherapy.* Glencoe, IL: Free Press.

Burke, P. J. (1991). Identity processes and social stress. *American Sociological Review, 56,* 836–849.

Burrus-Bamel, L. L., & Bamel, G. (1985). Leisure and recreation. In J. E. Birren & K. W. Schaie (Eds.), *Handbook of the psychology of aging* (pp. 848–863). New York: Van Nostrand Reinhold.

Buss, D. M. (1996). The evolutionary psychology of human social strategies. In E. T. Higgins & A. W. Kruglanski (Eds.), *Social psychology: Handbook of basic principles* (pp. 3–38). New York: Guilford.

Busse, E. W., & Blazer, D. G. (1980). Disorders related to biological functioning. In E. W. Busse & D. G. Blazer (Eds.), *Handbook of geriatric psychiatry* (pp. 390–414). New York: Van Nostrand.

Cain, W. S., & Stevens, J. C. (1989). Uniformity of olfactory loss in aging. *Annals of the New York Academy of Sciences, 561,* 29–38.

Calasanti, T. M., & Hendricks, J. (1986). A sociological perspective on nutrition research among the elderly: Toward conceptual development. *Gerontologist, 26,* 232–238.

Call, V., Sprecher, S., & Schwartz, P. (1995). The incidence and frequency of marital sex in a national sample. *Journal of Marriage and Family, 57,* 639–652.

Cameron, C. (1973). A theory of fatigue. *Ergonomics, 16,* 633–648.

Cameron, L., Leventhal, E. A., & Leventhal, H. (1993). Symptom representations and affect as determinants of care seeking in a community dwelling, adult sample population. *Health Psychology, 12,* 171–179.

Cannon, W. B. (1915). *Bodily changes in pain, hunger, fear, and rage.* New York: Appleton.

Cannon, W. B. (1932). *The wisdom of the body.* New York: W. W. Norton.

Cantor, N., & Zirkel, S. (1990). Personality, cognition, and purposive behavior. In L. Pervin (Ed.), *Handbook of personality: Theory and research* (pp. 135–164). New York: Guilford.

Carstensen, L. L. (1992). Selectivity theory: Social activity in life-span context. *Annual Review of Gerontology and Geriatrics, 11,* 195–217.

Carstensen, L. L. (1993). Motivation for social contact across the life span: A theory of socioemotional selectivity. *Nebraska Symposium on Motivation, 40,* 209–254.

Casey, K. L. (1978). Neural mechanisms of pain. In E. C. Carterette & M. P. Friedman (Eds.), *Handbook of perception* (Vol. VIB): *Feeling and hurting* (pp. 183–230). New York: Academic Press.

Chadda, R., & Kulhara, P. (1987). Prevalence of various depressive symptoms in major depressive disorders. *Indian Journal of Psychological Medicine, 10,* 1–5.

Chamberlain, K., & Zika, S. (1990). The minor events approach to stress: Support for the use of daily hassles. *British Journal of Psychology, 81,* 469–481.

Chambre, S, M. (1984). Is volunteering a substitute for role loss in old age? An empirical test of activity theory. *Gerontologist, 24,* 292–298.

Chapman, C. R. (1978). The hurtful world: Pathological pain and its control. In E. C. Carterette & M. P. Friedman (Eds.), *Handbook of perception* (Vol. VIB): *Feeling and hurting* (pp. 264–299). New York: Academic Press.

Chappell, N. L. (1990). Aging and social care. In R. H. Binstock & L. K. George (Eds.), *Handbook of aging and the social sciences* (3rd ed., pp. 438–454). San Diego: Academic Press.

Chappell, N. L., & Badger, M. (1989). Social isolation and well-being. *Journals of Gerontology, 44,* S169–S176.

Cheng, S. (1992). Loneliness–distress and physician utilization in well-elderly females. *Journal of Community Psychology, 20,* 43–56.

Chipperfield, J. G. (1993). Perceived barriers in coping with health problems: A twelve-year longitudinal study of survival among elderly individuals. *Journal of Aging and Health, 5,* 123–139.

Chiriboga, D. A. (1992). Paradise lost: Stress in the modern age. In M. A. Wykle, E. Kahana, & J. Kowal (Eds.), *Stress and health among the elderly* (pp. 35–71). New York: Springer.

Chiriboga, D. A., & Pierce, R. C. (1993). Changing contexts of activity. In J. R. Kelly (Ed.), *Activity and aging: Staying involved in later life* (pp. 42–59). Newbury Park, CA: Sage.

Clark, L. A., Watson, D., & Reynolds, S. (1995). Diagnosis and classification: Challenges to the current system and future directions. *Anuual Review of Psychology, 46,* 121–153.

Clary, E. G., Snyder, M., & Stukas, A. A. (1996). Volunteers and motivation: Findings from a survey. *Nonprofit and Voluntary Sector Quarterly, 25,* 485–505.

Clayton, V. P., & Birren, J. E. (1980). The development of wisdom across the life span: A reexamination of an ancient topic. In P. B. Baltes & O. G. Brim, Jr. (Eds.), *Life-span development and behavior* (Vol. 3, pp. 103–135). New York: Academic Press.

Clipp, E. C., & Elder, G. H., Jr. (1996). The aging veteran of World War II: Psychiatric and life course insights. In, P. E. Ruskin & J. A. Talbott (Eds.), *Aging and posttraumatic stress disorders.* Washington, DC: American Psychiatric Press.

Cnaan, R. A., Handy, F., & Wadsworth, M. (1996). Defining who is a volunteer: Conceptual and empirical considerations. *Nonprofit and Voluntary Sector Quarterly, 25,* 364–383.

Cofer, C. N., & Appley, M. H. (1964). *Motivation, theory, and research.* New York: Wiley.

Coffey, C. E. (1994). Anatomic imaging of the aging human brain: Computed tomography and magnetic resonaance imaging. In C. Coffey & J. L. Cummings (Eds.), *Textboook of geriatric neuropsychiatry* (pp. 159–194). Washington, DC: American Psychiatric Press.

Cohen, G. D. (1990). Psychopathology and mental health in the mature and elderly adult. In J. E. Birren, & K W. Schaie (Eds.), *Handbook of the psychology of aging* (3rd ed., pp. 359–374). San Diego: Academic Press.

Cohen, S., & Herbert, T. B. (1996). Health psychology: Psychological factors and physical disease from the perspective of human psychoneuroimmunology. *Annual Review of Psychology, 47,* 113–142.

Cohen, S., Kessler, R. C., & Gordon, L.U. (1995). Strategies for measuring stress in studies of psychiatric and physical disorders. In S. Cohen, R. C. Kessler, & L. U. Gordon (Eds.), *Measuring stress: A guide for health and social scientists* (pp. 3–26). New York: Oxford University Press.

Cohen, S., & Rodriguez, M. S. (1995). Pathways linking affective disturbances and physical disorders. *Health Psychology, 14,* 374–380.

Cohen, S., & Williamson, G. M. (1991). Stress and infectious disease in humans. *Psychological Bulletin, 109,* 5–24.

Cohler, B. J. (1991). Life course perspectives on the study of adversity, stress, and coping: Discussion of papers from the West Virginia conference. In E. M. Cummings, A. L.Greene, & K. H. Karraker (Eds.), *Life-span developmental psychology: Perspectives on stress and coping* (pp. 297–326). Hillsdale, NJ: Erlbaum.

Coleman, D., & Iso-Ahola, S. E. (1993). Leisure and health: The role of social support and self-determination. *Journal of Leisure Research, 25,* 111–128.

College of Business Administration, University of South Carolina. (1991). *The economic impact of the senior living industry in South Carolina.* Columbia, SC: Author.

Collins, L. M. (1996). Measurement of change in research on aging: Old and new issues from an individual growth perspective. In J. E. Birren & K W. Schaie (Eds.), *Handbook of the psvchology of aging* (4th ed., pp. 38–56). San Diego: Academic Press.

Comfort, A. (1980). Sexuality in later life. In J. E. Birren & R. B. Sloan (Eds.), *Handbook of mental health and aging* (pp. 885–892). Englewood, NJ: Prentice Hall.

Considine, M. (Ed.). (1977). *Van Nostrand's scientific encyclopedia* (5th ed.). New York: Van Nostrand.

Cook, A. J., & Thomas, M. R. (1994). Pain and the use of health services among the elderly. *Journal of Aging and Health, 6,* 155–172.

Cooke, R. G., Warsh, J. J., Stancer, H. C., Hasey, G. M., et al. (1990). Effect of concurrent medical illness on dexamethasone suppression test results in depressed inpatients. *Canadian Journal of Psychiatry, 35,* 31–35.

Corby, N., & Solnick, R. L (1980). Psychosocial and physiological influences on sexuality in the older adult. In J. E. Birren & R. B. Sloan (Eds.), *Handbook of mental health and aging* (pp. 893–921). Englewood Cliffs, NJ: Prentice Hall.

Costa, P. T., Jr., & McCrea, R. R. (1985a). *The NEO Personality Inventory Manual.* Odessa, FL: Psychological Assessment Resources.

Costa, P. T., Jr., & McCrea, R. R. (1985b). Hypochondriasis, neuroticism, and aging: When are somatic complaints unfounded? *American Psychologist, 40,* 19–28.

Costa, P. T., Jr., & McCrea, R. R. (1988). From catalog to classification: Murray's needs and the five-factor model. *Journal of Personality and Social Psychology, 55,* 258–265.

Costa, P. T., Jr., & McCrea, R. R. (1990). Personality: Another hidden factor in stress research. *Psychological Inquiry, 1,* 22–24.

Costa, P. T. Jr. & McCrae, R. R. (1995). Design and analysis of aging studies. In E. J. Massoro (Ed.), *Handbook of Physiology: Section 11. Aging* (pp. 25–36), New York: Oxford University Press.

Costa, P. T., Somerfield, M. R., & McCrea, R. R. (1996). Personality and coping: A reconceptualization. In M. Zeidner & N.S. Endler (Eds.), *Handbook of coping: Theory, research and applications* (pp. 44–61). New York: Wiley.

Cotman, C. W., Kahle, J. S., & Korotzer, A. R. (1995). Maintenance and regulation in brain of neurotransmission, trophic factors, and immune responses. In E. J. Massoro (Eds), *Handbook of physiology: Section 11. Aging* (pp. 345–362). New York: Oxford University Press.

Cousins, S. (1996). Exercise cognition among elderly women. *Journal of Applied Sport Psychology, 8,* 131–145.

Cowart, B. J. (1989). Relationships between taste and smell across the adult lifespan. *Annals of the New York Academy of Sciences, 561,* 39–55.

Coyne, J. C., & Downey,G. (1991). Social factors and psychopathology: Stress, social support, and coping process. *Annual Review of Psychology, 42,* 401–425.

Crandall, R., & Thompson, R. (1978). The social meaning of leisure in Uganda and America. *Journal of Cross-Cultural Psychology, 9,* 469–481.

Cristofalo, V. J. (1996). Ten years later: What have we learned about human aging from studies of cell cultures? *Gerontologist, 36,* 737–741.

Cross, G. S. (1993). *Time and money: The making of consumer culture.* London: Routledge.

Cross, S., & Markus, H. (1991). Possible selves across the life span. *Human Development, 34,* 230–255.

Crumbaugh, J. C., & Maholick, L. T. (1964). An experimental study in existentialism: The psychmetric approach to Frankl's concept of noogenic neurosis. *Journal of Clinical Psychology, 20,* 200–207.

Csikszentmihalyi, M. (1975). *Beyond boredom and anxiety.* San Francisco: Jossey-Bass.

Csikszentmihalyi, M., & Kleiber, D. A. (1991). Leisure and self-actualization. In B. L. Driver, P. J. Brown, & G. L. Peterson (Eds.), *Benefits of leisure* (pp. 91–102). State College, PA: Venture.

Csikszentmihalyi, M., & Rathunde, K. (1993). The measurement of flow in everyday life: Toward a theory of emergent motivation. *Nebraska Symposium on Motivation, 40,* 57–97.

Cuba, L., & Longino, C. F., Jr. (1991). Regional retirement migration: The case of Cape Cod. *Journals of Gerontology, 46,* S33–S42.

Cumming, E., & Henry, W. E. (1961). *Growing old: The process of disengagement.* New York: Basic Books.

Cunningham, W. R., Sepkoski, C. M., & Opel, M. R. (1978). Fatigue effects on intelligence test performance in the elderly. *Journals of Gerontology, 33,* 541–545.

Cutler, S. J., & Hendricks, J. (1990). Leisure and time across the life course. In R. H. Binstock & L. K. George (Eds.), *Handbook of aging and the social sciences* (3rd ed., pp. 169–185). San Diego: Academic Press.

Dannefer, D. (1988a). Differential gerontology and the stratified life course: Conceptual and methodological issues. *Annual Review of Gerontology and Geriatrics, 8,* 3–36.

Dannefer, D. (1988b). What's in a name? An account of the neglect of variability in the study of aging. In J. E. Birren & V. L. Bengtson (Eds.), *Emergent theories of aging* (pp. 356–384). New York: Springer.

Darko, D. F., Wilson, N. W., Gillin, J. C., & Golshan, S. (1991). A critical appraisal of mitogen-induced lymphocyte proliferation in depressed patients. *American Journal of Psychiatry, 148,* 337–344.

Datan, N., Rodeheaver, D., & Hughes, F. (1987). Adult development and aging. *Annual Review of Psychology, 38,* 153–180.

Dean, K. (1992). Health-related behavior: Concepts and methods. In M. G. Ory, R. P. Abeles, & P. D. Lipman (Eds.), *Aging, health, and behavior* (pp. 27–56). Newbury Park, CA: Sage.

de Castro, J. M. (1991). The relationship of spontaneous macronutrient and sodium intake with fluid ingestion and thirst in humans. *Physiology and Behavior, 49,* 513–519.

de Castro, J. M. (1993). Age related changes in spontaneous food intake and hunger in humans. *Appetite, 21,* 255–272.

de Castro, J. M. (1994). Family and friends produce greater social facilitation of food intake than other companions. *Physiology and Behavior, 56,* 445–455.

Deci, E. L. (1992). On the nature and functions of motivation theories. *Psychological Science, 3,* 167–171.

Deci, E. L., & Ryan, R. M. (1985). *Intrinsic motivation and self-determination.* New York: Plenum Press.

Deci, E. L., & Ryan, R. M. (1991). A motivational approach to self: Integration in personality. *Nebraska Symposium on Motivation, 38,* 237–288.

Deimling, G. T. (1994). Caregiver functioning. *Annual Review of Gerontology and Geriatrics, 14,* 257–280.

Delisle, M. A. (1988). What does solitude mean to the aged? *Canadian Journal on Aging, 7,* 358–371.

DeLongis, A., Coyne, J. C., Dakof, G., Folkman, S., & Lazarus, R. S. (1982). Relationship of daily hassles, uplifts, and major life events to health status. *Health Psychology, 1,* 119–136.

Dement, W., Richardson, G., Prinz, P., Carskadon, M., *et al.* (1985). Changes of sleep and wakefulness with age. In C. E. Finch & E. L. Schneider (Eds.), *Handbook of the biology of aging* (pp. 692–717). New York: Van Nostrand Reinhold.

DePaola, S. J., & Ebersole, P. (1995). Meaning in life categories of elderly nursing home residents. *International Journal of Aging and Human Development, 40,* 227–236.

Deptula, D., Sing, R., & Pomara, N. (1993). Aging, emotional states, and memory. *American Journal of Psychiatry, 150,* 429–434.

Depue, R. A., Luciana, M., Arbisi, P., Collins, P., & Leon, A. (1994). Dopamine and the structure of personality: Relation to agonist-induced dopamine activity to positive emotionality. *Journal of Personality and Social Psychology, 67*, 485–498.

DeVries, H. A., Brodowicz, G. R., Robertson, L. D., Svoboda, M. D., *et al.* (1989). Estimating physical working capacity and training changes in the elderly at the fatigue threshold. *Ergonomics, 32*, 967–977.

DeVries, H. A., Tichy, M. W., Housh, T. J., Smyth, K. D., *et al.* (1987). A method for estimating physical working capacity at the fatigue threshold (PWCFT). *Ergonomics, 30*, 1195–1204.

Diehl, M., Coyle, N., & Labouvie-Vief, G. (1996). Age and sex differences in strategies of coping and defense across the life span. *Psychology and Aging, 11*, 127–139.

Dienstbier, R. A. (Ed.). (1991). *Nebraska Symposium on Motivation, 38.*

Dinges, D. F., & Kribbs, N. B. (1991). Performing while sleepy: Effects of experimentally induced sleepiness. In T. H. Monk (Ed.), *Sleep, sleepiness, and performance: Human performance and cognition* (pp. 97–128). New York: Wiley.

Diokno, A. C., Brown, M. B., & Herzog, A. R. (1990). Sexual function in the elderly. *Archives of Internal Medicine, 150*, 197–200.

Dishman, R. K. (1994). Prescribing excersise intensity for healthy adults using perceived exertion. *Medicine and Science in Sports and Exercise, 26*, 1087–1094.

Ditto, B., Miller, S., & Maurice, S. (1987). Age differences in the consistency of cardiovascular response patterns on healthy women. *Biological Psychology, 25*, 23–31.

Dixon, R. A., & Bäckman, L. (1995). Concepts of compensation: Integrated, differentiated, and Janus-faced. In R. A. Dixon & L. Bäckman (Eds.), *Compensating for psychological deficits and declines: Managing losses and promoting declines* (pp. 3–19). Mahwah, NJ: Erlbaum.

Dollard, J. Miller, N. E., Doob, L. W., Mowrer, O. H., & Sears, R.R. (1939). *Frustration and aggression.* New Haven, CT: Yale University Press.

Dorfman, L. T., Holmes, C. A., & Berlin, K. (1996). Wife caregivers of frail elderly veterans: Correlates of caregiver satisfaction and caregiver strain. *Family Relations, 45*, 46–55.

Dowd, J. J. (1975). Aging as exchange: A preface to a theory. *Journal of Gerontology, 30*, 584–594.

Driver, B. L., Brown, P. J., & Peterson, G. L. (1991). Research on leisure benefits: An introduction to this volume. In B. L. Driver, P. J. Brown, & G. L. Peterson (Eds.), *Benefits of leisure* (pp. 3–11). State College, PA: Venture.

Duck, S. (1994). Attaching meaning to attachment. *Psychological Inquiry, 5*, 34–38.

Duck, S., & Montgomery, B. M. (1991). The interdependence among interaction, substance, theory, and methods. In B. M. Montgomery & S. Duck (Eds.), *Studying interpersonal interaction* (pp. 3–15). New York: Guilford.

Duffy, E. (1962). *Activation and behavior.* New York: Wiley.

Duffy, M. E., & MacDonald, E. (1990). Determinants of functional health of older persons. *Gerontologist, 30*, 503–509.

Dunbar, H. F. (1943). *Emotions and bodily changes: A survey of literature on psychosomatic interrelationships, 1910–1933* (2nd ed.). New York: Columbia University Press.

Dura, J. R., & Kiecolt-Glaser, J. K. (1990). Sample bias in caregiving research. *Journals of Gerontology, 45,* P200–P204.

Dweck, C. S. (1992). The study of goals in psychology. *Psychological Science, 3,* 165–167.

Dyck, M. J. (1987). Assessing logotherapeutic constructs: Conceptual and psychometric status of the Purpose in Life and Seeking of Noetic Goals tests. *Clinical Psychology Review, 7,* 439–447.

Easterlin, R. A. (1996). The economic and social implications of demographic patterns. In R. H. Binstock & L. K. George (Eds.), *Handbook of aging and the social sciences* (4th ed., pp. 73–93). San Diego: Academic Press.

Edgerton, V. R., & Hutton, R. S. (1990). Nervous system and sensory adaptation. In C. Bouchard, R. J. Shephard, T. Stephens, J. R. Sutton, *et al.* (Eds.), *Exercise fitness and health.* Champaign, IL: Human Kinetics Books.

Edinger, J. D., Morey, M. C., Sullivan, R. J., Higgenbotham, M. B., *et al.* (1993) Aerobic fitness, acute exercise, and sleep in older men. *Sleep, 16,* 351–359.

Edwards, J. N., & Booth, A. (1994). Sexuality, marriage, and well-being: The middle years. In A. S. Rossi (Eds.), *Sexuality across the life course* (pp. 233–259). Chicago: University of Chicago Press.

Edwards, R. H. T. (1981). Human muscle function and fatigue. In R. Porter & J. Whelan (Eds.), *Physiological mechanisms* (pp. 1–18). London: Pitman Medical.

Eisdorfer, C. (1967). New dimensions and a tentative theory. *Gerontologist 7,* 14–18.

Eisdorfer, C. (1968). Arousal and performance: Experiments in verbal learning and a tentative theory. In G. A. Talland (Ed.), *Human aging and behavior: Recent advances in theory and research* (pp. 189–216). New York: Academic Press.

Eisdorfer, C., & Wilkie, F. (1977). Stress, disease, aging and behavior. In J. E. Birren & K. W.Schaie (Eds.), *Handbook of the psychology of aging* (pp. 251–276). New York: Van Nostrand Reinhold.

Ekerdt, D. J. (1986). The busy ethic: Moral continuity between work and retirement. *Gerontologist, 26,* 239–244.

Elahi, D., Dyke, M. M., & Andres, R. (1995). Aging, fat metabolism, and adiposity. In E. J. Massoro (Ed.), *Handbook of physiology: Section 11. Aging* (pp. 147–170). New York: Oxford University Press.

Elahi, V. K., Elahi, D., Andres, R., Tobin, J. D., *et al.* (1983). A longitudinal study of nutritional intake in men. *Journals of Gerontology, 38,* 162–180.

Elder, G. H. (1974). *Children of the Great Depression: Social change in life experiences.* Chicago: University of Chicago Press.

Elder, G. H., & Clipp, E. C. (1994). Introduction to the special section on military experience in adult development and aging. *Psychology and Aging, 9,* 3–4.

Elder, G. H., George, L. K., & Shanahan, M. J. (1996). Psychosocial stress over the life course. In B. Kaplan (Ed.), *Psychosocial stress: Perspectives on struc-*

ture, theory, life course, and methods (pp. 247–292). San Diego: Academic Press.

Elias, M. F., & Elias, P. K. (1977). Motivation and activity. In J. E. Birren & K. W. Schaie (Eds.), *Handbook of the psychology of aging* (pp. 359–383). New York: Van Nostrand Reinhold.

Entwistle, D. R. (1972). To dispel fantasies about fantasy-based meaures of achievement motivation. *Psychological Bulletin, 77,* 377–391.

Erikson, E. H. (1963). *Childhood and society* (2nd ed.). New York: Norton.

Farran, C. J. (1997). Theoretical perspectives concerning positive aspects of caring for elderly persons with dementia: Stress/adaptation and existentialism. *Gerontologist, 37,* 250–256.

Faucheux, B. A., Dupuis, C., Baulon, A., Lille, F., & Bourliér, F. (1983). Heart rate reactivity during minor mental stress in men in their 50s and 70s. *Gerontology, 29,* 149–160.

Faucheux, B. A., Lille, F., Baulon, A., Landau, J., *et al.* (1989). Heart rate and blood pressure reactivity during active coping with a mental task in healthy 18- to 73-year old subjects. *Gerontology, 35,* 19–30.

Faulkner, J. A., Brooks, S. V., & Zerba, E. (1991). Skeletal muscle weakness and fatigue in old age: Underlying mechanisms. *Annual Review of Gerontology and Geriatrics, 10,* 147–166.

Feldman, H. A., Goldstein, I., Hatzichristou, D. G., Krane, R. J., & McKinlay, J. B. (1994). Impotence and its medical and psychological correlates: Results of the Massachusetts Male Aging Study. *Journal of Urology, 151,* 54–61.

Felton, B. J., & Berry, C. (1992). Groups as social network members: Overlooked sources of social support. *American Journal of Community Psychology, 20,* 253–261.

Ferraro, K. F. (1992). Self and other-people referents in evaluating life problems. *Journals of Gerontology, 47,* S105–S114.

Ferraro, K. F. (1993). Are Black older adults health-pessimistic? *Journal of Health and Social Behavior, 34,* 201–214.

Filipp, S.-H. (1996). Motivation and emotion. In J. E. Birren & K W. Schaie (Eds.), *Handbook of the psychology of aging* (4th ed., pp. 218–235). San Diego: Academic Press.

Finch, C. E., & Landfield, P.W. (1985). Neuroendocrine and autonomic functions in aging mammals. In C. E. Finch, & E. L. Schneider (Eds.), *Handbook of the biology of aging* (2nd ed., pp. 567–594). New York: Van Nostrand Reinhold.

Fineman, S. (1977). The achievement motive construct and its measurement: Where are we now? *British Journal of Psychology, 68,* 1–22.

Fischer, L. R., Mueller, D. P., & Cooper, P. W. (1991). Older volunteers: A discussion of the Minnesotta Senior Study. *Gerontologist, 31,* 183–194.

Fishbein, M., & Ajzen, I. (1975). *Belief, attitude, intention, and behavior: An introduction to theory and research.* Reading, MA: Addison-Wesley.

Fitting, M., Rabins, P., Lucas, M. J., & Eastham, J. (1986). Caregivers for dementia patients: A comparison of husbands and wives. *Gerontologist, 26,* 248–252.

Florini, J. R. (1989). Limitations of interpretation of age-related changes in hormone levels. Illustration by effects of thyroid hormones on cardiac and skeletal muscles. *Journals of Gerontology, 44,* B107–B109.

Foa, U. G. (1993). Interpersonal and economic resources. In U. G. Foa, J. Converse III, K. Y. Törnblom, & E. B. Foa (Eds.), *Resource theory: Explorations and applications* (pp. 13–30). San Diego: Academic Press.

Foley, D. J., Monjan, A. A., Brown, S. L., Simonick, E. M., *et al.* (1995). Sleep complaints among elderly persons: An epidemiologic study of three communities. *Sleep, 18,* 425–432.

Folkman, S. (1991). Coping across the life span: Theoretical issues. In E. M. Cummings, A. L.Greene, & K. H. Karraker (Eds.), *Life-span developmental psychology: Perspectives on stress and coping* (pp. 3–19). Hillsdale, NJ: Erlbaum.

Francis, D. (1984). *Will you still need me, will you still feed me, when I'm 84?* Bloomington: Indiana University Press.

Frankl, V. E. (1962). *Man's search for meaning: An introduction to logotherapy.* Boston: Beacon.

Frankl, V. E. (1967). *Psychotherapy and existentialism: Selected papers on logotherapy.* New York: Simon & Schuster.

Freeman, G. L. (1944). Using the interview to test stability and poise. *Public Personnel Review, 5,* 89–94.

Freud, A. (1946). *The ego and the mechanisms of defence.* New York: International Universities Press.

Friedman, H. S. (1990). Personality and disease: Overview, review, and preview. In H. S. Friedman (Ed.), *Personality and disease* (pp. 3–13). New York: Wiley.

Friedman, L., Brooks, J. O., III, Bliwise, D. L., Yesavage, J. A., & Wicks, D. S. (1995). Perceptions of life stress and chronic insomnia in adults. *Psychology and Aging, 10,* 352–357.

Friedman, M., & Rosenman, R. H. (1959). Association of specific overt behavior patterns with blood and cardiovascular findings: Blood cholesterol level, blood clotting time, incidence of arcus senilis, and clinical coronar artery disease. *Journal of the American Medical Association, 162,* 1286–1296.

Friedsam, H., & Martin, H. (1963). A comparison of self and physicians' health ratings in an older population. *Journal of Health and Social Behavior, 4,* 179–183.

Frolkis, V. V. (1977). Aging of the autonomic nervous system. In J. E. Birren & K. W. Schaie (Eds.), *Handbook of the psychology of aging* (pp. 177–189). New York: Van Nostrand Reinhold.

Fry, C. L. (1996). Age, aging, and culture. In R. H. Binstock & L. K. George (Eds.), *Handbook of aging and the social sciences* (4th ed., pp. 118–136). San Diego: Academic Press.

Fry, P. S. (1989a). Mediators of stress in older adults: Conceptual and integrative frameworks. *Canadian Psychology, 30,* 636–649.

Fry, P. S. (1989b). Mediators of perception of stress among community-based elders. *Psychological Reports, 65,* 307–314.

Fuhrer, R., & Wessely, S. (1995). The epidemiology of fatigue and depression: A French primary-care study. *Psychological Medicine, 25,* 895–905.

Furchtgott, E. F., & Busemeyer, J. K. (1979). Heart rate and skin conductance during cognitive process as a function of age. *Journal of Gerontology, 34,* 183–190.

Furry, C. A., & Schaie, K. W. (1979). Pretest activity and intellectual performance in middle aged and older persons. *Experimental Aging Research, 5,* 413–421.

Furry, C. A., & Baltes, P. B. (1973). The effect of age differences in ability–extraneous performance variables on the assessment of intelligence in children, adults, and the elderly. *Journal of Gerontology, 28,* 73–80.

Garry, P. J., Rhyne, R. L., Halioua, L. & Nicholson, C. (1989). Changes in dietary patterns over a 6-year period in an elderly population. *Annals of the New York Academy of Science, 561,* 104–112.

Gatz, M., Bengtson, V. L., & Blum, M. J. (1990). Caregiving families. In J. E. Birren & K W. Schaie (Eds.), *Handbook of the psychology of aging* (3rd ed., pp. 404–426). San Diego: Academic Press.

Gatz, M., & Karel, M. J. (1993). Individual change in perceived control over 20 years. *International Journal of Behavioral Development, 16,* 305–322.

Gatz, M., Kasl-Godley, J. E., & Karel, M. J. (1996). Aging and mental disorder. In J. E. Birren & K W. Schaie (Eds.), *Handbook of the psychology of aging* (4th ed., pp. 365–382). San Diego: Academic Press.

Geen, R. G. (1991). Social motivation. *Annual Reviews of Psychology, 42,* 377–399.

Geen, R. G., Beatty, W. W., & Arkin, R. M. (1984). *Human motivation: Physiological, behavioral, and social approaches.* Boston, MA: Allyn & Bacon.

George, L. K. (1990). Social structure, social processes, and social-psychological states. In R. H. Binstock & L. K. George (Eds.), *Handbook of aging and the social sciences* (3rd ed., pp. 186–204). San Diego: Academic Press.

George, L. K. (1996a). Social factors and illness. In R. H. Binstock & L. K. George (Eds.), *Handbook of aging and the social sciences* (4th ed., pp. 229–252). San Diego: Academic Press.

George, L. K. (1996b). Missing link: The case for a social psychology of the life course. *Gerontologist, 36,* 248–255.

Gergen, M. M., & Gergen, K. J. (1986). The discourse of control and the maintenance of well-being. In M. M. Baltes & P. B. Baltes (Eds.), *The psychology of control and aging* (pp. 119–138). Hillsdale, NJ: Erlbaum.

Gershenfeld, M. A., & Newman, J. (1991). *Love, sex, and intimacy after 50.* New York: Fawcett Columbine.

Gintner, G. G., Hollandsworth, J. G., & Intrieri, R. C. (1986). Age differences in cardiovascular reactivity under active coping conditions. *Psychophysiology, 23,* 113–120.

Gober, P., & Zonn, L. E. (1983). Kin and elderly amenity migration. *Gerontologist, 23,* 288–294.

Goffman, E. (1961). *Asylums:Essays on the social situation of mental patients and other inmates.* New York: Anchor Books.

Goldberg, A. P., & Hagberg, J. M. (1990). Physical exercise in the elderly. In E. L. Schneider & J. W. Rowe (Eds.), *Handbook of the biology of aging* (3rd ed., pp. 407–428). San Diego: Academic Press.

Goldstein, D. S., McCarty, R., Polinsky, R. J., & Kopin, I. J. (1983). Relationship between plasma norepinephrine and sympathetic neural activity. *Hypertension, 5*, 552–563.

Gordon, C., Gaitz, C. M., & Scott, J. (1976). Leisure and lives: Personal expressivity across the life span. In R. H. Binstock & E. Shanas (Eds.), *Handbook of aging and the social sciences* (pp. 310–341). New York:Van Nostrand Reinhold.

Gove, W. R. (1994). Why we do what we do: A biopsychosocial theory of human motivation. *Social Forces, 73*, 363–394.

Goya, R. G. (1991). The immune-neuroendocrine homeostatic network and aging. *Gerontology, 37*, 208–213.

Grady, C. L., & Rapoport, S. I. (1992). Cerebral metabolism in aging and dementia. In J. E. Birren, R. B. Sloan, & D. G. Cohen (Eds.), *Handbook of mental health and aging* (2nd ed., pp. 201–228). San Diego: Academic Press.

Graham, D. F., Graham, I., & MacLean, M. J. (1991). Going to the mall: A leisure activity of urban elderly people. *Canadian Journal on Aging, 10*, 345–358.

Gray, A., Jackson, D. N., & McKinlay, J. B. (1991). The relation between dominance, anger, and hormones in normally aging men: Results from the Massachusetts male aging study. *Psychosomatic Medicine, 53*, 375–385.

Greenwood, J. D. (1991). *Relations and representations: An introduction to the philosophy of social psychological science.* London: Routledge.

Grembowski, D., Patrick, D., Diehr, P., Durham, M., *et al.* (1993). Self-efficacy and health behavior among older adults. *Journal of Health and Social Behavior, 34*, 89–104.

Grimsby, L., Hannerz, J., Borg, J., & Hedman, B. (1981). Firing properties of single human motor units on maintained maximal voluntary effort. In H. T. Edwards (Ed.), *Human muscle fatigue: Physiological mechanisms. Ciba Symposium, 82*, 157–177.

Gupta, V., & Korte, C. (1994). The effects of a confidant and a peer group on the well-being of single elders. *International Journal of Aging and Human Development, 39*, 293–302.

Gutmann, D. (1977). The cross-cultural perspective: Notes toward a comparative psychology of aging. In J. E. Birren & K. W. Schaie (Eds.), *Handbook of the psychology of aging* (pp. 302–326). New York: Van Nostrand Reinhold.

Gutmann, D. (1992). Culture and mental health in later life. In J. E. Birren, R. B. Sloan, & G. D. Cohen (Eds.), *Handbook of mental health and aging* (2nd ed., pp. 75–97). San Diego: Academic Press.

Gutmann, E. (1977). Muscle. In C. E. Finch & L. Hayflick (Eds.), *Handbook of the biology of aging* (pp. 445–469). New York: Van Nostrand Reinhold.

Haan, N., Millsap, R., & Hartka, E. (1986). As time goes by: Change and stability in personality over fifty years. *Psychology and Aging, 1*, 220–232.

Haas, W. H., III, & Serow, W. J. (1993). Amenity retirement migration process: A model and preliminary evidence. *Gerontologist, 33,* 212–220.

Haggard, E. A. (1943). Experimental studies in affective processes. I. Some effects of cognitive structure and active participation on certain autonomic reactions during and following experimentally induced stress. *Journal of Experimental Psychology, 33,* 257–284.

Hall, G. S. (1922). *Senescence.* New York: Appleton.

Halter, J. B. (1995). Carbohydrate metabolism. In E. J. Massoro (Ed.), *Handbook of physiology: Section 11. Aging* (pp. 119–145). New York: Oxford University Press.

Hansell, S., Sherman, G., & Mechanic, D. (1991). Body awarness and medical care utilization among older adults in an HMO. *Journals of Gerontology, 46,* S151–S159.

Harkapaa, K., Jarvikoski, A., Mellin, G., Hurri, H., *et al.* (1991). Health locus of control beliefs and psychological distress as predictors for treatment outcome in low-back pain patients: Results of a 3-month follow-up of a controlled intervention study. *Pain, 46,* 35–41.

Harlow, H. F., Harlow, M. K., & Meyer, D. R. (1950). Learning motivated by a manipulative drive. *Journal of Experimental Psychology, 40,* 228–234.

Harlow, L. L., & Newcomb, M. D. (1990). Towards a hierarchical model of meaning and satisfaction in life. *Multivariate Behavioral Research, 25,* 387–405.

Harman, S. M., & Talbert, G. B. (1985). Reproductive aging. In C. E. Finch & E. L. Schneider (Eds.), *Handbook ofthe biology of aging* (2nd ed., pp. 457–510). New York: Van Nostrand Reinhold.

Harootyan, R. A., & Vorek, R. E. (1994). Volunteerng, helping, and gift giving in families and communities. In V. E. Bengtson & R. A. Harootyan (Eds.), *Intergenerational linkages: Hidden connections in American society* (pp. 77–111). New York: Springer.

Harre, R., & Lamb, R. (Eds.). (1983). *The encyclopedic dictionary of psychology.* Cambridge, MA: MIT Press.

Harrison, Y., & Horne, J. A. (1996). Long-term extension to sleep: Are we really chronically sleep deprived? *Psychophysiology, 33,* 22–30.

Hattie, J., & Marsh, H. W. (1996). Future directions in self-concept research. In B. A. Bracken (Ed.), *Handbook of self-concept: Developmental, social, and clinical considerations* (pp. 421–462). New York: Wiley.

Haug, M. R., Breslau, N., & Folmar, S. J. (1989). Coping resources and selective survival in mental health of the elderly. *Research on Aging, 11,* 468–491.

Hausman, P. B., & Weksler, M. E. (1985). Changes in the immune response with age. In C. E. Finch, & E. L. Schneider (Eds.), *Handbook of the biology of aging* (2nd ed., pp. 414–432). New York: Van Nostrand Reinhold.

Havighurst, R. J. (1952). *Developmental tasks and education.* New York: David McKay.

Haxby, J. V., & Rapoport, S. I. (1986). Abnormalities of regional brain metabolism in Alzheimer's disease and their relation to functional impairment.

Progress in Neuro-Psychopharmacology and Biological-Psychiatry, 10, 427–438.

Hays, J. C., Kasl, S., & Jacobs, S. (1994). Past personal history of dysphoria, social support, and psychological distress following conjugal bereavement. *Journal of the American Geriatric Society, 42,* 712–718.

Hays, J. C., Schoenfeld, D. E., & Blazer, D. G. (1996). Determinants of poor self-rated health in late life. *American Journal of the Geriatric Psychiatry, 4,* 188–196.

Hayslip, B., Galt, C. P., Lopez, F. G., & Nation, P. C. (1994). Irrational beliefs and depressive symptoms among younger and older adults: A cross-sectional comparison. *International Journal of Aging and Human Development, 38,* 307–326.

Hayward, L., Mant, A., Eyland, E., Hewitt, H., *et al.* (1992). Sleep disordered breathing and cognitive function in a retirement village population. *Age and Aging, 21,* 121–128.

Hazan, C., & Shaver, P. R. (1994). Deeper into attachment theory. *Psychological Inquiry, 5,* 68–79.

Heatherton, T. F., & Weinberger, J. L. (Eds.). (1994). *Can personality change?* Washington, DC: American Psychological Association.

Heckhausen, H. (1967). *The anatomy of achievement motivation.* New York: Academic Press.

Heckhausen, J., & Krueger, J. (1993). Developmental expectations for the self and most other people: Age grading in three functions of social comparison. *Developmental Psychology, 29,* 539–548.

Heckhausen, J., & Schulz, R. (1993). Optimisation by selection and compensation: Balancing primary and secondary control in life span development. *International Journal of Behavioral Development, 16,* 287–303.

Heckhausen, J., & Schulz, R. (1995). A life span theory of control. *Psychological Review, 102,* 284–304.

Heemstra, M. L. (1986). An efficiency model of information processing. In G. R. J. Hockey, M. G. H. Coles, & A. W. K. Gaillard (Eds.), *Energetics and human information processing* (pp. 233–242). Dordrecht, Netherlands: Nijhoff.

Hegsted, D. M. (1989). Nutrition and the chemical senses: Problems and opportunities. *Annals of the New York Academy of Sciences, 561,* 1–11.

Heidrich, S. (1994). The self, health, and depression in elderly women [Special issue: Feminist research methods in nursing research]. *Western Journal of Nursing Research, 16,* 544–555.

Heller, K., Thompson, M. G., Trueba, P. E., Hogg, J. R., *et al.* (1991). Peer support telephone dyads for elderly women: Was this the wrong intervention? *American Journal of Community Psychology, 19,* 75–83.

Hendrick, C., & Hendrick, S. S. (1994). Attachment theory and close adult relationships. *Psychological Inquiry, 5,* 38–41.

Hendricks, J. (1996). Qualitative research: Contribution and advances. In R. H. Binstock & L. K. George (Eds.), *Handbook of aging and the social sciences* (4th ed., pp. 52–72). San Diego: Academic Press.

Hendricks, J., Calasanti, T. M., & Turner, H. B. (1988). Foodways of the elderly: Social research considerations. *American Behavioral Scientist, 32,* 61–83.

Herbert, T. B., & Cohen, S. (1996). Measurement issues in research on psychosocial stress. In B. Kaplan (Ed.), *Psychosocial stress: Perspectives on structure, theory, life course, and methods* (pp. 295–332). San Diego: Academic Press.

Herman, C. P. (1996). Human eating: Diagnosis and prognosis. *Neuroscience and Biobehavioral Reviews, 20,* 107–111.

Hershey, L. A., & Whitney, C. M. (1988). Drugs and the elderly. In C. S. Kart, E. K. Metress, & S. P. Metress (Eds.), *Aging, health, and society* (pp. 262–272). Boston: Jones & Bartlett.

Hertzog, C. (1987). Applications of structural equation models in gerontology. *Annual Review of Gerontology and Geriatrics, 7,* 265–293.

Hewitt, P. L., & Flett, G. L. (1996). Personality traits and coping processes. In M. Zeidner & N. S. Endler (Eds.), *Handbook of coping: Theory, research and applications* (pp. 410–433). New York: Wiley.

Hickey, T., & Stilwell, D. L. (1991). Health promotion in older people: All is not well. *Gerontologist, 31,* 822–829.

Hilgard. E. R. (1987). *Psychology in America: A historical survey.* San Diego: Harcourt Brace Jovanovich.

Hill, C. A., & Preston, L. K. (1996). Individual differences in the experience of sexual motivation: Theory and measurement of dispositional sexual motives. *Journal of Sex Research, 33,* 27–45.

Hill, R. D., & Vandervoort, D. (1992). The effects of state anxiety on recall performance in older learners. *Educational Gerontology, 18,* 597–605.

Hinde, R. A. (1993). Epilogue. In U. G. Foa, J. Converse, Jr., K. Y. Törnblom, & E. B. Foa (Eds.), *Resource theory: Explorations and applications* (pp. 271–274). San Diego: Academic Press.

Hinkle, L. E., Jr. (1987). Stress and disease: The concept after 50 years. *Social Science and Medicine, 25,* 561–566.

Hinrichsen, G. A. (1991). Adjustment of caregivers to depressed older adults. *Psychology and Aging, 6,* 631–639.

Hobfoll, S. E. (1988). *The ecology of stress.* New York: Hemisphere.

Hobfoll, S. E. (1989). Conservation of resources: A new attempt at conceptualizing stress. *American Psychologist, 44,* 513–524.

Hobfoll, S. E., & Freedy, J. R. (1990). The availability and effective use of social support. *Journal of Social and Clinical Psychology, 9,* 91–103.

Hoch, C. C., Buysse, D. J., Monk, T. H., & Reynolds, C. F., III (1992). Sleep disorders and aging. In J. E. Birren, R. B. Sloane, & G. D. Cohen (Eds), *Handbook of mental health and aging* (2nd ed., pp. 557–581). San Diego: Academic Press.

Hoch, C. C., Reynolds, C. F., Jennings, J. R., Monk, T., *et al.* (1992). Daytime sleepiness and performance among healthy 80 and 20 year olds. *Neurobiology of Aging, 13,* 353–356.

Hochbaum, G. M. (1958). *Participation in medical screening programs: A socio-psychological study* (Publication No. 572). Washington: U.S. Public Health Service.

Hochschild, R. (1990). Can an index of aging be constructed for evaluating treatments to retard aging rates? A 2,462 person study. *Journals of Gerontology, 45,* B187–B214.

Hockey, G. R. J. (1986). A state control theory of adaptation and individual differences in stress management. In G. R. J. Hockey, M. G. H. Coles, & A. W. K. Gaillard (Eds.), *Energetics and human information processing* (pp. 285–298). Dordrecht, Netherlands: Nijhoff.

Hockey, G. R. J., Coles, M. G. H., & Gaillard, A. W. K. (Eds.). (1986). *Energetics and human information processing.* Dordrecht, Netherlands: Nijhoff.

Hockey, J., & James, A. (1993). *Growing up and growing old: Ageing and dependency in the life course.* Newbury Park, CA: Sage.

Hodson, D. S., & Skeen, P. (1994). Sexuality and aging: The hammerlock of myths. *Journal of Applied Gerontology, 13,* 219–235.

Hogan, D. P., Eggebeen, D. J., & Clogg, C. C. (1993). The structure of intergenerational exchanges in American families. *American Journal of Sociology, 98,* 1428–1458.

Hoge, D. R. (1996). Religion in America: The demographics of belief and affiliation. In E. P. Shafranske (Ed.), *Religion and the clinical practice of psychology* (pp. 21–41). Washington, DC: American Psychological Association Press.

Holahan, C. J., Moos, R. H., & Schaefer, J. A. (1996). Coping, stress, resistance and growth. In M. Zeidner & N. S. Endler (Eds.), *Handbook of coping: Theory, research and applications* (pp. 24–43). New York: Wiley.

Holahan, C. K. (1988). Relation of life goals at age 70 to activity participation and health and psychological well-being among Terman's gifted men and women. *Psychology and Aging, 3,* 286–291.

Holding, D. H. (1983). Fatigue. In G. R. J. Hockey (Ed.), *Stress and fatigue in human performance* (pp. 145–168). New York: Wiley.

Holmes, H. H., & Rahe, R. H. (1967). The social readjustment rating scale. *Journal of Psychosomatic Research, 11,* 213–218.

Holroyd, K. A., & Lazarus, R. S. (1982). Stress, coping, and somatic adaptation. In L. Goldberger & S. Breznitz (Eds.), *Handbook of stress: Theoretical and clinical aspects* (pp. 21–35). New York: Free Press.

Homans, G. C. (1961). *The human group.* New York: Harcourt, Brace & World.

Hooker, K. (1992). Possible selves and perceived health in older adults and college students. *Journals of Gerontology, 47,* P85–P95.

Hooker, K., Frazier, L.D., & Monahan, D J. (1994). Personality and coping among caregivers of spouses with dementia. *Gerontologist, 34,* 386–392.

Hooker, K., & Kaus, C. R. (1994). Health-related possible selves in young and middle adulthood. *Psychology and Aging, 9,* 126–133.

Horwath, C. C. (1989). Socio-economic and behavioral effects on the dietary habits of elderly people. *International Journal of Biosocial and Medical Research, 11,* 15–30.

Hothersall, D. (1990). *History of psychology.* New York: McGraw-Hill.

House, J. S., Umberson, D., & Landis, K. R. (1988). Structures and processes of social support. *Annual Review of Sociology, 14,* 293–318.

Hoyle, R. H. (1995). The structural equation modeling approach: Basic concepts and fundamental issues. In R. H. Hoyle (Ed.), *Structural equation modeling: Concepts, issues, and applications* (pp. 1–15). Thousand Oaks, CA: Sage.

Hudson, J. I., Pope, H. G., Sullivan, L. E., Waternaux, C. M., *et al.* (1992). Good sleep, bad sleep: A meta analysis of polysomnographic meaures in insomnia, depression, and narcolepsy. *Biological Psychiatry, 32,* 958–975.

Hutchinson, R. (1994). Women and the elderly in Chicago's public parks. *Leisure Sciences, 16,* 229–247.

Idler, E. L. (1992). Self-assessed health and mortality: A review of studies. *International Review of Health Psychology, 1,* 33–54.

Idler, E. L. (1993). Age differences in self-assessment of health: Age changes, cohort differences or survivorship? *Journals of Gerontology, 48,* S289–S300.

Ingvar, D. H. (1982). Mental illness and regional brain metabolism. *Trends in Neurosciences, 5,* 199–203.

Jackman, R. W., & Miller, R. A. (1996). The poverty of political culture. *American Journal of Political Science, 40,* 697–716.

Jackson, C. L., & Day, F. A. (1993). Locational concentrations of military retirees in the United States. *Professional Geographer, 45,* 55–65.

Jackson, J. S., Antonucci, T. C., & Gibson, R. C. (1990). Cultural, racial, and ethnic minority influences on aging. In J. E. Birren, & K W. Schaie (Eds.), *Handbook of the psychology of aging* (3rd ed., pp. 103–123). San Diego: Academic Press.

Jägerstad, M., Norden, Ä., & Åkesson, B. (1979). Relation between dietary intake and parameters of health status. *Scandinavian Journal of Gastroenterology, 14*(Suppl. 52), 236–295.

James, W. (1890). *The principles of psychology* (Vol. 2). New York: Holt.

Janis, I. L. (1983). Stress inoculation in health care: Theory and research. In D. Meichenbaum & Jaremko, M. E. (Eds.) *Stress reduction and prevention* (pp. 67–99). New York: Plenum Press.

Janus, S. S., & Janus, C. L. (1993). *The Janus report on sexual behavior.* New York: Wiley.

Jennings, J. R., Nebes, R. D., & Yovetich, N. A. (1990). Aging increases the energetic demands of episodic memory: A cardiovascular analysis. *Journal of Experimental Psychology: General, 119,* 77–91.

Jensen, M. P., & Karoly, P. (1992). Comparative self-evaluation and depressive affect among chronic pain patients: An examination of selective evaluation theory. *Cognitive Therapy and Research, 16,* 297–308.

Jones, C. J., & Meredith, W. (1996). Patterns of personality changes across the life span. *Psychology and Aging, 11,* 57–65.

Jones, D. C., & Vaughan, K. (1990). Close friendships among senior adults. *Psychology and Aging, 5,* 451–457.

Jutras, S., & Veilleux, F. (1991). Informal caregiving: Correlates of perceived burden. *Canadian Journal on Aging, 10*, 40–55.

Kagan, J. (1996). Three pleasing ideas. *American Psychologist, 51*, 901–908.

Kahana, R. J. (1978). Psychoanalysis in later life: Discussion. *Journal of Geriatric Psychiatry, 11*, 37–49.

Kahneman, D. (1973). *Attention and effort*. Englewood Cliffs, NJ: Prentice Hall.

Kane, R. L., & Kane, R. A. (1990). Health care for older people: Organizational and policy issues. In R. H. Binstock & George (Eds.), *Handbook of aging and the social sciences* (3rd ed., pp. 415–437). San Diego: Academic Press.

Kanner, A. D., Coyne, J. C., Schaefer, C., & Lazarus, R. S. (1981). Comparison of two modes of stress measurement: Daily hassles and uplifts versus major life events. *Journal of Behavioral Medicine, 4*, 1–39.

Kaplan, H. B. (1996). Themes, lacunae, and directions in research on psychosocial stress. In H. B. Kaplan (Ed.), *Psychosocial stress: Perspectives on structure, theory, life course, and methods* (pp. 369–403). San Diego: Academic Press.

Kaplan, M. (1961). Toward a theory of leisure for social gerontology. In R. Kleemeier (Ed.), *Aging and leisure* (pp. 389–412). New York: Oxford University Press.

Karl, F. (1991). Outreach counseling and educational activities in district. *Educational Gerontology, 17*, 487–493.

Karuza, J., Zevon, M. A., Gleason, T. A., Karuza, C. M., & Nash, L. (1990). Models of helping and coping, responsibility attributions, and well-being in community elderly and their helpers. *Psychology and Aging, 5*, 194–208.

Kasl, S. V. (1992). Stress and health among the elderly: Overview of issues. In M.A. Wykle, E. Kahana, & J. Kowal (Eds.), *Stress and health among the elderly* (pp. 5–34). New York: Springer.

Katz, I. R. (1996). On the inseparability of mental and physical health in aged persons: Lessons from depression and medical comorbidity. *American Journal of Geriatric Psychiatry, 4*, 1–16.

Katzman, R. (1995). Human nervous system. In E. J. Massoro (Ed.), *Handbook of physiology: Section 11. Aging* (pp. 325–362). New York: Oxford University Press.

Kaufman, A. V., & Adams, J. P. (1987). Interaction and loneliness: A dimensional analysis of the social isolation of a sample of older southern adults. *Journal of Applied Gerontology, 6*, 389–404.

Kaufman, J. E. (1996). Personal definitions of health among elderly people: A link to effective health promotion. *Family and Community Health, 19*(2), 58–68.

Kausler, D. H. (1990). Motivation, human aging, and cognitive performance. In J. E. Birren & K W. Schaie (Eds.), *Handbook of the psychology of aging* (3rd ed., pp. 171–182). San Diego: Academic Press.

Keefe, F. J., & Williams, D. A. (1990). A comparison of coping strategies in chronic pain patients in different age groups. *Journals of Gerontology, 45*, P161–P165.

Keil, J. E., Sutherland, S. E., Knapp, R. G., Waid, L. R., et al. (1992). Self-reported sexual functioning in elderly blacks and whites: The Charleston Heart Study experience. *Journal of Aging and Health, 4,* 112–125.

Kelly, H. H. (1992). Common-sense psychology and scientific psychology. *Annual Review of Psychology, 43,* 1–23.

Kemeny, M. E., Cohen, F., Zegans, L. S., & Conant, M. A. (1989). Psychological and immunological predictors of genital herpes recurrence. *Psychosomatic Medicine, 51,* 195–208.

Kennedy, H. G. (1988). Fatigue and fatiguability. *British Journal of Psychiatry, 153,* 1–5.

Kenyon, G. M. (1988). Basic assumptions in theories of human aging. In J. E. Birren & V. E. Bengtson (Eds.), *Emergent theories of aging* (pp. 3–18). New York: Springer.

Kenyon, G. M. (1996). The meaning/value of personal story telling. In J. E. Birren, G. M. Kenyon, J.-E. Ruth, Schroots, J. J. F., & Svensson, T. (Eds.), *Aging and biography: Explorations in adult development* (pp. 21–38). New York: Springer.

Kernis, M. H. (1995). Efficacy, agency, and self-esteem: Emerging themes and future directions. In M. H. Kernis (Ed.), *Efficacy, agency, and self-esteem* (pp. 237–253). New York: Plenum Press.

Kerr, D. S., Campbell, L. W., Hao, S. Y., & Landfield, P. W. (1989). Corticosteroid modulation of hippocampal potentials: Increased effect with aging. *Science, 245,* 1505–1509.

Kessler, R. C. (1997). The effects of stressful life events on depression. *Annual Review of Psychology, 48,* 191–214.

Kessler, R. C., Price, R. H., & Wortman, C. B. (1985). Social factors in psychopathology: Stress, social support, and coping processes. *Annual Review of Psychology, 36,* 531–572.

Killeen, M. (1990). The influence of stress and coping on family caregivers' perception of health. *International Journal of Aging and Human Development, 30,* 197–211.

Kinchla, R. A. (1992). Attention. *Annual Review of Psychology 43,* 711–742.

Kincade, J. E., Rabiner, D. J., Bernard, S. L., Woomert, A., Kkonrad, T. R., et al. (1996). Older adults as a community resource: Results from a national survey of self-care and aging. *Gerontologist, 36,* 474–482.

Kinsey, A. C., Pomeroy, W. B., & Martin, C. E. (1948). *Sexual behavior in the human male.* Philadelphia: W. B. Saunders.

Kinsey, A. C., Pomeroy, W. B., Martin, C. E., & Gebhart, P. H. (1953). *Sexual behavior in the human female.* Philadelphia: W. B. Saunders.

Kirkcaldy, B., & Cooper, C. L. (1992). Work attitudes and leisure preferences: Sex differences. *Personality and Individual Differences, 13,* 329–334.

Kleiber, D. A., & Ray, R. O. (1993). Leisure and generativity. In J. R. Kelly (Ed.), *Activity and aging: Staying involved in later life* (pp. 106–117). Newbury Park, CA: Sage.

Klinger, E. (1977). *Meaning and void: Inner experience and the incentives in people's lives.* Minneapolis: University off Minnesota Press.

Koch, S. (1941). Logical character of the motivation concept. *Psychological Review, 48,* 15–38.

Koch, S. (1976). Language communities, search cells, and the psychological studies. *Nebraska Symposium on Motivation, 23,* 477–569.

Koch, S. (1993). "Psychology" or "the psychological studies"? *American Psychologist, 48,* 902–904.

Koenig, H. G. (1994). *Aging and God: Spiritual pathways to mental health in midlife and later years.* Binghamton, NY: Haworth Pastoral Press.

Kogan, N. (1990). Personality and aging. In J. E. Birren & K W. Schaie (Eds.), *Handbook of the psychology of aging* (3rd ed., pp. 330–346). San Diego: Academic Press.

Kohn, R. R. (1997). Heart and cardiovascular system. In C. E. Finch & L. Hayflick (Eds.), *Handbook of the biology of aging* (pp. 281–317). New York: Van Nostrand Reinhold.

Kohrs, M. B., & Czajka-Narins, D. M. (1986). Assessing the nutritional status of the elderly. In E. A. Young (Ed.), *Nutrition, aging, and health* (pp. 25–29). New York: Liss.

Koland, F. (1994). Contrasting cultural profiles between generations: Interests and common activities in three intramilial generations. *Aging and Society, 14,* 319–340.

Kopin, I. J. (1995). Definitions of stress and sympathetic neuronal responses. *Annals of the New York Academy of Sciences, 771,* 19–30.

Kramer, B. J. (1993). Marital history and the prior relationship as predictors of positive and negative outcomes among wife caregivers. *Family Relations, 42,* 367–372.

Kramer, B. J. (1997a). Gain in the caregiving experience: Where are we? What next? *Gerontologist, 37,* 218–232.

Kramer, B. J. (1997b). Differential predictors of strain and gain among husbands caring for wives with dementia. *Gerontologist, 37,* 239–249.

Krause, N. (1988). Stressful life events and physician utilization. *Journals of Gerontology, 43,* S552–S561.

Krause, N. (1990a). Perceived health problems, formal/informal support, and life satisfaction among older adults. *Journals of Gerontology, 45,* S193–S205.

Krause, N., (1990b). Illness behavior in later life. In R. H. Binstock & L. K. George (Eds.), *Handbook of aging and the social sciences* (3rd ed., pp. 228–244). San Diego: Academic Press.

Krause, N., & Baker, E. (1992). Financial strain, economic values, and somatic symptoms in later life. *Psychology and Aging, 7,* 4–14.

Krause, N., & Borawski-Clark, E. (1994). Clarifying the functions of social support in later life. *Research on Aging, 16,* 251–279.

Krause, N., Jay, G., & Liang, J. (1991). Financial strain and psychological well-being among the American and Japanese elderly. *Psychology and Aging, 6,* 170–181.

Kromhout, D., Coulander, C. D., Obermann, G. L., Van Kampen-Donker, M., *et al.,* (1990). Changes in food and nutrient intake in middle-aged men from

1960 to 1985 (the Zutphen Study). *Journal of Clinical Nutrition, 51,* 123–129.

Kuhl, J. (1986). Aging and models of control: The hidden costs of wisdom. In M. M. Baltes & P. B. Baltes (Eds.), *The psychology of control and aging* (pp. 1–33). Hillsdale NJ: Erlbaum.

Kuhl, J. (1994). A theory of action and state orientation. In J. Kuhl & J. Beckmann (Eds.), *Volition and personality: Action versus state orientation* (pp. 9–46). Seattle, WA: Hogrefe & Huber.

Labouvie-Vief, G., Chiodo, L. M., Goguen, L. A., *et al.* (1995). Representation of self across the life span. *Psychology and Aging, 10,* 404–415.

Lacey, J. I. (1967). Somatic response patterning and stress: Some revisions of activation theory. In M. H. Appley & R. Trumbull (Eds.), *Psychological stress* (pp. 14–42). New York: Appleton–Century–Crofts.

Lacey, J. I., & Lacey, B. C. (1970). Some autonomic–central nervous system interrelationships. In P. Black (Ed.), *Physiological correlates of emotion* (pp. 205–227). New York: Academic Press.

Lachman, M. E. (1986). Locus of control in aging research: A case for multidimensional and domain specific assessment. *Psychology and Aging, 1,* 34–40.

Lair, C. V., & Moon, W. H. (1972). The effects of praise and reproof on the performance of middle aged and older subjects. *Aging and Human Development, 3,* 279–284.

Lakatta, E. G. (1985). Heart and circulation. In C. E. Finch & E. L. Schneider (Eds.), *Handbook of the biology of aging.* (2nd ed., pp. 377–413). New York: Van Nostrand Reinhold.

Lakatta, E. G. (1990). Heart and circulation. In E. L. Schneider & J. W. Rowe (Eds.), *Handbook of the biology of aging* (3rd ed., pp. 181–216). San Diego: Academic Press.

Lalonde B., Hooyman, N., & Blumhagen, J. (1988). Long-term outcome effectiveness of a health promotion program for the elderly: The Wallingford Wellness Project. *Journal of Gerontological Social Work, 13,* 95–112.

Lamberty, G. J., Bieliauskas, L. A., & Holt, C. S. (1994). Depressive symptom covariation in geriatric clinic patients. *Clinical Gerontologist, 15,* 15–27.

Landfield, P. W. (1988). Hippocampal neurobiological mechanisms of age-related memory dysfunction. *Neurobiology of Aging, 9,* 571–579.

Landreville, P., & Vezina, J. (1992). A comparison between daily hassles and major life events as correlates of well-being in older adults. *Canadian Journal on Aging, 11,* 137–149.

Landrine, H., & Klonoff, E. A. (1992). Culture and health-related schemas: A review and proposal for interdisciplinary integration. *Health Psychology, 11,* 267–276.

Lang, F. R., & Carstensen, L. L. (1994). Close emotional relationships in late life: Further support for proactive aging in the social domain. *Psychology and Aging, 9,* 315–324.

Lapierre, S., Bouffard, L., & Bastin, E. (1993). Motivational goal objects in later life. *International Journal of Aging and Human Development, 36,* 279–292.

Larson, R., Mannell, R., & Zuzanek, J. (1986). Daily well-being of older adults with friends and family. *Psychology and Aging, 1,* 117–124.

Laumann, E. O., Gagnon, J. H., Michael, R. T. & Michaels, S. (1994). *The Social organization of sexuality.* Chicago: University of Chicago Press.

Lawton, M. P. (1985). Activities and leisure. *Annual Review of Gerontologv and Geriatrics, 5,* 127–164.

Lawton, M. P. (1993). Meanings of activity. In J. R. Kelly (Ed.), *Activity and aging: Staying involved in later life* (pp. 25–41). Newbury Park, CA: Sage.

Lawton, M. P. (1994). Personality and affective correlates of leisure activity participation by older people. *Journal of Leisure Research, 26,* 138–157.

Lawton, M. P., Kleban, M. H., Rajagopal, D., & Dean, J. (1992). Dimensions of affective experience in three age groups. *Psychology and Aging, 7,* 171–184.

Lawton, M. P., & Lawrence, R. H. (1994). Assessing health. *Annual Review of Gerontology and Geriatrics, 14,* 23–56.

Lawton, M. P., Moss, M., & Fulcomer, M. (1987). Objective and subjective uses of time by older people. *International Journal of Aging and Human Development, 24,* 171–188.

Lawton, M. P., Moss, M., Kleban, M. H., Glicksman, A., & Rovine, M. (1991). A two-factor model of caregiving appraisal and psychological well-being. *Journals of Gerontology, 46,* P181–P189.

Lazarus, A. A. (1990). Stressing or depressing? *American Psychologist, 45,* 562.

Lazarus, R. S. (1990a). Theory-based stress measurement. *Psychological Inquiry, 1,* 3–13.

Lazarus, R. S. (1990b). Author's response. *Psychological Inquiry, 1,* 41–51.

Lazarus, R. S. (1991). *Emotion and adaptation.* New York: Oxford University Press.

Lazarus, R. S. (1993). From psychological stress to the emotions: A history of changing outlooks. *Annual Review of Psychology, 44,* 1–21.

Lazarus, R. S., Deese, J., & Osler, S. F. (1952). The effects of psychological stress upon performance. *Psychological Bulletin, 49,* 293–317.

Lazarus, R. S., & DeLongis, A. (1983). Psychological stress and coping in aging. *American Psychologist, 38,* 245–254.

Lazarus, R. S., & Folkman, S. (1984). *Stress appraisal and coping.* New York: Springer.

Leahey, T. H. (1991). *A history of modern psychology.* New York: Prentice-Hall.

Leiblum, S. R., Baume, R. M., & Croog, S. H. (1994). The sexual functioning of elderly hypertensive women. *Journal of Sex and Marital Therapy, 20,* 259–270.

Leigh, B. C., Temple, M. T., & Trocki, K. F.(1993). The sexual behavior of US adults: Results from a national survey. *American Journal of Public Health, 83,* 1400–1408.

Leont'ev, A. N. (1978). *Activity, consciousness, and personality* (M. J. Hall, Trans.). Englewood Cliffs, NJ: Prentice-Hall.

Lepore, S. J. (1995). Measurement of chronic stressors. In S.Cohen, R. C. Kessler, & L. U. Gordon (Eds.), *Measuring stress: A guide for health and social scientists* (pp. 102–120). New York: Oxford University Press.

Levendusky, P. G. (1978). Effects of social incentives on task performance in the elderly. *Journal of Gerontology, 33,* 562–566.

Levenson, H. (1974). Activism and powerful others: Distinctions within the concept of internal–external control. *Journal of Personality Assessment, 38,* 377–383.

Levenson, R. W., Carstensen, L. L., Friesen, W. V., & Ekman, P. (1991). Emotion, physiology, and expression in old age. *Psychology and Aging, 6,* 28–35.

Leventhal, E. A., Easterling, D., Leventhal, H., & Cameron, L. (1995). Conservation of energy, uncertainty reduction, and swift utilization of care among the elderly: Study II. *Medical Care, 33,* 988–1000.

Leventhal, E. A., Leventhal, H., Schaefer, P., & Easterling D. (1993). Conservation of energy, uncertainty reduction, and swift utilization of medical care among the elderly. *Journals of Gerontology, 48,* P78–P86.

Leventhal, H., Diefenbach, M., & Leventhal, E. A. (1993). Illness cognition: Using common sense to understand treatment adherence and affect cognition interactions. *Cognitive Therapy and Research, 16,* 143–163.

Leventhal, H., & Everhart D. (1979). Emotion, pain, and physical illness. In C. Izard (Ed.), *Emotions in personality and psychopathology* (pp. 263–298). New York: Plenum Press.

Levin, J. D. (1992). *Theories of the self.* Washington, DC: Hemisphere.

Levkoff, S., Cleary, P. D., & Wetle, T. (1987). Diffrences in the appraisal of health between aged and middle-aged adults. *Journals of Gerontology, 42,* 114–120.

Levy, J. A. (1994). Sex and sexuality in later life stages. In A. S. Rossi (Ed.), *Sexuality across the life course* (pp. 287–309). Chicago: University of Chicago Press.

Lewis, G., & Wessely, S. (1992). The epidemiology of fatigue: More questions than answers. *Journal of Epidemiology and Community Health, 46,* 92–97.

Lieberman, M. A. (1992). Limitations of psychological stress model: Studies of widowhood. In M. A. Wykle, E. Kahana, & J. Kowal (Eds.), *Stress and health among the elderly* (pp. 133–150). New York: Springer.

Lipsitz, L. A. (1989). Altered blood pressure homeostasis in advanced age: Clinical and research implications. *Journals of Gerontology, 44,* M179–M183.

Litvin, S. J., Albert, S. M., Brody, E. M., & Hoffman, C. (1995). Marital status, competing demands, and role priorities of parent-caring daughters. *Journal of Applied Gerontology, 14,* 372–390.

Locke, E. A., & Latham, G. P. (1990). *A theory of goal setting and task performance.* Englewood Cliffs, NJ: Prentice Hall.

Long, J. (1989). A part to play: Men experiencing leisure through retirement. In W. R. Bytheway, T. Keil, P. Allatt, & A. Bryman (Eds.), *Becoming and being old: Sociological approaches to later life* (pp. 55–71). London: Sage.

Lopata, H. Z. (1993). The support systems of American urban widows. In M. S. Stroebe, W. Stroebe, & R. O. Hansson (Eds.), *Handbook of bereavement: Theory, research, and intervention* (pp. 381–396). New York: Cambridge University Press.

Losier, G. F., Bourque, P. E., & Vallerand, R. J. (1993). A motivational model of leisure participation in the elderly. *Journal of Psychology, 127,* 153–170.

Lowenthal, M. F., & Robinson, B. (1976). Social networks and isolation. In R. H. Binstock & E. Shanas (Eds.), *Handbook of aging and the social sciences* (pp. 432–256). New York: Van Nostrand Reinhold.

Lund, D. A., Caserta, M. S., & Dimond, M. F. (1993). The course of spousal bereavement in later life. In M. S. Stroebe, W. Stroebe, & R. O. Hansson (Eds.), *Handbook of bereavement: Theory, research, and intervention* (pp. 240–254). New York: Cambridge University Press.

Macklis, R. (1997). *Radiation Research Society News, 30*(3), 3.

Maddi, S. R. (1970). The search for meaning. *Nebraska Symposium on Motivation, 18,* 137–186.

Maddox, G. L., & Douglas, E. B. (1973). Self-assessment of health: A longitudinal study of elderly subjects. *Journal of Health and Social Behavior, 14,* 87–93.

Madsen, K. B. (1974). *Modern theories of motivation.* Copenhagen, Denmark: Munksgaard.

Maes, M., Jacobs, M., Suy, E., Minner, B., *et al.* (1990). Prediction of the DST results in depressives by means of urinary-free cortisol excretion, dexamethasone levels, and age. *Biological Psychiatry, 28,* 349–357.

Maes, M., Leventhal, H., & de Ridder, D. T., D. (1996). Coping with chronic diseases. In M. Zeidner & N. S. Endler (Eds.), *Handbook of coping: Theory, research , and applications* (pp. 221–251). New York: Wiley.

Magnusson, D., & Törestad, B. (1993). A holistic view of personality: A model revisited. *Annual Review of Psychology, 44,* 427–451.

Makinodan, T. (1997). Immunity and aging. In C. E. Finch & L. Hayflick (Eds.), *Handbook of the biology of aging* (pp. 379–408). New York: Van Nostrand Reinhold.

Mangione, C. M., Marcantonio, E. R., Goldman, L., Cook, E. F., *et al.* (1993). Influence of age on measurement of health status in patients undergoing elective surgery. *Journal of the American Geriatrics Society, 41,* 377–383.

Mannell, R. C. (1993). High-investment activity and life satisfaction among older adults: Committed serious leisure and flow activities. In J. R. Kelly (Ed.), *Activity and aging: Staying involved in later life* (pp. 125–145). Newbury Park, CA: Sage.

Manu, P., Matthews, D. A., Lane, T. J., Tennen, H., *et al.* (1989). Depression among patients with a chief complaint of chronic fatigue. *Journal of Affective Disorders, 17,* 165–172.

Margolin, L., & White, L. (1987). The continuing role of physical attractiveness in marriage. *Journal of Marriage and the Family, 49,* 21–27.

Mariotti, S., Franceschi, C., Cossarizza, A., & Pinchera, A. (1995). The aging thyroid. *Endocrine Reviews, 16,* 686–715.

Markides, K. S., Lee, D. J., Ray, L. A., & Black, S. A. (1993). Physicians' ratings of health in middle and old age: A cautionary note. *Journals of Gerontology, 48,* S24–S27.

Markus, H., & Cross, S. (1990). The interpersonal self. In L. A. Pervin (Ed.), *Handbook of personality: Theory and research* (pp. 576–608). New York: Guilford.

Markus, H., & Herzog, A. R. (1992). The role of the self-concept in aging. *Annual Review of Gerontologv and Geriatrics, 11,* 110–143.

Markus, H., & Nurius, P. (1986). Possible selves. *American Psychologist, 41,* 954–969.

Marriot Seniors Volunteerism Study. (1991). Washington, DC: Marriot Senior Living Services.

Marsh, G. R., & Thompson, L. W. (1977). Psychophysiology of aging. In J. E. Birren & K. W. Schaie (Eds.), *Handbook of the psychology of aging* (pp. 219–248). New York: Van Nostrand Reinhold.

Marshall, V. W. (1996). The state of theory in aging and the social sciences. In R. H. Binstock & L. K. George (Eds.), *Handbook of aging and the social sciences* (4th ed., pp. 12–30). San Diego: Academic Press.

Martin, C. E. (1981). Factors affecting sexual functioning in 60–79 year old married males. *Archives of Sexual Behavior, 10,* 399–420.

Maslow, A. (1973). *The farther reaches of human nature.* New York: Viking.

Massoro, E. J. (1995). Aging: Current concepts. In E. J. Massoro (Ed.), *Handbook of physiology: Section 11. Aging* (pp. 3–21). New York: Oxford University Press.

Masters, W. H., & Johnson, V. E. (1966). *Human sexual response.* Boston: Little, Brown.

Matthews, K. A. (1992). Myths and realities of the menopause. *Psychosomatic Medicine, 54,* 1–9.

Matthias, R. E., Lubben, J. E., Atchison, K. A., & Schweitzer, S. O. (1997). Sexual activity and satisfaction among very old adults: Results from a community-dwelling Medicare population survey. *Gerontologist, 37,* 6–14.

Maxson, P. J. , Berg, S., & McClearn, G. (1996). Multidimensional patterns of aging in 70- year-olds: Survival differences. *Journal of Aging and Health, 8,* 320–333.

McAdams, D. P. (1994). Can personality change? Levels of stability and growth in the personality across the life span. In T. F. Heatherton & J. L. Weinberger (Eds.), *Can personality change?* (pp. 299–313). Washington, DC: American Psychological Association.

McCarter, R. J. M. (1995). Energy utilization. In E. J. Massoro (Eds.), *Handbook of physiology: Section 11. Aging* (pp. 95–118). New York: Oxford University Press.

McClelland, D. C. (1961). *The achieving society.* Princeton, NJ: Van Nostrand.

McClelland, D. C. (1992). Motivational configurations. In C. P. Smith, J. W. Atkinson, & J. Veroff (Eds.), *Motivation and personality: Handbook of thematic content analysis* (pp. 87–99). New York: Cambridge University Press.

McClelland, D. C., Koestner, R., & Weinberger, J. (1989). How do self-attributed and implicit motives differ? *Psychological Review, 96,* 690–702.

McClelland, D. C., & Winter, D. G. (1969). *Motivating economic achievement.* New York: Free Press.

McCrea, R. R. (1982). Age differences in the use of coping mechanisms. *Journal of Gerontology, 37,* 454–460.

McCrea, R. R., & Costa, P. T., Jr. (1986). Personality, coping, and coping effectiveness in an adult sample. *Journal of Personality, 54,* 385–405.

McCrea, R. R., & Costa, P. T., Jr. (1988). Psychological resilience among widowed men and women: A 10-year follow-up of a national sample. *Journal of Social Issues, 44*(3), 129–142.

McDowd, J. M., & Birren, J. E. (1990). Aging and attentional processes. In J. E. Birren & K W. Schaie (Eds.), *Handbook of the psychology of aging* (3rd ed., pp. 222–233). San Diego: Academic Press.

McEwen, B. S., DeKloet, E. R., & Rostene, W. (1986). Adrenal steroid receptors and actions in the nervous system. *Physiological Reviews, 66,* 1121–1188.

McFadden, S. H. (1996). Religion, spirituality, and aging. In J. E. Birren & K W. Schaie (Eds.), *Handbook of the psychology of aging* (4th ed., pp. 162–177). San Diego: Academic Press.

McGandy, R. B., Barrows, C. H., Spanias, A., Meredith, A., *et al.* (1966). Nutrient intakes and energy expenditure in men of different ages. *Journals of Gerontology, 21,* 581–587.

McIntosh, W. A., Fletcher, R. D., Kubena, K. S., & Landmann, W. A. (1995). Factors associated with sources of influence/information in reducing red meat by elderly subjects. *Appetite, 24,* 219–230.

McIntosh, W. A., Shifflet, P. A., & Picou, J. S. (1989). Social support, stressful events, strain, dietary intake, and the elderly. *Medical Care, 27,* 140–153.

McKinlay, J. B., & Feldman, H. A. (1994). Age-related variation in sexual activity and interest in normal men: Results from the Massachusts Male Aging Study. In A. S. Rossi (Eds.), *Sexuality across the life course* (pp. 261–285). Chicago: University of Chicago Press.

McKinlay, J. B., McKinlay, S. M., & Brambilla, D. (1987). The relative contributions of endocrine changes and social circumstances to depression in middle-aged women. *Journal of Health and Social Behavior, 28,* 345–363.

McReynolds, P. (1990). Motives and metaphors: A study in scientific creativity. In D. E. Leary (Ed.), *Metaphors in the history of psychology* (pp. 133–172) Cambridge, UK: Cambridge University Press.

Mechanic, D. (1992). Health and illness behavior and patient–practitioner relationship. *Social Science and Medicine, 34,* 1345–1350.

Mehrabian, A., & Blum, J. S. (1996). Temperament and personality as functions of age. *International Journal of Aging and Human Development, 42,* 251–269.

Melamed, S., Meir, E. I., & Samson, A. (1995). The benefits of personality–leisure congruence: Evidence and implications. *Journal of Leisure Research, 27,* 25–40.

Mellinger, G. D., Balter, M. B., & Uhlenhut, E. H. (1985). Insomnia and its treatment: Prevalence and correlates. *Archives of General Psychiatry, 42,* 225–232.

Mellinger, J. C., & Erdwins, C. J. (1985). Personality correlates of age and life roles in adult women. *Psychology of Women Quarterly, 9,* 503–514.

Melzack, R. (1993). Pain: Past, present and future. *Canadian Journal of Experimental Psychology, 47,* 615–629.

Melzack, R., & Katz, J. (1992). The McGill Pain Questionnaire: Appraisal and current status. In D. C. Turk & R. Melzack (Eds.), *Handbook of pain assessment* (pp. 152–168). New York: Guilford.

Melzack, R., & Wall, P. D. (1965). Pain mechanisms: A new theory. *Science, 150,* 971–979.

Mendes de Leon, C. F., Kasl, S. V., & Jacobs. S. (1994). A prospective study of widowhood and changes in symptoms of depression in a community sample of the elderly. *Psychological Medicine, 24,* 613–624.

Merskey, H. (1978). Pain and personality. In R. A. Sternbach (Ed.), *The psychology of pain* (pp. 111–127). New York: Raven.

Midlarsky, E., & Kahana, E. (1994). *Altruism in later life.* Thousand Oaks, CA: Sage.

Miller, B., McFall, S., & Montgomery, A. (1991). The impact of elder health caregiver involvement and global stress on two dimensions of caregiver burden. *Journals of Gerontology, 46,* S9–S19.

Miller, R. A. (1990). Aging and the immune response. In E. L. Schneider & J. W. Rowe (Eds.), *Handbook of the biologv of aging* (3rd ed., pp. 157–180). San Diego: Academic Press.

Miller, R. A. (1995). Immune system. In E. J. Massoro (Eds.). *Handbook of physiology: Section 11. Aging* (pp. 555–590). New York: Oxford University Press.

Miner, S. (1995). Racial differences in family support and formal service utilization among older persons: A nonrecursive model. *Journals of Gerontology: Psychological and Social Sciences, 50B,* S143–S153.

Mischel, T. (1976). Psychological explanations and their vicissitudes. *Nebraska Symposium on Motivation, 23,* 133–204.

Mitchell, E. D., & Mason, B. S. (1934). *The theory of play.* New York: Barnes.

Mobily, K. E., Lemke, J. H., & Gisin, G. J. (1991). The idea of leisure repertoire. *Journal of Applied Gerontology, 10,* 208–223.

Mobily, K. E., Lemke, J. H., Ostiguy, L. J., Woodard, R. J., *et al.* (1993). Leisure repertoire in a sample of midwestern elderly: The case for exercise. *Journal of Leisure Research, 25,* 84–99.

Moen, P., Robinson, J., & Fields, V. (1994). Women's work and caregiving roles: A life course approach. *Journals of Gerontology: Social Sciences, 49,* S176–S186.

Molander, B., & Bäckman, L. (1989). Age differences in heart rate patterns during concentration in a precision sport: Implications for attentional functioning. *Journals of Gerontology, 44,* P80–P87.

Molander, B., & Bäckman, L. (1994). Attention and performance in miniature golf across the life span. *Journals of Gerontology, 49,* P35–P41.

Monat, A., & Lazarus, R. S. (1985). Stress and coping: Some current issues and controversies. In A. Monat & R. S. Lazarus (Eds.), *Stress and coping: An anthology* (2nd ed., pp. 1–16). New York: Columbia University Press.

Monk, A. (1988). Aging, loneliness, and communications. *American Behavioral Scientist, 31,* 532–563.

Monk, T. H. (1991). Sleep and circadian rhythms. *Experimental Gerontology, 26,* 233–243.

Monk, T. H., Buysse, D. J., Reynolds, C. F., Jarrett, D. B., et al. (1992). Rhythmic or homeostatic influences on mood, activation, and performance in young and old men. *Journals of Gerontology, 47,* P221–P227.

Monk, T. H., Reynolds, C. F., III, Buysse D. J., Hoch, C. C., et al. (1991). Circadian characteristics of healthy 80-year-olds and their relationship to objectively recorded sleep. *Journals of Gerontology, 46,* M171–M175.

Monk, T. H., Reynolds, C. F., Machen, M. A., & Kupfer, D. J. (1992). Daily social rhythms in the elderly and their relation to objectively recorded sleep. *Sleep, 15,* 322–329.

Moody, H. R. (1988). Toward a critical gerontology: The contribution of the humanities to theories of aging. In J. E. Birren & V. L. Bengtson (Eds.), *Emergent theories of aging* (pp. 19–40). New York: Springer.

Moody, H. R. (1992). *Ethics in an aging society.* Baltimore: Johns Hopkins University Press.

Mooradian, A. D. (1990). Biomarkers of aging: Do we know what to look for? *Journals of Gerontology, 45,* B183–B186.

Moorman, C., & Matulich, E. (1993). A model of consumers' preventive health behaviors: The role of health motivation and health ability. *Journal of Consumer Research, 20,* 208–228.

Moos, R. H., Swindle, R. W. (1990a). Person–environment transaction and the stressor appraisal–coping process. *Psychological Inquiry, 1,* 30–32.

Moos, R. H., & Swindle, R. W. (1990b). Stressful life circumstances: Concepts and measures. *Stress Medicine, 6,* 171–178.

Mor-Barak, M. E., Miller, L. S., & Syme, L. S. (1991). Social networks, life events, and health of the poor frail elderly: A longitudinal study of the buffering versus the direct effect. *Family and Community Health, 14*(2), 1–13.

Morgan, D. G., & May, P. C. (1990). Age-related changes in synaptic neurochemistry. In E. L. Schneider & J. W. Rowe (Eds.), *Handbook of the biologv of aging* (3rd ed., pp. 219–254). San Diego: Academic Press.

Morgan, D. G., May, P. C., & Finch, C. E. (1987). Dopamine and serotonin systems in aged human and rodent brain: Effects of age and neurodegenerative disease. *Journal of the American Geriatrics Society, 35,* 334–345.

Morgan, D. G., May, P. C., & Finch, C. E. (1988). Neurotransmitter receptors in normal human aging and Alzheimer's disease. In A. K. Sen & T. Y. Lee (Eds.), *Receptor ligands in neurological disorders* (pp. 120–147). Cambridge, UK: Cambridge University Press.

Morgan, D. L., Schuster, T. L., & Butler, E. W. (1991). Role reversals in the exchange of social support. *Journals of Gerontology, 46,* S278–S287.

Morley, J. E. (1990). Nutrition and aging. In W. R. Hazzard, R. Andres, & E. L. Bierman (Eds.), *Principles of geriatric medicine* (2nd ed., pp. 48–59). New York: McGraw-Hill.

Morley, J. E., & Morley, P. M. K. (1996). Psychological and social factors in the pathogenesis of weight loss. *Annual Review of Gerontology and Geriatrics, 15,* 83–109.

Moss, M. S., & Lawton, M. P. (1982). Time budgets of older people: A window on four lifestyles. *Journals of Gerontology, 37,* 115–123.

Moss, M. S., Lawton, M. P., Kleban, M. H., & Duhamel, L. (1993). Time use of caregivers of impaired elders before and after institutionalization. *Journals of Gerontology, 48,* S102–S111.

Moss, M. S., Moss, S. Z., Rubinstein, R. L., & Resch, N. (1995). Impact of elderly mother's death on middle age daughters. *International Journal of Aging and Human Development, 37,* 1–22.

Moynihan, J. A., & Cohen, N. (1992). Stress and immunity. In N. Schneiderman, P. McCabe, & A. Baum (Eds.), *Stress and disease processes: Perspectives on behavioral medicine* (pp. 27–54). Hillsdale, NJ: Erlbaum.

Mulder, G. (1986). The concept and measurement of mental effort. In G. R. J. Hockey, M. G. H. Coles, & A. W. K. Gaillard (Eds.), *Energetics and human information processing* (pp. 175–198). Dordrecht, Netherlands: Nijhoff.

Mulligan, T., & Moss, C. R. (1991). Sexuality and aging in male veterans: A cross sectional study of interest, ability, and activity. *Archives of Sexual Behavior, 20,* 17–25.

Mulligan, T., & Palguta, R. F. (1991). Sexual interest, activity, and satisfaction among male nursing home residents. *Archives of Sexual Behavior, 20,* 199–204.

Mullins, L. C., & Mushel, M. (1992). The existence and emotional closeness of relationships with children, friends, and spouses: The effect of loneliness among older persons. *Research on Aging, 14,* 448–470.

Mullins, L. C., Mushel, M., Cook, C., & Smith, R. (1994). The complexity of interpersonal relationships among older persons: An examination of selected emotionally close relationships. *Journal of Gerontological Social Work, 22,* 109–130.

Mullins, L. C., Smith, R., Colquitt, R., & Mushel, M. (1996). An examination of the effects of self-rated objective indicators of health condition and economic condition on the loneliness of older people. *Journal of Applied Gerontology, 15,* 23–37.

Mullins, L. C., & Tucker, R. D. (1992). Emotional and social isolation among older French Canadian seasonal residents in Florida: A comparison with the English Canadian seasonal residents. *Journal of Gerontological Social Work, 19*(2), 83–106.

Murphy, C. W., Cain, W. S., & Hegsted, D. M. (Eds.). (1989). Nutrition and the chemical senses in aging: Recent advances and current research needs. *Annals of the New York Academy of Sciences, 561.*

Murray, H. A. (1938). *Explorations in personality.* London: Oxford University Press.

Naliboff, B. D., Benton, D., Solomon, G. F., Morley, J. E., Fahey, J. L., *et al.* (1991). Immunological changes in young and old adults during brief laboratory stress. *Psychosomatic Medicine, 53,* 121–132.

National Institute of Mental Health. (1995). Basic behavioral science research: A national investment—emotion and motivation. *American Psychologist, 50,* 838–845.

Neiss, R. (1988). Reconceptualizing arousal: Psychobiological states in motor performance. *Psychological Bulletin, 103,* 345–366.

Nelson, E. A., & Dannefer, D. (1992). Aged heterogeneity: Fact or fiction? The fate of diversity in research. *Gerontologist, 32,* 17–23.

Nelson, J. B., & Castell, D. O. (1990). Aging of the gastrointestinal system. In W. R. Hazzard, R. Andres, & E. L. Bierman (Eds.), *Principles of geriatric medicine* (2nd ed., 593–609). New York: McGraw-Hill.

Nelson, J. F. (1995). The potential role of selected endocrine systems in aging processes. In E. J. Massoro (Eds.), *Handbook of physiology: Section 11. Aging* (pp. 377–394). New York: Oxford University Press.

Neugarten, B. L., & Associates (1964). *Personality in middle and late life.* New York: Atherton.

Niemi, I. (1993). Systematic error in behavioural meaurement: Comparing results from interview and time budget studies. *Social Indicators Research, 30,* 229–244.

Nieswiadomy, M., & Rubin, R. M. (1995). Change in expenditure patterns of retirees 1972–1973 and 1986–1987. *Journal of Gerontology, 50B,* S274–S290.

Noakes, T. D. (1988). Implications of exercise testing for prediction of athletic performance: A contemporary perspective. *Medicine and Science in Sports and Exercise, 20,* 319–330.

Norris, F. H., & Murrell, S. A. (1987). Older adult family stress and adaptation before and after bereavement. *Journal of Gerontology, 42,* 606–612.

Norton, R. A. (1995). Gastrointestinal disease in the aged. In W. Reichel (Eds.), *Care of the elderly: Clinical aspects of aging* (4th ed., pp. 198–205) Baltimore: Williams & Wilkins.

Novick, N., Cauce, A. M., & Grove, K. (1996). Competence self-concept. In B. A. Bracken (Ed.), *Handbook of self-concept: Developmental, social, and clinical considerations* (pp. 210–258). New York: Wiley.

Nurmi, J. E. (1992). Age differences in adult life goals, concerns, and their temporal extension: A life course approach to future-oriented motivation. *International Journal of Behavioral Development, 15,* 487–508.

Nurmi, J. E., Pulliainen, H., & Salmela-Aro, K. (1992). Age differences in adults' control beliefs related to life goals and concerns. *Psychology and Aging, 7,* 194–196.

O'Connor, B. P. (1995). Family and friend relationships among older and younger adults: Interaction motivation, mood and quality. *International Journal of Aging and Human Development, 40,* 9–29.

O'Connor, B. P., & Vallerand, R. J. (1990). Religious motivation in the elderly: A French-Candian replication and an extension. *Journal of Social Psychology, 130,* 53–59.

O'Leary, A. (1990). Stress, emotion, and human immune function. *Psychological Bulletin, 108,* 363–382.

Okun, M. A. (1994). The relation between motives for organizational volunteering and frequency of volunteering by elders. *Journal of Applied Gerontology, 13,* 115–126.

Okun, M. A., & Di Vesta, F. J. (1976). Cautiousness in adulthood as a function of age and instructions. *Journals of Gerontology, 31,* 571–576.

Opler, M. K. (1967). Cultural induction of stress. In M. H. Appley & R. Trumbull (Eds.), *Psychological stress: Issues in research* (pp. 209–233). New York: Appleton–Century–Crofts.

O'Rand, A. M. (1996). The cumulative stratification of the life course. In R. H. Binstock & L. K. George (Eds.), *Handbook of aging and the social sciences* (4th ed., pp. 188–207). San Diego: Academic Press.

Ouslander, J. G., & Beck, J. C. (1982). Defining the health problems of the elderly. *Annual Review of Public Health, 3,* 55–83.

Palmore, E. B. (1981). *Social patterns in normal aging: Findings from the Duke Longitudinal Study.* Durham, NC: Duke University Press.

Pandolf, K. B. (1978). Influence of local and central factors in dominating rated perceived exertion during physical work. *Perceptual and Motor Skills, 46,* 683–698.

Pargament, K. I. (1996). Religious methods of coping: Resources for the conservation and transformation of significance. In E. P. Shafranske (Eds.), *Religion and the clinical practice of psychology* (pp. 215–239). Washington, DC: American Psychological Association Press.

Parker, J. D., & Endler, N. S. (1996). Coping and defense: A historical overview. In M. Zeidner & N.S. Endler (Eds.), *Handbook of coping: Theory, research, and applications* (pp. 3–23). New York: Wiley.

Parker, S. R. (1982). *Work and retirement.* London: George Allen & Unwin.

Parkes, C. M. (1987). *Bereavement: Studies of grief in adult life* (2nd ed.). Madison, CT: International Universities Press.

Parkes, C. M. (1995). Guidelines for conducting ethical bereavement research. *Death Studies, 19,* 171–181.

Parmelee, P. A., Katz, I. R., & Lawton, M. P. (1991). The relation of pain to depression among institutionalized aged. *Journals of Gerontology, 46,* P15–P21.

Passuth, P. M., & Bengtson, V. L. (1988). Sociological theories of aging: Current perspectives and future directions. In J. E. Birren & V. L. Bengtson (Eds.), *Emergent theories of aging* (pp. 333–355). New York: Springer.

Pasternak, R. E., Reynolds, C. F., Hoch, C. C., Buysse, D. S., *et al.* (1992). Sleep in spousally bereaved elders with subsyndromal depressive symptoms. *Psychiatry Research, 43,* 43–53.

Patrick, D. L., & Bergner, M. (1990). Measurement of health-status in the 1990s. *Annual Review of Public Health, 11,* 165–183.

Pearce, S. D. (1991). Toward understanding the participation of older adults in continuing education. *Educational Gerontology, 17,* 451–464.

Pearlin, L. (1982). The social contexts of stress. In L. Goldberger & S. Breznitz (Eds.), *Handbook of stress: Theoretical and clinical aspects* (pp. 367–380). New York: Free Press.

Pearlin, L. I., Aneshensel, C. S., Mullan, J. T., & Whitlatch, C. J. (1996). Caregiving and its social support. In R. H. Binstock & L. K. George (Eds.), *Handbook of aging and the social sciences* (4th ed., pp. 283–302). San Diego: Academic Press.

Pearlin, L. I., Mullan, J. T., Semple, S. J., & Skaff, M. M. (1990). Caregiving and the stress process: An overview of concepts and their measures. *Gerontologist, 30*, 583–594.

Pearlin, L. I., & Schooler, C. (1978). The structure of coping. *Journal of Health and Social Behavior, 19*, 2–21.

Perkins, H. W., & Harris, L. B. (1990). Familial bereavement and health in adult life course perspective. *Journal of Marriage and the Family, 52*, 233–241.

Persson, G., & Svanborg, A. (1992). Marital coital activity in men at the age of 75: Relation to somatic, psychiatric and social factors at the age of 70. *Journal of the American Geriatric Society, 40*, 439–444.

Pervin, L. A. (1992). The rational mind and the problem of volition: Review of E. A. Locke & G. P. Latham, *A theory of goal setting*. *Psychological Science, 3*, 162–164.

Pervin. L. A. (1994a). A critical analysis of current trait theory. *Psychological Inquiry, 5*, 103–113.

Pervin, L. A. (1994b). Further reflection on current trait theory. *Psychological Inquiry, 5*, 169–178.

Pervin, L. A. (1994c). Personality stability, personality change, and the question of process. In T. F. Heatherton & J. L. Weinberger (Eds.), *Can personality change?* (pp. 315–330). Washington, DC: American Psychological Association Press.

Peters, G. R., & Rappoport, L. (1988). Behavioral perspectives on food, nutrition, and aging. *American Behavioral Scientist, 32*, 5–16.

Peterson, C., Maier, S. F., & Seligman, M. E. P. (1993). *Learned helplessness: A theory for the age of personal control*. New York: Oxford University Press.

Pfeiffer, E. (1969). Sexual behavior in old age. In In E. W. Busse & E. Pfeiffer (Eds.), *Behavior and adaptation in late life* (pp. 151–162). Boston: Little, Brown.

Pfeiffer, E. (1977). Psychopathology and social pathology. In J. E. Birren & K W. Schaie (Eds.), *Handbook of the psychology of aging* (pp. 650–671). New York: Van Nostrand Reinhold.

Phillips, P. A., Rolls, B.J., Ledingham, J. G. G., Forsling, M. L., *et al.* (1984). Reduced thirst after water deprivation in healthy elderly men. *New England Journal of Medicine, 311*, 753–759.

Pierce, G. R., Sarason, I. G., & Sarason, B. R. (1996). Coping and social support. In M. Zeidner & N.S. Endler (Eds.), *Handbook of coping: Theory, research, and applications* (pp. 434–451). New York: Wiley.

Pietrini, P., Horwitz, B., Grady, C. L., Maisog, J., *et al.* (1992). A positron emission tomography (PET) study of cerebral glucose metabolism (rCMRglc) and blood flow (rCBF) in normal human aging. *Gerontologist, 32* (Special Issue II. 242, Abstract).

Pietrini, P., & Rapoport, S. I. (1994). Functional neuroimaging: Positron-emission tomography in the study of cerebral blood flow and glucose utilization in human subjects at different ages. In C. E. Coffey & J. L. Cummings (Eds.), *Textbook of geriatric neuropsychiatry* (pp. 195–213). Washington, DC: American Psychiatric Association Press.

Plomin, R., Lichtenstein, P., Pedersen, N. L., McClearn, G. E., & Nesselroade, J. R. (1990). Genetic influence on life events during the last half of the life span. *Psychology and Aging, 5,* 25–30.

Pollock, K. (1988). On the nature of social stress: Production of a modern mythology. *Social Science and Medicine, 26,* 381–392.

Popper, K. R. (1991). Of clouds and clocks: An approach to the problem of rationality and the freedom of man. In D. Cicchetti, & W. M. Grove (Eds.), *Thinking clearly about psychology: Vol. I. Matters of public interest* (pp. 100–139). Minneapolis: University of Minnesota Press.

Potts, M. K., Hurwicz, M. L., Goldstein, M. S., & Berkanovic, E. (1992). Social support, health-promotive beliefs, and preventive health behaviors among the elderly. *Journal of Applied Gerontology, 11,* 425–440.

Powell, D. A., Milligan, W. L., & Furchtgott, E. (1980). Peripheral autonomic changes accompanying learning and reaction time performance in older people. *Journal of Gerontology, 35,* 57–65.

Price, D. D., & Harkins, S. W. (1992). Psychophysical approaches to pain measurement and assessment. In D. C. Turk & R. Melzack (Eds.), *Handbook of pain assessment* (pp. 111–134). New York: Guilford.

Prinz, P. (1977). Sleep patterns in the healthy aged: Relationship with intellectual function. *Journal of Gerontology, 32,* 179–186.

Prinz, P. N., Dustman, R. E., & Emmerson, R. (1990). Electrophysiology and aging. In J. E. Birren & K. W. Schaie (Eds.), *Handbook of the psychology of aging* (3rd ed., pp. 135–149). San Diego: Academic Press.

Prohaska, T. R., Leventhal, E. A., Leventhal, H., & Keller, M. L. (1985). Health practices, and illness cognition in young, middle-aged, and elderly adults. *Journals of Gerontology, 40,* 569–578.

Quinn, J. F., & Burkhauser, R. V. (1990). Work and retirement. In R. H. Binstock & L. K. George (Eds.), *Handbook of aging and the social sciences* (3rd ed., pp. 308–327). San Diego: Academic Press.

Rabbitt, P. (1986). Models and paradigms in the study of stress effects. In G. R. J. Hockey, M. G. H. Coles, & A. W. K. Gaillard (Eds.), *Energetics and human information processing* (pp. 155–174). Dordrecht, Netherlands: Nijhoff.

Rakover, S. S. (1990). *Metapsychology: Missing links in behavior, mind, and science.* New York: Paragon House.

Rakover, S. S. (1992). Outflanking the mind–body problem: Scientific progress in the history of psychology. *Journal for the Theory of Social Behavior, 22,* 145–173.

Rakowski, W. (1992). Disease prevention and health promotion with older adults. In M. G. Ory, R. P. Abeles, & P. D. Lipman (Eds.), *Aging, health, and behavior* (pp. 239–275). Newbury Park, CA: Sage.

Rakowski, W., Fleishman, J. A., Mor, V., & Bryan, S. A. (1993). Self-assessment of health and mortality among older persons: Do questions other than global self-rated health predict mortality? *Research on Aging, 15,* 92–116.

Rakowski, W., Hickey, T., & Dengiz A. M. (1987). Congruence of health and treatment perceptions among older patients and providers of primary care. *International Journal of Aging and Human Development, 25,* 63–77.

Rakowski, W., Julius, M., Hickey, T., & Halter, J. B. (1987). Correlates of preventive health behavior in late life. *Research on Aging, 9,* 331–355.

Rakowski, W., Julius, M., Hickey, T. Verbrugge, L. M., & Halter, J. B. (1988). Daily symptoms and behavioral responses: Results of a health diary with older adults. *Medical Care, 26,* 278–297.

Ralston, P. A. (1993). Health promotion for rural black elderly: A comprehensive review. *Journal of Gerontological Social Work, 20,* 53–78.

Rapkin, B. D., & Fischer, K. (1992a). Personal goals of older adults: Issues in assessment and prediction. *Psychology and Aging, 7,* 127–137.

Rapkin, B. D., & Fischer, K. (1992b). Framing the construct of life satisfaction in terms of older adults' personal goals. *Psychology and Aging, 7,* 138–149.

Rappoport, L., & Peters, G. R. (1988). Aging and the psychosocial problematics of food. *American Behavioral Scientist, 32,* 31–40.

Raskind, M. A., Peskind, E.R., Veith, R. C., Beard, J. C., *et al.* (1988). Increased plasma and cerebrospinal fluid norepinephrine in older men: Differential suppression of clonidine. *Journal of Clinical Endocrinology and Metabolism, 66,* 438–443.

Ray, D. C., Raciti, M. A., & MacLean, W. E. (1992). Effects of perceived responsibility on help-seeking decisions among elderly persons. *Journals of Gerontology, 47,* P199–P205.

Read, S. J., Jones, D. K., & Miller, L. C. (1990). Traits as goal-based categories: The importance of goals in the coherence of dispositional categories. *Journal of Personality and Social Psychology, 58,* 1048–1061.

Reich, J. W., & Zautra, A. J. (1991). Experimental and measurement approaches to internal control in at-risk older adults. *Journal of Social Issues, 47*(4), 143–158.

Rejeski, W. J. (1985). Perceived exertion—an active or passive process? *Journal of Sport Psychology, 7,* 371–378.

Reker, G. T. (1994). Logotheory and logotherapy: Challenges, opportunities, and some empirical findings. *International Forum for Logotherapy, 17,* 47–55.

Reker, G. T., Peacock, E. J., & Wong, P. T. P. (1987). Meaning and purpose in life and well-being: A life-span perspective. *Journal of Gerontology, 42,* 44–49.

Reker, G. T., & Wong, P. T. P. (1988). Aging as an individual process. Toward a theory of personal meaning. In J. E. Birren & V. L. Bengtson (Eds.), *Emergent theories of aging* (pp. 214–246). New York: Springer.

Reymond, M. J., Donda, A., & Lemarchand-Béraud, T. (1989). Neuroendocrine aspects of aging: Experimental data. *Hormone Research, 31,* 32–38.

Reynolds, C. F., III, Hoch, C. C., Buysse, D. J., Houck, P. R., *et al.* (1992). Electroencephalographic sleep in spousal bereavement and bereavement-related depression of late life. *Biological Psychiatry, 31,* 69–82.

Reynolds, C. F., III, Kupfer, D. J., Taska, L. S., Hoch, C. C., *et al.* (1985). Sleep and healthy seniors: A revisit. *Sleep, 8,* 20–29.

Reynolds, C. F., III, Monk, T. H., Hoch, C. C., Jennings, J. R., *et al.* (1991). Electroencephalographic sleep in the healthy "old old": A comparison with the "young old" in visually scored and automated measures. *Journals of Gerontology, 46,* M39–M46.

Richardson, G. S. (1990). Circadian rhyhms and aging. In E. L. Schneider & J. W. Rowe (Eds.), *Handbook of the biology of aging* (3rd ed., pp. 275–305). San Diego: Academic Press.

Riddick, C. C., & Stewart, D. G. (1994). An examination of the life satisfaction and importance of leisure in the lives of older female retirees: A comparison of blacks to whites. *Journal of Leisure Research, 26,* 75–87.

Riggs, K. E. (1996). Television use in a retirement community. *Journal of Communication, 46,* 144–158.

Riley, M. (1992). Aging in the twenty-first century. In N. E. Cutler, D. W. Gregg, & M. P. Lawton (Eds.), *Aging, money, and life satisfaction: Aspects of financial gerontology* (pp. 23–36). New York: Springer.

Riley, M. W. (1994). Aging and society: Past, present, and future. *Gerontologist, 34,* 436–446.

Ritchie, J. C., Belkin, B. M., Krishnan, K. R., Nemeroff, C. B., *et al.* (1990). Plasma dexamethasone concentration and the dexamethasone suppression test. *Biological Psychiatry, 27,* 159–173.

Roberto, K. (1992). Coping strategies of older women with hip fractures: Resources and outcomes. *Journals of Gerontology, 47,* P21–P26.

Roberts, S. B., Fuss, P., Heyman, M. B., Evans, W. J., *et al.* (1994). Control of food intake in older men. *Journal of the American Medical Association, 272,* 1601–1606.

Robinson, D. N. (1985). *Philosophy of psychology.* New York: Columbia University Press.

Rodgers, W. L., & Herzog, A. R. (1987). Interviewing older adults: The accuracy of factual information. *Journals of Gerontology, 42,* 387–394.

Rodin, J. (1986). Aging and health: Effects of the sense of control. *Science, 233,* 1271–1276.

Rodin, J., McAvay, G., & Timko, C. (1988). A longitudinal study of depressed mood and sleep disturbances in elderly adults. *Journals of Gerontology, 43,* P45–P53.

Rodin, J., & Salovey, P. (1989). Health psychology. *Annual Review of Psychology, 40,* 533–579.

Rodin, J., Timko, C., & Harris, S. (1985). The construct of control: Biological and psychological correlates. *Annual Review of Gerontology and Geriatrics, 5,* 3–55.

Rogers, J., & Bloom, F. E. (1985). Neurotransmitter metabolism and function in the aging nervous system. In C. E. Finch & E. L. Schneider (Eds.), *Handbook of the biology of aging* (2nd ed., pp. 645–691). New York: Van Nostrand Reinhold.

Rogers, R. W. (1975). A protection motivation theory of fear appeals and attitude change. *Journal of Psychology, 91,* 93–114.

Rolls, B. J., Dimeo, A. K., & Shide, D. J. (1995). Age related impairments in the regulation of food intake. *American Journal of Clinical Nutrition, 62,* 923–931.

Rook, K. S. (1990). Parallels in the study of social support and social strain. *Journal of Social and Clinical Psychology, 9,* 118–132.

Rosenblatt, P. C. (1993). Grief: The social context of private feelings. In M. S. Stroebe, W. Stroebe, & R. O. Hansson (Eds.), *Handbook of bereavement: Theory, research, and intervention* (pp. 102–111). New York: Cambridge University Press.

Rosenbloom, C. A., & Whittington, F. J. (1993). The effects of bereavement on eating behaviors and nutrient intakes in elderly widowed persons. *Journals of Gerontology, 48,* S223–S229.

Ross, E. (1968). Effects of challenging and supportive instructions on verbal learning in older persons. *Journal of Educational Psychology, 59,* 261–266.

Roth, L. (1929). *Spinoza.* Boston: Little, Brown.

Rothbaum, F., Weisz, J. R., & Snyder, S. S. (1982). Changing the world and changing the self: A two process model of perceived control. *Journal of Personality and Social Psychology, 42,* 5–37.

Rotter, J. B. (1966). Generalized expectancies for internal versus external control of reinforcements. *Psychological Monographs: General and Applied, 80* (Whole No. 609), 1–28.

Rotter, J. B. (1975). Some problems and misconceptions related to the construct internal versus external control of reinforcement. *Journal of Consulting and Clinical Psychology, 43,* 56–67.

Roy, C. S., & Sherrington, C. S. (1890). On the regulation of the blood supply of the brain. *Journal of Physiology, 11,* 85–108.

Rubinstein, R. L., Kilbride, J. C., & Nagy, S. (1992). *Elders living alone: Frailty and the perception of choice.* New York: Aldine de Gruyter.

Ruff, G. E., & Korchin, S J. (1967). Adaptive stress behavior. In M. H. Appley & R. Trumbull (Eds.), *Psychological stress: Issues in research* (pp. 297–306). New York: Appleton Century.

Runnels, B. L., Garry, P. J., Hunt, W. C., & Standefer, J. C. (1991). Thyroid function in a healthy elderly population: Implications for clinical evaluation. *Journals of Gerontology, 46,* B39–B44.

Russell, D. W. (1996). UCLA Loneliness Scale (Version 3): Reliability, validity, and factor stucture. *Journal of Personality Assessment, 66,* 20–40.

Russell, D. W., & Cutrona, C. E. (1991). Social support, stress, and depressive symptoms among the elderly: Test of a process model. *Psychology and Aging, 6,* 190–201.

Russo, J., Vitaliano, P. P., Brewer, D. D., Katon, W., & Becker, J. (1995). Psychiatric disorders in spouse caregivers of care recipients with Alzheimer's disease and matched controls: A diathesis–stress model of psychopathology. *Journal of Abnormal Psychology, 104,* 197–204.

Rust, J. O., Barnard, D., & Oster, G. D. (1979). WAIS Verbal-Performance differences among elderly when controlling for fatigue. *Psychological Reports, 44,* 489–490.

Ruth, J.-E., & Coleman, P. (1996). Personality and aging: Coping and management of the self in later life. In J. E. Birren & K W. Schaie (Eds.), *Handbook of the psvchology of aging* (4th ed., pp. 308–322). San Diego: Academic Press.

Ruth, J-E., & Öberg, P. (1995). Ways of life: Old age in a life perspective. In J. E. Birren, G. M. Kenyon, J.-E. Ruth, J. J. F. Schroots, & T. Svensson (Eds.), *Aging and biography: explorations in adult development* (pp. 167–186). New York: Springer.

Ryan, R. M. (1993). Agency and organization: Intrinsic motivation, autonomy and the self in psychological development. *Nebraska Symposium on Motivation, 40,* 1–56.

Rychlak, J. F. (1993). A suggested principle of complimentarity for psychology: In theory not method. *American Psychologist, 48,* 933–942.

Ryff, C. D. (1989a). Beyond Ponce de Leon and life satisfaction: New directions in quest of successful aging. *International Jouurnal of Behavioral Development, 12,* 35–55.

Ryff, C. D. (1989b). In the eyes of the beholder: Views of psychological well-being among middle-aged and older adults. *Psychology and Aging, 4,* 195–210.

Ryff, C. D. (1991). Possible selves in adulthood and old age: A tale of shifting horizons. *Psychology and Aging, 6,* 286–295.

Ryff, C. D., & Essex, M. J. (1992). Psychological well-being in adulthood and old age: Descriptive markers and explanatory processes. *Annual Review of Gerontology and Geriatrics 11,* 144–171.

Ryff, C. D., & Keys, C.-L. M. (1995). The structure of psychological well-being revisited. *Journal of Personality and Social Psychology, 69,* 719–727.

Sagan, L. A. (1987). What is hormesis and why haven't we heard about it before? *Health Physics, 52,* 521–533.

Sagy, S., & Antonovsky, A. (1994). The reality worlds of retirees: An Israeli case-control study. *Journal of Psychology, 128,* 111–128.

Salthouse, T. A. (1991). *Theoretical perspectives on cognitive aging.* Hillsdale, NJ: Erlbaum.

Sanders, C. M. (1993). Risk factors in bereavement outcome. In M. S. Stroebe, W. Stroebe, & R. O. Hansson (Eds.), *Handbook of bereavement: Theory, research, and intervention* (pp. 255–267). New York: Cambridge University Press.

Sapolsky, R. M. (1992). *Stress, the aging brain, and the mechanisms of neuron death.* Cambridge, MA: MIT Press.

Sapolsky, R. M. (1990). Adrenocortical function, social rank, and personality among wild baboons. *Biological Psychiatry, 28*(10), 862–878.

Sapolsky, R., & McEwen, B. (1988). Why dexamethasone resistance: Two possible neuroendocrine mechanisms. In A. Schatzberg & C. Nemeroff (Eds.), *The hypothalamic–pituitary–adrenal axis: Physiology, pathophysiology and psychiatric implications* (pp. 155–171). New York: Raven.

Sappington, A. A. (1990). Recent psychological approaches to the free will versus determinism issue. *Psychological Bulletin, 108,* 19–29.

Sarason, I. G., Pierce, G. R., & Sarason, B. R. (1994). General and specific perceptions of social support. In W. R. Avison & I. H. Gotlib (Eds.), *Stress and mental health: Contemporary issues and prospects for the future* (pp. 151–177). New York: Plenum Press.

Schachter, S. (1959). *The psychology of affiliation: Experimental studies of the sources of gregariousness.* Stanford, CA: Stanford University Press.

Schaefer, J. A., & Moos, R. H. (1992). Life crises and personal growth. In B. N. Carpenter (Ed.), *Personal coping: Theory, research, and application* (pp. 149–170). Westport, CT: Praeger.

Schaie, K. W., & Willis, S. L. (1991). *Adult development and aging* (3rd ed.). Boston: Little, Brown.

Schaie, K. W., & Willis, S. L. (1996). *Adult development and aging* (4th ed.). New York: HarperCollins.

Scharlach, A. E., Runkle, M. C., Midanik, L. T., & Soghikian, K. (1994). Health conditions and service utilization of adults with elder care responsibilities. *Journal of Aging and Health, 6,* 336–352.

Scheer, B. T. (1953). *General physiology* (2nd ed.). New York: Wiley.

Schiavi, R. C., Schreiner-Engle, P., Mandeli, J., Schanzer, H., et al. (1990). Healthy aging and male sexual functions. *American Journal of Psychiatry, 147,* 766–771.

Schiavi, R. C., Schreiner-Engle, P., White, D., & Mandeli, J. (1991). The relationship between pituitary–gonadal function and sexual behavior in healthy aging men. *Psychosomatic Medicine, 53,* 363–374.

Schiavi, R. C., & Seagraves, R. T. (1995). The biology of sexual functions. *Psychiatric Clinics of North America, 18,* 7–23.

Schneiderman, N., McCabe, P., & Baum, A. (Eds.). (1992). *Stress and disease processes.* Hillsdale, NJ: Erlbaum.

Schreiner-Engle, P., Schiavi, R. C., White, D., & Ghizzani, A. (1989). Low sexual desire in women: The role of reproductive hormones. *Hormones and Behavior, 23,* 221–234.

Schroots, J. J. F., & Birren, J. E. (1990). Concepts of time and aging in science. In J. E. Birren & K. W. Schaie (Eds.), *Handbook of the psychology of aging* (3rd ed., pp. 45–64). San Diego: Academic Press.

Schultz, D. (1977). *Growth psycholgy: Models of the healthy personality.* New York: Van Nostrand Reinhold.

Schulz, R., Heckhausen, J., & Locher, J. L. (1991). Adult development, control and adaptive functioning. *Journal of Social Issues, 47*(4), 177–196.

Schulz, R., O'Brien, A. T., Bookwala, J., & Fleissner, K. (1995). Psychiatric and physical morbidity effects of dementia caregiving: Prevalence, correlates, and causes. *Gerontologist, 35,* 771–791.

Schulz, R., Visintainer, P., & Williamson, G. M. (1990). Psychiatric and physical morbidity effects of caregiving. *Journals of Gerontology, 45,* P181–P191.

Schulz, R., & Williamson, G. M. (1991). A 2-year longitudinal study of depression among Alzheimer caregivers. *Psychology and Aging, 6,* 569–578.

Schwartz, J. B., Gibb, W. J., & Tran, T. (1991). Aging effects on heart rate variation. *Journals of Gerontology, 46,* M99–M106.

Schwarzer, R. (1992). Self-efficacy in the adoption and maintenance of health behaviors: Theoretical approaches and a new model. In R. Schwarzer (Eds.), *Self-efficacy: Thought control of action* (pp. 217–243). Washington: Hemisphere.

Schwarzer, R., & Leppin, A. (1991). Social support and health: A theoretical and empirical overview. *Journal of Social and Personal Relationships, 8,* 99–127.

Schwarzer, R. & Schwarzer, C. (1996). A critical survey of coping instruments. In M. Zeidner & N. S. Endler (Eds.), *Handbook of coping: Theory, research, and applications* (pp. 107–132). New York: Wiley.

Seligman, M. E. P. (1991). *Learned optimism.* New York: Knopf.

Selye, H. (1946). The general adaptation syndrome and the diseases of adaptation. *Journal of Clinical Endocrinology, 6,* 117–230.

Selye, H. (1956). *The stress of life.* New York: McGraw-Hill.

Selye, H. (1974). *Stress without distress.* Philadelphia: Lippincott.

Selye, H. (1982). History and present status of the stress concept. In L. Goldberger & S. Breznitz (Eds.), *Handbook of stress: Theoretical and clinical aspects* (pp. 7–17). New York: Free Press.

Sharma, R. P., Pandey, G. N., Janicak, P. G., Peterson, J., et al. (1988). The effects of diagnosis and age on the DST: A metaanalytic aproach. *Biological Psychiatry, 24,* 555–568.

Shaver, K. G. (1992). Blame avoidance: Toward an attributional intervention program. In L. Montada, S.-H. Filipp, & M. J. Lerner (Eds.), *Life crises and experiences of loss in adulthood* (pp. 163–178). Hillsdale, NJ: Erlbaum.

Shephard, R. J. (1987). *Physical activity and aging* (2nd ed.). Rockville, MD: Aspen.

Shewchuk, R. M., Foelker, G. A., Camp, C. J., & Blanchard-Field, F. (1992). Factorial invariance issues in the study of adult personality: An example using Levenson's locus of control scale. *Experimental Aging Research, 18,* 15–24.

Shewchuk, R. M., Foelker, G. A., & Niederehe, G. (1990). Measuring locus of control in elderly persons. *International Journal of Aging and Human Development, 30,* 213–224.

Shifflett, P. A., & McIntosh, W. A. (1986). Food habits and future time: An exploratory study of age-appropriate food habits among the elderly. *International Journal of Aging and Human Development, 24,* 1–16.

Shock, N. W. (1977). System integration. In C. E. Finch & L. Hayflick (Eds.), *Handbook of the biology of aging* (pp. 639–665). New York: Van Nostrand Reinhold.

Shuchter, S. R., & Zisook, S. (1993). The course of normal grief. In M. S. Stroebe, W. Stroebe, & R. O. Hansson (Eds.), *Handbook of bereavement: Theory, re-*

search, and intervention (pp. 23–43). New York: Cambridge University Press.

Sidney, K. H., & Shephard, R. J. (1977). Perception of exertion in the elderly. Effects of aging, mode of exercise, and physical training. *Perceptual and Motor Skills, 44,* 999–1010.

Silver, A. J., & Morley, J. E. (1992). Role of the opioid system in the hypodipsia associated with aging. *Journal of the American Geriatrics Society, 40,* 556–560.

Silverstein, M., & Litwak, E. (1993). A task-specific typology of intergenerational family structure in later life. *Gerontologist, 33,* 258–264.

Silverstein, M., & Zablotsky, D. L. (1996). Health and social precursors of later life retirement-community migration. *Journal of Gerontology Series B: Psychological and Social Sciences, 51B,* S150–S156.

Simon, H. (1995). The information-processing theory of mind. *American Psychologist, 50,* 507–508.

Skaff, M. M., & Pearlin, L. I. (1992). Caregiving: Role engulfment and the loss of self. *Gerontologist, 32,* 656–664.

Skinner, B. F. (1987). *Upon further reflection.* Englewood Cliffs, NJ: Prentice Hall.

Slife, B. D., & Williams, R. N. (1995). *What's behind the research: Discovering hidden assumptions in the behavioral sciences.* Thousand Oaks, CA: Sage.

Smedslund, J. (1991). The pseudoempirical in psychology and the case for psychologic. *Psychological Inquiry, 2,* 325–338.

Smith, J., & Baltes, P. B. (1993). Differential psychological ageing: Profiles of the old and very old. *Ageing and Society, 13,* 551–587.

Smith, L. N., Patterson, T. L., & Grant, I. (1990). Avoidant coping predicts psychological disturbance in the elderly. *Journal of Nervous and Mental Disease, 178,* 525–530.

Smith, T. W., & Williams, P. G. (1992). Personality and health: Advantages and limitations of the five-factor model. *Journal of Personality, 60,* 395–423.

Smits, C. H. M., Deeg, D. J. H., & Bosscher, R. J. (1995). Well-being and control in older persons: The prediction of well-being from control measures. *International Journal of Aging and Human Development, 40,* 237–251.

Solomon, L. R., & Lye, M. (1990). Hypernatraemia in the elderly patient. *Gerontology, 36,* 171–179.

Sonderegger, T. B. (Ed.). (1992). Psychology of aging. *Nebraska Symposium on Motivation, 39.*

Sorkin, B. A., Rudy, T. E., Hanlon, R. B., Turk, D. C., *et al.* (1990). Chronic pain in old and young patients: Differences appear less important than similarities. *Journals of Gerontology, 45,* P64–P68.

Spangler, W. D. (1992). Validity of questionnaire and TAT measures of need for achievement: Two meta-analyses. *Psychological Bulletin, 112,* 140–154.

Speake, D. L., Cowart, M. E., & Pellet, K. (1989). Health perceptions and lifesyles of the elderly. *Research in Nursing and Health, 12,* 93–100.

Spence, J. T., & Helmreich, R. L. (1983). Achievement-related motives and behaviors. In J. T. Spence (Ed.), *Achievement and achievement motives: Psy-*

chological and sociological approaches (pp. 1–74). San Francisco: Free-man.

Spiro, A., III., Schnurr, P. P., & Aldwyn, C. M. (1994). Combat-related posttrau-matic stress disorder symptoms in older men. *Psychology and Aging, 9,* 17–26.

Stagner, R. (1977). Homeostasis, discrepancy, dissonance: A theory of motives and motivation. *Motivation and Emotion, 1,* 103–138.

Stagner, R. (1985). Aging in industry. In J. E. Birren, & K W. Schaie (Eds.), *Handbook of the psychology of aging* (2nd ed, pp. 789–817). New York: Van Nostrand Reinhold.

Stanley, D., & Freysinger, V. J. (1995). The impact of age, health, and sex on the frequency of older adults' leisure activity participation: A longitudinal study. *Activities, Adaptation, and Aging, 19*(3), 31–42.

Starr, B. D. (1985). Sexuality and aging. *Annual Review of Gerontology and Geriatrics, 5,* 97–126.

Staudinger, U., & Baltes, P. B. (1996). Interactive minds: A facilitative setting for wisdom-related performance? *Journal of Personality and Social Psychology, 71,* 746–762.

Stebbins, R. A. (1992). *Amateurs, professionals, and serious leisure.* Montreal: McGill–Queen's University Press.

Stebbins, R. A. (1996). Volunteering: A serious leisure perspective. *Nonprofit and Voluntary Sector Quarterly, 25,* 211–224.

Steinbach, U. (1992). Social networks, institutionalization, and mortality among elderly people in the United States. *Journals of Gerontology, 47,* S183–S190.

Steinkee, E. E. (1994). Knowledge and attitudes of older adults about sexuality in aging: A comparison of two studies. *Journal of Advanced Nursing, 19,* 477–485.

Stenback, A. (1980). Depression and suicidal behavior in old age. In J. E. Birren & R. B. Sloan (Eds.), *Handbook of mental health and aging* (pp. 616–652). Englewood Cliffs, NJ: Prentice Hall.

Sternbach, R. A. (1978). Psychological dimensions and perceptual analyses, in-cluding pathologies of pain. In E. C. Carterette & M. P. Friedman (Eds.), *Handbook of perception* (Vol. VIB): *Feeling and hurting* (pp. 231–261). New York: Academic Press.

Stevens, D. P., & Truss, C. V. (1985). Stability and change in adult personality over 12 and 20 years. *Developmental Psychology, 21,* 568–584.

Stoller, E. P. (1993). Interpretations of symptoms by older people: A health diary study of illness behavior. *Journal of Aging and Health, 5,* 58–81.

Stoller, E. P., & Forster, L. E. (1994). The impact of symptom interpretation on physician utilization. *Journal of Aging and Health, 6,* 507–534.

Stoller, E. P., & Pugliesi, K. L. (1989). The transition to the caregiving role: A panel study of helpers of elderly people. *Research on Aging, 11,* 312–320.

Stone, A. A. (1992). Selected methodological concepts: Mediation and moder-ation individual differences, aggregation strategies, and variability of replicates. In N. Schneiderman, P. McCabe, & A. Baum (Eds.)., *Stress and disease processes: Perspective in behavioral medicine* (pp. 55–72). Hillsdale, NJ: Erlbaum.

Strack, S., & Feifel, H. (1996). Age differences, coping, and the adult life span. In M. Zeidner & N. S. Endler (Eds.), *Handbook of coping: Theory, research, and applications* (pp. 485–501). New York: Wiley.

Strain, L. A. (1991). Use of health services in later life: The influence of health beliefs. *Journals of Gerontology, 46,* 143–150.

Streib, G. F. (1993). The life course of activities and retirement communities. In J. R. Kelly (Ed.), *Activity and aging: Staying involved in later life* (pp. 246–263). Newbury Park, CA: Sage.

Stroebe, M. S., Gergen, M. M., Gergen, K. J., & Stroebe, W. (1992). Broken hearts or broken bonds: Love and death in historical perspective. *American Psychologist, 47,* 1205–1212.

Stroebe, M. S., Hansson, R. O., & Stroebe, W. (1993). Contemporary themes and controversies in bereavement research. In M. S. Stroebe, W. Stroebe, & R. O. Hansson (Eds.), *Handbook of bereavement: Theory, research, and intervention* (pp. 457–475). New York: Cambridge University Press.

Stroebe, M. S., & Stroebe, W. (1993). The mortality of berreavement: A review. In M. S. Stroebe, W. Stroebe, & R. O. Hansson (Eds.), *Handbook of bereavement: Theory, research, and intervention* (pp. 175–195). New York: Cambridge University Press.

Stroebe, M. S., Stroebe, W., & Hansson, R. O. (Eds.). (1993). *Handbook of bereavement: Theory, research, and intervention.* New York: Cambridge University Press.

Stylianos, S. K., & Vachon, L. S. (1993). The role of social support in bereavement. In M. S. Stroebe, W. Stroebe, & R. O. Hansson (Eds.), *Handbook of bereavement: Theory, research, and intervention* (pp. 397–410). New York: Cambridge University Press.

Subbotsky, E. (1995). The development of pragmatic and non-pragmatic motivation. *Human Development, 38,* 217–234.

Sussman, M. B. (1976). The family life of old people. In R. H. Binstock & E. Shanas (Eds.), *Handbook of aging and the social sciences* (pp. 218–243). New York: Van Nostrand Reinhold.

Talbert, G. B. (1977). Aging of the reproductive system. In C. E. Finch & L. Hayflick (Eds.), *Handbook of the biology of aging* (pp. 318–356). New York: Van Nostrand Reinhold.

Talbott, M. M. (1990). The negative side of the relationship between older widows and their adult children: A mother's perspective. *Gerontologist, 30,* 595–603.

Talkington-Boyer, S., & Snyder, D. K. (1994). Assessing impact on family caregivers to Alzheimer's disease patients. *American Journal of Family Therapy, 22,* 57–66.

Taylor, S. E., & Aspinwall, L. G. (1996). Mediating and moderating processes in psychosocial stress: Appraisal, coping, resistance, and vulnerability. In

H. B. Kaplan (Ed.), *Psychosocial stress: Perspectives on structure, theory, life course, and methods* (pp. 71–110). San Diego: Academic Press.

Tesser, A., Martin, L. L., & Cornell, D. P. (1996). On the substitutability of self-protective mechanism. In P. M. Gollwitzer & J. A. Bargh (Eds.), *The psychology of action: Linking cognition and motivation to behavior* (pp. 48–68). New York: Guilford.

Thayer, R. E. (1989). *The psychobiology of mood and arousal.* New York: Oxford University Press.

Thoits, P. A. (1991). Patterns in coping with controllable and uncontrollable events. In E. M. Cummings, A. L.Greene, & K. H. Karraker (Eds.), *Life-span developmental psychology: Perspectives on stress and coping* (pp. 235–258). Hillsdale, NJ: Erlbaum.

Thomas, L. E. (1982). Sexuality and aging: Essential vitamin or popcorn? *Gerontologist, 22,* 240–243.

Thompson, L. W., Gong, V., Haskins, E., & Gallagher, D. (1987). Assessment of depression and dementia during the late years. *Annual Review of Gerontology and Geriatrics, 7,* 295–324.

Thompson, R. A. (1992). Maturing the study of aging: Discussant's comments. *Nebraska Symposium on Motivation, 39,* 245–259.

Timiras, P. S. (1988). *Physiological basis of geriatrics.* New York: Macmillan.

Timko, C., & Moos, R. H. (1989). Choice, control, and adaptation among elderly residents of sheltered care settings. *Journal of Applied Social Psychology, 19,* 636–655.

Tinsley, H. E., Teaff, J. D., Colby, S. L., & Kaufman, N. (1985). A system for classifying leisure activities in terms of the psychological benefits of participation reported by older persons. *Journal of Gerontology, 40,* 172–178.

Tokarski, W. (1993). Later life activity from European perspectives. In J. R. Kelly (Ed.), *Activity and aging: Staying involved in later life* (pp. 60–67). Newbury Park, CA: Sage.

Tornstam, L. (1992). The quo vadis of gerontology: On the scientific paradigm of gerontology. *Gerontologist, 32,* 318–326.

Tran, V. L., Wright, Jr., & Chatters, L. (1991). Health, stress, psychological resources, and subjective well-being among older blacks. *Psychology and Aging, 6,* 100–108.

Troll, L. E. (1980). Interpersonal relations: Introduction. In L. W. Poon (Eds.), *Aging in the 1980's* (pp. 435–440). Washington, DC: American Psychological Association Press.

Trumbull, R., & Appley, M. H. (1986). A conceptual model for the examination of stress dynamics. In M. H. Appley & R. Trumbull (Eds.), *Dynamics of stress: Physiological, psychological, and social perspectives* (pp. 21–45). New York: Plenum Press.

Turk, D. C., & Melzack, R. (Eds.). (1992). *Handbook of pain assessment.* New York: Guilford.

Turner, B. F. (1988). Reported changes in preferred sexual activity over the adult years. *Journal of Sex Research, 25,* 289–303.

Turner, R. J., & Wheaton, B. (1995). Checklist measurement of stressful life events. In S. Cohen, R. C. Kessler, & L. U. Gordon (Eds.), *Measuring stress: A guide for health and social scientists* (pp. 29–58). New York: Oxford University Press.

Uchino, B. N., Kiecolt-Glaser, J. K., & Cacioppo, J. T. (1992). Age-related changes in cardiovascular response as a function of chronic stressor and social support. *Journal of Personality and Social Psychology, 63,* 839–846.

Umberson, D. (1992). Gender, marital status, and the social control of health behavior. *Social Science and Medicine, 34,* 907–917.

U.S. Bureau of the Census. (1996). *Current population reports: Special studies 65+ in the United States* (pp. 23–190). Washington, DC: U.S. Government Printing Office.

Vallerand, R. J., O'Connor, B. P., & Hamel, M. (1995). Motivation in later life: Theory and assessment. *International Journal of Aging and Human Development, 41,* 221–238.

Vande Kemp, H. (1996). Historical perspective: Religion and clinical psychology in America. In E. P. Shafranske (Ed.), *Religion and the clinical practice of psychology* (pp. 71–112). Washington, DC: American Psychological Association Press.

Van den Berg, C. J. (1986). On the relation between energy transformations on the brain and mental activities. In G. R. J. Hockey, M. G. H. Coles, & A. W. K. Gaillard (Eds.), *Energetics and human information processing* (pp. 131–135). Dordrecht, Netherlands: Nijhoff.

Verbrugge, L. M., Gruber-Baldini, A. L., & Fozard, J. L. (1996). Age differences and age changes in activities: Baltimore Longitudinal Study. *Journal of Gerontology Series B: Psychological and Social Sciences, 51B,* S30–S41.

Vermeulen, A. (1991). Androgens in the aging male. *Journal of Endocrinology and Metabolism, 73,* 221–224.

Veroff, J., Atkinson, J. W., Feld, S. C., & Gurin, G. (1960). The use of thematic apperception to assess motivation in a nationwide inerview study. *Psychological Monographs, 74* (Whole No. 499).

Veroff, J, Reuman, D., & Feld, S. (1984). Motives in American men and women across the adult life span. *Developmental Psychology, 20,* 1142–1158.

Vitaliano, P. P., Russo, J., Bailey, S. L., Young, H. M., & Mc Cann, B. S. (1993). Psychosocial factors associated with cardiovascular reactivity in older adults. *Psychosomatic Medicine, 55,* 64–177.

Vitaliano, P. P., Russo, J., Young, H. M., Teri, L. & Maiuro, R. D. (1991). Predictors of burden in spouse caregivers of individuals with Alzheimer's disease. *Psychology and Aging, 6,* 392–402.

Vitiello, M. V., Prinz, P. N., Avery, D. H., Williams, D. E., et al. (1990). Sleep is undisturbed in elderly, depressed individuals who have not sought health care. *Biological Psychiatry, 27,* 431–440.

Von Korff, M. (1992). Epidemiologic survey methods: Chronic pain assessment. In D. C. Turk & R. Melzack (Eds.), *Handbook of pain assessment* (pp. 391–408). New York: Guilford.

von Mering, O., & Weniger, F. L. (1959) Social-cultural background in the aging individual. In J. Birren (Eds.), *Handbook of aging and the individual* (pp. 279–335). Chicago: University of Chicago Press.

Walker, S. N., Volkan, K., Sechrist, K. R., & Pender, N. J. (1988). Health-promoting life styles of older adults: Comparisons with young and middle-aged adults, correlates and patterns. *Advances in Nursing Science, 11,* 76–90.

Waller, K. V., & Bates, R. C. (1992). Health locus of control and self-efficacy beliefs in a healthy elderly sample. *American Journal of Health Promotion, 6,* 302–309.

Walz, T. H., & Blum, N. S. (1987). *Sexual health in later life.* Lexington, MA: Lexington Books.

Wang, H. S., & Busse, E. W. (1975), Correlates of regional cerebral blood flow in elderly community residents. In A. M. Harper, W. B. Jennett, J. D. Miller, & J. O. Rowan (Eds.), *Blood flow and metabolism in the brain* (pp. 8.17–8.18). London: Churchill Livingstone.

Warburton, D. M. (1986). A state model for mental effort. In G. R. J. Hockey, M. G. H. Coles, & A. W. K. Gaillard (Eds.), *Energetics and human information processing* (pp. 217–232). Dordrecht, Netherlands: Nijhoff.

Watson, D., & Pennebaker, J. W. (1989). Health complaints, stress, and distress. Exploring the central role of negative affectivity. *Psychological Review, 96,* 234–254.

Watson, R. I. (1978). *The Great Psychologists* (4th ed.). New York: Harper & Row.

Weber, M. (1958). *The Protestant ethic and the spirit of capitalism.* New York: Scribner.

Weinberger, J. L. (1994). Can personality change? In T. F. Heatherton & J. L. Weinberger (Eds.), *Can personality change?* (pp. 333–350). Washington, DC: American Psychological Association.

Weiner, B. (1992). *Human motivation: Metaphors, theories, and research.* Newbury Park, CA: Sage.

Weiner, H. (1992). *Perturbing the organism: The biology of stressful experience.* Chicago: University of Chicago Press.

Weiner, M. F. (1989). Age and cortical suppression by dexamethasone in normal subjects. *Journal of Psychiatric Research, 23,* 163–168.

Weinstein, N. D. (1993). Testing four competing theories of health-protective behavior. *Health Psychology, 12,* 324–333.

Weisenberg, M. (1977). Pain and pain control. *Psychological Bulletin, 84,* 1008–1044.

Weisse, C. S. (1992). Depression and immunocompetence: A review of the literature. *Psychological Bulletin, 111,* 475–489.

Weisz, J. R. (1982). Can I control it? The pursuit of veridical answers across the life span. In P. B. Baltes & O. G. Brim, Jr. (Eds.), *Life-span development and behavior* (pp. 234–300). New York: Academic Press.

Welford, A. T. (1958). *Aging and human skill.* London: Oxford University Press.

Welford, A. T. (1992). Psychological studies of aging: Their origins, development, and present challenge. *International Journal of Aging and Human Development, 34,* 185–197.

Wenger, G. C., Davies, R., Shabtahmasebi, S., & Scott, A. (1996). Social isolation and loneliness in old age: Review and model refinement. *Aging and Society, 16,* 333–358.

Wethington, E., Brown, G. W., & Kessler, R. C. (1995). Interview measurement of stressful life events. In S. Cohen, R. C. Kessler, & L. U. Gordon (Eds.), *Measuring stress: A guide for health and social scientists* (pp. 29–70). New York: Oxford University Press.

Wheaton, B. (1996). The domains and boundaries of the stress concept. In B. Kaplan (Ed.), *Psychosocial stress: Perspectives on structure, theory, life course, and methods* (pp. 29–70). San Diego: Academic Press.

White, R. W. (1959). Motivation reconsidered: The concept of competence. *Psychological Review, 66,* 297–333.

Widlocher, D. (1982). La notion de fatigue. *Psychologie Medicale, 14,* 1979–1980.

Wigdor, B. T. (1980). Drives and motivations with aging. In J. E. Birren, & R. B. Sloan (Eds.), *Hanbook of mental health and aging* (pp. 245–261). Englewood Cliffs, NJ: Prentice Hall.

Wiggins, J. S., & Pincus, A. L. (1992). Personality strucure and assessment. *Annual Review of Psychology, 43,* 473–504.

Williamson, G. M., & Schulz, R. (1992a). Pain, activity restrictions, and symptoms of depression among community-residing elderly adults. *Journals of Gerontology, 47,* P367–P372.

Williamson, G. M., & Schulz, R. (1992b). Physical illness and symptoms of depression among elderly outpatients. *Psychology and Aging, 7,* 343–351.

Williamson, G. M., & Schulz, R. (1995). Activity restriction mediates the association between pain and depressed affect: A study of younger and older adult cancer patients. *Psychology and Aging, 10,* 369–378.

Willis, S. L. (1992). Cognition and everyday competence. *Annual Review of Gerontology and Geriatrics, 11,* 80–109.

Wills, T. A. (1991). "Peer support telephone dyads for elderly women: Was this the wrong intervention?": Comment. *American Journal of Community Psychology, 19,* 75–83.

Winn, R. L., & Newton, N. (1982). Sexuality in aging: A study of 106 cultures. *Archives of Sexual Behavior, 11,* 283–298.

Wiseman, R. F. (1980). Why older people move: Theoretical issues. *Research on Aging, 2,* 141–154.

Wolinsky, F. D. (1990). *Health and health behavior among elderly Americans: An age-stratification perspective.* New York: Springer.

Wolinsky, F., & Arnold, C. L. (1988). A different perspective on health and health services utilization. *Annual Review of Gerontology and Geriatrics, 8,* 71–101.

Wolinsky, F. D., & Johnson, R. J. (1992). Perceived health status and mortality among older men and women. *Journals of Gerontology, 47,* S304–S312.

Wong, D. F., Broussolle, E. P., Wand, G., Villemagne, V., et al. (1988). *In vivo* measurement of dopamine receptors in the human brain by position emission tomography: Age and sex differences. *Annals of the New York Academy of Sciences, 515,* 203–214.

Wood, L. A. (1989). Social relationships among the rural elderly: A multi-method approach. In L. E. Thomas (Ed.), *Research on adulthood and aging: The human science approach* (pp. 205–224). Albany: State University of New York Press.

Woodruff-Pak, D. S. (1985). Arousal, sleep and aging. In J. E. Birren & K. W. Schaie (Eds.), *Handbook of the psychology of aging* (2nd ed., pp. 261–295). New York: Van Nostrand Reinhold.

Woodworth, R. S. (1938). *Experimental psychology.* New York: Holt.

Worthington, E. L., Kurusu, T. A., McCollogh, M. E., & Sandage, S. J. (1996). Empirical research on religion and psychotherapeutic processes and outcomes: A 10-year review and research prospectus. *Psychological Bulletin, 119,* 448–487.

Wortman, C. B., & Silver, R. C. (1989). The myths of coping with loss. *Journal of Consulting and Clinical Psychology, 57,* 349–357.

Wright, R. A., Brehm, J. W., Crutcher, W., Evans, M. T., & Jones, A. (1990). Avoidant control difficulty and aversive incentive appraisals: Additional evidence of an energization effect. *Motivation and Emotion, 14,* 45–73.

Wundt, W. (1887). *Grundzüge der physiologischen Psychologie* (3rd ed.). Leipzig: Engelmann.

Wurtman, J. J., Lieberman, H., Tsay, R., Nader, T., *et al.* (1988). Calorie and nutrient intakes of elderly and young subjects measured under identical conditions. *Journals of Gerontology, 43,* B174–B180.

Wysocki, C. J., & Gilbert, A. N. (1989). *National Geographic* smell survey: Effects of age are heterogeneous. *Annals of the New York Academy of Sciences, 561,* 12–28.

Yates, F. E., & Benton, L. A. (1995). Loss of integration and resiliency with age: A dissipative destruction. In E. J. Massoro (Ed.), *Handbook of physiology: Section 11. Aging* (pp. 591–610). New York: Oxford University Press.

Young, P. T. (1961). *Motivation and emotion.* New York: Wiley.

Zarit, S. H., Reevers, K. E., & Bach-Peterson, J. (1980). Relatives of the impaired elderly: Correlates of burden. *Gerontologist, 20,* 649–655.

Zarit, S. H., & Teri, L. (1992). Interventions and services for family caregivers. *Annual Review of Gerontology and Geriatrics, 11,* 287–310.

Zautra, A. J., Affleck, G., & Tennen, H. (1994). Assessing life events among older adults. *Annual Review of Gerontology, 14,* 324–352.

Zeidner, M., & Saklofske, D. (1996). Adaptive and maladaptive coping. In M. Zeidner & N. S. Endler (Eds.), *Handbook of coping: Theory, research and applications* (pp. 505–531). New York: Wiley.

Zika, S., & Chamberlain, K. (1992). On the relation between meaning in life and psychological well-being. *British Journal of Psychology, 83,* 133–145.

Zuckerman, M. (1995). Good and bad humors: Biochemical bases of personality and its disorders. *Psychological Science, 6,* 325–332.

Zung, W. W. K. (1980). Affective disorders. In E. W. Busse & D. G. Blazer (Eds.), *Handbook of geriatric psychiatry* (pp. 338–367). New York: Van Nostrand Reinhold.

Index

Acetylcholine, 25
Achievement motivation, 279–287
  cultural factors in, 281–283, 287
  measurement of, 280–282, 287
  relationship to goals, 284–286
  vicarious, 287
Activation, 37–38
Activities
  age-differentiated, 304
  autotelic, 293–294
  of older people, 272–273
  time-budget continuum of, 295–296
  see also Leisure
Activities of daily living (ADLs) impair-
     ments, as stress cause, 208
Activities of Daily Living Scale, 212
Activity theory, of social relationships,
     267, 275, 276
Adaptation
  cognition in, 8
  as coping, 188, 189, 190, 193, 204
  to loss, 285–286
  to stress, 143
Adenosine triphosphatase, 55
Adjustment, 188, 322
Adler, Alfred, 249
Adrenal cortex, 28–29
Adrenal medulla, 29–30
Adrenocorticotrophic hormone (ACTH),
     27, 28, 29
Adult education, 311–312
Affective disorders, sleep patterns in, 46–47
African Americans, health behaviors of, 133
Aging
  "Alzheimerization" of, 18–19, 322
  biomarkers of, 14–15

Aging (*cont.*)
  cellular, 27
  continuum of, 18
  definitions of, 14–17
  existential theories of, 248
  normal, differentiated from pathologi-
    cal, 68–69
  psychological markers of, 15–17
  sociological markers of, 15–17
  stress of, 154–156
  successful, 2, 10, 110, 252, 325
    possible selves and, 244
    self-concept in, 240, 246
Alcmaeon, 107
Allport, G.W., 8, 247
Altruism, 175–176
  in caregiving, 217
  in volunteering, 317, 318–329, 320
Alzheimer's disease
  cerebral metabolism in, 24
  choline acetyltransferase in, 25
  cognitive function in, effect of sleep on,
    48
  dopamine in, 26
  eating habits in, 84
  hypercortisolism in, 28–29
  neural plaques of, 40
Alzheimer's disease patients
  caregivers for, 208–209, 210–211,
    220–221
  age of, 219–220
  depression in, 219
  motivation of, 216–217
"Alzheimerization," of aging, 18–19, 322
American Psychological Association
  (APA), 325–326

Androgens, 95
Anemia, 35
Anger, testosterone in, 33
Animal experimentation, in motivation
     research, 7–8, 12
*Annual Review of Gerontology and Geri-
     atrics*, 100–101
Annual Review of Psychology, 4, 9, 11–12,
     147
Anorexia, 31, 83
Antibodies, 34
Antidepressants, as fatigue cause, 55–56
Antihistamines, as fatigue cause, 55–56
Antonovsky, H., 150–151
Anxiety
     during competitive situations, 166–168
     coping and, 191
     death-related, 250
     pain perception and, 74
Apathy, 250
Appetite
     in illness, 84
     see also Anorexia; Eating
Aristippos, 65
Aristotle, 2, 4, 202, 233, 289, 296
Arousal
     cerebral metabolism in, 23
     emotional, 121, 268–269
     energetic, 52
Arthritis, 35
     effect on eating habits, 84
     effect on leisure activities, 309–310
Atomic bomb survivors, 146
Attachment, 259
     differentiated from social support, 266
     intrinsic motive for, 263–264
     in parent–child relationship, 274
     relationship to dependency, 270
Attention-demanding task performance,
     effect of fatigue on, 56
Autoantibodies, 35
Autobiography, 248, 256–257
Autoimmune disease, 35
Autonomic nervous system
     in arousal, 23
     effect of stress on, 161–169, 185
Autonomy, 285
     consciousness and, 247
     during development, 243, 274–275

Autonomy (*cont.*)
     during retirement, 303
     in Western societies, 115
Autotelic activities, 293–294
Avoidance behavior, 191, 195

Basal metabolic rate (BMR), 21
Baumeister, R.F., 252
B cells, 35
Beck Depression Inventory, 59
Behavior, age factors in, 1–2, 10
Behavioral medicine, 111–112
Behaviorism, 8, 188, 232, 279
Beliefs, 324
Bereavement
     coping with, 223
     definition of, 222
     as stress cause, 222–230
          measurement of, 223–225
          effect of social support on, 225–226
Bible, 2, 74
Biological Abstracts, 140
Biological deterioration, age-related, 267,
     322
Biological factors, in aging, 21–40
     cardiovascular functions, 37–39, 40
     cerebral metabolism, 22–24
     endocrine system, 27–37
     neurotransmitters, 24–26
Biological theories, of stress, 144–147,
     184–185
Biomarkers, for aging, 14–16
Blood flow
     cerebral, 22–24
     diastolic, during cognitive tasks,
          163–164, 165
     systolic
          aging-related increase in, 38
          during cognitive tasks, 163, 164, 165
Body fat, effect on glucose tolerance, 32
Body-self neuromatrix, 74
Boredom, 250
Bourque, P.E., 296–297
BP: *See* Blood pressure
Brain
     metabolic activity of, 22–24
     see also Central nervous system
Brown-Sequard, Charles, 32
"Busy ethic," 291

Caloric intake, aging-related decrease in, 84–85
Cancer, immune dysfunction as risk factor for, 35
Carbohydrate metabolism, 31–32
Cardiac output, 38, 54
Cardiovascular disease
  personality factors in, 111–112
  sexual behavior in, 99, 100
Cardiovascular reactivity, stress-related, 162–169, 185
Cardiovascular system, aging-related changes in, 37–39, 40
Caregivers
  for Alzheimer's disease patients, 208–209, 210–211, 220–221
  age of, 219–220
  depression in, 219
  motivation of, 216–217
  bereavement in, 227–228
  burden of, 210, 211, 212–213, 214, 217–218, 220
  coping by, 211, 213
  for dementia patients, 209
  health of, 215–216
  loss of self by, 219–220
  for older parents, 174, 210, 217, 219
  self-efficacy of, 214
  stress experienced by, 168–169, 209–222
    age factors in, 218–220
    models of, 210–214
    motivation and, 216–217
    outcome measurement of, 214–216
    social support effects in, 220–222
    spousal factors in, 217–218
Caregiving
  by adult children, 174, 210, 217, 219
  as leisure activity, 307
  as life satisfaction source, 211–212, 213, 214, 220, 221
  by spouse, 209–210
  as stressor, 208
Catecholamines, 25–26, 30
Cautiousness, 284
Central nervous system
  in arousal, 23
  interaction with immune system, 35
  neurotransmitters of, 24–25

Central nervous system (cont.)
  in sexual behavior function, 95
Children
  adult, as caregivers, 174, 210, 217, 219
  death of, 226, 229
Cholecystokinin, 82
Cholesterol, dietary intake of, 86
Choline acetyltransferase, 25
Churchill, Winston, 307
Circadian rhythm, of sleep, 44–46
Cognition, in adaptation, 8
Cognitive function, effect of sleepiness on, 48
Cognitive-motivational theory, 6
Cognitive-psychological theories
  of health behaviors, 112–113
  of leisure, 293
Cognitive psychology, 8, 232
Cognitive task performance
  cerebral metabolism during, 22–24
  effect of fatigue on, 56–58
Cognitive theory
  in experimental laboratory geropsychology, 170
  of stress, 147–152
Coherence, sense of, 121–122, 150–151, 251, 255
Cohort effects
  in coping, 196–197, 198, 202
  in gerontological research, 323
  in leisure, 307–309
Combat, as stress cause, 14–16, 146
Communication technology, 270
Competence, 117
  relationship to self-efficacy, 241
Computer technology, educational use of, 312
Concentration camps, 249, 251
Confidants, 273–274
Conflict, psychological, as fatigue cause, 59
Conflict resolution, as coping strategy, 202
Conscientiousness, 118
Consciousness, 247
Conservation of resources theory, of stress, 151–152
Continuity theory
  of leisure, 306–307
  of social relationships, 267, 276

Control, personal, 74
  aging-related decrease in, 177–181, 184
  as coping mechanism, 191, 199–200
  personal responsibility and, 180,
    181–183
  primary, 177, 178, 199, 238, 239
  secondary, 177, 178, 199
    cognitive adaptations in, 238–239
  self-concept and, 238–239
  self-efficacy and, 241
  sense of purpose and, 252–253
  stress and, 177–184
Conversion disorders, 50
Coping, 187–206
  anticipatory, 189
  behavior-focused, 191
  with bereavement, 223
  by caregivers, 211, 213
  cognitive, 8, 191, 192
  control and, 199–200
  definitions of, 109, 188–190, 191,
    192, 204
  emotional responsivity and, 189
  emotion-focused, 191, 192–193, 198,
    201, 213
  inappropriate, 191–192
  measurement of, 208–209
  problem-focused, 191, 192–193, 195,
    198–199, 201
  with psychosocial stressors, 108–109
  styles and strategies of, 190–197,
    204–206
    age factors in, 198–202
    assessment of, 193–194
    assimilative versus accommodative,
      199, 238
    in bereavement, 228
    cohort effects in, 196–197, 198, 202
    contextual factors in, 195
    cultural factors in, 196–197
    life transitions and, 196–197
    motivation in, 197
    noncoping, 192
    in pain, 72, 78, 200
    personality factors in, 189, 194, 196,
      197, 200
    religion, 203–204, 205–206
    relationship to stress and personal
      control, 179
    social support, 196

Coping (cont.)
  styles and strategies of (cont.)
    theories of, 190–193
    wisdom, 202–203, 205–206
Coronary artery disease, 38
Corticosteroids, interaction with insulin,
  31–32
Cortisol, 28, 28–29
Costa, P.T., 149–150, 153, 185
Counterculture movement, 112
Crisis growth, 146–147
Csikszentmihalyi, M., 293–294, 295,
  297–298
Cultural factors
  in achievement motivation, 281–283,
    287
  in bereavement, 223
  in emotional isolation, 270
  in food habits, 85–86, 87, 88–89
  in health behaviors, 110
  in health care services utilization,
    131–132
  in motivation, 324
  in mourning, 222
  in sexuality, 96–97
CV: See Cardiovascular reactivity
Cytokines, 25

Daily hassles, 157, 174, 190
  coping strategies for, 195
  definition of, 142
Darwin, Charles, 65, 144
Daughters, as caregivers, 210, 217, 219
Death
  of children, 226, 229
  of parents, 226, 229
  of spouse, 208, 226
  see also Bereavement
Death acceptance, 253, 254
Death anxiety, 250
Defense mechanisms, 201–202, 204, 234
  avoidance-related, 191
  Freudian theory of, 188, 194
Dehydration, 90
Dementia
  Alzheimer's-type: See Alzheimer's
    disease
  sleep patterns in, 45
Dementia patients, caregivers for, 209
Denial, 191

Dental health, effect on eating habits, 82, 84
Dependability, in social relationships, 261
Dependency, relationship to attachment, 270
Depression
  bereavement-related, 223–224
  in caregivers, 215, 219
  cognitive function in, effect of sleep on, 48
  as existential sickness, 250
  as fatigue cause, 50, 59, 62–63
  hormonal factors in, 28–29
  hypercortisolism in, 28–29
  immunocompetence deficit in, 36–37
  loss-related, 52–53
  during menopause, 34
  pain perception in, 75–77
  relationship to health, 127–128
  religious amotivation-related, 203–204
  sleep patterns in, 46, 47, 48
  social support and, 174
  thyroid disorders-related, 31
  as undernutrition cause, 84
Descartes, René, 6
Desires, 280
Despair, 190–191
Developmental theory, Erikson's, 190–191, 196, 243, 274–275
Dewey, John, 232
Dexamethasone suppression test, 28–29
Diabetes mellitus, 27
  effect on eating habits, 84
  effect on sexual behavior, 99, 100
Diagnostic and Statistical Manual of Mental Disorders (DSM), 59, 111
Dilthey, Wilhelm, 247
Disasters, 156
Discomfort, 65, 68
Disease
  definition of, 107
  differentiated from illness, 69
  infectious, immune factors in, 34, 35
Disengagement theory, of social relationships, 266–267, 276, 301
Distress, definition of, 142
Dominance, 284
  testosterone in, 33
Dopamine, 26
Drinking, 81, 90, 290

Drugs
  as fatigue cause, 55–56
  see also specific drugs

Eating, 81–89
  biological factors in, 81, 82–83
  economic factors in, 89
  food habits in, 85–87, 88–89
  food preferences in, 84–85, 233
  general health and, 84
  hedonic factors in, 81, 84, 87
  as leisure activity, 290
  psychosocial factors in, 83, 84, 87–89
  time spent in, 302
Ecclesiastes (XII:1–7), 2
Ecological-cognitive theory, of leisure, 295
Ecological studies, of stress and coping, 207–230
  of bereavement, 222–230
  of caregiving, 209–222
    age factors in, 218–220
    models for, 210–214
    motivation assessment in, 216–217
    outcome measurements in, 214–216
    social support effects in, 220–222
    spousal factors in, 217–218
Edwards Personal Preference Schedule, 281–282
Efficacy, 252
Egocentrism, 235
Ego integrity, 190–191, 325
Egoism, 175
Eisenhower, Dwight D., 307
Elderhostels, 312
Elders Life Stress Inventory, 47
Electrodermal response levels, during cognitive tasks, 162–164
Electroencephalogram (EEG), 42–43
Electromyogram (EMG), 55, 63–64
Electrooculogram (EOG), 42
Emotion
  fatigue and, 59
  hierarchy of, 11
  illness and, 66
  multidimensional theory of, 68
  relational theory of, 120, 191
Emotion and Adaptation (Lazarus), 189
Encyclopedic Dictionary of Psychology (Harre and Lamb), 187–188

Endocrine system, aging-related changes in, 27–34
Environmental reaction, motivation as, 5–6
Epinephrine, adrenal secretion of, 29–30
Equilibrium, 139, 154
Erectile dysfunction, 95, 99, 100
Ergonomics, 51
Erikson, Erik, developmental theory of, 190–191, 196, 243, 274–275
Escapism, as coping strategy, 198, 201, 205
Estradiol, 32–33
Estrogens, 33, 34
Exchange convoy model, of social relationships, 265–266, 268, 287
Exercise, 133, 135–137
    cardiovascular effects of, 39
    effect on glucose tolerance, 32
    intrinsic motivation for, 310
Exertion, perceived, rating of, 60–62
Exhaustion, as stress response, 53
Existentialism, 247, 248, 256
Expectancies/expectations, 238
    effect of loss on, 245
    in perception of fatigue, 61–62
    self-efficacy, 117, 118
Experience-sampling method (ESM), 294
Experimental psychology, 7–8
Experimental Psychology (Woodworth), 59
Extroversion, relationship to coping, 189

Family
    nontraditional, 260
    as social support, 261, 277
Fantasy, 280
Fat
    body content of, effect on glucose tolerance, 32
    dietary intake of, 86
Fatigue, 49–64, 69
    acute, 51
    central, 56–58
        differentiated from peripheral, 53–54
    chronic, 50, 51
    definitions of, 51–52, 56
    incidence/prevalence among older persons, 45, 49–50
    mental, 49, 56–58

Fat (cont.)
    perception of, 59–63
    peripheral, 54–56, 59–60
        differentiated from central, 53–54
    phasic, 56
    physical indices for, 55, 63–64
    as physiological impairment, 53–54
    theoretical analysis of, 52
    thyroid disorders-related, 31
Field studies, versus laboratory studies, 208–209
Financial strain, effect on perception of personal control, 180–181
Fitness: See Physical fitness
Flexible Goal Adjustment scale, 199, 205
Flight–fight reaction, 166
Flow theory, of leisure, 293–294, 300
Fluid intake, 81, 90, 290
Follicle-stimulating hormone, 33
Food, symbolic value of, 89
Food habits, 85–87, 88–89
Food preferences, 84–85, 233
Frankl, V., 249–250, 251, 253
Free association, 280
Freud, Anna, 194
Freud, Sigmund, 9, 65, 94, 188, 194, 248, 249–250, 280
Freudian theory, 232
    influence on psychosomatic medicine, 111, 137
Friends/friendship, 261, 266
    companionship provided by, 277
    reciprocity in, 264
    as social support, 264, 267, 274
Frustration, 140
Frustration-aggression hypothesis, of stress, 160
Fulfillments, 252
Future meaning/orientation, 249, 251, 252, 254

Galvanic skin response, 140
Gastrointestinal disorders, effect on eating habits, 82, 90
Gate control theory, of pain, 66–68
General adaptation syndrome, 53, 141, 144
General Health Questionnaire, 59
Generalized resistance resources, 150, 191, 202–203

General Social Survey, 97
Generativity, 190, 287, 325
Genetic factors, in motivation, 13
Geriatric Depression Scale, 47
Geriatric Life Events Scale, 73
Geritol, 62
Gerodynamics, 17
Gerontology
    behavioral, 3
    development of, 3
Gestalt psychology, 232
Gifted individuals, Terman Study of, 274,
    276, 284–285
Glucagon, 31–32
Glucocorticoids, 28, 29, 31, 144
Glucose tolerance, 31–32
Goals, 8–9, 12
    accommodative, 202
    achievement motivation and, 284–286
    adjustment of, 234, 238
        age-related, 241, 244, 245
        as coping strategy, 198–199, 205
        loss-related, 239
        stress-related, 197
    affiliative, 259
    as consciousness component, 247
    in leisure, 299, 301–302
    life satisfaction and, 242
    major, 291–292
    purposes as, 252
    of social relationships, 259, 268
    transcendental, 256
    well-being and, 245
Goal seeking, age-related decline in, 254
Grandma Moses, 307
Grief, 222, 223, 228
Grier, Roosevelt, 301
Growth hormone, 31–32

Hall, G. Stanley, 325–326
Hamilton Rating Scale for Depression, 36,
    59
Handbook of Bereavement (Stroebe,
    Stroebe, and Hansson), 226
Handbook of Mental Health and Aging
    (Burren et al.), 50
Handbook of Self-Concept (Bracken),
    234
Handbook of the Biology of Aging
    (Gutman), 3, 27

Handbook of the Psychology of Aging
    (Burren and Schaie), 58, 81, 162, 239,
    279
Hassles Scale, 159–160
Health
    definition of, 107, 108–109
    effect of bereavement on, 226–227, 228
    future expectations about, 244–245
    effect on leisure activities, 306,
        309–310, 320
    effect on meaning of life, 256
    effect on motivation, 13
    self-assessment of, 123–128, 137
    effect on self-esteem, 240
    effect on sexual behavior, 99–100
Health behaviors, 107–138
    as antecedents of illness, 109
    as consequences of illness, 109
    cultural factors in, 110
    personality factors in, 111
    possible selves and, 245
    relationship to perception of health
        status, 123–128
    theories and models of, 110–123
        of behavioral medicine and health
            psychology, 111–112
        commonsense model, 120–121
        health beliefs, 113
        health consumer, 122–123
        locus of control-self-efficacy
            expectancies, 113–117
        protection motivation, 118
        of psychosomatic medicine, 111
        salutogenic, 121–122
        sociological-behavioral, 119
        synthesis of social-cognitive and
            behavioral theories, 119–120
Health beliefs, effect on health care ser-
    vices utilization, 131
Health belief theory, 113
Health care services utilization, 128–132
    behavioral model of, 119
    by caregivers, 216
    cultural factors in, 131–132
    influence of pain on, 73
    locus of control in, 115–116
    psychosocial factors in, 131–132
Health consumer model, of health behav-
    iors, 122–123
Health-promotion behaviors, 132–137

Health psychology, 111–112
Health status, perception of, 123–128
Heart rate
  age-related changes in, 38–39, 40
  in cognitive tasks, 38–39, 162–164, 165
  in competitive situations, 166–168
  in fatigue, 54, 56
  in physical exertion, 60, 62
  in stress, 37, 208
Hedonic factors, in eating and drinkng,
  81, 84, 87
Hedonic tone, 295
Hedonism, 65
Hippocampus
  aging of, 29
  relationship to pituitary-adrenal system,
  29
Hippocrates, 107, 111
Hiroshima atomic bomb survivors, 146
Hobfoll, S.E., 151–152
Homeodynamics, 139
Homeostasis, 18, 39–40, 139
  biological, 249–250
  of body fluids, 90
  cognitive, 6
  failure of, 145
  social, 5
  sympathetic-adrenal system in, 141
Hormesis, 145–147
Hormones
  adrenal, 27–30
  effect on immune system, 35
  pituitary, 27–29, 32–34
  see also specific hormones
HR: See Heart rate
Human Relations Area Files, 96
Humors, theory of, 107, 111
Hypernatremia, 90
Hypersomnia, 47
Hypertension
  effect on eating habits, 84
  effect on sexual behavior, 99–100
Hypochondriasis, 63, 74–75, 129
Hypokalemic drugs, as fatigue cause,
  55–56
Hypothalamic–pituitary–adrenal axis
  in depression, 28, 29
  interaction with immune system, 35
  in stress, 141, 184–185
Hypothalamo–pituitary–thyroid axis,
  30–31

Illness
  chronic, pain associated with, 71
  "commonsense" model of, 120–121
  differentiated from disease, 69
  food intake in, 84
  emotional factors in, 66
  fatigue associated with, 53, 62–63
  psychosomatic, 69
  relationship to neuroticism, 127
  signs and symptoms of, 69, 72–73
  stress as risk factor for, 34
  as stressor, 208
Immune system
  aging-related changes in, 34–37
  stress-related dysfunction of, 226–227
Immunization theory, of information
  processing, 238
Impotence, 95, 99, 100
Independence, 285
Infectious disease, immune factors in, 34,
  35
Information processing
  immunization theory of, 238
  metaphors for, 7
Information seeking, as coping strategy,
  198
Insomnia, 47
Instinct, 9, 11
Insulin, 31–32
Integrity, 190–191, 325
Introspection, 280

James, William, 232–233
Janus Report, 97
Japanese atomic bomb survivors, 146

Kames, Lord, 289
Kaplan, M., 293, 298
Klinger, E., 250–251
Knowledge, as wisdom, 202, 203

Laboratory studies
  field studies versus, 170–171, 208–209
  subjects in, 324
Lactic acid, in fatigue, 54, 63–64
Lawton, M.P., 295, 297
Lazarus, R.S., 147–149, 152, 153,
  170–171, 185–186
Learned helplessness, 233
Learning tasks, stress response in, 185
Leisure, 289–320

Leisure (*cont.*)
  activities of
    adult education, 311–312
    caretaking, 307
    effect of health on, 306, 309–130, 320
    in retirement communities, 291,
      313–315
    volunteering, 315–319, 320
  amenity migration and, 312–315, 320,
    325
  casual, 296
  classification of, 303–304
  definition of, 289, 297
  determinants of, 306–311
    cohort effects, 307–309
    cultural factors, 307–309
    personality factors, 311
    previous life experiences, 306–307
    socioeconomic status, 310–311
  developmental, 295
  elements of, 293
  experiential, 295
  goals of, 299, 301–302
  increased time available for, 291, 292,
    302
  life-course analysis of, 304–305, 306–307
  as life goal, 291–292
  motivation in
    assessment of, 300–302
    attribution of, 298–300
  serious, 289, 296, 297, 300
  social, 295
  social relationships and, 20, 301
  theories of, 292–293
  work differentiated from, 290–291, 295,
    297
  as work equivalent, 312–313
Lewin, Kurt, 8, 332
Life, purpose or meaning of, 247–257
  empirical studies of, 253–256
  measurement of, 253–256
  relationship to control, 252–253
  theories of, 249–252, 257
Life Attitude Profile, 253–254
Life-course analysis, of leisure, 304–305,
  306–307
Life crises, coping with, 146
Life difficulties, 140
Life events, stressful, 142
Life expectancy
  as biomarker of aging, 14–15

Life expectancy (*cont.*)
  increase in, 65
  relationship to health behavior, 110
Life experiences, effect on leisure activities, 306–307
Life histories, 256
Life problems, 140
Life satisfaction
  caregiving as source of, 213–212, 213,
    214, 220, 221
  leisure activities as source of, 310
  measurement of, 255–256
  relationship to goals, 242
Life-span development, 248
Life stages/transitions
  developmental theory of, 190–191, 243,
    274–275
  definition of, 196
  as social stress cause, 196–197
  time frames for, 196–197
Life stories, 248
Limbic system, 27, 74
Locus of control, 177, 181
  external, 113, 116
  in health behaviors, 113–117, 135, 136
  internal, 113, 115–116, 117
    relationship to healthful lifestyle,
      135, 136
  measurement scales for, 114–115,
    116–117
  perceived versus actual, 114
  see also Control, personal
Loneliness, 269–272, 277
Losier, G.F., 296–297
Loss
  adaptation to, 285–286
  aging-related, 52–53, 251–252
  compensation for, 239
  effect on expectations, 245
  as fatigue cause, 52–53
  as goal adjustment cause, 239, 242
  of self, by caregivers, 219–220
Luteinizing hormone, 32–33
Lymphocytes, 35–36

Maddi, S.R., 250, 253
Malingering, 292
Marital happiness, relationship to sexual
  behavior, 101
Marital status, effect on health beliefs and
  behaviors, 134–135

Marriage, as meaningful experience, 255
Maslow, A., 247
Massachusetts Institute of Technology Clinical Research Center, 85
Massachusetts Male Aging Study, 100
May, R., 247
McCrea, R.R., 149–150, 153, 185
McGill Pain Questionnaire, 70, 75–67
Meaning
  of life, 247–257
    empirical studies of, 253–256
    measurement of, 253–256
    relationship to control, 252–253
    search for, 237, 253
    theories of, 249–252, 257
    will to, 249–250
Medicine
  behavioral, 111–112
  psychosomatic, 111, 137
  see also Health care services utilization
Menopause, 95–96
  hormonal factors in, 33–34
Metaphors, for motivation, 4–6, 19
Migration, amenity, 312–315, 320, 325
Military retirees, 314–315
Mind-body dualism, 6
Mineralocorticoids, 28
Minnesota Multiphasic Personality Inventory (MMPI), 74, 218
Monoamine oxidase inhibitors, as fatigue cause, 55–56
Mood disorders, 50
Mortality
  relationship to self-perception of health, 124–127
  relationship to widowhood, 229
Motivation
  in aging, 2–3
  biological, relationship to social motivation, 325
  biological factors in, 21–40
    cardiovascular system, 37–39
    cerebral metabolism, 22–24
    endocrine system, 27–34
    immune system, 34–37
    neurotransmitters, 24–26
  for caregiving, 216–217
  components of, 3–4
  in coping, 197

Motivation (cont.)
  current research in, 7–9
  definitions of, 3–7, 9–11
  effectance, 117
  extrinsic, in leisure, 294, 295, 296–297, 297–298
  genetic factors in, 13
  intrinsic
    in caregiving, 216–217
    in leisure, 293–294, 295, 296, 297–298, 310
  in leisure, 293–294, 295, 296, 297–298, 310
  metaphors for, 4–6, 19
  temporal framework for, 13–14
  theories of, 4
Motives
  biological, 11–13
  classification of, 11–13
  definition of, 197
  functional anatomy of, 7
  hierarchy of, 11
  needs as, 12
  social, 11–13
Motor function, aging-related decline in, 1, 3
Mourning, definition of, 222
Muscle fiber, aging-related decrease in, 54
Muscle strength, aging-related decline in, 55

Naps, 49
Narcissism, 235
Narcolepsy, 47
Narratives, 237
National Health and Nutrition Examination, 228
National Health Interview Survey, 133
National Institute of Mental Health, 41
National Opinion Survey Research, 228
National Research Council, Recommended Dietary Allowances of, 86
National Survey of Black Americans, 136
Natural disasters, 156
Natural killer cells, 35–36, 37, 164
Nebraska Symposium on Motivation, 4, 7, 9–10, 232, 250
Need(s), 7, 279–280
  biological, 6–7

Need(s) (*cont.*)
  of elderly persons, 17
  hierarchy of, 11
  for leisure, 291
  for meaning, 252
  as motives, 12
  for sleep, 41
NEO (neuroticism, extroversion, open-
    ness) Personality Inventory, 194
Neobehaviorism, 7–8
Nephropathy, 35
Nerve growth factor, 25
Neurasthenia, 50
Neuroleptics, as fatigue cause, 55–56
Neuromatrix, body-self, 74
Neuromuscular transmission, fatigue-
    related impairment of, 54–56, 59–60
Neuropeptides, 35
Neurosis, as lack of purpose, 250
Neuroticism
  relationship to coping, 189
  relationship to illness, 127
Neurotransmitters, 24–26
Neurotrophic factors, 25
Nihilism, 250
Nonevents, as stressors, 157
Norepinephrine, 25–26
  adrenal secretion of, 29–30
  interaction with insulin, 31–32
Nursing home residents
  meaning of life among, 256
  sexual activity preferences of, 98
Nutrition programs, for the elderly, 88

Obesity
  physiological factors in, 83
  relationship to eating habits, 86
Olfaction, aging-related changes in, 84
Opioids, role in hunger and thirst, 82, 90
Overeating, 82–83
Oxygen consumption, in fatigue, 54, 55,
    63–64

Pain
  aging-related increase in, 71
  avoidance of, 65
  chronic, 72, 78
  chronic illness-related, 65
  coping strategies for, 72, 78, 200
  gate control theory of, 66–68

Pain (*cont.*)
  measurement of, 68–72, 69–71
  multidimensionality of, 67–68, 74
  perception of, 68–72, 123–124, 125
    aging-related changes in, 71–72
    cultural factors in, 73–74
    in depression, 75–77
    personality factors in, 74–78
Pain thresholds, 71
Pancreas, 31–23
Parent-child relationship, 256, 266
Parents
  bereavement in, 229
  death of, 208, 226
Parkinson's disease, 26
Past, review and evaluation of, 251
Pathos, 66
Performance: *See* Task performance
Personality
  psychosocial factors in, 324
  stability of, 236–237
Personality factors
  in cardiovascular disease, 111–112
  in coping, 189, 194, 196, 197, 200
  in emotional isolation, 269–270
  in health behaviors, 111
  in leisure activities, 311
  in motivation, 323–324
  in pain perception, 74–78
  in social relationships, 272
Personality traits, motivation as, 5
Pessimism, 126
Phenomenological–existential movement,
    247–248
Phenomenology, 247
Physical activity
  age-related decrease in, 1
  see also Exercise
Physical attractiveness, of sexual partners,
    96–97, 102
Physical fitness
  cardiovascular effects of, 39
  effect on sleep patterns, 47–48
Physical strength
  aging-related decrease in, 1
  see also Muscle strength
Physics, 247
Pituitary gland, 27
Pituitary–gonadal hormones, 32–34
Play, 289, 290, 293

Pleasure
  effect on meaning of life, 256
  in sexual behavior, 98
Pleasure principle, 249–250
Polysomnograph (PSG), 42, 47–48
Positron emission tomography (PET), 22
Posttraumatic stress disorder, 13–14, 158
Power, will to, 249
Prescription drugs, effect on appetite, 82
Preventive health behaviors, 132–137
Problem-solving skills, 146, 190
Prolactin, 32–33
Protection motivation theory, of health
     behavior, 118
Protestant Reformation, 115
Psychiatric/psychological disorders
  bereavement-related, 228–229
  in caregivers, 215
  sleep patterns in, 46–47
Psychological Abstracts, 139–140,
     187–188, 195, 202, 210, 232
Psychological markers, of aging, 15–17
Psychology
  cognitive, 8, 232
  dynamic, 2–3
  experimental, 7–8
  Gestalt, 232
  Golden Age of Theory in, 8
  health, 111–112
Psychoneuroimmunology, 34, 36
Psychopathology
  relationship to search for meaning, 250
  see also Psychiatric/psychological
     disorders
Psychosocial factors
  in eating habits, 83, 84, 87–89
  in health care utilization, 131–132
  in motivation, 13
  in personality, 324
  in sexuality, 93, 104
  as stress cause, 322–323
Psychosocial theories, of stress, 147–154,
     184, 185–186
Psychosomatic illness, 69
Psychosomatic medicine, 111, 137
Public health, 132
Pulse wave velocity, 165
Purpose, of life, 247–257
  empirical studies of, 253–256
  measurement of, 253–256

Purpose, of life (*cont.*)
  relationship to control, 252–253
  theories of, 249–252, 257
Purpose in Life attitude scale, 253,
     254–255

Quality of life
  in old age, 109
  see also Life satisfaction

Rating of perceived exertion (RPE) scale,
     60–62
Reaction time tasks
  diastolic blood pressure during, 163,
     164, 165
  effect of fatigue on, 58
Reciprocity
  in friendship, 264
  in social relationships, 272
  in social support, 175
Recommended Dietary Allowances (RDA),
     86
Recreation, 289, 290
Reinforcement theory, of social relation-
     ships, 265
Reker, G.T., 251–252
Religion
  as coping strategy, 203–204, 205–206
  relationship to life satisfaction, 252
Relocation, residential
  as amenity migration, 312–315, 320
  effect on psychological well-being, 255
Repression, 191
Residential patterns, effect on social
     contacts, 309
Resource theory, of social relationships,
     266
Respiration, sleep-related disturbances of,
     44–45
Respite care, 215
Responsibility
  denial of, as coping strategy, 201, 205
  for health care, 130
  relationship to personal control, 180,
     181–183
Resting energy expenditure (REE), 83
Retirement
  forced, 238
  leisure time in, 302–303
  self-identity in, 237–238

Retirement (*cont.*)
  as stress cause, 155
Retirement communities, leisure activities
  in, 291, 313–315
Risk aversion, 131
Risk taking, relationship to health behaviors, 112
Roles
  aging-related changes in, 237–238
  multiple, 73
Role strain, 197
Role theory, of caregiving, 216
Rural areas, attitudes toward health care
  in, 133

Salutogenic theory
  of health behaviors, 121–122
  of stress, 150–151
Satiety, 82, 83, 90
Secondary gain, 75
Sedentary lifestyle, effect on sleep patterns, 47–48
Self, 231–246
  aging-related changes in
    models of, 238–241
    role changes and, 237–238
  components of, 232–235
  loss of, by caregivers, 219–220
  material, 232
  multifactorial nature of, 232–235,
    245–246
  social, 232
  social motivation and, 231–232
  spiritual, 232
  stability of, 235–237, 246, 248
  temporal aspects of, 235, 243–245, 246
Self-acceptance, 254, 255
Self-care, 128
Self-concept, 232
  aging-related changes in, 241
  effect of role changes on, 237–238
  homeostasis in, 234
  model of, 234, 235
  relationship to control, 238–239
  in successful aging, 240, 246
Self-confidence, 255
Self-defense mechanisms:
See Defense mechanisms
"Self-defense zoo," 234 Self-determination theory, of leisure, 296–297

Self-efficacy, 117, 122
  of caregivers, 214
  control and, 241
  definition of, 233
  goal changes and, 238
  health behaviors and, 136
  stress response and, 240–241
Self-enhancement, 233
Self-esteem, 234
  assessment of, 235
  cross-sectional studies of, 240
  definition of, 233
  determinants of, 234
  effect of social support on, 242–243
Self-estimation, 232
Self-evaluation, 236
Self-feelings, 232
Self-identity, during retirement, 237–238
Selfishness, 234
Self-knowledge, 233, 255
Self-motives, classification of, 233
Self-perception, aging-related changes in,
  241
Self-preservation, 232
Self-protection, 233
Self-reports, 256–257
Self-seekng, 232
Self-worth, 252
Selves
  definition of, 233
  past, 235, 243–244, 245
  possible, 235, 243–245, 246
  present, 235, 243–244
Selye, H., stress model of, 140–141, 143,
  144, 152, 184
Senescence (Hall), 325–326
Senior Citizens Center, 291
Serotonin, 26
Sexuality, 93–105
  as biological drive, 93
  biological factors in, 94–96, 103–104
  cultural factors in, 96–97
  gender differences in, 93–94
  hormonal factors in, 32–34
  motivations in, 93–94
  physical health and, 99–100
  psychosocial factors in, 93, 104
  psychological well-being and, 100–103
  surveys of, 97–99
Shepherd's Centers, 312

Sibling relationships, 266
Skin conductance, in stress, 37
Skinner, B.F., 8, 49
Sleep, 41–49
    circadian rhythm of, 44–46
    disturbances of, 41
        cognitive effects of, 48
        depression-related, 59
        epidemiology of, 42
        neuropsychiatric factors in, 46–48
    need for, 41
    NREM, 42–44
    physiological indices for, 42–44
    REM, 42, 44, 46
    slow-wave, 42, 43–44, 46, 48
    stages of, 42–44
Sleep apnea, 44–45
Sleepiness, daytime, 48, 49
Smell, sense of, aging-related impairment
    of, 84
SOC: See Coherence, sense of
Social cognitive theory, of health behav-
    iors, 136
Social contacts, effect of residential pat-
    terns on, 309
Social contract, 259
Social exchange theory, 287
    of caregiving, 216
    of social relationships, 264–266, 276
Social integration, 261
Social interactions
    aging-related decrease in, 325
    differentiated from social relationships,
        260–261, 275–276
    as leisure activity, 303, 305, 307,
        308–309
Social isolation, 269–272, 277
    widowhood-related, 225
Social networks, 261–262
    age-related decrease in, 273
Social Readjustment Rating Scale, 158,
    159–160
Social relationships, 259–277
    benefits of, 273–275
    definitions of, 260–263
    factors affecting, 272–275
    goals of, 259, 268
    effect on health beliefs and behaviors,
        134–135
    effect on health services utilization, 119

Social relationships (cont.)
    long-term longitudinal study of, 275
    effect on meaning of life, 256
    negative, 264
    effect on nutrition, 87–88
    personality factors in, 272
    quality of, 273
    effect on self-concept, 243
    sense of coherence associated with, 122
    sexual behavior in, 103, 104
    as stress moderator, 172
    taxonomy of, 261–263
    theories of, 263–269
        disengagement–activity–continuity,
            266–267, 276, 301
        exchange convoy model of, 265–266,
            268, 287
        intrinsic motive, 263–264
        social exchange, 264–266
        socioemotional selectivity, 267–269,
            273, 276–277
    see also Family; Friends/friendship
Social Science Citation Index, 140
Social support
    behavioral, 261
    in bereavement, 225–226, 229
    for caregivers, 168, 214, 215, 220–221
    classification of, 172–173
    cognitive, 261
    control and, 179
    as coping strategy, 196, 201
    family as, 261
    formal versus informal sources of,
        173–174
    friends as, 264, 267, 274
    health beliefs and, 134–135
    intergenerational exchanges in, 175–176
    perception of, 172–173
    personality factors in, 176, 177
    reciprocity in, 265–266
    self-esteem and, 242–243
    stress response and, 168, 169, 172–
        177, 186
Socioeconomic factors
    in food habits, 87–89
    in health behaviors, 136
    in leisure activities, 310–311
Socioemotional selectivity theory, of
    social relationships, 267–269, 273,
    276–277

Sociological markers, of aging, 15–17
Socrates, 65
Somatoform disorders, 111
Spinoza, Baruch, 2
Spirituality, 203
Spiritual self, 232
Spouse
  as caregiver, 213, 217–218, 219
  death of, 208, 226; see also Widowhood
State–Trait Anxiety Inventory, 47
Stebbins, R.A., 295–296, 297
Stereotypy, situational, 162
Strain, 140, 142
  chronic, relationship to negative life
    events, 213
  role-related, 197
Stress, 39–40, 139, 186
  acute, 140
  adaptation to, 143
  aging and, 154–156
  autonomic nervous system effects of,
    161–169, 185
  beneficial effects of, 145–147
  bereavement-related, 222–230
    measurement of, 223–225
    effect of social support on, 225–226
  biological effects of, 161–169
  buffering factors in
    multiple roles, 73
    sense of coherence, 251
  in caregivers, 168–169, 209–222
    age factors in, 218–220
    models of, 210–214
    motivation and, 216–217
    outcome measurement of, 214–216
    social support effects in, 220–222
    spousal factors in, 217–218
  classification of, 156–157
  definitions of, 52, 140, 141–144, 184,
    197
  effect on eating habits, 84
  as exhaustion cause, 53
  fatigue and, 52–53
  frustration–aggression hypothesis of,
    160
  heart rate in, 37, 208
  hypothalamic–pituitary–adrenocortical
    system in, 27
  immune system effects of, 34, 35,
    36–37

Stress (cont.)
  insomnia-related, 47
  as intervening variable, 147
  laboratory versus field studies of,
    208–209
  leisure and, 305
  multidimensional theory of, 70
  negative social relationships-related, 264
  pain and, 68
  perception of, 73
  physiological versus psychological,
    147–149, 152–154
  psychological effects of, 170–184
    personal control and, 177–184, 186
    social support and, 172–177, 186
  psychosocial, 108–109
    effect on illness/health behavior,
      119–120
  self-efficacy and, 240–241
  Selye's model of, 140–141, 143, 144,
    152, 184
  theories of, 144–154
    biological, 144–147, 184–185
    Lazarus', 147–149, 152, 153, 185–186
    psychometric, 149–150
    psychosocial, 147–154, 184
Stress Interview, 140
Stress management, 190, 205
Stressors
  assessment of, 208
  biological versus psychosocial, 142–144
  chronic, domains of, 213
  classification of, 156–157
  definition of, 141–142
  interdependency of, 152–154
  laboratory studies of, 170–181
    of autonomic nervous system,
      161–169
  measurement of, 157–161, 157–161
  outcomes measurement of, 161
  primary, 142
  psychosocial, 322–323
  secondary, 142
Stress resistance, 146
Suffering, 68
Sun City, Arizona, 314
"Support banks," 175, 256–266
Sympathetic-adrenal system, 141
Sympathetic nervous system, neurotransmitters of, 25–26

Symptoms, 69
  interpretation of, 72–73

Task performance
  attention-demanding, effect of fatigue
    on, 56
  cognitive
    cerebral metabolism during, 22–24
    effect of fatigue on, 56–58
  effect of fatigue on, 54–58
    chronic factors in, 56–58
    peripheral factors in, 54–56
  heart rate during, 38–39, 162–164, 165
  rating of perceived exertion for, 60–62
Taste, sense of, aging-related changes in, 84
T cells, 35, 37, 37
Television viewing, 312
Tenacious Goal Pursuit scale, 199, 205
Terman Study, of gifted individuals, 274,
    275, 284–285
Testosterone, 32–33, 95
Thematic apperception test, 280–281, 283
Theory of Goal Settings and Task Perfor-
    mance (Locke and Latham), 8–9
Thirst, 81, 90
Threats, 142
Thurston's Primary Abilities Test, 58
Thymus, involution of, 35
Thyroid gland, 30–31
Thyroid-releasing hormone, 30–31
Thyrotropin, 30–31
Thyroxine, 30–31
Tremors, effect on eating habits, 84
Type A personality, 112

Underfeeding, 83
United States National Survey of Families
    and Households, 98
Urbanization, 235

Vallerand, R.J., 296–297
Values, 324
  conflicting, 251
  as consciousness component, 247
  reconstruction of, 252
Veterans
  posttraumatic stress disorder in, 14–16
  spousal caregivers for, 214

Vinci, Leonardo da, 37
Viral infections, effect on eating habits,
    84
Virtue, 289
Vision loss, aging-related, 84
"Vitality in Later Life" (American Psy-
    chology Association), 3
Vitamin supplements, 62
V_{O2max}, in fatigue, 54, 55, 63–64
Volunteer Functions Inventory, 317
Volunteering, 315–319, 320
  altruism in, 317, 318–319, 320
  prevalence of, 317–318
Vulnerability, 118

Water deprivation, 90
Weakness, thyroid disorders-related, 31
Wechsler Adult Intelligence Scale, 58
Well-being, psychological
  coping as component of, 189
  measurement scale for, 254–256
  relationship to sexuality, 100–103
  subjective, 16
Widowhood, 96, 143, 155, 222
  effect on eating habits, 84, 88
  as mortality risk factor, 229
  social support during, 225–226
Will
  freedom of, 249
  to live, 109, 125
  to meaning, 249–250
  to power, 249
Wisdom, 202–203, 205–206, 245
Women, sexuality of, 33–34, 99, 100, 102
  biological factors in, 95–96
  cultural factors in, 96–97
Wong, D.F., 251–252
Work, as meaningful experience, 255
Work ethic, 154, 290, 291
Work motivation theory, of caregiving,
    216
World Health Organization, health defini-
    tion of, 108

Yerkes–Dodson law, of performance-
    motivation relationship, 56–57

Zung Self-Rating Scale for Depression, 59